THE
SOVIET
ESTIMATE

THE
SOVIET
ESTIMATE

U.S. INTELLIGENCE ANALYSIS
& SOVIET STRATEGIC FORCES

JOHN PRADOS

PRINCETON UNIVERSITY PRESS
PRINCETON, NEW JERSEY

Published by Princeton University Press,
41 William Street, Princeton, New Jersey 08540
In the United Kingdom: Princeton University Press,
Guildford, Surrey

Dial Press edition, 1982
First Princeton hardcover printing, 1986
First Princeton Paperback printing, 1986

LCC 85-43379
ISBN 0-691-07685-5
ISBN 0-691-02235-6 (pbk.)

Printed in the United States of America by
Princeton University Press,
Princeton, New Jersey

To Jill
with
Love

Mei Yao-ch'en: When confronted by the enemy respond to changing circumstances and devise expedients. How can these be discussed beforehand?

Reply: . . . if the estimates made in the temple before hostilities indicate victory it is because calculations show one's strength to be superior to that of his enemy; if they indicate defeat, it is because calculations show that one is inferior. With many calculations, one can win; with few one cannot. How much less chance of victory has one who makes none at all.

—Sun Tzu, verse 28

CONTENTS

INTRODUCTION

In the United States it is the function of the "intelligence community" to inform senior officials, and through them the wider public, of threats to the national security. This "community" is composed of a group of organizations, the best known of which is the Central Intelligence Agency. Among the others, however, are the intelligence branches of the armed services, the Defense Intelligence Agency, the National Security Agency, the National Reconnaissance Office, and the State Department's Bureau of Intelligence and Research.

Intelligence mainly provides answers through the medium of the "estimate." This is defined by the Joint Chiefs of Staff as an analysis of a foreign situation, development, or trend. It identifies major elements, interprets their significance, and appraises the future possibilities. Such estimates are produced by almost all the organizations comprising the intelligence community. The community also collectively produces reports called "national intelligence estimates," which state the agreed views of all the agencies on some item of national importance. Made in addition to daily reports on current events, these are the most important product of the intelligence community.

The growth of Soviet military power has been one of the most significant and disturbing trends of postwar history. In at least one area—the strategic nuclear forces that directly threaten the United States—the Soviets have made such progress that it is now disputed whether conditions reflect "parity" with the U.S. or even actual Soviet nuclear "superiority." Throughout the period in which the Soviets have been developing their strategic nuclear power, U.S. intelligence has provided estimates of their activities. These have been, perhaps, the most vital estimates produced by the intelligence community. There have been other issues of equal or greater importance to American security: European recovery and crises over Germany in the 1940s; Korea, China, and the Middle East in the 1950s; Viet Nam and the Middle East in the 1960s and 1970s; and most recently Iran. All have been crucial international issues, which figured as subjects for national intelligence estimates. But looming behind these regional events has been Soviet power, which over the entire period figures as the prime intelligence subject.

In the 1960s periodic and explicit statements by Defense Secretary Robert McNamara described Soviet nuclear forces and programs in considerable detail, based on the national intelligence estimates. Today, however, numerous commentators tell us that much of that information was in error, that intelligence "systematically underestimated" both the pace and scope of Soviet strategic force developments. Were the national intelligence estimates wrong? Was the CIA mistaken, duped, or manipulated? In view of the great public concern over Soviet military power it seems important to find out.

Basically, therefore, this book is a study of the effectiveness of U.S. intelligence. I have selected this one major substantive area, Soviet strategic nuclear forces, and I try to tell the story of U.S. intelligence reporting about that area by relating the national intelligence estimates to information which has since become available about Russia.

In the years since 1945 there has occurred a tremendous evolution of military technology and consequent heightened levels of risk and threat. The story of the Soviet estimate is told with reference to these technological developments. At first the threat was a question of Soviet development of the atomic weapon, then of long-range air attack against the United States. This was followed by the development of intercontinental ballistic missiles and the expansion of such missile forces. The quest for a viable ballistic-missile defense has also been an important issue, as has the invention of multiple-warhead missiles. In later years the verification of arms control agreements received great emphasis. Intelligence reporting on crisis situations provides a useful counterpoint to the longer-term questions of strategic-force growth. Each of these subjects is discussed here. Some distortion results from adopting this topical method rather than rendering a strictly chronological account but I felt that a subject-by-subject approach offered the best method for understanding the effectiveness of intelligence. And since at any one time only one particular technology was regarded as the dominant threat to the United States, this distortion is minimal.

Intelligence has always been a sensitive area of government. Traditionally intelligence estimates are closely held and information pertaining to intelligence organizations themselves is often vague and incomplete. This reflects a quite proper concern for security. Restriction of source material due to security considerations has posed problems for this effort.

In general the sources pertinent to an intelligence study are the same sort relevant to any study of policy-making in the executive branch. These are primarily congressional documents, memoirs, executive documents, and periodicals. In addition there are secondary-source accounts of United States foreign policy and defense planning in the period after 1945. Some of these sources are authoritative, for example statements by presidents or secretaries of defense that explain, advocate, or defend their policies. Accusations of intelligence wrongdoing in the mid-1970s resulted in a series of congressional and executive investigations, which have opened an important window on intelligence activities. In particular the reports and hearings of the Church Committee in the U.S. Senate and the Pike Committee in the House of Representatives contain much useful background information. The executive branch's Murphy Commission report and appendices have also been valuable.

Certain documentary sources on intelligence estimates have always been part of the public record. These consist principally of the dialogues between defense and foreign policy officials and elected representatives in congressional hearings. Testimony and questions posed for the record reveal many useful details. Intelligence officials formally met with congressional committees at least 175 times between 1955 and 1974. Some of these hearings have also produced committee prints, which form part of the record. Of course the congressional documents are subject to security deletions and to classification in toto in certain cases.

A major breakthrough in making information available has resulted from the Freedom of Information Act (5 U.S.C. 552 et seq.) and the prior institution of Executive Order 11652, which regulates the declassification of information held by the executive branch. Both provide for the review of specific classified material and its possible release. This, combined with the reduction of mandatory declassification to a period of twenty years, have opened up the immediate post-1945 archives and have revealed some records of later years as well. The Presidential Library system, the National Archives, and private microfiche production have provided a vital means of access to the documentary sources recently made available. Unfortunately declassification requests entail numerous delays and the staffs who service requests are zealous guardians of the classification system. The CIA may, in fact, have been exempted from the Freedom of Information Act by the time this volume goes to press.

The 1975 congressional investigations, which former Defense Intelligence Agency chief Lieutenant General Samuel V. Wilson termed "the intelligence inquisition," have encouraged the publication of memoirs by former intelligence officials and secondary accounts of intelligence operations. The number of these books already approaches two dozen. They furnish useful detail, some material on intelligence morale, and other features, but do not include any accounts by officials who worked exclusively as intelligence analysts.

Another important resource is press coverage of U.S. defense planning and intelligence activities. In fact, a surprisingly large amount of information about intelligence estimates is part of the public record in this form. A word about the practice of "leaking" is in order here. In the course of foreign and military policy debates the substance of decision and information documents is often passed along to journalists. Actually such "leaks" are not limited to documents but often include opinions on certain policies that are intended to influence the setting in which decisions are made. Every effort has been made to check the veracity of information provided for the record by leaks. The reader should note, however, that in some instances the fact that a leak has occurred is itself significant. With regard to the intelligence community in particular, very few of the debates over Soviet nuclear forces passed unmarked by some degree of leaking on the part of officials, and the practice was adopted both in support of and in opposition to policy. Information provided in this manner must be used with caution—though it can be revealing, it is often misleading.

The documentary and periodical record has been supplemented with interviews conducted with a number of former intelligence officials. All such interviews were requested and granted on the basis of confidentiality and this has been preserved here. No interview has been directly cited nor has any interviewee been directly quoted. No information provided by interviews was used if it could not be confirmed by other sources. The same is true of information provided by correspondence and by panel discussions presented at various times by public interest groups in Washington, D.C., and New York City. No effort was made to gain access to classified materials through these interviews. The former officials generally proved to be courteous and helpful and their contributions are gratefully acknowledged. Having said all this it is necessary to reemphasize that a lack of access to certain sources was the major limitation on this study.

The intelligence community employs over one hundred thousand people; some seventy-six thousand have passed through the CIA alone, and that agency was hiring at a rate of eleven hundred a year in 1975. No single account can cover every aspect of even a single intelligence issue. By its nature this book must be an initial effort, one showing only the broad outlines. Detailed accounts remain to be supplied for the technical collection programs, the offices in the various agencies, the armed services intelligence units, particularly the National Security Agency and National Reconnaissance Office, and for the intelligence activities of the Office of the Secretary of Defense. Yet there are some indications that the window on intelligence may already be closing. In view of this the need for such studies is even more pressing. The analysis of the intelligence function of government in the United States has yet to reach any advanced stage. To help lay the foundation for future work this book provides source notes and an extensive bibliography.

This study would have been impossible without the aid and assistance of many persons. I wish to thank the staffs of the Columbia University libraries, the New York Public Library, the Library of Congress, and the libraries of the University of Michigan (Ann Arbor) and New York University. At the Dwight D. Eisenhower Library, National Archives and Reference Service, invaluable help was provided by John E. Wickman and archivist Herbert Pankratz. At the Lyndon Baines Johnson Library, National Archives and Reference Service, similar cooperation was extended by archivists Martin I. Elzy, Tina Lawson, Claudia Anderson, and Nancy Smith. Vital logistics help has been furnished by Harlene Hipsh, Lee Euler, Joseph Prados, and Edward Gragert. For comments on earlier versions of the manuscript I am indebted to William T. R. Fox, Richard Pious, Morton H. Halperin, Richard K. Betts, John Huizenga, and Ms. Roothee Benzenberg. Editorial aid has been cheerfully and selflessly provided by Kevin Zucker prior to submission and by Douglas Stumpf of The Dial Press. The errors of omission and commission are my own.

—John Prados
Washington, D.C., December 1980

Note on the Princeton University Press Edition

Issues of intelligence analysis are no less pressing today as when this book was originally written. There remains a considerable need for better understanding of what is intelligence and how information is manipulated in support of political programs. Issues of management and organization also retain their importance. As developments have continued over the past five years, an Afterword has been added to this text bringing up to date the various themes raised. The Afterword (see p. 300) deals with management questions, recent substantive issues, arms control compliance, espionage, and intelligence collection management. The Afterword follows but does not supplant the formal conclusion of the book. That conclusion, and the main text of the study, have stood the test of time and have not been altered for this edition.

I am grateful to Mr. Loren Hoekzema of the Princeton University Press for the editorial skill and interest that makes this edition possible.

—John Prados
Washington, D.C., October 1985

THE
SOVIET
ESTIMATE

CHAPTER ONE
THE SOVIET INTELLIGENCE MISSION

It was ten fifty A.M. The cold November winds did not penetrate into the interior of Cheyenne Mountain, which houses the underground headquarters of the North American Aerospace Defense Command (NORAD). This facility outside Colorado Springs has the responsibility for tracking and assessing all aerospace threats to the continental United States. That morning, November 9, 1979, a NORAD technician was feeding the computers with data for a planned war-game exercise. But a mechanical error occurred in the computer system and the data was transferred to the "live" lines, which display the readouts of all the monitoring systems designed to detect strategic nuclear attack on the United States. The warning system then read this spurious data as real Soviet missile launches from both the land and the sea, causing indicators to light up simultaneously at NORAD headquarters, Pacific headquarters in Honolulu, and the National Military Command Center in the Pentagon. An alert was ordered, ten fighter interceptors "scrambled" from air bases in the United States and Canada, the President's airborne command-post plane was manned and readied for launch, and 116 Strategic Air Command bombers prepared for takeoff on further command. Fortunately the computer error was quickly detected because the warning was flashing on only one of the sensor types; other systems reported no Soviet missiles in flight. Duty officers immediately suspected a false alarm and within six minutes the alert readiness status was canceled.

This disturbing incident was followed by two more in June 1980. Before dawn on June third, and again on June sixth, an integrated circuit computer data chip in the NORAD system failed, again alerting U.S.

defenses to a Soviet simultaneous missile launch. The same alert measures were taken, and in one case an airborne command-post plane was
actually launched from Guam. It took twenty minutes to secure from a
six-minute alert. Nor are these isolated instances. In late 1973, bombers
were actually launched when a computer miscalculated the trajectory
of a Russian missile in flight and plotted that it would hit a U.S. airbase
in California. Several incidents occurred in the 1950s and '60s. On one
occasion defenses were alerted when detection mechanisms were trig-
gered by radar beams reflected off the moon. In 1950 there was an alert
resulting from radar detection of birds in flight off the Atlantic seaboard.

In each case war was averted because reasonable minds prevailed.
Officers on duty at NORAD and other places disbelieved their machine
warnings. But *why* did they? Why did not the military machinery simply
gear up on the assumption that the NORAD alerts were correct? Apart
from the "fail-safe" backup machines to give contradictory indications,
and the fact that similar false alarms had occurred previously, it is a
safe bet to assume that the men at NORAD and the Pentagon relied on
their perceptions of the international situation. No international crisis
was under way, and no behavior by the Russians pointed to a Soviet
nuclear attack on the United States. Therefore when the warning indicators went off, our officers looked for corroborative information and
found none.

Even more importantly, they *knew* enough about the state of Soviet
military readiness to doubt that a massive attack could be launched "out
of the blue." This knowledge came, of course, from our intelligence
agencies, the most famous of which is the Central Intelligence Agency
(CIA).

The present United States intelligence community has evolved only since
the end of World War II.

At that time our major intelligence organization was the Office of
Strategic Services (OSS), which had compiled a brilliant record during
the war. Headed by William J. ("Wild Bill") Donovan, OSS had put
agents behind enemy lines, arranged the surrender of German armies
in Italy, and compiled some very sharp analyses of foreign intentions
and capabilities. These analyses, called "estimates," were the specific
province of the OSS Research and Analysis (R&A) Branch, which had
acquired considerable skill in their formulation and presentation.

Following the war President Harry S Truman acted on recommendations to reorganize U.S. intelligence for the postwar period, and this
resulted in the dismantling of OSS. In his executive order 9621, issued
on September 20, 1945, Truman directed that the secret, intelligence-

gathering components of OSS be transferred to the Army where they would be known as the Strategic Services Unit (SSU), while the R&A branch went to the State Department. Neither arrangement proved to be particularly felicitous. Although the SSU was a strong organization with seven major field stations, it was largely isolated in the War Department, and its head, General John Magruder, who had run all OSS secret intelligence operations before the transfer to SSU, resigned in February 1946. In the State Department the R&A analysts, for their part, discovered that the State Department's regional bureaus were actually opposed to intelligence reports on their areas from an office over which they had no control. The secretary of state, James F. Byrnes, took little interest in the office and did not press for acceptance of its recommendations within his department. Consequently the Interim Research and Intelligence Service (the new name for R&A) became essentially moribund and its specialty of formulating estimates was allowed to atrophy.

This system proved to be unsatisfactory, even for Truman, who had had little love for intelligence and who had been happy to abolish the OSS. On January 22, 1946, the President sent a memorandum to the secretaries of state, war, and navy ordering a new restructuring of intelligence. There would now be a National Intelligence Authority, a senior executive body composed of the three secretaries and a representative of the President. Under their authority would be a Central Intelligence Group (CIG) whose foremost duty would be to "accomplish the correlation and evaluation of intelligence relating to the national security, and the appropriate dissemination within the government of the resulting strategic and national policy intelligence."[1] President Truman appointed Admiral Sidney Souers, a St. Louis businessman, as director of central intelligence (DCI) to assist the national authority and head the CIG.

The formation of CIG followed the recommendations of the Eberstadt Report of 1945. This report closely followed the thinking of Secretary of the Navy James Forrestal and advocated a National Security Council (NSC) to serve the President and the continuation of the Joint Chiefs of Staff (JCS) as the central military command body reporting to the President. The report also recommended the formation of a central intelligence body, and this became the CIG formed in 1946.

While the Eberstadt Report found its way through Congress and the bureaucracy, Admiral Souers began to put the CIG on its feet, mainly by absorbing the SSU. The OSS group at the State Department was left alone, to be disbanded in 1947,[2] while the CIG was essentially staffed with personnel recruited from the military and the SSU, which became CIG's Office of Special Operations, the clandestine service. Within CIG the clandestine service was complemented by an Office of Research and Evaluation (ORE), which had explicit responsibility for the compilation of estimates. The secondary status accorded ORE, however, is shown by the fact that in March 1946 its total professional staff numbered only twenty-nine among the CIG staff of several hundreds.

CIG was rapidly given assignments by the director of central intelligence. In his directive CIG-9, of May 9, 1946, Admiral Souers ordered it to "produce the highest possible quality intelligence on the USSR in the shortest possible time," and also ordered that the greatest care be taken to ensure the secrecy of even the existence of this operation.[3] As a result the early Soviet operations were organized under the title of "strategic intelligence digest." Subsequently Admiral Souers resigned from government service and was replaced on June 10, 1946, by Air Force General Hoyt Vandenberg, a sharp and hard-driving nephew of the chairman of the Senate Foreign Relations Committee. Vandenberg infused the CIG with a sense of action. For the first time ORE was authorized to conduct independent analyses of issues. By the end of 1946 CIG total manpower stood at two thousand and the ORE employed some three hundred professionals.

Early in 1947 the internal struggle over unification of the armed forces came to a head. Recommendations of the Eberstadt Report were included in draft legislation sent to President Truman. The CIG would be transformed by the proposed legislation into a Central Intelligence Agency (CIA), in keeping with the widespread feelings within CIG that the group could not work effectively suspended as it was between the State, War, and Navy departments. Only wartime Army Chief of Staff General George Marshall spoke against statutory establishment of the agency, writing Truman on February seventh that CIA's powers seemed almost limitless in the proposed legislation and thus required more definition. However, the provision to which CIA would later trace its authority to conduct covert operations was adopted with little change from the January 22, 1946, document directing formation of the CIG.

The proposed legislation went to the Congress on February 26, 1947, and in his accompanying letters Truman gave major attention to the debate over military unification, while not even mentioning CIA. Much the same thing happened in Congress. There were heated exchanges over whether the Joint Chiefs of Staff should be continued and over the powers to be invested in a secretary of defense, but testimony on the proposed Central Intelligence Agency was quick and pro forma. The National Security Act of 1947 was passed by Congress and signed into law by President Truman on July 26.

.   .   .

In the first years of its existence the CIA spent much effort developing a capability for covert operations. The evolution of analytical intelligence proceeded more slowly. One review of intelligence community development has concluded that between 1947 and 1950 "the CIA never fulfilled its estimates function, but continued to expand its independent intelligence production," mostly with information culled from the State Department's diplomatic reporting.[4] Analysis was still centered at the Office of Research and Evaluation (ORE), which was drafted into CIA but retitled as the Office of Reports and Estimates. The ORE was composed of a number of analysts who specialized in regional areas, plus a group of staff editors. Editors reviewed the assessments made and included them in CIA's intelligence publications.

The system led in practice to both duplication of effort and conflicts between the regional offices and the publications editors. These were settled in favor of the regional offices by 1949. At that time there were no more than a handful of analysts in ORE's Global Survey Division who were attempting to circulate joint intelligence estimates, approved generally by intelligence community members. The procedure for approving an estimate, or "coordinating," as it became known, was entirely ad hoc. The resulting estimates were noncommittal in order to achieve general approval and overly long, as coordination did not prevent the inclusion of dissents from other intelligence outfits.

Some of the earliest coordinated intelligence estimates were those produced in the context of the beginnings of the Cold War. When an estimate of Soviet reactions to the British withdrawal from Greece and Turkey was presented in March 1947, the CIG was asked for an in-depth assessment of Soviet intentions to be coordinated among the intelligence agencies. Preliminary work was completed by February 1947, "based on the most painstaking preparatory work in the history of intelligence, and involving extensive scientific investigation of both overt and covert intelligence material."[5] Among the sources used were the records of the Hitler-Molotov discussions in Berlin that had been held in November 1940, which presumably could shed light on Stalin's basic geostrategic thinking.[6] In any case, the CIG regarded its intelligence assessment as "foolproof," defended it against criticisms, and took the basic position that the Soviet Union would not risk a global war or interfere militarily with American actions in the Cold War.

Shortly after the formation of the CIA severe doubts about Soviet intentions began to develop. Western-Soviet difficulties arose over the occupation of Germany and Austria, the status of the port city of Trieste, and Soviet activities in Eastern Europe. Winston Churchill warned of an "Iron Curtain" separating the Soviet occupation areas from the West as early as 1946. In February 1948 a coup in Prague replaced the Czech parliamentary democracy with a Soviet-sponsored government. The U.S. commander in Germany, General Lucius D. Clay, warned in a famous cable on March 5 that

> I have felt and held that war was unlikely for at least two years. Within the last few weeks, I have felt a subtle change in Soviet attitude which I cannot define but which now gives me a feeling that it may come with dramatic suddenness.[7]

This statement electrified Washington. At the Pentagon and CIA, officials immediately began to refine their appraisals of Soviet intentions. James V. Forrestal, who had been appointed the first secretary of defense, huddled with the intelligence chiefs of the armed services for two days and came up with a prediction that proved true—that the Russians might blockade Berlin but were not about to start a war. For its part the CIA on March sixteenth was willing to go no further than the rather tentative prediction that the probability of war would not be high for the next sixty days, extending this prediction beyond two months only on April second.

The Air Force disagreed with both assessments, predicting that war was imminent. This was only the latest of a string of disagreements by the youngest of the military intelligence services. Whereas the Office of Naval Intelligence had been formed in 1882 and the Army's G-2 in 1903, there was no distinct air intelligence until November 1940, when an intelligence division was created in the staff of the chief of the Air Corps. This was later expanded into an A-2 section under the Air Force's deputy chief of staff for operations with the mission to "(a) insure the prevention of strategic, tactical, or technological surprise from any source, and (b) provide air intelligence required for the planning and conduct by the [Air Force] of the operations of war."[8] Since 1945 the Air Force had taken the position that the Soviet Union posed a threat to the United States, and in 1947 and 1948 believed there was nothing to prevent the Soviets from attempting to utilize their superior ground forces in Europe.

This type of disagreement presented basic problems of coordination among intelligence agencies: how to assign which mission to which group and how to reflect disagreements within the intelligence estimates. The subject assignments of intelligence were a matter for superior directive. At the very first meeting of the National Security Council (NSC), on September 26, 1947, the director of central intelligence submitted his suggestions for intelligence community organization. Subsequently, at its meeting on December twelfth the NSC discussed and approved these, with some modifications. The heads of the armed service intelligence units, the State Department's Office of Intelligence and Research, the FBI, and the Atomic Energy Commission, were constituted as a top-level executive committee chaired by the director of central intelligence and called the Intelligence Advisory Committee (IAC). The IAC became the interagency board that approved operations and reviewed estimates.

A second NSC intelligence directive was approved on January 13, 1948, and established categories of intelligence. This directive distinguished between *basic* and *national* intelligence, the former consisting of "encyclopedic information of a more or less permanent and static nature," to be entered in a National Intelligence Survey. National intelligence, by contrast, was defined as integrated departmental information covering the broad aspects of national security and transcending the competence of any single organization. The use of the term "integrated" was significant: the National Security Council wanted the CIA and the other IAC-member agencies to consider in concert their positions on specified issues of interest to the NSC.[9]

This point was reinforced by the director of central intelligence, Rear Admiral Roscoe H. Hillenkoetter, in his directive 3/2, of September 13, 1948. Here Hillenkoetter commented on the purpose of the interagency participation in drafting national intelligence:

> Departmental participation in the preparation of national intelligence reports and estimates is undertaken to ensure that authorized recipients
> a. are presented with national intelligence that comprises all the best available expert knowledge and opinion;
> b. are aware, in the case of disputed points, of the views of the departments on substantive matters within their special fields of responsibility and interest.[10]

Hillenkoetter, head of the Pacific Fleet Intelligence Center during the war, had experienced numerous intelligence disputes, some over relatively fine points. Thus in his directive he noted that "[any] dissent published in a national intelligence paper should present a distinct difference of opinion on which CIA and the dissenting intelligence organization have found it impossible to agree."

Despite such executive orders it proved to be extremely difficult to achieve cooperation from the whole intelligence community on the drafting of estimates. Partly as a result there was widespread feeling at CIA that intelligence estimates were not receiving sufficient attention at the NSC. The CIA could not secure agreement on treating the more controversial subjects and thus tended to produce reports of minimal utility and interest. For instance, the monthly "Estimate on the World Situation," produced by Ludwell Montague's Global Survey Division at CIA, mostly paralleled press accounts although they did contain some information from secret sources. In the editions from December 1947 to May 1948 the monthly estimates focused mainly on Eastern Europe, France, and Italy, were drily written, and contained very little information on military and strategic matters.

During a survey of the activities, organization, and personnel of the CIA undertaken by President Truman and his advisors, Allen W. Dulles, Matthias F. Correa, and William H. Jackson, the low morale among CIA estimators became apparent. It was learned that there were at least five proposals floating around CIA for the creation of some kind of central estimates staff, several of them emanating from within the ORE. The final Dulles-Jackson-Correa Report of January 1949 was quite critical of the intelligence community on a number of issues. The report asserted that the NSC had not gone far enough in defining the scope and limits of departmental versus national intelligence, particularly in the scientific and technical areas. Barring a few exceptions like the coordinated estimates on Berlin, "whose occurrence was largely fortuitous," the CIA had not carried out its function of producing national intelligence. The procedure by which ORE produced estimates, based on its own information and circulated to other departments for comment, did not fill the need for national intelligence estimates. Not only did the other agencies not feel themselves full participants, ORE and CIA complicated the problem by offering its publications in competition to theirs. As the report observed,

> A national intelligence report or estimate as assembled and produced by the Central Intelligence Agency should reflect the coordination of the best intelligence opinion, based on all available information. It should deal with matters of wide scope relevant to the determination of basic policy, such as the assessment of a country's war potential, its preparedness for war, its strategic capabilities and intentions, its vulnerability to various forms of direct attack or indirect pressures.[11]

Comparison between this ideal and the community product in 1948–1949 brought forth the conclusion that

> the principle of the authoritative national intelligence estimate does not yet have established acceptance in the government. Each department still depends more or less on its own intelligence estimates and establishes its plans and policies accordingly.[12]

The report recommended that an "Estimates Division" be formed at CIA to produce analyses with joint information and contributions from all the intelligence agencies.

There was no immediate action on the recommendations of the Dulles-Jackson-Correa Report. Rather, until after the start of the Korean War in 1950 the CIA's Special Estimates series was the only joint intelligence product out of eleven CIA publications. Complaints continued. During July 1949 a senior analyst at ORE noted a tendency for papers scheduled to be coordinated to focus on short-term problems that could be narrowly defined. In 1950, however, President Truman's desire for a judgment on Soviet war aims in Korea broke the bottleneck that had held back the national intelligence estimates. In the summer of 1950 the CIA again adopted ad hoc procedures to achieve consensus on a half dozen short national estimates, which mostly held that the Soviets would not resort to war over Korea.

It was evident that the ad hoc approach to drafting national estimates could not continue. In the fall of 1950 Admiral Hillenkoetter was posted to a fleet command in the Far East. He was replaced as director of central intelligence by General Walter Bedell Smith, who had been chief of staff to General Eisenhower during the war, and had recently returned from Moscow after serving three years as ambassador. "Beetle" Smith had the military prestige needed to smooth relations between CIA and military intelligence units and was personally quite interested in national intelligence. Smith had held a high opinion of the OSS Research and Analysis Branch during World War II and now wanted to see something like it at CIA. He offered the job of deputy director to William H. Jackson, participant in the Dulles-Jackson-Correa Report, along with full support to implement the 1949 report's recommendations. Jackson immediately accepted and was sworn in on October 7, 1950.

Smith next asked Professor William L. Langer, the Harvard historian who had actually headed OSS Research and Analysis, to come to Washington and help organize an Office of National Estimates. This office was to be formally charged with the compilation of National Intelligence Estimates (NIEs). "Beetle" Smith was willing to give Langer carte blanche for the creation of this "estimates division" and mentioned the figure of a thousand staff slots. As Langer later put it,

I hastily packed a bag, leaving my wife to follow with the family. After long discussions between the general and myself, the organization was decided on . . . and I was instructed to take any personnel from any part of the agency. I eventually assembled a staff of fifty or sixty, which Smith was sure would prove inadequate. I pled with him that I did not want so large an office that much of the time would be lost in administration. He finally yielded, on my promise to add to the staff if necessary, but it was never increased.[13]

The Office of National Estimates (ONE) was formally created on November 13, 1950. Langer opted for a high-quality ONE with a two-tier hierarchy. The larger part of ONE was a support staff, which drafted suggestions for NIEs, assembled contributions from other offices, and summarized information in preparation of the initial drafts of the estimate papers. Smith let it be known that he expected all military and other agencies to participate actively in this drafting, accomplished at ONE by the Estimates Staff under Ray Cline. Each NIE was then assigned to a senior analyst from a small Board of National Estimates (BNE) whose task was to negotiate acceptable language with the representatives of other agencies and then formulate a final draft, which would go for approval to the IAC. It was difficult to get the various agencies to send over representatives who were both competent on the subject matter and empowered to speak for their superiors but, Langer recalls, "the drive and overriding authority of General Smith made for rapid progress."

By January 1951 Smith had successfully channeled CIA's main efforts toward formal national intelligence estimates and a breakthrough was made with the dissemination of twelve of these documents, reportedly without any substantive dissents. The matter of dissents continued to attract attention during the tenure of Bedell Smith as director of central intelligence. He favored an arrangement under which the text of an NIE would be mainly CIA language and then all dissents would be recorded. Langer at ONE argued that estimates "littered" with dissents would be of no value except to inform policy makers of the existence of large differences of opinion and he wanted to concentrate on achieving agreement on the general content of each estimate. Smith let his ONE chief go ahead, but exercised a firm hand at meetings of the IAC when the draft NIEs came up for review. Finally, the military services challenged CIA on the nature and style of NIEs, maintaining that they should be factual and descriptive rather than speculative. Here Langer argued that the NIEs must be problem oriented in order to satisfy policy makers. In this position he was supported by the CIA's deputy director, William H. Jackson.

As more NIEs were produced, the procedure for their formulation was better accepted. The forum for discussion of organizations' views on substantive intelligence questions more and more was seen to lie in the

IAC and its permanent subcommittees. Before "coordination" at the Intelligence Advisory Committee the draft NIE would have been formulated at the Board of National Estimates by compromise among the CIA and other intelligence agencies. Prior to that the paper would have been drafted by ONE's Estimates Staff based on "contributions" from all the interested agencies. Most of 1951 was spent in a steadfast effort

> to reduce the procedures for drafting NIEs to an orderly set of instructions that would ensure cooperation and contributive efforts by State and the military agencies while also maintaining CIA control of the content and the intellectual integrity of the final document.[14]

The ONE staff director adopted the practice of himself reviewing each draft estimate a first time before it had even been sent to the senior analysts on the Board.

On January 9, 1953, the acting director of central intelligence, Allen Dulles, issued an intelligence directive specifically covering the production of NIEs. Dulles envisioned a regular program of NIEs covering certain topics, and of Special National Intelligence Estimates (SNIEs), according to a list submitted to the IAC by the BNE before the first of the year. In preparing this list BNE was to consult the National Security Council Planning Staff, several interagency committees of the IAC, and certain independent groups as well. Additional estimates, usually SNIEs, might be required by circumstances and would be initiated by requests to the IAC at periodic intervals.

According to this directive the normal preparation sequence for an NIE comprised four phases. First the BNE would circulate "terms of reference" outlining the scope and content of the study and what offices would contribute on each question. The ONE Estimates Staff would then solicit the contributions and assemble a first-draft NIE from these. The draft would then go to BNE where it would be reviewed with the contributory agencies and rewritten. Then the IAC would review the result and insert dissents in the form of footnotes to the estimate, or CIA could agree to rewrite the text so as to reflect the dissenting positions. In the last stage the finished NIE would be published over the signature of the director of central intelligence as the considered opinion of the entire community. Continuing the dissent provisions instituted in 1948, the 1953 directive stated, "Any agency may dissent to any feature of an estimate. Such dissents identify the dissenter and will state the dissenter's position on the issue."[15] With minor changes this system then prevailed for over two decades.

Of the first dozen NIEs several papers were produced on the subject of Soviet actions and motivations. One paper, NIE 11, specifically dealt with Soviet intentions and capabilities, and the NIE 11 series remained an annual one concerning Soviet activities, perhaps the single most crucial output of the intelligence community over the long term. Although the series changed format on occasion as different areas of interest developed with respect to the Russians, and was eventually supplemented by assorted specialized reports and monographs, NIE 11 remains central to any study of U.S. intelligence analysis of Soviet strategic developments.

CHAPTER TWO
INTERCONTINENTAL ATTACK

The United States is largely surrounded by oceans rather than powerful neighboring states. In the years before World War II this meant that the U.S. was essentially immune to direct attack because potential enemies simply could not mount operations across the transoceanic distances required. The atomic bomb, with its unprecedented destructive force demonstrated at Hiroshima and Nagasaki, changed all that. Teamed with the long-range bomber, atomic weapons could destroy whole cities at intercontinental distances. The United States could be attacked directly over the Pole. In the context of the Cold War, the question of when Russia would develop the atomic bomb and the strategic bomber cast a lengthened shadow and dimmed hopes for the continued military invulnerability of the United States.

The A-bomb was the wartime creation of the Manhattan Project, a large-scale weapons development program in the United States conducted in secrecy and at great cost. It happened that the first test of the bomb occurred in July 1945, at the same time that allied leaders were meeting at the summit conference at Potsdam. When, on July twenty-fourth, President Truman casually informed Josef Stalin that the U.S. was testing a weapon of unusual destructive power, the Soviet dictator remarked only that he was glad to hear it. But later, in the fall of 1945 at a London meeting of the "Big Four" foreign ministers, the Soviet delegate went out of his way to declare that Russia would not be intimidated by American possession of the atomic weapon.

Moscow maintained silence on the issues of atomic energy and weapons, and did not respond favorably when the possibility of international control over atomic energy through the United Nations was raised under the Acheson-Lilienthal plan. Analysis of public military doctrine in the Soviet Union in the late 1940s supports the impression that the Soviets minimized the importance of the atomic factor, implying disinterest in weapons of this type. Rather, they stressed "permanently operating factors": greater military capability, productive capacity, popular will, and the traditional principles of war.

The doctrine of "permanently operating factors" remained in effect only in public, however. The Soviets were already engaged in a strong atomic research program. By the time of Truman's statement to Stalin at Potsdam the Russians had already had an atomic laboratory under nuclear physicist Igor Kurchatov for almost two years. Though Stalin appeared unconcerned to American observers, that same night, according to Marshal Georgi K. Zhukov, he discussed the development with Zhukov and foreign minister Vyacheslav Molotov. The latter is reported to have said, " 'We'll have to talk it over with Kurchatov and get him to speed things up.' "[1] Two weeks later, on the day following the atomic bombing of Hiroshima, Stalin put his secret police chief Lavrenti P. Beria in charge of the administration of the Soviet atomic program.

In 1945 the Soviets already possessed a base upon which to build such a program. Russian physicists had worked at Cambridge before the war, and in Denmark with Niels Bohr. Others had done important theoretical work at home. One paper, for example, concluded that uranium was capable of natural fission, a hypothesis which has only recently been confirmed by field work in Africa. In 1937 physicists placed a cyclotron in limited operation at the Moscow Radium Institute which, although not as large as Berkeley's thirty-seven-inch-diameter cyclotron, was the first such mechanism in Europe. Beam energy on the cyclotron was gradually increased until it was ready for full-scale experimental work in 1941. The hypothesis that a nuclear chain reaction was sustainable was first advanced in the Soviet Union in April 1939, and a Special Committee for the Problem of Uranium was formed in 1940. This group included Kurchatov, engineer V. I. Vernadskii, and physicists Abraham Yoffe, Peter Kapitsa, Yuri Khariton, and A. P. Vinogradov. Vernadskii also headed the Commission on Isotopes which had formed in 1939. It has been suggested that this early work was conducted independently by the Soviet Academy of Sciences with little cognizance on the part of the Soviet government.[2]

The Academy held an all-union conference on isotopes on April 16–17, 1940. That November there was another conference on the physics of atomic nuclei. Physicist Peter Kapitsa envisioned an atomic explosion as early as his presentation on October 12, 1940:

Theoretical calculations show that, whereas a modern high explosive bomb can destroy an entire city block, an atom bomb, even one of small size, if it can be manufactured, could easily destroy a major capital city with several million inhabitants.[3]

The potentialities of such a weapon are said to have been suggested by the scientists to Stalin rather than conceived independently by the Soviet leadership. In any case atomic research ground to a complete halt after the German invasion of Russia when the scientists were drawn into work on more immediate needs for the war effort.

The situation changed in 1943 when the tide turned on the Russian front. It was then that the atomic research laboratory was formed under Kurchatov. Also that year Kurchatov was voted a full Academician by the Soviet Academy of Sciences. Meanwhile, in April, the Soviet Purchasing Commission in the United States signified its interest in purchasing eight tons each of uranium oxide and uranyl nitrate salts from which fissionable materials could be extracted.[4] Nevertheless the Kurchatov laboratory was small, numbering fewer than fifty physicists, and was no match for the American Manhattan Project. Not until 1944 did the Russians begin construction of their first atomic reactor, the F-1 unit at Leningrad, and a first chain reaction was not achieved until Christmas 1946.

When Beria was given administrative control over the atomic program in August 1945, he set up an "engineering council" to oversee atomic work under Boris L. Vannikov, an official from the production ministries. Soviet interest was clearly shown after the release of the semiofficial "Smyth Report," which detailed the history of the Manhattan Project. This was translated into Russian and thirty thousand copies were published in early 1946. At least one prominent physicist, Peter Kapitsa, was placed under house arrest after 1947 for refusal to work in the Soviet weapons program. In June 1946 Vannikov was relieved of all other duties and placed in charge of the First Main Directorate, a supraministerial agency with the sole task of directing the weapons program. Vannikov, scientists, engineers, and a representative of Beria sat together on the steering committee.

The Russians occasionally broke their silence on atomic matters. In a speech on November 6, 1945, Molotov warned that there could be no secrets of great technical significance that could remain in one country or one "narrow group" of nations for long. There was limited press coverage of the Bikini series of atomic tests held by the United States in 1946. Stalin himself told French journalist Alexander Werth in an interview on September 24, 1946, that "monopoly possession of the atomic bomb cannot last long." In May 1947 Andrei Gromyko, then a rising Soviet diplomat assigned to the UN, declared that atomic monopoly was an illusion. Molotov himself reiterated this theme even more strongly in a speech on November sixth, when he stated that the "secret" of the atomic bomb "has long ago ceased to exist."

Naturally there was intense interest in the U.S. on the question of when the Soviets might actually achieve the atomic bomb. A number of scientists and engineers from the Manhattan Project, and, it is reported, Kurchatov himself when queried by Stalin in 1945, believed it would take Russia about five years. Some U.S. military officers, like General Leslie R. Groves, who had headed the Manhattan Project, expected the Russian A-bomb to be a problem for their grandchildren. Vannevar Bush, scientist in charge of the wartime Office of Scientific Research and Development, which had supervised all military research in the United States, had a much more practical attitude. Bush wrote President Truman in September 1945 to caution that there was no secret to the A-bomb, rather, " 'the secret resides principally in the details of construction of the bombs themselves and in the manufacturing process.' "[5]

As time passed without evidence of a Soviet atomic explosion, observers tended to draw confirmation for their belief in the five-year interval. Thus persistent but unconfirmed reports in the French press, in both 1947 and 1948, that the Russians had tested a bomb were discounted in the United States. In 1948 a statement made by Soviet deputy foreign minister Andrei Vishinsky that the U.S. had no monopoly on atomic weapons was countered by press reports that the Joint Chiefs of Staff anticipated the advent of the Soviet A-bomb sometime in 1952. Physicist J. Robert Oppenheimer wrote in a personal letter to a Navy admiral that

> one important factor [is] the time necessary for the Soviet Union to carry
> ·out the program for atomic energy to obtain a significant atomic armament.
> With all recognition for the need for caution in such predictions, I tend to
> believe that for a long time to come the Soviet Union will not have achieved
> this objective.[6]

Oppenheimer's opinions and the American press reports in fact reflected the official intelligence estimates provided for the JCS. The JCS was served by the Joint Intelligence Group (JIG), which was modeled along British lines and composed of representatives of Army, Navy, and Air Force intelligence. The earliest JIG reports in 1945 had used the five-year interval as its prediction for the Soviet A-bomb. In November 1947 the JIG projected that the Soviets might develop some type of atomic weapon between 1950 and 1953. One year later the prediction was mid-1953. The most recent study of this question found only one estimate that differed from the "five-year prediction." This was a report from General McDonald's Air Force intelligence unit, which stated that

" 'it is possible that the Soviets are at present on the brink of success in the development of an atomic bomb' " and envisioned Soviet bomb production starting in the 1949–1951 period.[7]

While the Air Force might not have agreed with the JIG estimates, everyone was aware that the available information was completely inadequate. Estimates were "five percent information and ninety-five percent construction." David Lilienthal, chairman of the Atomic Energy Commission, noted in his diary on March 17, 1949, that "in my opinion our sources of information about Soviet progress are so poor as to be actually merely arbitrary assumptions."[8] The United States knew only that Soviets were interested in the A-bomb and that they had gained access to the uranium mines around Joachimsthal in Czechoslovakia. There were also reports from German sources after 1948 that uranium mining had begun in the Soviet Union itself.

In the U.S. an Atomic Energy Commission (AEC) had been formed in 1947 to handle all aspects of both peaceful atomic energy and nuclear weapons, including the U.S. interest in Soviet atomic weapons. One of the first proposals considered by the AEC commissioners was concerned with developing the capability of detecting any Soviet atomic test. This proposal was supported by commissioner Admiral Lewis Strauss, and meetings were held on the matter with General Hoyt Vandenberg, head of the old CIG. The Navy supported this AEC recommendation, as did General Vandenberg, against the opposition of his own service, the Air Force, which felt that aircraft used for atomic detection purposes would thus be diverted from their mission of strategic bombing. In any case, a study group called the Long-Range Detection Panel was formed to review the situation. President Truman approved the initiative and in September 1947 authority to operate a detection system was given to the Air Force. During the SANDSTONE atomic test series of 1948 technicians developed a system by which information on the nature and explosive yield of an atomic test could be derived from analysis of radioactivity in the particulate debris generated by an atomic explosion and suspended in the atmosphere. Subsequently the activation of the Long-Range Detection System was accomplished with the installation of air sample collectors aboard B-29 bombers in a unit known as AFOATS One, which became operational in early 1949.

A functional detection system enabled officials to be confident that Russian atomic testing could be discovered when it occurred. Although there were complaints as late as June 1949 that the system was too expensive, the need for information prevailed. The essential points were made in a paper by the Policy Planning Staff of the State Department dated August 16, 1949:

It would be of the utmost importance for us to know when the U.S.S.R. has successfully tested a bomb in order to anticipate and counter possible changes in Soviet foreign policy which might result therefrom, and to know whether a shift in its foreign policy was the result of possession of atomic bombs. We cannot know whether the U.S.S.R. would make the knowledge public if it did possess the atomic bomb; however, we would be in a position to know the truth of what the U.S.S.R. said publicly.[9]

The U.S. acquired an atomic detection capability just in time, as it turned out. On September 3, 1949, an observation bomber routed over the Sea of Japan brought back samples which, after analysis, were confirmed to have come from an atomic explosion. The news was a surprise to the U.S. government. Secretary of State Dean Acheson was informed as he attended the United Nations General Assembly session in New York. AEC Chairman Lilienthal was vacationing on Martha's Vineyard and the Pentagon had to resort to parachuting a general officer onto the island who then hitchhiked to Lilienthal's home to convey the report. Immediate consultations were held in Washington after which President Truman decided to release a public announcement of the Soviet explosion, which was done on September twenty-second.

The Russian technical achievement was impressive. Certainly it shook those who did not expect a Soviet bomb for another five years. Herbert York has remarked retrospectively that

even more impressive was the time it took [the Soviets] to go from the first chain-reacting pile [reactor] . . . to a first bomb test. The periods in the [American and Soviet] cases differ by only eighteen days out of a total [elapsed] time of two and a half years.[10]

The existence of a Soviet atomic bomb moved the United States to review its defense policies and to decide upon the development of an even more powerful nuclear weapon, the hydrogen bomb, in which an atomic weapon would serve merely as the trigger for the explosive device.

Russia was also aware of the possibilities inherent in a hydrogen (or "thermonuclear") bomb, which would provide a much greater explosive yield for a given amount of fissionable material in the weapon. The scientists responsible for the Soviet A-bomb almost immediately began to work toward the new weapon. The basic conceptual breakthrough occurred in 1950 when physicists Andrei D. Sakharov and I. Ogarkin calculated that a thermonuclear chain reaction could be created in the instant prior to the disintegration of the atomic trigger. Work continued in this area until some months after Stalin's death, in 1953, when Soviet

Premier Georgi Malenkov declared that, as with atomic power, the United States possessed no monopoly on thermonuclear fusion and hence on the hydrogen bomb. The first Russian "H-bomb" test followed within a week when, on August eighth, the Soviets fired a tower device called JOE IV. This thermonuclear explosion, however, may have been of only four hundred to seven hundred kilotons yield, making it little larger than a fission weapon fired by the U.S. in 1952, and considerably smaller than the first United States thermonuclear blast in November of that year. One advantage the Soviet device did have was that it was already "weaponized," or configured in a deliverable nuclear bomb, whereas the American weapon had yet to undergo this process.

In any case, once the basic breakthrough had been made to an atomic arsenal, it was only a question of the Soviets improving their weapons and increasing their stockpile. It became crucial for U.S. intelligence to predict the size of the stockpile and its effect on Soviet behavior. Reaction was immediate. On February 10, 1950, the ORE released an estimate of the effects of Soviet possession of the bomb upon the security of the United States. The estimate projected the size of the Soviet nuclear arsenal at 100 bombs by 1953 and 200 before the end of 1955; predicted that having the bomb would make the Russians more venturesome internationally; and posited that a Soviet strike with 200 bombs might prove decisive in knocking the U.S. out of a future war. It did not comment on how large a stockpile the Russians might *need* to deliver 200 weapons on target but it did foresee that the "critical date" for this size attack would not occur before 1956–1957.

The CIA's estimate differed from that of the JCS, which was given in a letter of January thirty-first as 10–20 Soviet bombs by mid-1950 and 70–135 for mid-1953. The difference impressed officials working on a major review of defense policy called NSC-68, who told Defense Secretary Louis Johnson that the ORE estimate gave the Russians a much greater capability than that forecast in the national intelligence estimate, from which the JCS figures had been drawn. Nevertheless, when it was issued on April fourteenth, NSC-68 carried forward the official NIE figures, estimating the Soviet stockpile at 10–20 for mid-year, 25–45 at mid-1951, 45–90 at mid-1952, 70–135 for mid-1953, and 200 atomic weapons by 1954. The NSC study noted that the estimate represented only the production capabilities of known or deducible Soviet plants and was admittedly based on incomplete coverage of Soviet activities, with the implication that ORE's more pessimistic estimate might be more accurate.

The recommendations for policy were that the U.S. should be prepared to wage a global war in the threat year 1954. Truman decided in

favor of the NSC-68 program later in 1950, but soon afterwards the
Korean War began and there was much concern over whether the Korean conflict would precipitate the general war which all men dreaded.
The CIA commented on this in NIE 3 of November 15, 1950, which
covered Soviet intentions and capabilities. It forecast that Russia would
have "to make good certain important deficiencies in atomic bomb
stockpile and in certain types of aircraft" before embarking on a war
course, and concluded that

> the probability is that the Soviet government has not yet made a decision
> directly to launch a general war over the Korean-Chinese situation. There is
> a good chance that they will not in the immediate future take such a deci-
> sion. At what point they *will* take a decision to launch a general war is not
> now determinable by intelligence.[11]

This judgment was somewhat modified in NIE 11 on Soviet intentions
in the current situation, which followed on December fifth:

> The possibility cannot be disregarded that the USSR may already have de-
> cided to precipitate global war in circumstances most advantageous to itself
> through the development of a general war in Asia. We are unable, on the
> basis of our present intelligence, to determine the possibility of such a deci-
> sion having in fact been made.[12]

Fortunately the war fears proved to be groundless. Perhaps Stalin's
stockpile was not large enough or his bombers not capable, or perhaps
Russia was simply not ready for war or did not want it. In any case
there were no Soviet atomic tests at all in 1950, and two in 1951.

Toward the middle 1950s useful information was obtained through
espionage. As part of an effort to maintain the credibility of Hans Felfe,
a West German intelligence officer who secretly worked for the Russians, Soviet intelligence passed Felfe a uranium ore sample from the
Czechoslovakian mines. Part of this sample found its way into the hands
of the CIA and enabled the U.S. to make accurate assessments of the
production potential of the mines. Nevertheless information on the overall tonnage of fissionable material and on the characteristics of Soviet
weapons tests were virtually the only raw data available to American
analysts.

The 1955 NIE projected the size of the Soviet stockpile for the end
of that year at 490 weapons, of which only fifteen were classed as large
(five hundred to one thousand kilotons) and 320 as medium (forty to
seventy kilotons) in size, but the estimate included the caveat that the
actual numbers could be as much as a third different from the figures

provided. In predicting the stockpile for mid-1958 the estimate outlined several assumptions with regard to the level of Soviet fissionable materials production and gave stockpile projections based on each assumption. All the plausible projections provided for expansion of the rate of Soviet production until 1958 (giving a base projection of 1,240 weapons in that year), and then posited either a leveling off, a continued steady-state expansion, or stepped-up production after that date.

Under the leveled-off hypothesis the NIE projected the Soviet stockpile at 1,540 nuclear weapons by mid-1959 and 1,850 by mid-1960. With steady-state expansion it forecast 1,570 weapons for 1959 and 1,960 the following year. The stepped-up production hypothesis led to a prediction of 1,760 weapons at mid-1959 and 2,450 for 1960. Thus the national estimate predicted an annual production rate for Soviet nuclear weapons ranging between 300 and 500 after 1958 with a rate averaging 250 annually before that date.

From the evidence available today it would appear that the Soviet weapons program progressed at something like the steady state expansion hypothesis. During 1954 there were one or two Soviet weapons tests. This increased in 1955 and in November of that year there was a second thermonuclear shot in the megaton range, which is reported to have resulted in two fatalities—a soldier thrown on the ground by concussion and a little girl killed by a falling wooden beam. The existing Soviet nuclear weapons test site at Semipalatinsk was supplemented in 1956 by a second site in the Soviet Arctic on the island of Novaya Zemlya, providing the Soviets with the capability of holding seven or eight atomic tests that year, including a sustained series begun on August 24, 1956. By 1958 press reports credited the Soviet Union with possession of over two thousand nuclear weapons. Russia had evidently entered an age of "nuclear plenty" as far as its weapons stockpile was concerned.

CHAPTER THREE
INTELLIGENCE RESOURCES

The necessity of predicting the emergence of Soviet atomic capability and weapon stockpiles must have served to point up the paucity of all kinds of information on developments behind the "Iron Curtain." The very existence of the Russian bomb then further accentuated the need for adequate intelligence collection programs; during this period we see the advent and development of important intelligence resources.

Translation and analysis of foreign publications was one of the first forms of information collection assigned to the CIA as a "matter of common concern." The CIA maintained a multimillion dollar budget for the acquisition of periodicals and photographs available abroad, produced numerous translations and reviews, and organized the whole into a comprehensive central archive available to analysts and operatives alike. Some information that was available to intelligence as a result of cooperation during World War II, such as the identities and locations of Soviet Army post offices, was instrumental in enabling intelligence to monitor the disposition of Soviet military units after the war. The CIA also took over the Foreign Broadcast Information Service and produced translations of foreign civilian radio transmissions. All this was primary information for analysts of Soviet programs.

A second intelligence source was espionage. Throughout much of this period there was intense competition and duplication of clandestine services because CIA's espionage branch was paralleled by the quasi-independent Office of Policy Coordination (OPC) headed by Frank Wisner. Internal division was reduced in 1952, when "Beetle" Smith forced a "shotgun wedding" between OPC and CIA's Office of Special Operations. Under the new organization espionage was the responsibility of the seemingly innocuous Directorate of Plans (DDP) with Wisner in command. Within DDP there were divisions for Eastern Europe and for Soviet Russia. The Soviet Russia division was led by Harry Rositzke, an "old hand" from the OSS with a Harvard Ph.D. in English literature. It focused on exploiting members of the East European and Russian emigré communities, many of whom were looking for places to live in the West between 1945 and 1950. Frank Lindsay's Eastern European Division also worked extensively among the refugees, as attested by the division's early-1950s budget of $100 million.

A special variety of espionage operations was the deliberate "penetration" attempt, in which the clandestine service would try to infiltrate agents into Russia, mostly emigrés who had agreed to return to their homeland as CIA agents. At this time the agent program received considerable emphasis. Indeed, building toward the hypothetical "war date" of 1954, the U.S. Air Force wanted to have agents stationed near every one of the two thousand-odd active Soviet military airfields. Rositzke has written that the CIA simply did not know enough about Russia to provide an agent with a solid "cover" story, even though there were numerous volunteers to take on the dangerous espionage missions. Agent losses were high—the Soviets claim to have captured twenty-three between 1951 and 1961—and the program was reportedly terminated in 1954. However, some intelligence gains from the agent programs included direct reports on the activities of heavy bombers at the airbase near Orsha, and, in 1952, a report demonstrating that an airfield at Providenaya Bay, in the Soviet Far East, was not capable of handling atomic weapons.[1]

At about the time agent operations were terminated, the Russians began to permit tourism and this opened up a new intelligence resource, so-called "legal" operations in which information was gleaned from the observations of tourists returning from the Soviet Union. In the "mounted" effort visitors to the Soviet Union were contacted in advance by the CIA, told what to look for, and debriefed upon their return. The "legal" operations became so widely used by the CIA that an entirely new organization, the Domestic Contact Service, was developed to service the need. "Legal" operations are said to have provided the first photographs of Russian surface-to-air missiles (SAMs), missile production plants, and the Soviet atomic-powered submarine. In 1953, despite the opposition of Ambassador George Kennan, the CIA was authorized for the first time to station officers at the Moscow embassy.

Besides tourists others were enlisted to help U.S. intelligence. An overwhelming majority of the German scientists and engineers who had been taken to Russia after the war later returned to the West. Most of them had little love for the Russians and were quite willing to share their experiences with Western intelligence officials. There was at least one full-scale conference between certain returned technicians and British and American intelligence analysts held under the auspices of the Air Force. The clandestine services maintained contact with other intelligence services and exchanged information with some of them. Cooperation with British intelligence was closest, including the exchange of NIEs for high level British estimates and the joint formulation of estimates on some subjects. Quadrennial conferences were also held where intelligence officials gathered from many countries to consider papers prepared in advance.

Another important resource was the knowledge of Soviet nationals. Some Russian military men defected to the West and their recollections accorded intelligence with vital firsthand information. A few others, because of disillusionment with Soviet society or for other motives, agreed to pass along intelligence information while continuing to work for the Soviet government or military. These latter, called "agents in place," provided important information on secret Soviet policy decisions. Indeed the stationing of CIA personnel in Moscow after 1953 was very probably related to the need to maintain contact with Soviet "agents in place." The value of these sources is illustrated by the fact that some of the earliest data on Russian bomber and missile development came from a defector in 1948, while an "agent in place," KGB major Peter Popov, furnished the CIA with material on Warsaw Pact military organization between 1953 and 1958.

"Human intelligence" had substantial limitations for American intelligence analysts. There was a windfall quality to its coverage since both agent and "legal" reports were scattered and intermittent and reflected contributors of uneven reliability. Moreover, since analysts were not informed of the identities of sources, they could not judge their reliability.

An alternative to "human intelligence" was offered by various types of machines designed to collect information. "Machine spies" or "national technical means," as they are now termed, supply periodic and precise coverage. Early forms included radio monitoring and aerial photography, both of which received powerful impetus during World War II. In addition, the machineries for technical collection—advanced radios, radars, radio direction finders, new kinds of cameras and film— promised even greater opportunities for systematic intelligence coverage. Thus technical means were highly attractive in the abstract: to the budgeteers there was the possibility of making intelligence "cost effective" for the first time; to the analyst there was the possibility of securing "hard" data in which they could have complete confidence; for the policy maker there was the knowledge that needed information would be in the system when required.

Technical collection programs were primitive in the immediate post-war years. Military authorities in cantonment areas along the borders of Eastern Europe monitored Soviet signals traffic as a routine measure. Aircraft packed with extra radio equipment conducted peripheral flights along the Iron Curtain to receive Soviet messages originating from farther away. Each of the armed services formed its own unit, termed a "security group" or a "security agency" to do this intelligence work. Centralized direction over this "signals intelligence" area was deemed so important that an interagency body called the United States Communications Intelligence Board (USCIB) was formed under the chairmanship of the director of central intelligence. In 1949 the USCIB ordered the separate units of the three services merged into an Armed Forces Security Agency which maintained its existence for some three years.

In November 1952 President Truman created a new agency to replace the Armed Forces Security Agency. Under an executive order of November fourth, which has remained secret to this day, Truman formed the National Security Agency (NSA) which has been responsible for conducting signals intelligence ever since. The secretary of defense became the executive authority for all NSA operations, and the USCIB became the advisory body to the director of the NSA. Under Army General Ralph J. Canine the NSA moved to Fort Meade, Maryland. On December 29, 1952, five weeks after his executive order, Truman issued a National Security Council Intelligence Directive which gave NSA its mission to collect signals intelligence. Drawing most of its personnel from the "security groups" of the individual services, the NSA central headquarters had about nine thousand officers by 1956. The agency's existence was officially acknowledged in the 1957 edition of the United States Government Manual. For the first time there was an intelligence organization wholly dedicated to technical collection programs.

At the time of NSA's creation the U.S. was already conducting some secret technical collection of Soviet communications. Principal among these was telephone tapping. The wiretaps of that period were so productive that agents called them "telephone sluices." Both sides knew that secrets passed along their telephone cables and developed methods of "scrambling" telephone conversations for unintended listeners. Carl Nelson, of the CIA's Office of Communications, discovered that U.S. scrambling codes could be broken by means of the interception and amplification of faint echoes of the real signals, called "artifacts," which traveled along the cables with the scrambled messages. It was soon established that Soviet scrambling equipment could be defeated by similar means and U.S. intelligence developed machinery for this purpose.

In the fall of 1951 Operation Silver was begun in Vienna to tap the

Russian telephone cables to that city. The Americans then discovered that British intelligence had maintained a telephone sluice into the Soviet embassy for nearly two years. But the British lacked the equipment to recover the real signals on the Soviets' "secure," or scrambled, channels. Anglo-American intelligence then pooled its resources for the telephone sluice while the U.S. also installed additional taps on other Soviet cables in and around Vienna. The success of the Vienna wiretaps was such that U.S. intelligence soon planned Operation Gold, a tap into the vital Berlin-Leipzig telephone cable, over which passed Russian communications between Moscow and their command in East Germany, as well as sensitive military teleprinter channels. Evidently this telephone sluice was suggested by the British, who found on the Berlin city master plans that the cable ran within three hundred yards of Rudow, in the American sector. A special task force was formed for Operation Gold under William K. Harvey of CIA. Working from West Berlin the Americans established an "experimental" radar station in Rudow. Under cover of the construction work a tunnel was built that carefully aimed to intersect with the Russian phone cable. Construction began in the summer of 1954 and was completed in early 1955 at a cost believed to have been between four and six million dollars.

The tapping of Soviet communications began in 1955 and continued for almost a year, after specific approval from President Dwight D. Eisenhower. There were some bad moments. On one occasion the Americans worried that settling of the ground would alert the East German farmer opposite that a tunnel ran under his field. During the winter there was a scare when, after a snow, it became apparent that heating units in the tunnel were melting the snow on top of it, a dead giveaway. The Americans had to turn off the heaters and rushed refrigerators into the tunnel to cool off the ground above. The tunnel was finally discovered by East German repairmen during a maintenance call in April 1956, reportedly after a warning to the Russians from British double-agent George Blake.

The information already gathered must have been considerable. Gold was rated a "brilliant success" by CIA's special programs manager Richard Bissell twelve years later, although it is worth noting that Bissell has since recalled that the "reams" of reports from Gold forced him to consider imposing a monthly quota in order to limit what the Berlin Station could send back from the sluice. This would presumably have forced Harvey's collectors to exercise some selectivity in what they thought important. Another CIA officer, analyst Victor Marchetti, has written that the Berlin wiretap "produced literally tons of trivia and gossip but little in the way of high-grade secret information."[2]

Aerial photography was a technical source that came of age during World War II. The use of overlapping sets of photographs and stereoscopes for interpreters of the finished pictures, plus the possibility of gathering sequential sets of photographs of the same locale over time, aided in photographic interpretation.[3] By 1945 there were specialized reconnaissance aircraft and units in both the Navy and the Air Force. After the war occasional photographs were taken by the peripheral aircraft flights along the Iron Curtain. There was also a program for some photo coverage of the interior. In the late 1940s the U.S. used a combination of the RB-50 aircraft (a modified B-29) with a jet reconnaissance plane of the RF-86 type strapped underneath. In this fashion the carrier aircraft would fly to a release point along the frontier, the jet would streak to a target up to a couple of hundred miles away, and then would escape before Soviet air defenses could react to the intrusion. Under a different program RB-36 aircraft based in Britain made flights north to monitor Soviet naval bases and nuclear test sites in the Arctic Ocean. These flights were called "Murmansk Runs" by the participating flight crews and the missions may occasionally have overflown Russia. In 1950 the Navy began development of the first aircraft specifically designed for an intelligence role, although that particular design was optimized for the collection of signals transmissions.

In order to cover the Soviet interior, intelligence technologists hit upon the idea of using high-altitude unmanned balloons. Although it was sponsored by CIA, only a handful of top intelligence officials knew of the balloon program. Scientists at the Office of Naval Research developed the large Skyhook balloons and others with the Air Force provided high-altitude cameras. The first Skyhook was launched from St. Cloud, Minnesota, on September 25, 1947, and one of these balloons may have been involved in the incident of January 7, 1948, in which Air Force pilot Captain Thomas Mantell was killed while chasing an unidentified flying object. The Skyhook balloon programs soon became massive, with over a hundred flights a year launched each by the Navy and the Air Force, which also used Skyhook for weather-data collection and other purposes.

For its intelligence role Skyhook was launched from Western Europe and allowed to drift across the Soviet Union. Radio commands sent when the balloons reached the vicinity of Japan would detach instrument packages from the balloons, parachuting them to earth for recovery. Later techniques were developed to allow in-flight recovery of the instrument capsules by specially equipped aircraft. This use of Skyhook in what was called the Moby Dick program was not very satisfactory. Many of the balloons crashed in Russia, and some were recovered by the Soviets. Equally problematic was the fact that the photo coverage depended upon the capriciousness of the wind so that it was not always easy even to tell what had been photographed.

At the same time the risks were growing for the manned aircraft programs. Almost forty aircraft were lost along the Iron Curtain or on the Berlin air corridors in the period 1945–1947. In October 1952 a reconnaissance plane was shot down by MIG's over the Sea of Japan. In July 1953 a Royal Air Force RB-57, an aircraft which then held the world altitude record, was almost lost to Soviet air defenses in the Ukraine. The situation clearly had to be remedied.

As early as the spring of 1949, when the CIA originally approached the Air Force to make arrangements for parachuting agents into Russia, the search for alternatives to the agent program raised the issue of a high-altitude aircraft using a precision camera. This proposal was given more serious consideration in 1954 when Eisenhower appointed James R. Killian to head a panel studying the question of reducing the possibility of a surprise attack on the United States.

The subcommittee of the Killian panel concerned with intelligence issues was chaired by Edwin Land, president of the Polaroid Corporation. Land strongly believed that cameras could be built capable of taking good photographs from a very high altitude. Consequently the subcommittee recommended that the U.S. develop and procure an aircraft specifically designed for overhead reconnaissance from high altitude.

The reconnaissance plane they had in mind was the U-2. It had been conceived by the Lockheed Corporation, and could be built largely from existing components right up to the airframe itself. Designed to fly at so high an altitude that it could not be touched by any Soviet air defense then in use, the plane, with its proven airframe, was also relatively inexpensive to develop.

The U-2 was approved by the IAC in late November 1954, and put before President Eisenhower during the first week of December. Killian recalls that Eisenhower listened carefully and asked many tough questions. He approved the development provided that the plane could be built secretly and not entangled in the Department of Defense bureaucracy. Director of Central Intelligence Allen Dulles met this requirement by offering to develop the U-2 under the CIA cloak, using the director's secret contingency fund for the initial financing. Lockheed was then authorized to build a U-2 prototype at its plant in Burbank, California. The initial program called for the manufacture of thirty planes at a cost of $35 million.

While Eisenhower approved development of the U-2, he was careful to instruct CIA to come back to the White House for authorization to establish operating bases. Eisenhower remarked,

> Well, boys, I believe the country needs this information and I'm going to approve it. But I'll tell you one thing. Someday one of these machines is going to get caught and we're going to have a storm.[4]

The U-2 made its debut in August 1955 and was substantially freed of bugs that same year. With later weight improvements, range increased from twenty-six hundred to thirty-two hundred miles, which allowed for more extensive missions. The U-2 flew above seventy thousand feet altitude and navigated by stellar fixes. On a flight the plane would locate its targets and then execute a dog-leg maneuver over the target, a far cry from the haphazard guidance of the Moby Dick balloons. Each U-2 flight carried enough film to produce some four thousand paired photos, which could be assembled into a mosaic of the points surveyed, over a strip of perhaps seven miles to either side of the plane's flight path.

Collection guidance for the U-2 was provided by an Ad Hoc Requirements Committee that was established in the summer of 1955. Each member served as the focal point within his organization for aerial photo coverage requests. The committee also served as liaison for the inter-departmental clearances necessary to approve each series of U-2 flights. Members included representatives from CIA, the State Department, and the armed service intelligence units. The committee would formulate flight profiles that were passed for approval to the White House through Eisenhower's military aide, Colonel Andrew Goodpaster. Returning U-2 films would be developed by a photographic-interpretation unit formed within CIA in 1953 and interested parties would contact their Ad Hoc Committee member for access to the interpreted pictures.

A first group of six U-2 pilots, all former military fliers, completed their training at Watertown Strip, Nevada, in April 1956. (Another pilot had been killed in the crash of a training flight.) All had undergone a process called "sheep-dipping" in the CIA which was to disguise their military background—they were officially employees of Lockheed Aircraft. Thus by 1956 the CIA had both planes and pilots; the U-2 was ready to be put into operation. Eventually twenty-two aircraft were procured at a cost some three million dollars under the original estimate.

In the summer of 1955, when the U-2 was nearing the end of its flight tests, the President quite unexpectedly chose to present a mutual overhead reconnaissance proposal to the Soviets as a disarmament mea-

32   THE SOVIET ESTIMATE

sure during the 1955 Geneva Summit conference. Aerial reconnaissance as a specific disarmament action was advocated within the U.S.
government by Nelson Rockefeller. Rockefeller commissioned certain
studies on the technical capabilities of aerial reconnaissance, passed the
studies along to President Eisenhower, and recommended that the possibility be taken up at Geneva. There is no evidence that Rockefeller or
his technical experts were apprised of the prospects for high-resolution
photography from the U-2. Rather they judged photographic coverage
of the Soviet Union to be feasible with aircraft already in use for the
purpose. Press reports of the period speculated that Russia could have
been covered by overflights over a period of thirty days, using a total of
thirty-four RB-47 aircraft at a cost of $15 million for each cover.

Eisenhower, who, of course, did know of the U-2 and of the imminence of requests to fund its deployment, was sufficiently attracted
to the Rockefeller recommendation that he ordered it receive detailed
study within government. Rockefeller held meetings at Paris on July
eighteenth and nineteenth with the President's disarmament commissioner, Harold Stassen; Chairman of the JCS, Admiral Arthur Radford;
and other high officials. Preliminary exchanges with other Western
leaders gave the President sufficient confidence in the aerial reconnaissance proposal that he planned to present it at Geneva. "Open Skies"
required that each country present the others with a "military blueprint"
of its force structure, following which each side would have legal rights
to a certain number of reconnaissance flights annually, over the others'
airspace and without restriction. The flights would verify that the posture and dispositions of the adversary's forces were not otherwise than
claimed. "Open Skies" was offered to the French, British, and Soviet
delegates by Eisenhower on the afternoon of July 21, 1955, in what the
President recalled was an atmosphere of great tension.

Eisenhower's presentation of the "Open Skies" plan at Geneva
stunned the audience. As if to increase the dramatic effect, his remarks
were followed by a very loud peal of thunder, which seemed to come
from nowhere. There was complete silence in the conference room. Soviet Premier Nikolai Bulganin initially saw some merit in "Open Skies,"
but Party Secretary Khrushchev, the real power in the Soviet delegation,
told Eisenhower privately that he did not agree with Bulganin—there
would be no action on the proposal. Although "Open Skies" was included in the outline plan for disarmament submitted to the United Nations Disarmament Subcommittee on August thirtieth, and although it
passed in the General Assembly by a vote of fifty-six to seven, the Soviets never did respond. "Open Skies" seems to have raised Russian fears
of legalizing Western intelligence-gathering in the Soviet Union. The

sole effect of the offer was to intensify the arms-control debate over whether "on-site" inspection was required as a provision of potential international agreements on disarmament and nuclear weapons.

In mid-August 1955 there was discussion of the use of the U-2 at the NSC. Eisenhower often conducted the most sensitive business in his administration among smaller groups after NSC meetings ended. He met with Allen Dulles and Richard Bissell from CIA, John Foster Dulles from State, Admiral Radford for the Joint Chiefs, and the President's aide General Goodpaster. The CIA requested that its U-2 unit be deployed overseas, and that the Air Force provide air basing and logistics support proper to the operation of a U-2 unit. As part of a briefing designed to illustrate U-2 potential, Eisenhower was shown pictures of his own favorite golf course at Augusta, Georgia. The pictures featured distinct images of golf balls on the putting green taken from fifty-five thousand feet. Eisenhower was an avid golfer. Needless to say, the CIA received permission to proceed with the U-2 program. But Eisenhower also continued the strict secrecy in which the program had been conducted.

Flights over Russia began in mid-1956. In June Bissell came in from CIA with Allen Dulles to get permission to fly the U-2 over Russia. After presenting the flight plans he was asked to wait outside while Eisenhower considered the matter with Allen Dulles and his brother Foster, the secretary of state. Goodpaster joined Bissell outside the meeting room to inform him of the decision.

"Well, you've been authorized to conduct overflights for ten days."

"You mean ten *flying* days," queried Bissell. "In other words bad days don't count."

Goodpaster answered, "It doesn't mean anything of the kind. It means ten days. You're free to go for ten days and it starts from now."[5]

Several days later the weather cleared and the flight program began. Partly as a result of this urgency, however, the U-2 flights coincided closely with the official visit of Twining's Air Force delegation as guests of the Soviet Air Force. The Twining visit ended in Leningrad on June thirtieth, at the Monino Air Force Academy. The next day the first U-2 flight covered Moscow, Leningrad, and the Soviet Baltic seacoast. Events following the second flight dispelled any doubts that the Russians knew of the U-2 flights; the Soviet Foreign Ministry lodged a secret protest against the intrusions. The United States made no reply. Instead, on July 9, 1956, NACA announced that the initial high-altitude weather data from the U-2 had been processed and that the plane had thus proved its worth.

Other signs of Soviet concern with the U-2 followed their diplomatic note. On July tenth a Tass bulletin mentioned a Soviet protest over violations of airspace. Four days later, during a reception at the French embassy in Moscow, Premier Nikolai Bulganin took aside the U.S. ambassador, Chester Bohlen, and asked him if he was familiar with the Soviet note delivered in Washington. Bohlen, who had learned of plans for the flights but was not informed of particulars, replied that he knew of the note but had no further information whatsoever. Bulganin claimed to have indisputable evidence through radar tracking of U.S. violations and emphasized the seriousness of the matter. On July twenty-third there was a further exchange between Marshal R. A. Rudenko, chief of staff of the Soviet Air Force and Western reporters, in which the Soviet officer warned that "all necessary measures" would be taken if the air intrusions continued.

The Americans temporarily stopped the U-2 overflights but six had already been made. Pictures of the Kremlin are said to have impressed Eisenhower much as had those of the golf balls, when a full-dress briefing was held for the President. Meanwhile, over the base at Lakenheath in mid-August, an incident occurred that could have drawn unwanted attention to the U-2's. This was the appearance of a UFO, which was sighted both visually and by radar one night. It is not known if the UFO incident is related to U-2 operations from Lakenheath but this, combined with worsening Anglo-American relations over the Suez matter, induced the Americans to transfer the main U-2 base to Wiesbaden. Respite was short lived, however. Use of the German U-2 base was partly compromised during September 1956 by the crash of a U-2 aircraft near Kaiserslautern in which the pilot was killed. To avoid possible revelation Eisenhower then canceled a flight series from the German bases in December.

One last group of CIA U-2 pilots completed their training in February 1957, after which the Air Force began to train their own pilots on the plane. By then the 1010 Detachment had been activated at Incirlik. The NATO airbase at Bodø, Norway, also came into use for U-2 flights. Bodø was well placed to monitor Russian activity at the Novaya Zemlya atomic test facility while Incirlik was within easy flight range of the Soviet missile test centers in the Ukraine. The secrecy of the program did not prove easy to maintain, however. Aside from Soviet radar observations there were oversights. For instance the U-2 used liquid hydrogen to help facilitate oxidation of fuel in its engine; but, the Air Force made no effort to preserve secrecy on the movements of liquid hydrogen, which required special procedures and equipment and was used for few things other than U-2 fueling. After the Kaiserslautern crash a Soviet embassy car was often found parked near the end of the runway at Wiesbaden, observing the takeoffs of aircraft, including the U-2.

After the initial effort most of the U-2 flights were part of daily missions along the periphery of the Soviet Union. Requests for photo coverage were collected by Bissell's Ad Hoc Requirements Committee. In view of the need for excellent flying weather to facilitate photography, the Bissell committee grouped its planned missions into quarterly programs for approval by the White House. Flight requests were cleared with John Foster Dulles through his assistant secretary of state Robert Murphy. Bissell then carried the requests to Goodpaster at the NSC. Sometimes the military advisor would be out and the recommendation would go to Major John S. Eisenhower, the President's son. Eisenhower discussed the risks and opportunities of each flight program with his secretaries of state and defense. Caution in approving flight plans prevailed throughout the Eisenhower administration; Bissell's private air force carried out far fewer intrusions than its planes were capable of. It is reported that only twenty to thirty actual penetrations of Soviet airspace were made before U-2 overflights ended in 1960.

Aside from the U-2, radar was the newest technical collection mechanism in the mid-1950s. The first large intelligence radar was a National Security Agency (NSA) facility erected near Samsoun, Turkey. Radar is a detection apparatus that functions by means of bouncing a radio beam off an object. The time required for the beam's outward and return pulses establishes the distance between the radar and the object. In addition certain characteristics of the returning beam pulse can be used to establish other information about the observed object, such as its altitude or size. Repeated observations are also able to establish speed and direction data. Radar had been widely proven in World War II and was a major element in continental air defense during the 1950s, but it had not previously been used for an intelligence application.

When the suggestion was made to construct an intelligence radar there was initial opposition within the Pentagon. In 1954 the support of Trevor Gardner, who believed that the U.S. had to exploit every conceivable intelligence method to trace Soviet missile progress, was instrumental in quieting opposition, particularly from the Air Force. With the USAF change of heart construction of the Turkish radar was quickly approved by President Eisenhower. By the summer of 1955 the radar was operational and able to track Soviet IRBM launches from Kapustin Yar. The Samsoun facility initially had a range of about one thousand nautical miles, which was insufficient to cover Soviet missiles throughout their flights, but advances in radar antenna technology were incorporated in the Turkish installation which, by 1957, extended beam range out to perhaps thirty-five hundred nautical miles. Thereafter, any Soviet missile that followed a trajectory taking it to forty miles or more altitude could be tracked by the U.S. radars. The success of the NSA project was such that when, in 1958, construction of an intelligence radar was proposed for Alaska, in order to observe the Soviet missiles during their reentry phase, the project had widespread support and was rapidly approved.

For some time the existence of the radar in Turkey was a closely held secret in the United States. However, a number of scientists were aware of the technical possibilities and some, such as Dr. William O. Baker of Bell Laboratories, encouraged government officials to rely on the novel technologies coming off the drawing boards. These advances were commonly covered in the technical literature. One such magazine, *Aviation Week,* published an article and editorial in its October 21, 1957, issue that described the Turkish radar installations and their work in monitoring Soviet missile progress.

This revelation caused immediate consternation in government. On October twenty-third, Deputy Secretary of Defense Donald Quarles received telephone calls on the radar article from both the Office of the Secretary of Defense and from the White House. Eisenhower apparently decided to take the issue up directly with *Aviation Week*'s publishers, McGraw-Hill in New York. A White House official met with Donald C. McGraw in his office on October twenty-ninth. According to a memorandum deposited in White House records, the publisher was told that

> the article contained some things that were true, some things that were untrue, and some things that were in between. I further stated that in the judgment of the President the publication of this article constituted a serious breach of security and that the President wanted Mr. McGraw personally to know of the gravity with which he viewed the event.

The unnamed White House official warned that it was entirely possible that there would be some follow-up by other government agencies and asked the New York publisher "what assurance he could convey to the President that better judgment would be used in the future."

Mr. McGraw told him that he had just returned to his office

> from a business trip throughout the southwestern states but that he was familiar with the article. He clearly had some notion about repercussions also because he was prepared with a response that he understood the material in the article was known to many persons both here and abroad and to the Russians. I stated that it was true that some of the facts were known to some people but that the article in *Aviation Week* was the first time some of the key facts had been published. I then tried to point out in general terms that the principal consequences were in directions other than telling something to the Russians.[6]

The New York publisher agreed that in the future an additional senior editor of *Aviation Week* would pass upon articles that had a clear national security aspect slated for the magazine. No legal action against McGraw-Hill followed this exchange, quite possibly because the administration did not wish to draw any further public attention to the article.

Initially, the armed services retained all authority for collecting raw information pertinent to their military roles and missions. But this became less acceptable, primarily to the CIA, as more and more factors were seen as relevant to the determination of military capabilities. The CIA bent a special effort to acquiring expertise in the scientific intelligence area. It formed an Office of Scientific Intelligence (OSI) to satisfy demands for technical analyses. As OSI grew in size and competence it began to perform analyses of weapons still in the development stages. The military saw this as an encroachment upon their area of intelligence concern. A new effort to resolve the issue of responsibilities was contained in DCID 3/4, promulgated on August 14, 1952. Here Director of Central Intelligence Walter Bedell Smith specified that "no complete separation of areas of interest is possible or necessarily desirable in scientific and technical intelligence activities" and, further, OSI was explicitly made responsible for analyses on "pertinent applied research and development," which came very close to specifying weapons "in development." [7] The order amounted to a license for CIA to produce estimates on "high technology" weapons. The Scientific Estimates Committee constituted under the IAC by DCID 3/4 proved essentially moribund, but the OSI had succeeded in establishing a definite military intelligence role. By 1955 OSI was performing research on technical intelligence matters in five divisions.

CHAPTER FOUR
THE BOMBER GAP

During World War II the Russians used their air force mainly in support of their ground troops. There were few Soviet attacks against targets in the enemy's interior, no aircraft specifically designed for this task, and no articulated doctrine of "strategic bombing" such as that which underlay the massive rear-area bombing carried out by the British and Americans. As was noted in an Air Force intelligence analysis of November 1946,

> The U.S.S.R. will remain predominantly a land power. The traditional conception of the Army as the only sure shield in defense and the only fully effective weapon in the attack will persist in the future. . . . [The Soviet Air Force] will remain essentially tactical in design.[1]

Such a view was consistent with the Soviets' emphasis on the "permanently operating factors" and the general Western appreciation of Soviet military doctrine.

Of course the Soviets had far more interest in strategic bombardment than the "permanently operating factors" would appear to indicate. They would need a heavy bomber to carry an atom bomb and the development of its technology was equally difficult. During the war the Soviets several times requested provision of heavy bombers under the Lend Lease program. Only one such aircraft was ever given to them and that was a B-24 which had developed mechanical trouble and had been forced to land at Yakutsk in late 1942. Near the end of the war the Russians themselves interned three B-29's which landed in the Soviet Far East after bombing missions over Japan. Despite American requests, these aircraft were never returned.

After the war, the Soviets demonstrated a lively interest in German bomber technology. A large organization had been formed within the Soviet Rear Services Staff explicitly for the exploitation of German technology. Said to be under the direction of Georgi Malenkov, the "Special

Construction Bureaus" had some sixty thousand to seventy thousand personnel. One participant who defected to the West in September 1946 felt that this effort "degenerated into the predatory looting of German industry."[2] In any case the Soviets shipped most of the aircraft factory machinery they encountered back to Russia along with perhaps two thousand German aeronautical engineers and workers. They also acquired the blueprints for, and one prototype of, a German heavy bomber, the Junkers Ju-287, which was a six-engine jet bomber with a design featuring forward-swept wings. Only one or two had been built.

It appears that the Russians took apart each of the types of heavy bombers available to them and created blueprints of the planes in this manner. They apparently decided that the U.S. B-29-type aircraft best suited their purposes. Stalin reputedly called in Andrei Tupolev, leader of a major Soviet aircraft design bureau, and gave him eighteen months to duplicate the B-29. Tupolev fulfilled the assignment and his bureau acquired the reputation of being the foremost Soviet bomber designers. The new bomber was designated the Tu-4 and first flew in 1947. Its existence was revealed in an air parade staged over Moscow in May 1948. This date met the predictions of the Central Intelligence Group, which, in its estimate ORE 3/1 of October 31, 1946, expected the Russians to develop and produce a bomber "with the approximate characteristics of the B-29" by 1948 and to achieve serial production of these planes before 1950.

In 1946 the Soviets had formed a Long-Range Air Force, evidently looking ahead to the operational use of large bombers. A 1948 defector who had been a technical expert in the Soviet Air Force, Lieutenant Colonel G. A. Tokayev, brought to the West the news that the Politburo was giving special attention to the Long-Range Air Force. By 1949 this force had enough Tu-4 bombers to equip three airfields in western Russia, and four years later the Soviets had deployed some one thousand Tu-4's, with monthly production ranging from ten to twenty-five aircraft.

The United States was quite concerned about the development of Soviet strategic attack capabilities. In July 1947 President Truman established an Air Policy Commission under Thomas K. Finletter to study the question of the future size of the United States Air Force. The Finletter Report, which was presented in January 1948, projected that by 1952 the Soviet Union would have a substantial atomic strike capability. The emergence of the Tu-4, which the Americans designated the Bull, seemed to confirm these fears. Almost as soon as news of the Soviet Joe I atomic shot became available, intelligence concluded that the Russians were now capable of detonating atomic weapons on American soil.

At one meeting Air Force intelligence representatives expressed interest in having the CIA acquire a Bull bomber complete with pilot for intelligence evaluation. Although this request was somewhat unrealistic, the Soviet Long-Range Air Force was subsequently monitored with especial care.

Although the size of the Soviet atomic bomb stockpile was only conjecture, with no "hard" evidence to support it, the limitations of Russian bombers were both visible and determinant. The Tu-4 Bull was not, in fact, really suitable for atomic attacks against the continental United States. The Bull's flight range was insufficient to reach a U.S. target and return to its Soviet base, even in the absence of American air defenses. Further, the Tu-4 could not refuel in flight, a capacity demonstrated by an American bomber in March 1949, and thus Bull's range could not be extended.

The main obstacle to an indigenous Soviet bomber design lay in the area of aircraft propulsion. Russian aircraft engines had too little power to lift the substantial weight required by a heavy bomber design. With the appearance of jet propulsion at the end of World War II the problem was further complicated because of the necessity of making the transition to a novel technology. In the late 1940s, however, the Russians were able to import fifty Rolls-Royce "Nene" engines from Great Britain. This enabled engine specialists to study jet propulsion techniques in detail, and the Soviets soon developed both jet and turboprop aircraft engines with significantly greater power. In 1953 the Soviet Union introduced a jet engine capable of fifteen thousand pounds of thrust, which was sufficient to power a high-performance aircraft.

By this time, design work on purely Soviet bomber aircraft was far enough advanced so that new aircraft prototypes soon followed the new engines. One heavy bomber was a jet model from the Myacheslav Design Bureau. This plane was given the designation Mya-4 by the Soviets and called Bison in the West. It had an air speed of 520–560 miles per hour and could carry a bomb load of ten thousand pounds over seven thousand nautical miles. Work on the Bison is thought to have begun in 1950. The first prototype was flown in 1953 and appeared for the first time in the Moscow air parade of May 1954. Another jet bomber, somewhat smaller than the Bison, was the Tupolev Tu-16 Badger. This aircraft first flew in 1952 and entered series production the next year. The Badger was a medium bomber and, although it became the workhorse of the Soviet aerial bombardment forces, it did not have the range for two-way intercontinental missions. A third bomber design, also from Tupolev, was the Tu-95 Bear. This was a turboprop heavy bomber without the Bison's speed, but able to carry a larger payload over a longer range, specifically about twenty-five thousand pounds for seventy-eight hundred nautical miles.

As the Soviets built up their heavy bomber force, they made an effort to gain propaganda mileage from their military developments. In the case of bombers the Russian practice was to flaunt them in the periodic air parades, when masses of Russian aircraft flew over Western (and Soviet) observers in tight formations. The air parades were a standard feature of the Soviet celebration of such occasions as May Day, Air Force Day, and the anniversary of the Soviet revolution. The flyovers were often the best opportunities for Western attachés to gain firsthand impressions of Soviet equipment. Typically, foreign observers would be shown to a reviewing stand along the flight path of the air parade. The Soviets would have been practicing formation flying for some weeks prior to the parade and when the day came their massed squadrons could be very impressive. The impression given is described by Vice Admiral Leslie C. Stevens, the U.S. naval attaché in Moscow from 1947 to 1949. Recounting the Tu-4 Bull's second appearance in 1949 he wrote

> [The air parade] began with a perfect formation of planes sweeping across the sky and spelling out "SLAVA STALINU" (Glory to Stalin). It continued with various formations, jet fighters and bombers. One squadron of fifteen heavy bombers roared overhead, indistinguishable, except in tiny details, from our B-29s. To build them in quantity is itself an accomplishment. It was for us during the war. The jets with extreme sweptback wings and tail looked like darting arrows, but the speed they showed was not startling.[3]

It was the Soviet practice of making these flyovers that catalyzed a famous intelligence dispute since called the "bomber gap."

The start of the "bomber gap" came with the appearance of a single Bison jet heavy bomber in the 1954 May Day air parade. At that time Air Force intelligence hypothesized that the Bison seen was the prototype model of a design probably begun during 1952, so that full-scale production was unlikely before 1956. To test this hypothesis the Air Force selected a group of U.S. airframe manufacturers, furnished them with the performance capabilities estimated for the Bison, and asked them to study how long it would take to put the plane in production, given Soviet engineering technology and machine-tool limitations. There is no indication that the American manufacturers were asked to evaluate Soviet aircraft-engine technology. The resulting contractor study foresaw a four-year production lead-time and thus supported the A-2 hypothesis.

More Bisons appeared in the 1955 May Day parade, casting doubt on the 1954 forecast, which had been reiterated in a February 1955 intelligence estimate. Reaction was immediate from the Strategic Air Command (SAC) intelligence director, Colonel James H. Walsh, and Air Force intelligence chief Major General John A. Samford. The secretary of defense, Charles E. Wilson, was apprised of their concern and on May thirteenth the Pentagon issued a press release which stated that

> the Soviets have recently elected to expose some new aircraft developments
> in air parade formation over Moscow. These observations establish a new
> basis for our estimate of Soviet production of the heavy jet bomber (Type
> 37) Myacheslav M[ya]-4 and of the medium bomber (Type 39) Tupolev Tu-
> 16.[4]

The implication was that if the Soviets had begun production earlier than previously believed, their strength must have been rising faster than had been thought.

At this time the NIE on Soviet intentions and capabilities through 1960 was in draft and about to go to the IAC for final review. The estimate was approved with no dissents on May 16, 1955. It cited current Russian heavy bomber strength at 20 Bisons and 20 Bears. This inventory was expected to rise to 80 of each by mid-1956, to 200 Bisons and 150 Bears by mid-1957, and to 350 and 250 respectively by mid-1958. Soviet bomber strength was expected to level off in 1959 at a level of 400 Mya-4 jets and 300 Bear turboprops. NIE 11-3-55 included the following caveat:

> There is no firm intelligence on the planned balance between the types and
> categories of long-range aircraft or on their future authorized organizational
> aircraft strengths; the above figures represent our estimate of the most
> probable way in which the Soviet Long-Range Aviation would be propor-
> tioned during the period and is predicated on the assumption(s) (a) that no
> change will occur in the total authorized number of aircraft in [individual]
> long-range units; (b) that the BEAR turboprop heavy bomber is currently in
> series production; and (c) that the U.S.S.R. is devoting a major aircraft pro-
> duction effort to the development of massive intercontinental air attack ca-
> pability.[5]

Measured against United States defense plans, by mid-1959 the Long-Range Air Force would be more powerful than the Strategic Air Command.

The judgments expressed in the NIE were then apparently confirmed by Soviet activity. The Russians scheduled another flyover for their Air Force Day ceremonies, only a couple of weeks prior to a scheduled Ge-

neva summit between Soviet and Western leaders. On the appointed
day the U.S. air attaché to the Soviet Union, Colonel Charles E. Taylor,
went out to Tushino airfield to watch the air parade. It appears that the
Soviets, perhaps engaged in posturing before the summit, executed a
deceptive flyover. Taylor saw first ten and then eighteen Bison jet
bombers fly past the reviewing stand, almost double the number that
had appeared in May and four times the number of modern B-52 jet
heavy bombers then in SAC. The flyover was deceptive because the
Soviets evidently pressed into service every available Bison and then
had the first serial of planes circle, out of sight of the reviewing stand,
to make a second pass overhead. Taking the exhibition at face value the
number of Bisons seen that day exceeded the total number with which
the Soviets were credited in the NIE.

The result of the Soviet deception was to encourage U.S. intelligence
to revise its projections of Soviet bomber strength upwards yet again.
As the director of central intelligence, Allen Dulles, later put it,

> Every indication pointed to [the Soviets] having adopted [the Bison] as a
> major element of their offensive strength and to an intention to produce
> these planes more or less as fast as they could.[6]

By the end of 1955 intelligence was predicting that the Soviet inventory
of Bisons alone would rise to between six hundred and eight hundred
by 1959 or 1960 while production of Bear bombers was expected to
reach twenty-five per month before the end of 1956. These predictions
were leaked and appeared in the press, resulting in the first public
charges of the existence of a "bomber gap."

The alarming news went to congressional leaders in greater detail in
early 1956 as the Eisenhower administration made its case for the fiscal
year 1957 defense budget. Already concerned over Russian progress in
the development of guided missiles, the Senate Armed Services Committee on February twenty-fourth decided to hold hearings on the airpower situation. Eisenhower attempted to head off the impending
investigation with a supplemental budget request for the current fiscal
year to increase production of Air Force B-52 bombers. But the chairman of the Senate Subcommittee on Airpower, Senator Stuart Symington (D-Missouri), who had himself been secretary of the Air Force from
1947 to 1949, was not mollified by the administration's budget initiative.
The Symington subcommittee opened its hearings on April 16, 1956,
and received testimony from a number of senior defense officials. Here
the Air Force saw an opportunity to win approval for enlarged bomber
production and for strengthening SAC. Air Force witnesses tended to

play up the supposed Russian lead in bombers and even asserted that SAC would dwindle to but half the size of the Soviet Long-Range Air Force by 1959.

Air Force preparations for the airpower hearings included consultations between headquarters in Washington and the SAC command at Offutt Air Base near Omaha. The intelligence chiefs, Samford at the capital and Colonel Robert N. Smith at Offutt, furnished figures on Soviet bomber strength that were worked up into a chart comparing Russian numbers with those planned for SAC. The chart was presented to the Symington subcommittee by SAC commander General Curtis LeMay during his testimony. LeMay asserted that the CIA agreed with the Soviet numbers. LeMay also indicated that it was only reasonable to project that the Russians would support their bomber force by providing dispersed bases and an aerial refueling capability for the planes.

Defense Secretary Charles Wilson disagreed with the Air Force and said so strongly. In one session Senator Symington even accused the secretary of "unconstitutionally contradicting" both Air Force Chief of Staff General Nathan Twining and CIA chief Allen Dulles. Wilson continued to object. "Engine Charlie" called his own press conference on May first to emphasize his view that U.S. defenses were adequate to the Soviet threat. Wilson held to this view before the Symington subcommittee in July. Moreover, he resisted the imputation that an Air Force warning on the Soviet bombers had been ignored in 1953. Rather, Wilson maintained that at the time, when information on the Soviet program was "very sketchy indeed," he had nevertheless approved the initiation of a second production line for the B-52. In his own testimony of June twenty-first Admiral Arthur F. Radford, the chairman of the Joint Chiefs of Staff, stated that "there is good reason to believe that we normally overestimate Communist capabilities in almost every respect."[7] Similarly both Navy and Army witnesses were less pessimistic than the Air Force, but to no avail. Between Eisenhower's requested supplementary and the additional increase approved by Congress in the wake of the airpower hearings, the Air Force budget grew by $928.5 million.

Before the airpower hearings ended, an Air Force delegation actually visited the Soviet Union for the first time since the war. Twining led the group, which arrived in Russia a mere four days after his Symington subcommittee testimony, in which he recommended the formation of six additional wings of B-52's. There were also delegations from twenty-seven other nations, which the Soviets guided on an eight-day lightning tour of Soviet Air Force installations as part of their Air Force Day commemorations. The U.S. team wished to discover how far the Soviets might be willing to expose their air progress to outside scrutiny and also "to attempt to measure their current and potential air strength and degree of readiness for global war, to the extent that conditions imposed by our hosts would allow and against the background of our existing assessments."[8]

The U.S. delegation flew into Moscow's Vnukovo airport and was received by Soviet chief marshal of aviation Pavel Zhigarev and other officials. There was an air parade at Tushino, a reception held by Marshal Zhukov, a ground aircraft exhibit at a Russian fighter base west of Moscow, visits to the Zhukovski Air Engineering Academy, two aircraft plants, an atomic power plant, and the Monino Air Force Academy. Twining noted in his report to President Eisenhower that Russian personnel had been "invariably unresponsive" when members of his party endeavored to converse "on serious professional lines" and that no one "succeeded in promoting a forthright exchange of views with anyone." Consequently, "we obtained no new information of significance."[9] Soviet officials had carefully controlled all interchanges and had consciously played down their strength. On this occasion, for example, only three Bison and four Bear bombers were seen in the Soviet flyover.

Upon the delegation's return to the U.S., Twining apparently told the President that Soviet Defense Minister Marshal Georgi K. Zhukov had objected to him that " 'I think you have the reports too high in estimating our strength,' " but American officials dismissed this remark as a well-coached leak.[10] If anything the Air Force delegation drew opposite conclusions, as illustrated by the daily reporting of *New York Times* correspondent Hanson Baldwin, who accompanied the Twining party. Similarly the secret text of Twining's report was echoed by General Thomas Power, who wrote later that "there could no longer be any doubt in our minds that the Soviets were rapidly reaching the point where they could successfully challenge our technological superiority."[11]

Despite these Air Force concerns, or perhaps because of them, a new NIE was drafted in August 1956, which continued the alarming predictions of Soviet strength favored by the Air Force, but only in the face of increasing opposition from the Army's G-2 and the Navy's Office of Naval Intelligence. The Air Force case was made by Major General Millard Lewis, who had replaced Samford in July. But by this time the Army had begun to see its organizational interests threatened and G-2's Major General Robert A. Schow questioned the Air Force case and dissented from the NIE of August, which stated current Soviet strength at 65 bombers (35 Bison and 30 Bear) and predicted 470 for mid-1958 and 800 (500 Bison and 300 Bear) for mid-1960. The director of naval intelligence, Rear Admiral Laurence H. Frost, also began to question the wide disparity between the relatively small number of Soviet bombers shown for the current inventory and the quite large numbers forecast for two and four years in the future.

In the face of this growing intelligence disagreement among the armed services, the CIA became more directly involved in the question of projecting the size of the Soviet bomber force. CIA had been building close ties with the MIT Center for International Studies, and MIT economist Max Millikan had been induced to come to Washington to head the Office of Research and Reports (ORR) that had replaced the older ORE. Millikan greatly improved the quality of economic research at CIA before his departure in 1953, and CIA analysts now used economic arguments to probe the Soviet bomber estimates. Analysts began to point out that with the Soviets' limited industrial base it would be quite difficult to provide the supporting forces and facilities required by the bomber force that the Air Force was predicting even if the Russians could somehow manufacture the planes themselves. This argument impressed ONE, which had the main responsibility for drafting the NIEs on Soviet forces, and it produced a paper on this subject which relied heavily on the ORR reporting. In addition to the support-forces argument ONE questioned whether, in fact, the Soviets might also be experiencing actual production difficulties. The 1955 NIE had predicted 160 heavy bombers for mid-1956 but the actual number by that time, as given in the 1956 NIE, was only sixty-five. Since both estimates expected a similar number of Soviet heavy bombers for the end of the period (1960), Soviet production would have to expand even more rapidly to meet the 1960 inventory figure than had been envisioned.

New information became available after the 1956 NIE was issued. For one thing American agents were able to get a sample of the type of metal used in the Bison's jet engines, from a wire coathanger taken off a Soviet Aeroflot civilian airliner. Metallurgical analysis of the sample showed that the heat resiliency of the material had been overrated by the U.S., thus leading directly to the realization that Bison performance capabilities were less than estimated. This raised questions about whether the Russians would want to deploy such a large force of these aircraft. Moreover, one of the early U-2 reconnaissance flights returned with photographs of Soviet bomber bases that demonstrated conclusively that there were far fewer heavy bombers than had been thought. Revision of the NIEs on Russian bomber strength began in December 1956.

By 1957 the prevailing opinion had completely changed. Allen Dulles informed Eisenhower to this effect early in the year. The new view was that the Soviets had only about fifty heavy bombers and that they might be building more of the turboprop Tupolev Bears than Bisons. Both Defense Secretary Wilson and Secretary of the Air Force Donald Quarles told congressional panels of the reduced projections in February testimony on the fiscal year 1958 military budget. Legislators were taken aback by reports of the new intelligence estimates and questioned officials, particularly Quarles, very closely. Representative Daniel Flood (D-Pennsylvania) interrogated Quarles and Twining in one such heated exchange.

Flood turned to Twining and asked, "What is the earliest date the Air Force and the Department of Defense, either or both, knew that the intelligence was fifty percent wrong on the heavy bomber figures on which the current fiscal budget was predicated?"

Twining replied, "I would just like to add this: I should emphasize that there is no change in our estimate of the number of these modern long-range bombers the Soviets could provide for their forces during the next two years. The change that has been made is to revise our estimates of long-range bomber strength today and in the near future."

"That is not responsive."

Secretary Quarles said that perhaps he could be responsive.

"That is not an answer," Flood reiterated.

Quarles then stated, "Throughout the period that the Congress was in session, and throughout the time of congressional action, we believed that the testimony given before the Senate subcommittee on the Air Force [sic] was the best summary of our intelligence and there was no intelligence to the contrary that came to my attention. . . . In the fall and early winter we did revise our estimates of the number of these bombers. Now, it was not sent to Congress. Congress was not in session at the time. So far as we could see it did not affect any matter before the Congress."[12]

An angry Stuart Symington wrote to Allen Dulles protesting the revised estimates, but Dulles only replied that press reports alleging reduced Soviet capabilities were substantially correct. Eisenhower also had his own views on the bomber matter, as recalled by aide Andrew Goodpaster:

> The President made his own determinations in this regard. Very quickly we found the Bomber Gap had a tendency to recede. It was something that each year was going to occur next year. But in fact it did not occur. The President's information and intelligence proved to be correct.[13]

The 1957 NIE on Soviet intentions and capabilities confirmed the downward revision of Soviet strength. The estimate was approved by the IAC on November twelfth. NIE 11-4-57 put current Soviet bomber numbers at 90–150 and noted that the Russians had finally introduced aerial refueling, but predicted that most of the tanker aircraft used for this were likely to be converted Bisons. It also cited evidence that the Soviets had established nuclear-weapons-handling facilities in the vicinity of their airbases. Most interesting was the hypothesis that the rate of formation of new bomber units, called regiments in the Soviet forces, had dropped since 1956. The key judgment was perhaps this:

> If recent heavy bomber production has in fact been as low as the preponderance of evidence indicates, a partial explanation may lie in the field of technical problems. For example, it is possible that larger-scale production has been delayed pending the availability of higher-thrust engines or other developments expected to improve performance characteristics. But we would believe it more likely that Soviet planners have deliberately decided on a relatively modest heavy bomber program.[14]

The estimate went on to note public statements by Premier Nikita S. Khrushchev that disparaged manned bombers; these could be intended "to prepare the Russian people for some deemphasis on the heavy bomber, or to cover up delays in production."

The outyear projections furnished in NIE 11-4-57 combined both Bison and Bear aircraft into a single range of figures. The Soviets were expected to have 150–250 by mid-1958, and 250–450 a year later. The projection for 1960 had now decreased to 400–600, a reduction of twenty-five percent from previous estimates. Bomber strength was expected to stabilize at this level until 1962. General Lewis of the Air Force dissented from the bomber range figures, inserting a footnote which effectively expanded the ranges by predicting that the Russians would deploy large numbers of tankers (300–500 by mid-1961) in addition to the bombers themselves. In contrast, CIA's deputy director of intelligence, Robert Amory, the Army G-2 chief Schow, and the Joint Chiefs' intelligence representative stated in another footnote that

> [we] believe that the above projected future strength of the heavy bombers is contrary to the available evidence and foreseeable trends. Past estimates predicted an extensive production program of heavy bombers. This program has failed to develop as anticipated. Despite this the present estimate still implies an extensive program even though reduced below previous estimates. Even the lower figures . . . would require an increase in bomber production which is not yet evident nor indicated by trends. In regard to the total numerical strength, the upper range of figures implies a continued buildup of total strength which is in seeming contradiction to the indicated trends.[15]

For the Navy, Director of Naval Intelligence Admiral Frost inserted a footnote to insist that Soviet bombers available in operational units would "almost certainly" approximate the lower end of the range.

As Goodpaster recalled, the "bomber gap" continued to recede. The net effect of evidence received in 1958 was to scale down drastically the projection of Bisons and Bears. President Eisenhower was told on June 17, 1958, of an intelligence report that put current Bison strength at eighty-five planes and Bears at fifty. The total of 135 Russian bombers was little more than half the upper-range figure of the reduced 1957 NIE. The 1958 NIE was approved by the United States Intelligence Board (USIB), which replaced the Intelligence Advisory Committee (IAC), on December twenty-third. In view of the belief that the Russians were nearly finished with their bomber production, the NIE projected Soviet bombers at 160–240. The next estimate on the subject was NIE 11-4-60, forwarded by the USIB in February 1960. It reduced the projection even further—to 120–180 Soviet heavy bombers. In actual fact the Russians built something less than 200 aircraft of the Bison and Bear types combined. Congress was told 125 in 1959, and one widely accepted total figure is 185. The "bomber gap" had disappeared.

Each reduction in the national estimate of Soviet bomber strength in itself accounted for a relative improvement in the combat power of SAC. Even though the situation envisioned by the Air Force in the 1955 air-power hearings never came to pass, President Eisenhower maintained a cautious attitude toward the subject. At a White House meeting on June 9, 1959, for example, Eisenhower questioned Air Force Chief of Staff General Thomas D. White as to the training Soviet bomber crews received. When White replied that his information indicated an extensive Soviet training effort, the President said that "there is reason not to get complacent over the fact that the estimate of Soviet bombers has been cut back."[16]

The "bomber gap" episode demonstrates that available information is of little use without objective analysis. Air Force behavior in the interpretation of the bomber threat shows that where organizational interests impinge or turn upon certain conclusions, objective analysis of intelligence is likely to suffer. This kind of problem can be mitigated to some extent by the opposition of organizations with different interests, in this case the other armed services, or by the presence of an independent and disinterested agency such as the CIA was intended to be. But the problem of the intelligence assessment "slanted" or "cooked" to meet certain needs cannot be eliminated simply by bureaucratic contention.

Another lesson to be learned from the "bomber gap" is that it is not *necessarily* bad to be wrong about the facts. The Air Force was quite wrong in its evaluation of the dimensions of the Russian bomber threat. Even so many of those responsible were rewarded. General Samford was promoted to head the National Security Agency. Colonel Robert Smith, who had helped prepare the airpower hearings testimony, remained at the head of SAC intelligence for a decade. Colonel James Walsh, Smith's predecessor at SAC, was promoted to general and became head of Air Force intelligence in 1958. In intelligence as in other arenas of bureaucratic politics, the rewards appear to have gone to those who support the interests of their organizations.

On the other hand the evidence also suggests that there are advantages in being right about questions of substance. The military services resisted CIA activity in the military intelligence field from the agency's inception. But the fact that CIA was more nearly correct about the bombers than at least one service gave the CIA credibility in this sphere.

One criticism made of the American success in correcting the "bomber gap" misestimates is that this was accompanied by a total misinterpretation of the focus of Soviet strategic effort. This view argues that the U.S. analysts erred in considering only an intercontinental bomber threat, thereby completely missing the Soviet buildup of medium bombers presumably aimed at Europe. This assertion is based on the fact that while the Soviets built few heavy bombers, they did produce large numbers of the Tupolev Tu-16 Badgers, enough to make up the difference between actual Soviet total bomber strength, including the Badgers, and the numbers projected in the NIEs.[17] While this account does not have the space to treat the Badger question in detail, it should be pointed out that this criticism implies that the NIEs projected few or no Badgers would be deployed. This was not the case. To cite just two examples, the 1955 NIE projected 700 Badgers for 1960, while the 1957 NIE predicted that Badger strength would peak in 1960 at 1,000–1,100 aircraft. This last figure is almost precisely the number of these medium bombers fielded by the Soviets. In all U.S. intelligence seems to have done quite well on the Soviet medium bomber.

CHAPTER FIVE
INSTANTANEOUS ATTACK

Beyond the threat from intercontinental bombers loomed a new instrument of war, the guided missile. In particular the intercontinental ballistic missile (ICBM), once the Soviets possessed it, would mean that devastating nuclear blows could be dealt against the United States almost instantaneously. Missile development represented the leading edge of military technology in the 1950s and was one of the most important intelligence issues of the time. Both the Soviet Union and the United States were aware of the potential offered by missiles and both superpowers worked hard to achieve this capability. It was feared that whichever side fielded a missile first might, for one fleeting moment, possess a decisive military advantage. This notion further increased the importance of early intelligence warning of Soviet missile development.

Like the atom bomb, Russian missiles did not appear out of a vacuum following World War II. They were the product of long Russian interest in rocket propulsion and space flight stretching back to the beginning of the twentieth century. Russian experts were among the pioneer space scientists, and Soviet enthusiasts also represented some of the earliest experimenters with rocket hardware in the period just before World War II. Theoretical and practical work done by these men provided the Soviets with a sizable technology base when serious interest in the creation of long-range missiles grew after 1945.

The most noted Russian rocket pioneer was Konstantin Tsiolkovsky (1857–1935), a man trained as a schoolteacher who became interested in rocket propulsion, in part, after reading Jules Verne. From about 1883 Tsiolkovsky began to focus his efforts on concepts of air and space travel. He proposed that in the absence of air, motion could only result from the application of Newton's third law, that is, every action brings an equal reaction in the opposite direction. Later Tsiolkovsky suggested the use of multistage rockets, or "step-rockets" as they were then called, to generate sufficient motive power to escape the earth's gravitational pull. Tsiolkovsky continued to produce papers on rockets until his death. His contributions included a formula that proposed theoretically unlimited velocity in space (1903), a paper on "cosmic step rockets" (1929), and papers on the jet airplane (1930), rocket fuel (1934), and the maximum speed attainable by a rocket (1935).

Ivan V. Meshchersky (1859–1935) made an important contribution by elaborating methods of calculating the ballistic path of a rocket in flight. Meshchersky, who became a professor at the St. Petersburg Polytechnic Institute, adapted Newtonian physics to describe the motion of an object of variable mass, as in the case of a rocket which constantly consumes its own mass (fuel) for propulsion. Fridrikh A. Tsander (1887–1933), a Lithuanian interested in rockets as early as 1907, emigrated to Moscow in the wake of the Russian revolution and, unlike Tsiolkovsky, whose innovations were uniformly conceptual, began to experiment with building rocket engines and other components. Soviet aerospace research was given additional impetus from the formation of the Zhukovsky Academy of Astronautics in 1919.

The 1930s brought the beginnings of a connection with the Soviet military as well as a period of increased institutional growth. At Moscow in 1931 Tsander formed a Group for the Study of Jet Propulsion (GIRD), which soon had branches all over Russia. In 1932 Sergei P. Korolyov (1906–66) established a Rocket Research Development Center in Moscow with a department for the construction of rocket engines, one for vehicles under Mikhail K. Tikhonravov (1900–), and one for rocket aircraft. The first rocket successfully launched in the Soviet Union flew on August 17, 1933, and there were six tests of this model between then and May 1934, including one that rose to an altitude of 4,920 feet.

The scientists' interest in rocket flight was diverted somewhat in the decade from 1935 to 1945 owing first to Stalin's great purges and then to World War II. The GIRD organizations were disbanded in 1935. Later many prominent scientists and engineers were imprisoned, including Korolyov, who supposedly had assisted in "wrecking" Soviet aircraft production through his interest in rockets. Also imprisoned were the nuclear physicist Igor Kurchatov and the talented aircraft designer Andrei Tupolev. These men and many others were employed in wartime research in prison camps during 1941–1945.

Whatever the Soviet government's attitude toward novel technologies, rockets proved themselves during World War II. The Gas Dynamics Laboratory in Leningrad developed more than 118 types of engines between 1932 and 1944 and these were used to power a variety of vehicles including a naval torpedo. Scientist A. G. Kostikov invented the Katyusha unguided ballistic rocket between 1936 and 1940 and this became a useful artillery weapon for Soviet armies in the war. A similar air-to-air rocket was used against the Japanese in the Manchurian campaign of 1940. Korolyov himself designed a rocket-powered glider and others extended his concept for building rocket-powered interceptor aircraft. Rocket units were also developed to assist heavy aircraft in their takeoffs from airfields. Most importantly, the Germans with their use of the large V-1 pulse-jet cruise missile and the V-2 guided ballistic missile demonstrated beyond doubt the military advantages of large rockets. Despite complete Allied air supremacy the Germans were able to bombard London with them in 1944–1945.

The Soviets were not slow to appreciate these trends. An article on the utilization of long-range rockets appeared in a Russian military journal as early as April 1944. In May 1946 General M. Gerasimov wrote that

> the significance of rocket artillery, which is difficult to detect but capable of firing projectiles with sufficient accuracy to destroy targets located hundreds and possibly thousands of kilometers away, will grow.[1]

As the war's end approached the Soviets were as interested in German rocket technology as they had been in German aviation development. On May 6, 1944, the Second Belorussian Front under Marshal Konstantin Rokossovsky captured Peenemünde, the Baltic Sea island where the Germans had located their missile research and development center. Later that year Soviet armies also captured the Lehesten facility in Poland, where the Germans had conducted missile flight tests and static-test firings of V-2 rocket engines. Other facilities that fell within the Soviet occupation zone at war's end were the Zentralwerke in the Harz Mountains where V-2's were assembled, the Mittelwerke Gmbtl plant in Thuringia, and another factory in Prague that had produced engines for the German Me-163 rocket fighter. Inspection and assessment of the German sites was carried out for the Russians by a colonel who was an instructor at the Zhukovsky Academy. Near the end of October 1946, in a massive and secretly orchestrated move, some six thousand German technicians and over twenty thousand members of their families were shipped off to Russia together with the German missile plants, some V-2 rocket engines that had been captured, and blueprints and engineering studies for other advanced long-range weapons. The German rocket plants were reassembled in the Soviet Union and provided the basis for a large-scale Russian missile program.

The Soviets were not entirely satisfied with their German acquisi-
tions, however. The commander of the Soviet Air Force, Marshal Pavel
F. Zhigarev, has been cited as saying in 1946 that, in the event of a
Soviet-American war, what was really needed were long-range rockets
capable of hitting targets on the North American continent. It happened
that two items taken from Germany in 1945 suggested such a weapon.
One was the plans for a long-range rocket, the second a complete engineering study, performed by Austrian scientist Eugen Sanger, demonstrating the feasibility of a "rocket bomber" which would "skip"
through the earth's upper atmosphere, giving it extremely high speed
and a range of ten thousand miles. There was enough interest in the
potential of both projects that high-level meetings were held in April
1947 to discuss them. Stalin was reported to have announced it a poor
bargain that Russia had smashed Germany and captured Berlin only to
have the Western Allies get away with the best German rocket scientists. On the substantive question at hand Stalin remarked that

> [an intercontinental] rocket would change the fate [sic] of the war. It could
> be an effective straitjacket for that noisy shopkeeper Harry Truman. We
> must go ahead with it, comrades! The problem of the creation of transatlan-
> tic rockets is of extreme importance to us.[2]

The next day a secret directive was issued that formed a state commission to study the problems of the Sanger project and the long-range
missile.

The Soviets eventually chose to emphasize missile development over
that of the Sanger project. Many of the deported Germans were settled
at Khimki outside Moscow and they were provided with a relatively high
standard of living in exchange for their work. They were now to go
beyond the task of reestablishing V-2 production in Russia to the goal
of innovating a longer-range rocket. For his part Sergei Korolyov, who
had been released from imprisonment in 1945, was named to head a
new rocket development group in late 1946 and assumed those duties
in February 1947.

By 1949–1950 the Russians had accumulated sufficient expertise to
begin phasing out the use of Germans altogether. The last service the
Germans are said to have performed was work on the guidance systems
for the Soviet missiles. After 1950 even this work was accomplished by
Soviet scientists. Following a period during which the Germans were
kept in Russia as a security measure, many of them left and proceeded
to the West. A few dedicated men remained in Russia and one German
scientist, M. K. Yangel (1911–1971), actually went on to become a So-

viet citizen and, from 1966 until his death, the chief designer of the
Soviet rocket program.

To achieve a truly intercontinental capability any Russian missile
would have to develop thrust sufficient to lift a payload of useful proportions out to a distance of fifty-five hundred miles. The early limiting
factor was the lack of rocket engines with this kind of thrust, and the
low thrust-to-weight ratios that characterized early Soviet rocket engines. A real ICBM would also require some means of stabilizing and
correcting the missile's trajectory in mid-flight, which was a very different problem from that of guidance systems for the relatively short-range
V-2.

In its early stages the Soviet ICBM program was reputedly called
"Project 333" for a three-thousand-pound payload carried to three thousand nautical miles aboard a three-stage rocket. These capabilities expanded as the Russians gained experience. According to Khrushchev,
Dr. Sergei P. Korolyov began work on a more promising and sophisticated ICBM design shortly after Stalin's death in 1953. Engines for the
big rocket were designed by the Gas Dynamics Laboratory with final
work in 1954, and the decision was made to solve the guidance problem
by means of radio commands from the ground using stations at intervals
along the missile's trajectory.

Political leaders began to make statements about the missiles much
as they had earlier about the atomic bomb. In his own statements over
the period 1955–1957 it appears that party secretary Nikita S. Khrushchev denigrated the future of manned bombers while extolling the
virtues of the rocket. On December 29, 1955, Premier Bulganin revealed, in the course of a speech, Soviet success in developing missiles.
Less than two months later foreign ministry official Anastas Mikoyan
asserted that, using planes or rockets, the Soviet Union could deliver a
nuclear weapon to any point on the globe. During his own state visit to
Great Britain, on April 23, 1956, Khrushchev stated his confidence that
Russia would soon have "a guided missile with a hydrogen warhead that
can fall anywhere in the world."[3]

While these statements may have been based more upon perceived
feasibility than actual accomplishment, it is clear at least that Soviet
leaders anticipated the advent of an ICBM capability. They also made
use of their medium-range rocket capability in 1956 to threaten Britain,
France, and Israel with nuclear retaliation over the Suez crisis, at a time
when these nations were isolated as a result of universal opposition (including that of the United States) to their invasion of Egypt. A Soviet
note to the British baldly stated that "other countries" need not use na-

val or air power to attack Britain and France but could use other methods "such as rocket technique." The threat came on the same day that Anglo-French troops first landed at the northern end of the Suez Canal. At the time, Anglo-American intelligence cooperation had been curtailed because of the British action, but Soviet "rocket rattling" drove the allies close together once again. CIA representative Chester Cooper told British officials that U.S. intelligence doubted whether the Soviets possessed either nuclear warheads or missiles in numbers sufficient to threaten Britain and France. Meanwhile, NATO commander General Alfred Gruenther, who was a close associate of President Eisenhower's, told the press that Soviet attacks on either Britain or France would be followed by the destruction of the Soviet Union "as surely as night follows day." American concern was backed up by over a thousand sorties by nuclear bombers of the Strategic Air Command.

Discussions of missile strategy among the Russians were heard more and more frequently. Defense Minister Marshal Georgi K. Zhukov referred to long-range and "mighty" missiles in his speech to the Twentieth Party Congress on Soviet military accomplishments. Between July 1955 and December 1956 the number of Soviet technical personnel assigned to research and development programs increased by almost a quarter. A 1957 Soviet article cited three advantages that would accrue to the owner of an ICBM: the missiles could be used with mobile launchers; they could operate under all weather conditions, even in a hostile air environment; and, the missiles would be capable of making surprise attacks from concealed positions.

Soviet dissident historians write that the final plans for Korolyov's ICBM design were accepted by the Soviet armed forces in 1954 and that preliminary development such as static-test firings of the engines occurred following the party congress in 1956. The rocket fuels and liquid oxygen used to drive the engines were volatile, the number of small things that could go wrong numerous, and the sheer complexity of the mechanism considerable. Nevertheless the technical difficulties were solved one after another. In 1957 a recommendation was made that the ICBM be used to place an artificial satellite into earth orbit, as both the U.S. and the Soviets had announced they would do for International Geophysical Year. With the T-3 missile, or the SS-6, as it would later be called in the West, the Russians had a missile powerful enough to orbit a substantial payload. Khrushchev was attracted by the possibility of beating the U.S. to a major scientific achievement such as orbiting a satellite, and he approved the recommendation.

On August 27, 1957, the Soviet Union issued an official statement that it had successfully flight-tested an ICBM. Another flight was slated to carry the planned artificial satellite. The satellite, called Sputnik, was developed in a very short time, and included radio transmitters that operated on frequencies that could be heard by amateur radio enthusiasts. Sputnik had a diameter of twenty-three inches and weighed 184 pounds. It was launched on October 4, 1957. This was followed on November fourth by the launching of a much larger space vehicle, the 1,118-pound Sputnik II, which carried more instruments plus a live dog into orbit. The SS-6 that launched these satellites could just as easily have carried a thermonuclear weapon. Russia had entered the space age, but the United States had yet to conduct a successful flight-test of its competing ICBM.

Perceptions of Soviet Missile Development

The early intelligence information on Soviet missile progress was piecemeal and of varying value. Broad outlines of the Russian effort were known, as was Soviet use of German technicians. The presence of a missile testing facility at Kapustin Yar, the only one between 1947 and 1956, was known from the spring of 1947.

In this early period the CIA benefited greatly from close cooperation with the British MI 6. According to one source, liaison reporting from other countries accounted for some seventy percent of the raw information reports to CIA in its early years. In 1948 a British communications intelligence team, posing as archeologists in Iran, evidently monitored the V-2 tests from Kapustin Yar. That same year a major source of information was gained when Colonel Georgi Tokaty-Tokaev, erstwhile deputy chairman of the Soviet State Commission on missile production, defected to Great Britain. By his own account Tokaty-Tokaev furnished information regarding Soviet policy discussions but not details of specific programs. He went on to publish reminiscences in several places and material from him began to turn up in other public-record analyses of Russian activities as early as the 1950 edition of Asher Lee's book on the Soviet Air Force.[4] In the meantime the British had passed all their missiles intelligence along to the Americans.

Guided missiles intelligence was perhaps one area where Anglo-American cooperation was closest. The two countries actually wrote joint estimates on the subject. One was prepared in 1949 using information available before January first of that year. Another early study was a joint Army-Navy-Air Force examination of the Soviet missile program that was coordinated by the British in 1948–1949. The assistant to the director of the Navy's Guided Missiles Division, Robert F. Freitag, later recalled that this effort convinced him that the Soviets were aiming at development of a *ballistic* missile capability rather than the cruise-type guided missiles then favored by the Navy. Despite alarm at the pace of Soviet progress, intelligence estimates on Soviet missile programs continued for a time to receive low priority. In 1950 the CIA had only three analysts who concentrated on this subject.

Another breakthrough in the available information occurred with the return of the German technicians who had worked in the early stages of the Soviet program. A joint conference of British and American intelligence officers with a number of these technicians was held on September 8–26, 1952. The United States Air Force also sponsored a similar conference at Wright-Patterson Air Force Base, location of its Air Technical Intelligence Center, in October 1952. The German technicians gave detailed information on their living conditions in Russia and the projects they had worked on. The material was developed into another Anglo-American joint intelligence report issued in July 1953. This report contained discussions of Soviet use of the V-2 rockets, the improvements they had made, and designs for a 240,000-pound-thrust engine, used to power the intermediate-range ballistic missiles. Expectations were that the Soviets would possess a missile with a 2,275-nautical-mile range by 1955–1957.

Because the Soviet launching site at Kapustin Yar was known, the Allies could make specific plans to watch it. Aerial reconnaissance missions flew periodically over this Ukrainian town under the joint cooperation program. The near loss of a Royal Air Force Canberra photo-recon plane during a mission in 1953 demonstrated that something more was needed and was crucial for the argument in favor of construction of the Turkish radar and the U-2 aircraft. Not only did Russian missile progress affect decisions on these new intelligence technologies, it also crystallized bureaucratic differences in the U.S. over intelligence organization. "Beetle" Smith's 1952 decision that separation of areas of intelligence concern was not possible or desirable in this area gave CIA a green light to expand its Office of Scientific Intelligence (OSI). To minimize conflict with the military intelligence groups, however, CIA was careful to assign an "acceptable" officer to head the OSI missile intelligence division. This man was Colonel Jack A. White, an officer on detached duty from the Army who had served with the Army missile program in the late forties and early fifties and had taught missile ballistics at Fort Bliss before coming to CIA. White's OSI division produced contributions on missiles for the National Intelligence Estimates. They were often contradicted, however, mainly by the Air Force, and feeling grew at CIA, especially within OSI, that an interagency panel should coordinate missiles intelligence contributions before they were sent to the BNE. Again the military services opposed formation of such a group, and Allen Dulles, who replaced Smith as director of central intelligence in 1953, for a long time refused to press for the interagency committee proposal.

By the mid-1950s the Air Force, concerned with the pace of Soviet missile progress, was no longer confining itself to NIE contributions. A stream of sensitive information began to flow from individuals in the Air Force directly to congressmen considered sympathetic to USAF views on military research and procurement. Senator Stuart Symington would often refer to his possession of information other than that contained in the NIEs. Similarly, Senator Henry Jackson (D-Washington), who first joined the Armed Services Committee in 1954, was provided with missile information by Lieutenant Colonel Vincent Ford, military aide to Trevor Gardner, in a series of clandestine meetings. One such meeting occurred in the spring of 1955 in which Ford and a subordinate, armed with briefcases of documents, described to Jackson the relative missile progress of the U.S. and Russia.[5]

Both Jackson and Symington took a pessimistic view of Soviet developments in their public statements. For example, in July 1954 Symington spoke of Soviet efforts to field an ICBM with a range of between four thousand and five thousand miles. In a television appearance the following year he warned that Eisenhower's NSC conceded the Soviets were ahead in the missile area. In February 1956 Symington claimed that the Russians were testing a missile with a range hundreds of miles longer than that of anything in the American arsenal. In January 1956 Senator Jackson made a major Senate speech in which he warned of a Soviet lead in intermediate-range ballistic-missile (IRBM) production. Both senators followed up these concerns at great lengths during the airpower hearings of 1956.

The available evidence indicates that presidential concern over Soviet missiles did not run far, if at all, behind that expressed by the senators. Eisenhower writes that "there was rarely a day when I failed to give earnest study to reports of our progress and to estimates of Soviet capabilities."[6] The NSC was briefed on missile programs in July 1955, and at a meeting on September eighth the President resolved that ICBM programs had to have the highest national priority. Two months later Eisenhower accorded the IRBM effort a priority equal to that on the ICBMs. Missiles were again discussed at the NSC during December and in February 1956. In May the relative technological positions of the United States and Soviet Union were considered, and in February 1957 the NSC approved another augmentation of an already rapidly rising missile-development budget.

An NIE dealing specifically with the Soviet missile programs was requested as early as 1954, as was one on Russian ability to orbit what was then called an "earth satellite vehicle" (ESV). The latter has been called a very successful estimate due to its almost exact prediction, made several years in advance, of the date at which a Soviet satellite could be launched. In addition there were annual NIEs produced on Soviet capabilities to attack the U.S., as well as annual NIEs on Soviet military power in general. Intelligence had a fair amount of knowledge concerning progress in Russian laboratory research and some technical information on Soviet missile tests. The early missile estimate, NIE 11-6-54, apparently judged that no firm current information existed on which Soviet rockets were available for operational use and which types were in development. The 1955 NIE on Soviet capabilities and probable actions did not modify this observation, but it did judge that the Russian missile program must be a large one given the number of "personalities" and activities associated with it. Moreover it predicted that there would not be an operational Soviet ICBM until about 1960.[7]

Analysts differed in their projections of a date for an operational Russian ICBM but, in general, few after 1954 expected the Soviets needed more than five years to perfect their ICBM. Differences in emphasis between the CIA and General John Samford's Air Force A-2 resulted partly from the fact that CIA's OSI and USAF's A-2 each made separate contributions on the national estimates. The feeling that there should be agreement on technical details of missile systems in advance of NIE compilation has already been observed.

In the period 1954–1956, as far as the Air Force was concerned, guided-missiles intelligence was *military* intelligence—not only should there be no interagency committee but the CIA had no business in this area in the first place. Very probably Dulles's awareness of this feeling accounted for his failure to press OSI claims. But in 1955 the Air Force intelligence organization came under heavy criticism from the Hoover Commission's task force studying intelligence activities. In an attempt to submerge itself within the intelligence community the Air Force began to support the IAC subcommittee structure. In addition there was an increasing trend in the administration to perform interagency "net assessments," which compared the military capabilities of the U.S. and Russia. The Science Advisory Committee, which served the President, was particularly noted for these, and this reliance on civilian studies alerted the Air Force to Eisenhower's opinion that military judgments were perhaps not the only ones of interest on such subjects as guided missiles. There was also congressional support for an interagency approach to missile intelligence—all this led General Samford to reverse the Air Force position.

As a result Allen Dulles took up the matter of an IAC subcommittee on missiles toward the end of 1955; he approached Defense Secretary Charles Wilson with a proposal to form a Guided Missiles Intelligence Committee (GMIC). Wilson was amenable to the initiative and, given Air Force concurrence, overrode continuing objections from the Navy, Army, and Joint Staff. On January 31, 1956, Dulles established terms of reference for the operation of GMIC. The committee was "to strengthen the community approach to problems in the field of guided missile intelligence and to give impetus to individual efforts." Military objections were then further mollified when Dulles appointed Colonel Jack White as the first GMIC chairman. White had managed to maintain his high reputation among military colleagues even while heading OSI's missiles division. White's successor as head of GMIC, Air Force Colonel Earl McFarland, was also well respected by military authorities. From 1956 GMIC produced the analyses of technical characteristics of Soviet missile systems that contributed to the NIEs. The analyses were also used by other offices to predict how many of each type of missile the Soviets might produce and how much their program must be costing.

These reforms coincided with increased public concern over Soviet military gains. In 1955 Walter Dornberger, former head of the German V-weapons program and then a contributor to the American one, published some alarming speculations on Russian missile plans. Dornberger warned that the Soviets might use shorter-range missiles in an attack from the sea. The rockets could be placed in cannisters and towed to points off the U.S. coast by submarines. A few days after the resignation of Trevor Gardner, the February 20, 1956, issue of *Newsweek* reported "mounting evidence" of an operational Soviet IRBM. The Alsop brothers, news commentators with close ties to the intelligence community, reported early in 1956 that it could be "rather positively stated" that no Soviet ICBM test had yet occurred. However, they believed that

> the Soviets have quite regularly telegraphed their weapons development punches, boasting about each new weapon as soon as they were confident that they had solved the design problem and were preparing for a test.

The Alsops went on to say that official U.S. forecasts invariably underestimated Soviet developments by at least two years and they cited an estimate that evidently predicted the first Russian ICBM test for 1958.[8] The administration made some efforts to allay public concern. At his press conference on April twenty-fifth President Eisenhower told the audience that

I know of no reason why . . . the Soviets should be making misstatements
in this field. And I certainly don't want to accuse them of any such thing.
But I do want to point out that there is a very, very long distance between a
laboratory capacity or capability of doing something and making an instrument, a really efficient, effective instrument of war.[9]

Allen Dulles went even further than the President when he appeared
on television and said, apropos of Khrushchev's claim in London of an
operational ICBM, that the Soviet party secretary was not given to minimizing things and his claims were "a little bit on the high side." Dulles,
who had at first refused to testify in the Senate's airpower hearings, and
then attempted to halt publication of even a censored version of his
testimony, was roundly criticized by Senator Jackson for saying on television what he would not reveal before Congress.

In the meantime evident Soviet progress, especially on the IRBM, led
the Air Force to request a revised NIE. Using new information gleaned
from technical collection, Khrushchev's public assertions, and Soviet
scientists attending international meetings on space exploration, the
NIE continued the prediction that the Russians would be able to orbit
a satellite in 1957, probably using an ICBM-type rocket for a booster.

After 1956 indications piled up with great rapidity, forcing the conclusion that the Russians were upon the verge of achieving their ICBM. A
1957 U-2 flight returned with evidence of Soviet missile activities at
Tyuratam, near the Aral Sea, much farther east than the Kapustin Yar
facility. Analysts at CIA's Office of Current Intelligence (OCI) associated the activity with preparations for a satellite launch using an ICBM
vehicle. On May 10, 1957, satellite programs were discussed at the NSC,
where it was customary to begin with a briefing on current items from
Allen Dulles. The preceding evening Dulles had met with his senior
subordinates, as usual, in order to decide what intelligence to give the
NSC. On this occasion he rejected the Tyuratam missile-activity report
with the claim that Eisenhower would not understand it. En route to
the NSC, however, Dulles asked OCI chief Ray Cline if the item was
truly vital. Upon being assured it was he decided to present it, even
though Cline, based upon the decision at the evening staff meeting, had
not brought along the report. At the meeting Dulles turned to Cline who
then related what he could remember of the Tyuratam report. Eisenhower leaned forward in his seat and asked if the Soviet missile cited in
the report had the range to reach the U.S. The CIA officer replied that
the rocket might reach Hawaii but not California. Dulles later told Cline
"he was exceedingly grateful that we had slipped that current intelligence item in when we did."[10]

Dulles was right. Warning the NSC was fortuitous. If there had not been some such near-term warning of the Russian missile test then subsequent criticisms of intelligence on the Soviet ICBM might have been even more scathing than was the case. *Aviation Week* reported in its May twentieth issue that the Soviet Union had actually tested an ICBM. On July 5, 1957, a Stewart Alsop column appeared which claimed U.S. government possession of "convincing evidence that the Soviets have tested their first experimental version of a very long range, multistage ballistic missile." Two days later a *New York Times* follow-up quoted a high Pentagon official as saying that he assumed the Alsop story to be true. In fact, it was later recorded, a U-2 flight in the summer of 1957 brought back pictures of the Soviet ICBM actually on its launch pad at Tyuratam, certainly proof positive of the culmination of Soviet efforts. On August 27, 1957, the Soviets claimed in a press statement that they had successfully tested the huge rocket.

Initial reaction to the Soviet test was limited to such attentive observers as Senator Symington. General awareness came more slowly, responding to the orbiting of Sputnik, first in October and then a month later. The Russian Sputniks electrified America as warnings of Soviet missile progress had failed to do. President Eisenhower made two speeches underlining his confidence in the military strength of the nation. Retiring Defense Secretary Charles Wilson called Sputnik a "neat technical trick." But administration efforts were unable to quell the resulting furor. A week after the launching of Sputnik II, the *Times* editorialized its conviction that the NSC should take immediate steps to place the U.S. ahead "in a race that is not so much a race for arms or even prestige, but a race for survival." On November twenty-fifth *Aviation Week* charged that Soviet Sputnik plans had been available to the government as early as June, in the form of a Rand Corporation study of Soviet astronautics. Stewart Alsop again sounded a keynote in his magazine article of December 1957:

> There is no doubt at all that strategic missiles will surely replace the manned bombers, as the longbow replaced the knights' swords. The prospect which immediately confronts us is that the Soviets will achieve this replacement before we do. There will then be a gap—in the Pentagon it is known simply and ominously as The Gap—during which we will be in somewhat the position of the mounted French knights at Crécy, sword in hand, facing the skilled British bowmen killing them at will.[11]

The reaction to Sputnik sparked a new Senate investigation, this time by Senator Lyndon Johnson's Preparedness Investigating Subcommittee of the Armed Services Committee. On October 9, 1957, the subcommittee staff heard preliminary briefings on American satellite efforts, which revealed that the people working on the U.S. program had given little thought to the military or political repercussions of the Soviet Union reaching orbit first, due to their assumption that the Russians could never do so. Two days later the subcommittee asked the Department of Defense for a report covering service roles and missions with respect to missile development, proposed satellite programs, the Vanguard satellite program specifically, and a report "on the Soviet satellite and missile program furnishing all information available."[12]

Senator Johnson clearly felt he had come upon an issue of utmost national importance in the question of a Soviet lead in the "race for space." He was encouraged in this belief by his close staff assistant George E. Reedy, Jr., who almost daily forwarded memos to Johnson on aspects of the missile investigation. In one such memo Reedy pointed out that the most important single point about Sputnik is what it revealed about the level of Soviet technology:

> The simple fact is that we can no longer consider the Russians to be behind us in technology. It took them four years to catch up to our atomic bomb and nine months to catch up to our hydrogen bomb. Now we are trying to catch up to their satellite. We can no longer consider ourselves as having a lead in anything other than industrial production.[13]

In another paper on November nineteenth Reedy criticized the methods adopted in the airpower hearings of 1956 and made recommendations that Johnson's hearings avoid sweeping statements about defense strategy, focus on specific and factual criticisms of the Eisenhower policies, and recognize that "a nation's strategy is not *solely* a question of bombers and guided missiles."[14] Four days later the advisor wrote Johnson that

> the proper approach would be to state frankly that we have lost a battle *and to present that loss as a challenge to the American people*. They need not be told that the Russian missile developments are meaningless or that they have been defeated. Neither statement is correct. *What they do need to be told is that they will be defeated—and freedom will be defeated—unless they respond to the Soviet challenge*.[15]

The Johnson subcommittee heard a great number of witnesses from the military and scientific communities through the end of 1957 and on into the new year. The hearings helped lay the groundwork both for a Department of Defense reorganization, requested by Eisenhower in

1958, and for the formation of the National Aeronautics and Space Administration (NASA) which would supplant the old National Advisory Committee on Aeronautics (NACA). The missile investigation also emphasized the Soviet advantage in scientific training and led to certain changes in United States educational policy with effects that persisted into the 1970s.

The NIE on Soviet missiles current at the time of Sputnik had been approved by the IAC on March 12, 1957. It predicted that the Soviets might have an ICBM ready for operational use by 1960–1961. Of course, this NIE was overtaken by the events themselves when the Russians first tested their ICBM and then launched Sputnik. Consequently the forecast was revised in the fall of 1957. The new prediction, contained in NIE 11-4-57, rolled back to 1959 the date at which the Russians could attain marginal missile capability with up to ten ICBMs in the field. With regard to IRBMs the NIE now expected the Soviets to achieve an initial operating capability sometime in 1958 with a missile of one thousand nautical miles range. Previous "firm evidence" of Soviet development of IRBMs in the sixteen-hundred-nautical-mile-range category was now discounted with the statement that "there are no current indications of development of ballistic missiles of ranges beyond about one thousand nautical miles save for the ICBM." The estimate did contain the caveat that these predictions should be considered tentative pending the completion of a special estimate being drafted in the intelligence community.[16]

How was this material presented to the Johnson subcommittee? In advance of the CIA presentation Karl Weber, deputy director of the OSI, took a summary of the CIA testimony to the subcommittee offices with the notion that Senator Johnson could cite it in open session or read from it as the formal CIA opinion. Allen Dulles himself would appear only in executive session, from which no testimony would be released. Senate staffers instead wished to use the CIA statement as a press release. The issue was not yet resolved when hearings opened and Allen Dulles, accompanied by OSI Director Herbert Scoville, appeared at the witness table. Dulles stated that the intelligence community had predicted "some time ago that the Soviets would have the capability of orbiting earth satellites during the year 1957, employing for that purpose the same propulsion developed in their missile programs." A review of Soviet IRBM efforts was given, along with an analysis of the implications of the two Soviet ICBM tests in the summer of 1957. As the Johnson subcommittee wished, a press release on Dulles's testimony was later issued, but much of the CIA's information on Soviet ICBMs and IRBMs was deleted.

Despite all precautions news of the intelligence predictions reached the public through the press. In early December *Newsweek* carried a story mentioning Allen Dulles and the NIE prediction of an operational Soviet ICBM by the end of 1959. For his part Senator Johnson drew dire conclusions, as he related in a letter to a constituent on January 9, 1958:

> So far, on the basis of lengthy investigation, we have determined that we are behind the Russians in ballistics [sic] missiles and may possibly soon be behind in all phases of military capabilities. I think there are three main reasons: (1) we underestimated the capabilities of the Russians; (2) we did not give our military program sufficient priority or sufficient money; and (3) it appears to take the Defense Department about twice as long to put a weapon system in operation as it does the Russians.[17]

Similar opinions were voiced by many Americans, even though Eisenhower attempted to defuse alarm on Soviet progress. Nevertheless concern over the Soviet military lead was of paramount importance for the remainder of Eisenhower's term in office. The Soviet Sputnik in a sense changed the terms of the intelligence debate over foreign missile progress by turning it into a political and public issue.

CHAPTER SIX
MASSIVE ATTACK

Defense required total success, given nuclear weapons, for to fail at destroying any part of attacking forces would permit devastating blows from the opponent. No conceivable defense was that good, even before the advent of the ICBM made all existing defenses instantly irrelevant. Concern with American vulnerability to a nuclear attack led to repeated calls from some quarters for a civil defense program that would provide fallout shelters for the great majority of the population. There was some discussion of civil defense in the Senate airpower hearings in 1956, and this was followed by more hearings explicitly on civil defense in early 1957. At that time the Federal Civil Defense Administration brought forward a plan to create a national shelter system at a cost of forty billion dollars. Since this amount was equal to the total annual spending for defense at the time, the NSC questioned the value of such a program. It was decided to request a study from a civilian advisory panel on the question of what means could be used to protect against nuclear attack. The resulting panel was caught up in the events surrounding Sputnik, and as it turned out, vulnerability in the broadest sense was its most vital theme.

The advisory panel was formed under White House aegis, within the Science Advisory Committee, which functioned under the Office of Defense Mobilization. The panel was ordered by NSC Action 1691-b(2) of April 4, 1957, which called for an evaluation of the civil defense shelter proposal as part of a study of active and passive defenses. Eisenhower's special assistant for national security affairs, Robert Cutler, and the acting science advisor, James R. Killian, recommended the appointment of H. Rowan Gaither as chairman of the group, to be called the Security Resources Panel (SRP). Gaither was a San Francisco lawyer, president of the Ford Foundation until early 1956, and one of the founders of that institution as well as of the Rand Corporation, on whose Board of Directors Gaither served, as chairman. Killian and Dr. Detlev Bronk of the Science Advisory Committee briefed Gaither on the nature of the SRP project and on May eighth the President wrote Gaither to request his participation in coming "to grips with one of the most important and perplexing problem areas affecting our future national security."[1] The SRP came informally to be called the Gaither Committee. In May and June an advisory panel, made up of technical experts and experienced government men, determined the structure of the project. A ten-member steering committee, under the direction of Robert C. Sprague and William C. Foster, directed each of four subpanels which dealt respectively with active defenses, passive defenses, socio-economic-political analysis, and evaluation of quantitative assessments. Among the sixty-five staff members recruited were representatives of nearly every organization in government that dealt in national security affairs. The staff included three people from the Office of the Secretary of Defense, three from the Air Force, one from the Army, and a number of physicists, some of whom had worked on the Manhattan Project or the Bikini atomic tests. Personnel from the Institute of Defense Analysis also figured widely in the makeup of the staff, particularly men from the Institute's Weapons Systems Evaluation Group. There were two men from Rand. The senior of two representatives from CIA was Richard M. Bissell, who ran the U-2 program. Bissell had been at both MIT and the Ford Foundation at the same time as Gaither himself.

As the SRP assembled Gaither held a series of conferences with defense officials which served to flesh out the terms of reference given for the panel study. There were two meetings with Deputy Defense Secretary Donald Quarles in late June. Committee members met with the Armed Forces Policy Council, consisting of the service secretaries and chiefs of staff, on July fifteenth. The next day Gaither, Sprague, and sixteen other members of the SRP's advisory and steering committees and the Office of Defense Mobilization's Science Advisory Committee met with President Eisenhower at the White House. Work began shortly afterwards.

Despite the substantial quantitative and analytical abilities of its members, the SRP functioned mainly as a consumer of reports rather than an initiator of analyses. Committee members questioned defense officials, examined budget and force planning documents, and evaluated other studies. Some of the staff members were given a full-dress inspection tour of SAC and its bases. Among the available reports was a March 1957 Pentagon study, chaired by Hector Skifter, which recommended that the Army continue to develop the Nike-Zeus antiballistic missile and that the Air Force be authorized to begin work on a ballistic-missile early-warning radar network. Another study of antiballistic missiles, which were "active defenses" in the parlance of the Gaither Com-

mittee, was completed at Rand later in 1957 and suggested that SAC
bases would be easier to defend against nuclear attack than cities. A
third report, done for the Army by the Operations Research Office at
Johns Hopkins, generally supported the Army program for active defense. As for NSC documents, steering-committee member James A.
Perkins recalled in 1960 that "there may have been an NSC paper that
bore on our security program that I did not see during the summer, but
I do not know what it was."[2] Sprague later specified that the Gaither
Committee had had access to NSC papers, Pentagon and Joint Chiefs
documents, annual war-gamings, nuclear weapons testing information
and service, and NIEs.

But cooperation with the Gaither Committee was not so complete as
the foregoing might seem to indicate. Although Richard Bissell worked
with the SRP, and although he made a case there for new intelligence
technologies, it is not clear whether the Gaither staff had any access to
U-2 pictures of Russia. Indeed, Eisenhower's possession of U-2 photographs has been given as his reason for discounting some of the Gaither
Committee's threat assessment. At the Department of Defense there was
additional foot-dragging from some of the armed services. In mid-August a battle developed over the Joint Chiefs' refusal to give the panel
two documents on Air Force capabilities. In the midst of this controversy Gaither suffered a heart attack, and leadership of the study fell to
Robert Sprague and his codirector William C. Foster. Meanwhile General Nathan F. Twining, who replaced Admiral Radford as Chairman of
the Joint Chiefs of Staff, confirmed his predecessor's refusal to give the
requested documents to the SRP.

One reason the Joint Chiefs might have been apprehensive about the
study is that SRP overstepped its original terms of reference. Initially
organized to do an analysis of the relative utility of civil defense versus
active defense, in the face of an imminent Soviet ICBM, the Gaither
Committee slowly broadened its area of inquiry. The one news leak on
the committee study, which appeared in August, made no mention of
civil defense at all and cited the committee's task as evaluating new
technological means of defense against atomic attack.

The advent of the Russian ICBM touched off crucial issues of U.S.
vulnerability and defense. Without missiles in the U.S. arsenal—the Atlas program had yet to produce an operational ICBM—SAC depended
entirely upon bombers for its war strength. If the bomber bases could
be attacked with missiles, then the time available to respond to such an
attack would shrink tremendously, from several hours in the case of a
bomber attack to the missile's flight time of perhaps half an hour. The
problem was further complicated by the fact that the United States at

the time did not even have a radar warning network designed to track ICBMs. The Distant Early Warning (DEW) Line was intended primarily to detect bombers. The Ballistic Missile Early Warning System (BMEWS) was still in the design stage, and even when that was ready the warning time in case of attack by missile could not be expected to increase by more than about twenty minutes. Moreover, this covered only attacks across the Pole; in the case of missiles launched from submarines the warning time could be expected to be less.

The United States government's declared policy with regard to nuclear weapons was that any attacker would be faced with an overwhelming retaliation from SAC. But the missile radar problem combined with SAC's reliance upon bombers meant that the Americans' *effective* force would be limited to the number of bomber aircraft able to take off before the missiles arrived at the bases. The number of surviving bombers would be far fewer than the inventory of aircraft in SAC, as the Gaither Committee found out to its horror. The lack of aircraft shelters on airfields minimized the potential number of surviving planes, while the single runways at most air bases limited the number of aircraft that could take off even if alerted. Steering committee codirector William C. Foster later said that work on the committee had been like spending ten hours a day staring straight into hell.[3]

On paper SAC was a huge striking force. There were 1,650 B-47 jet medium bombers, 150 prop-jet B-36 heavy bombers, and 214 B-52 jet heavy bombers. Production of new B-52 jets continued at seventeen a month and the activation of a new B-52 bomber wing was scheduled for November 1957. On the other hand, over 2,000 aircraft were concentrated at twenty-nine airbases within the United States, an average of 70 planes per base, and only one or a few of these aircraft could take off from one base at any one time. There was an official program for SAC dispersal, but sixteen air bases that had been funded from 1956 through 1958 were still under construction while SAC had never practiced dispersal to civilian airports on a large scale. Moreover, there were press reports that the Air Force had curtailed in-flight training missions by B-47 and B-36 bombers for budgetary reasons. This occurred at a time when the B-52 force was less than fully operational since, as late as October 1957, only 119 of the deployed B-52 bombers had yet been incorporated into the war plan.

Beginning in November 1956 SAC experimented with a system of holding a portion of its aircraft on continuous ground alert, ready to take off. This Operation Try-Out was accomplished with two B-47 wings and two wings of KC-97 air tankers of the 38th Air Division at Hunter Air Force Base in Georgia. It was succeeded on October 1, 1957, by two similar exercises. Despite ground alert and dispersal, however, the

Gaither Committee found that the maximum number of loaded aircraft SAC could launch in a *two-hour* period was 134 bombers, including only eight B-52's, compared to a missile flight time of *half an hour*.

It is no wonder that SRP members felt themselves in the face of great national peril. As James Perkins put it, "It seemed to us that the nature of the threat was not fully determined or fully considered." Thus, "the government did not have its eyes open in the summer and fall of 1957."[4] Essentially the same feeling was voiced by another panel member in 1976, who recalled that the crucial problem at the time of the Gaither Committee was "the speed with which the U.S. Air Force could achieve adequate early warning facilities and an appropriate alert posture."[5] As for the *raison d'être* of the SRP, a civilian shelter program, Gaither staff director Jerome Wiesner emerged from the study convinced that such a program was not really feasible and that the only practicable course was to prevent the outbreak of nuclear war through the preservation of a credible deterrent.[6]

In its delineation of the Soviet threat the Gaither Report emphasized the "dynamic development and exploitation" of military technology by the Soviets. The report made no extended comment on the Russian ICBM but did suggest that the Russians had "probably" surpassed the U.S. in ICBMs. The Soviets were credited definitely with tests of a 950-nautical-mile missile and with a 700-nautical-mile missile in production for at least a year. The judgment that the Soviet ICBM would soon be available for combat use was implicit in the future "timetable" included in the Gaither Report. There, under "Period B," beginning in 1959 or early in 1960 and extending until 1961 or '62, it was projected that the Soviets might have a "significant" delivery capability on missiles with megaton (one thousand kiloton) warheads; that the U.S. would not have such a capability at that time; and that the United States would probably not have achieved either early warning by radar or an active defense against ICBM attack. The implications were explicitly stated in the body of the Gaither Report:

> By 1959, the USSR may be able to launch an attack with ICBMs carrying megaton warheads, against which SAC will be almost completely vulnerable under present programs. By 1961–1962, at our present pace, or considerably earlier if we accelerate, the United States could have a reliable early warning capability against a missile attack, and SAC forces should be on a 7 to 22 minute operational "alert." The next two years seem to us critical. If we fail to act at once, the risk, in our opinion, will be unacceptable.[7]

While the SRP was drafting its report, the Soviets launched their first Sputnik. This achievement lent additional plausibility to SRP's projections and additional urgency to its recommendations.

Sputnik II, a much larger satellite, was launched on November third. The following morning senior Gaither Committee members met with Eisenhower to present their conclusions orally. Rowan Gaither himself returned to Washington for the meeting. The President discovered that the cost of the programs recommended by the committee were substantial, but he was glad to agree with the SRP that a civil defense shelter program should have a relatively low priority. The President was uncomfortable with the findings on SAC vulnerability and asked the committee to check its figures. On November fifth an item in *The New York Times* reported that a secret study of the entire scope of national defense was about to be reported to the NSC. Discussions of the SRP report's recommendations had already begun in Quarles's office. Preparations continued for the NSC presentation, set for November seventh. On the sixth some seventy SRP staff members went to the White House to receive personal thanks from the President.

At nine on the morning of November seventh there was an especially large gathering for the NSC. Present were twenty members of the SRP, Eisenhower, his secretaries of state, defense, and treasury, the full Joint Chiefs of Staff, the service secretaries, and other NSC, White House, and defense officials. Allen Dulles and his deputy director for intelligence, Robert Amory, attended for the CIA and distributed a new intelligence estimate appraising the civil defense shelter system of the Soviet Union. The Gaither Committee panelists then briefed the contents of their report using tables and charts to illustrate their points. The panelists had augmented the information on SAC vulnerability previously disclosed to the President and the presentation was even stronger. Eisenhower alternated between watching the briefers and following their comments in a copy of the Gaither Report spread out on his knees. Aside from recommendations to adopt an "alert" posture for SAC and to build missile detection radars, the Gaither Committee also made a variety of programmatic recommendations with a total price tag of $44.22 billion over five years. These included an increase in the planned initial procurement of Atlas from 80 to 600 missiles, with all but the first group to be placed in hardened missile sites; the initial procurement of IRBMs increased from 60 to 180 missiles; and a high priority for development of an underwater-fired intermediate-range missile, Polaris. There was an intelligence recommendation urging the "exploitation of all means presently at our disposal to obtain both strategic warning and hard intelligence, even if some risks have to be taken, together with the vigorous development of new techniques."[8]

President Eisenhower did not agree with all of the SRP's recommendations. The President felt that "the panel had failed to take into account certain vital information and other considerations." On November fourth Eisenhower had reminded Gaither and his associates of the presence of numerous SAC bases overseas. Of the NSC presentation Eisenhower remarked that he was most impressed with the SAC vulnerability argument and that the report "contained certain useful distillations of data and some interesting suggestions" but that the President, unlike an advisory panel, must take into account conflicting purposes and still keep costs within bounds. The SRP report as a whole "could not be accepted as a master blueprint for action."[9] President Eisenhower did send most of the report's recommendations to specific agencies for comment, but no action at all was taken to increase ICBM and IRBM procurement, a program thought to cost a total of about $3.7 billion.

Part of the reason for Eisenhower's attitude stemmed from the SRP's enlargement of its area of inquiry. When Gaither and other members of the steering committee had met with him in July, Eisenhower had given them both an extended due date of October and explicitly told them to exclude any "detailed examination of national security policies and programs for the purpose of recommending specific modifications, changes, or amendments (as did the Killian Technology Capabilities Panel)."[10] Eisenhower evidently felt that by addressing such matters as missile procurement, IRBM squadrons based overseas, and spending on conventional armaments (for which $5.5 billion was recommended), the Gaither Committee had made exactly the kind of "broad brush" options paper he did not want.

A second reason for the cool reception given the SRP report was that its recommendations were isolated within the bureaucracy. Although the report asked for more spending for all the services, and might have expected their support on this account, it received none. For its part the State Department was also cool. John Foster Dulles had argued at the NSC on November seventh that the report was based only on military considerations rather than the entire "international struggle" and that a shelter program in the U.S. would adversely affect relations with NATO Europe. When the departmental responses to the Gaither Report began to come into the White House around Christmas of 1957, it rapidly became clear just how little support it had. And since none of the committee members had current authority in government, there was no way they could press from within the executive for implementation of the SRP recommendations.

Finally the Gaither Report became a political issue, which cannot have aided its chances for implementation. The same Soviet Sputniks that underlined the urgency in Gaither's message also put Eisenhower under a great deal of pressure on his management of defense spending and commitment to a balanced budget. Bits and pieces of the Gaither Report leaked and appeared in the press until Chalmers Roberts of *The Washington Post* published a very detailed article in that paper on December 20, 1957. The tone of the report was notably at variance with the upbeat mood of Eisenhower's own speeches in November. Within a day of the Roberts exposé there were fully eight public reactions from United States senators alone.

Lyndon Baines Johnson was but one of many who tried to convince Eisenhower to release the Gaither Report to the public, or at least the Senate. LBJ was running his ballistic missiles hearings at the time and consequently had a presumptive "need to know." First Johnson associated himself with requests from other senators. When this route brought no action the senator met with presidential political advisor Bryce Harlow and also asked John Foster Dulles to press for release of the report from within the administration. Harlow politely refused. For his part Foster Dulles had no intention of pressing for release of a document which, if made public, would force him into a split with the President. Eisenhower did not wish to set the precedent of releasing NSC papers to the Congress and invoked the doctrine of "executive privilege" and the confidentiality of advisory opinions. Lawyers for Johnson's Permanent Investigating Committee met with Harlow again in late December, and were told that Eisenhower was "sympathetic in principle" but that precedent was the overriding consideration. Committee counsel replied that Senators Johnson and Styles Bridges were equally anxious to protect the precedents. Later LBJ's representatives agreed to meet with James R. Killian, newly appointed as presidential science advisor, in lieu of seeing the Gaither Report itself.[11]

The meeting with Killian occurred on December 27, 1957, while departmental responses to the Gaither Report were flowing into the White House. Killian took the position that virtually all the factual material in the Gaither Report was contained in testimony already received in Johnson's committee hearings. Killian felt that the Johnson committee might lack some "amplification" of testimony on the anticipated attrition rate of SAC and on whether it was large enough to carry out its mission in the event of war with Russia. He admitted that some testimony on the U.S. air defense system and on planned shelter programs might also be helpful, but this was all that the Senate got out of the White House. On January 15, 1958, President Eisenhower wrote to Senator Johnson and officially refused to release the report of the SRP.

Some senior members of the Gaither panel subsequently engaged in a publicity campaign to warn of serious dangers to the United States. Senator Henry Jackson quoted Gaither in a television appearance in April

1958. Jerome Wiesner and Robert Sprague filmed a television interview that July, and there was a lecture series on campuses. Recommendations similar to those in the SRP report concerning defense budget increases were brought forward in the public Rockefeller Report, which involved participation of some of the SRP people. All this contributed to widespread questioning of Eisenhower's leadership. Secretary of Defense Neil H. McElroy later observed that

> the Gaither Report really was responsible for a good deal of pressure from the Congress on the administration, and it would be my guess that President Eisenhower had questions at times as to whether the Gaither Report should have been requested, ordered at all, because it seemed to create more problems than it solved.[12]

Eisenhower himself was mostly interested in measures to disperse and alert bases of the SAC. The President's concern was reflected by many in the defense establishment and the wider intellectual community that served it, as typified by one young defense analyst, Daniel Ellsberg, then moving up through Rand, who felt that preventing a surprise attack upon the United States was the central military problem of the time.

Intelligence and the Race for Operational ICBMs

However, the Gaither Report's recommendations were not totally ignored. In fact McElroy told Eisenhower on December 5, 1957, that the supplementary budget request shortly to be submitted for 1958 should be "as large an amount as seemed solid and justified."[13] The figure $1.6 billion was mentioned but the President opined that two thirds of the money was really needed more to stabilize public opinion than for military purposes. Nevertheless the Department of Defense and the CIA had submitted their comments on the Gaither Report by the end of the year and on January 6, 1958, these were discussed at the NSC. A package of additional funds was requested, over and above that included in the original supplement. A first increment of $1.37 billion won approval on January seventh, the major part of which was intended for SAC alert and dispersal, ballistic missile warning radars, and an acceleration of the ICBM program. Eisenhower made an additional supplemental request for $1.45 billion in new obligational authority on April second.

Meanwhile a Special National Intelligence Estimate (SNIE) was compiled in the wake of Sputnik, completed in December 1957, and approved by the IAC on January 5, 1958. A November NIE had predicted a nominal Soviet ICBM capability, with perhaps ten rockets, emerging during 1959. The SNIE predicted nominal capability for mid-1958 at the earliest but an increase between then and mid-1959, and also added an assessment that the Soviets might accumulate one hundred ICBMs between mid-1959 and mid-1960. The credibility of the estimate at this time was enhanced by the fact that current intelligence had been able to provide advance notice of Soviet preparations for launching Sputnik III which, evidently due to technical problems, was not actually orbited until May 15, 1958.

The basis for constructing the estimates on Soviet missile development was later explained in some detail by Allen Dulles in a speech to the Institute of Aeronautical Sciences meeting in New York. Dulles referred to the emphasis Nikita Khrushchev had placed upon missiles, the requirements the Soviet command might set for the missiles in the future, the missile's role in Soviet doctrine, Russian missile production capacity, and finally current Soviet inventories of these weapons. All these were factors in the final estimate and Dulles conceded that all were to some extent interdependent judgments. Dulles also specified that knowledge of the state of the art in technical development plus American experience in the same field were useful guides in judging others' capabilities. The intelligence chief sounded a cautionary note about the estimates:

> It is difficult to predict how much emphasis will be given to any particular weapons system until the research and development stage are completed, tests of effectiveness have been carried out, and the factories have been given the order to proceed with serial production.[14]

These were the difficulties exactly faced by estimators in the winter of 1958. Under the circumstances the conclusions in the SNIE of January had to be considered highly tentative. Intelligence searched for additional information on the Soviet SS-6 ICBM.

Very little was known with confidence about Soviet missile forces. Russian abilities to produce an ICBM, create a doctrine for its use, and absorb such missiles into its forces were certainly unknowns. Intelligence was nevertheless compelled to predict a date for initial operating capability (IOC), or the earliest practical use, of such an ICBM force. American analysts did know that the Russians had accumulated considerable experience with rockets and missiles. The Soviet artillery branch had organized a Special Purpose Rocket Brigade to handle missions in this field as early as 1948. The unit grew to a strength of three to four thousand by 1951, when it was further expanded to become a division, servicing battlefield tactical rockets and also missiles of the V-2 type. Troop training with medium-range ballistic missiles (MRBM) like the T-1 was thought to have begun in 1953 or 1954. At a time when American techniques required a week or two to fuel and prepare a missile for launch, Russian troops were accomplishing the same thing, in the field, in a matter of hours. During 1957 there were press reports that the Soviets had formed a separate service arm in their military for rocket utilization. Although this report proved premature, that year the Russians did test their ICBM, and in 1958 it became known that the Soviets had formed an umbrella organization to coordinate military research and development under Konstantin N. Rudnev (1911–1980), formerly a deputy minister for armaments. There did not seem to be any obstacles to prevent the Soviets from immediately integrating intercontinental missiles with nuclear warheads into their strategic forces.

Statements from the Soviet leadership in general tended to reinforce the impression that the Russians would proceed rapidly with ICBM deployment. Premier Nikita Khrushchev, in speeches and conversations with Western visitors during this period, was extremely optimistic about Soviet missile prospects. Khrushchev claimed that the Soviet ICBM could launch ten or twelve satellites at once if need be. Later Khrushchev's statements began to imply that the Soviet Union had an existing production line for long-range missiles, that missiles were being turned out "like sausages." By 1959 the Soviet leader boasted that a single factory was capable of producing 250 missiles in a year.

Khrushchev's missile claims were impressive and they were supported by the Sputniks. Intelligence analysts in Washington viewed his statements to some degree as authoritative and cited them in the NIEs. But the claims were misleading indicators of Soviet achievement; they were vague and attempted to evoke a generalized threat of ballistic missile potential in place of a specific demonstration of Soviet missile power. The best scholarly examination of Soviet statements over the 1958–1960 period holds that in fact the Russians deliberately chose to practice a missile deception in their foreign policy.[15] If so, then the references to Khrushchev's statements contained in the NIEs were doubly damaging, for there is evidence that the Soviets had access to copies of the national estimates until about 1961. They were supplied by Colonel William H. Whalen, an officer on the Joint Staff and intelligence advisor to the Army Chief of Staff, who was recruited by the Soviet KGB in 1959.[16] Khrushchev probably was encouraged by the success of his deception to continue misleading the U.S. with regard to Soviet missile capability.

The predictions made in both the November NIE and the January SNIE were upward revisions of the Soviet ICBM threat. Both estimates envisioned the threat sooner than previous predictions, either in terms of date by which the Soviets might achieve an IOC or the numbers of rockets the Soviets were expected to have by a given date. The January SNIE predicted a near-term threat for the first time—IOC by mid-1958 and an inventory of one hundred SS-6's by mid-1959. This might tempt the Russians to try their hand at a disarming strike against SAC before the radar warning net could be completed. These views were taken up at the White House where, at the very least, they were accepted by the President's Science Advisory Committee. The scientists realized that the Soviets needed to perfect their SS-6 before deploying it. As participants in or monitors of the U.S. ICBM program they also had a firm idea of the time lags involved. Yet at a conference with Eisenhower on February 4, 1958, the President was told that the Russians were about one year ahead of the United States on missile propulsion technologies. Although the Soviets were also said to be a year behind in nuclear warhead design, they had selected a much simpler operational concept—a very large missile to loft an admittedly heavier warhead—and so might expect IOC in a shorter period of time. Committee chairman James R. Killian went even further on April seventeenth when he reported to Eisenhower that at least five SS-6's had been tested, of which three nose cones returned to earth, and that "with the background of their proven 700-mile and 1,000-mile missiles, the Soviets could complete all the necessary test shots within the next six months."[17]

President Eisenhower worked very hard to preserve a middle ground in 1958. He tried to rein in some of the most pessimistic fears that were being expressed, cautioning that Soviet developments must not be overly dramatized. On January 3, 1958, the President told his cabinet that Russian possession of an ICBM before the U.S. would be "by no means catastrophic."[18] To the Scientific Advisory Committee meeting on February fourth

> the President said that in evaluating material of this kind it is necessary to consider relative probabilities. Until an enemy has enough operational capability to destroy most of our bases simultaneously and thus prevent retaliation by us our deterrent remains effective.[19]

Later in March the President criticized a CIA estimate of the world situation to one of his advisors with the remark that it could have been written by high school students. Killian remarked that one morning I received a telephone call from [Eisenhower] out of the blue. He wanted me to know, he said, that his own judgment led him to the conclusion that we would not be involved in any hostilities during the coming five years and that the Soviets were not as strong as many claimed.[20]

General Andrew Goodpaster, who served as the President's staff assistant throughout the period, believes that, as in the case of the bomber gap, Eisenhower made his own determinations on the missile question. The present evidence along with Eisenhower's news conference statements of the period certainly lend weight to Goodpaster's impression. It seems he was extremely judicious in taking an early nonalarmist stance on Soviet missile progress and then maintaining this position despite widespread and frequently heated criticism.

In the case of the Russian missiles the testing history of the rocket was important in establishing the date for IOC. Scientists and intelligence analysts agreed that a certain number of flight tests was required to correct design flaws in propulsion and guidance systems and other missile components. The number of missile tests required varies with the rocket. Although in no case is it known with confidence in advance of any test program, it is usually estimated at twenty to thirty.

On January 16, 1958, Allen Dulles gave the NSC a full-dress briefing on Soviet missile progress. According to the CIA's tabulation no Russian ICBMs had been tested in 1955 or 1956, while in 1957 there were the two Sputnik shots and at least two ICBM shots at less than full range. There may have been some failures as well. So at the time of the NSC briefing the total number of Soviet ICBM firings stood at less than ten. On January seventeenth Twining appeared before the Johnson subcommittee and insisted "we are not—today—in my judgment in a position of inferior military strength vis-à-vis the Soviet Union."[21]

There was an ICBM shot from Tyuratam in April 1958, and the Soviets launched their Sputnik III in May (after a delay of almost five months), but a long hiatus followed, lasting into 1959. On the basis of the ICBM test evidence the Russians might have been a third to halfway through the development stage on the SS-6. A revised national estimate on Soviet missile capabilities was ordered into production in May 1958 and completed the next month. At the time the NIE was released, there had been no additional ICBM tests for two months, and delays and failures were known. Yet the estimate went on to predict truly massive numbers of Soviet missiles and at a relatively early date: up to one hundred in 1959, five hundred in 1960 and one thousand by 1961. At a meeting with Eisenhower on June seventeenth, Allen Dulles asserted that the net effect of delays in the Soviet program would be "to retard by six months to a year the dates on which the Soviets are expected to have an initial operational ICBM capability." In reply Eisenhower commented to Dulles and his director of scientific intelligence, Herbert Scoville, who also attended, that he could not understand how the Soviet missile difficulties were reflected in this estimate.[22]

As if the intelligence that the Soviets would be the first to achieve an ICBM initial operating capability were not enough, the political situation was soon complicated by the leak of the range of Soviet missile strengths projected in the national estimates. Joseph and Stewart Alsop, prominent journalists with very good connections to the intelligence community, including friendships with Dulles, Bissell, and Frank Wisner of CIA, raised in their column the disturbing question implied by the Soviet figures:

> At the Pentagon they shudder when they speak of the "gap," which means the years 1960, 1961, 1962, and 1963. They shudder because in these years, the American government will flaccidly permit the Kremlin to gain an almost unchallenged superiority in the nuclear striking power that was once our specialty.[23]

The allusion to a "gap" was a reiteration of the formula used to describe the alleged bomber disparity and had already been used by Stewart Alsop in an article some months before. The description stuck and people began to speak of the "missile gap" much as they had of the "bomber gap" before it.

The Alsop figures lent credibility to the charges that the administration was not doing enough on defense, especially in the wake of Sputnik. It was not generally known how much Eisenhower had, in fact, done. He had approved an expansion of the Atlas program from four to nine squadrons (sixty-three ICBMs), had blocked cancellation of the Titan II missile, and increased planned acquisition of that type by seven squadrons. In addition the Polaris fleet ballistic missile had been accelerated and the Air Force convinced to accept a program for a solid-fuel ICBM called Minuteman. There were reports that SAC had succeeded in substantially increasing the number of bombers ready for takeoff on fifteen-minute alert. Further, the administration had also advanced the scheduled dates for the construction of BMEWS radars in Alaska and Scotland while a third BMEWS installation was already under construction at Thule, Greenland. Finally the United States had begun to explore the technical feasibility of mounting infrared detection equipment aboard satellites to provide maximum warning of any Soviet missile launches.

There had been proposals to do much more—for example to triple the

size of the Atlas deployment. Support for that measure came from both
the Air Force and certain defense contractors involved in that program.
Eisenhower saw the Minuteman as much more reliable and promising
and his refusal to accede to "full scale" deployment of Atlas aroused
considerable dissatisfaction in some quarters. The Air Force Chief of
Staff, General Thomas D. White, and the JCS Chairman, "Nate" Twining, who was also from USAF, generally supported the President's policies. But predictions of the huge numbers of Soviet missiles were seized
upon and reiterated by other Air Force spokesmen. In a speech to the
Air Force Association on September 27, 1958, Secretary of the Air Force
James H. Douglas stated that

> we must concede that during the past year [the Soviets] have fired several
> ballistic missiles to intercontinental ranges. We concede them operational
> missiles with ranges of less than a thousand miles. Their achievements
> with ballistic missiles and satellites have emphasized the high technical
> quality of their military power, and calls for us to consider the probable
> scope of the Soviet missile threat. We expect that the Soviets will have a
> very small number of intercontinental range missiles in an operational unit
> during the next year, and that they can have a substantial number available
> by 1960.[24]

Although Secretary Douglas was careful to include passages in his
speech that indicated confidence in the strength of U.S. forces, some in
the Air Force simply thought that "the Russians are coming." General
Thomas S. Power, by now head of SAC, had addressed the same audience as Douglas in 1957 and said that the Russian military buildup was
designed to provide capabilities for aggression and would be used "when
they think they are stronger than we are."[25] Opinions in Air Force Intelligence followed the patterns prevalent in that service as a whole.
Starting with fiscal year 1958 the intelligence function in USAF had
been converted from a staff section (A-2) to an officially titled Assistant
Chief of Staff for Intelligence (ACSI). In 1958 the office of the ACSI
was dominated by men who were prepared to believe that Russia was
creating a "missile gap" in its favor. Contributions from ACSI had been
a major force in the high ICBM projection contained in the May 1958
NIE. In July 1958 Major General James H. Walsh was brought back
from Great Britain, where he had commanded SAC's Seventh Air Division, to take over ACSI. General Walsh had been director of intelligence
at SAC during the "bomber gap." Now he believed that the reason the
Soviets did not appear to be building so many bombers was precisely
because they had chosen instead to accelerate their missile programs.
   Under Walsh were a number of Air Force analysts with similar views.
A CIA officer has been quoted as saying that " 'to the Air Force every

flyspeck on film was a missile.' "[26] On another occasion a newly hired professional analyst for CIA's Office of Scientific Intelligence was given an orientation briefing by the Air Force that was designed to refute many elements of the CIA's own official position. In the period from 1957 to 1960 ACSI was almost weekly presenting its view to the intelligence community that the Soviets were deploying hundreds of ICBMs.

During 1958 the dispute over Soviet missile progress was intensified, given the approach of the Soviets' projected IOC and the lack of new data. Nothing was derived from the Turkish radars unless the Soviets launched missiles, and no missiles flew after the Sputnik launch on May third. Moreover, during 1958 there were few U-2 overflights of Russia so that there was minimal photographic coverage of Russian test sites or potential deployment areas. This did not mean that the intelligence on Soviet missiles was not discussed; indeed the topic was raised in the NSC at least nine times during 1958. It did mean that the Air Force, CIA, and others involved with this intelligence issue were forced to extrapolate from outdated evidence. Thus there developed at least two competing interpretations of Soviet ICBM test history. The Air Force position was that the Soviets were satisfied with the amount of testing they had conducted already and would now proceed to deploy the SS-6. The CIA's Office of Scientific Intelligence maintained that the Soviet halt reflected real difficulties with the SS-6 program and that Russian ICBM deployment would be correspondingly delayed. This conflict remained unresolved through 1958.

In general, the administration continued to warn against taking too seriously the number ranges included in the estimates. During January 1959 Defense Secretary McElroy told the Senate Appropriations Committee that he could not "overemphasize the importance of the word 'could' in this type of estimate. It is not intended to mean that the Soviet Union will actually produce the numbers of missiles that have been estimated."[27] Under tough questioning from Senator Johnson's subcommittee, McElroy made much the same point. He felt that the main threat was still Russian bombers rather than ICBMs, that there was no evidence the Soviets were farther along toward an operational ICBM than the U.S., and that, while conceding the Russians a capability to build large numbers of missiles if they chose to do so, no one "can be inside of the Russian mind" and know the Soviets' actual decisions. McElroy also recalled the experience of the bomber estimates and pointed to how they had been exaggerated:

> Twining himself, when he was Chief of Staff of the Air Force, came back from Russia and testified that this was something we had to be very appre-

hensive of; they had the capacity to produce great numbers, they did not make the national determination to do so; and they may do this in the case of the ICBMs.[28]

The new assessment of Soviet progress presented at the 1959 hearings and based upon the recently revised NIEs projected one hundred ICBMs for 1960, three hundred for 1961, five hundred for 1962, and perhaps one thousand to fifteen hundred for 1963. Although these figures were quite large, they represented a reduction from the May 1958 estimate.

Defense Secretary McElroy's assertions were not taken at face value. Instead the "missile gap" revelations had made Soviet power a sensitive issue in American politics and concerns continued to run very high. Even Adlai Stevenson, normally unflappable and a very thoughtful politician, returned from an extensive tour of Russia in 1958 to tell his speechwriters that the magnitude of the Soviet challenge had been "borne in upon him" that summer.[29] The alarmist stance of many politicians, however, can be related to posturing in advance of the 1960 election, for which both Symington and Johnson intended to be the Democratic Party's nominee.

Symington, especially, was quite upset with the Eisenhower administration due to its attitude toward the putative Russian missile threat. The senator's interest focused specifically on the national estimates. Symington had been responsible for the airpower hearings of 1956 and was the only U.S. senator who had ever sat on the NSC, having been Truman's secretary of the Air Force from 1947 to 1949. He was regarded as a favorable advocate by the Air Force. In any case, in 1958 after Armed Services had been briefed on the CIA's most recent estimate of Soviet missiles, Symington went to the White House to complain that the national estimates did not reflect real Russian capabilities. The senator claimed he had obtained "other" intelligence. President Eisenhower asked the senator if he would not like to go out to the CIA's offices, around the Reflecting Pool down by the Potomac, and see how the estimates were actually made. Symington agreed and became the first legislator to meet with the Board of National Estimates at CIA on official business. The BNE explanation did not satisfy Symington, who wrote the President on August 29, 1958, to reiterate his views. Symington feared that the Soviets had more missiles than they were credited with. When the December NIE came in with a further *reduction* of the Soviet ICBM projection the senator was quite angry, and he proved to be one of the most aggressive questioners in the January 1959 hearings. In February he inserted the text of this letter to Eisenhower into the

Congressional Record, causing the administration some embarrassment.

Symington was not without kindred lights inside the executive. The source of his "other intelligence" presumably held similar views, as did the sources for the 1958 leaks to the Alsops. Something of this view existed at the White House in the President's Science Advisory Committee (PSAC). There the chemist George Kistiakowsky had made himself a "one-man panel on guided missiles" under Killian. At a meeting with the President on January 12, 1959, held to discuss the results of the Geneva conference, Killian told Eisenhower that Kistiakowsky's impressions of Soviet missile capability "ran counter to our best intelligence estimates." Killian said it was PSAC's position that Russia already had an operational long-range missile force. The President replied that he might accept that the Russians had achieved an IOC, but that the real question concerned the numbers and accuracy of the Soviet ICBMs,[30] However, the PSAC contention was regarded as serious enough so that on January thirtieth Eisenhower had a full-dress briefing on U.S.-Soviet missile capabilities given to his cabinet after the regular meeting.

The Russians resumed ICBM testing in April 1959 and conducted an intense series of flights of the SS-6 through the remainder of the year, including the first full-range five-thousand-nautical-mile test of any Soviet ICBM. In 1959 the Soviets also formed their Strategic Rocket Forces (SRF) as an independent arm of their armed forces under Marshal of Aviation Mitrofan I. Nedelin. The indications were not all positive for the Soviets, however. Some evidence existed that the Soviets had had numerous launch or in-flight missile failures, and there was also the long hiatus in the flight-test program. The Soviets evidently had postponed launch of their Sputnik III for five months due to various technical problems. Even more telling was evidence that the successful Lunik shot at the beginning of 1959 had been preceded by three failures. Such reports cannot have encouraged belief in a combat-ready Soviet ICBM.

Even the Air Force had begun to step back from its pessimism of 1958. In the fiscal year 1960 hearings Jim Douglas, who had made a fairly alarming speech before the Air Force Association the previous September, now maintained that in view of the Soviet test lag it was difficult to see how the SS-6 could attain IOC during 1959 or the Russians deploy the significant numbers of missiles in 1959 that he had predicted. Unofficially Hanson Baldwin, military correspondent of *The New York Times,* wrote that

despite the repeated alarms in Washington, hard evidence of Soviet capability of launching long range missiles is still absent . . . several such reports have been investigated and were found to be erroneous.[31]

Other writers asserted the opposite. Thomas W. Phillips, a retired Army brigadier general, wrote in a January 1959 article that at least seven ICBM launching sites had been discovered in western Russia and that the Japanese had reported the existence of five others in the Soviet Far East. Drew Pearson reported Soviet IRBM sites in Eastern Europe and under construction in Albania. In a mid-July Senate speech, Lyndon Johnson charged that his hearings had developed the "fact" that the Eisenhower administration defense program conceded to the Russians at least a three-to-one advantage in ICBMs over the next few years. But McElroy held firm. In June 1959 he told a press audience that the Russians might achieve IOC, with perhaps ten missiles, by the end of the year but this would be neck and neck with the United States.

Not only were the indicators of Soviet activity inconclusive but the difficulties in collecting information were legion. As has already been noted, the U-2, was of limited utility at this time. The aircraft had been exhibiting mechanical difficulties. At least two Lockheed and five SAC pilots were killed in U-2 crashes between 1956 and 1958 and indeed, SAC grounded all its U-2's on July 10, 1958, after two fatal crashes had occurred in a twenty-four-hour period. There was peripheral coverage of the Soviets from Bodø, Norway, but no U-2 overflights of Russia. The U-2 operations were reduced even further when a crash at Atsugi in Japan almost revealed the existence of this secret photo reconnaissance program. Despite difficulties, however, information was substantial enough to warrant ten NSC briefings on Soviet missile intelligence during 1959 together with four more detailed exchanges between CIA's Office of Scientific Intelligence and the PSAC. At one meeting on June sixteenth, OSI Director Herbert Scoville assessed the newest SS-6 tests and described unusual "luminous phenomena" which had accompanied them.

In making judgments on fragmentary data such as that on the Soviet missiles, analysts were constantly being thrown back to assessing probabilities and intentions. This was not a problem unique to intelligence—PSAC was concerned about much the same thing, as attested by Jim Killian:

> We who spoke for science never succeeded in making clear the difference between *probability* and *possibility*. . . . I made one major effort by asking Robert Bacher to prepare an analysis in depth of why scientific assessment was not tantamount to political assessment in such fields as test detection and monitoring negotiations.[32]

The state of knowledge was important because, in the political climate surrounding the "missile gap," analysts without a substantial amount of information were inclined to give the benefit of the doubt to the Russian rocket developers in what would later become known as "worst case" analysis. Thus in a memorandum to the President of August 18, 1959, Allen Dulles noted that

> while there is presently some difference of opinion concerning the date at which the Soviets are likely to achieve a first operational capability with ten ICBMs, the consensus is that this will be achieved either in 1959 or in 1960.

In this memo, whose statements regarding Russia had been cleared through the USIB, the main conclusion was that

> based on the findings of competent American military authority and on intelligence regarding Soviet military developments we conclude that the military position of the USSR relative to that of the U.S. is improving. Given the continuation of present programs by both the U.S. and USSR the latter will make further gains in relative military power during the next few years.[33]

In a similar vein a week later Kistiakowsky attended a USIB meeting to listen to the presentation of the Hyland panel report on the Soviet missile program and noted that it had been "a really excellent report which should do a lot to silence those who maintain the threat is imaginary."[34]

But Allen Dulles had his own organization engaged in the formulation of a new set of national estimates. These were completed in December 1959 and their presentation at the fiscal year 1961 budget hearings led intelligence into renewed political dispute over the "missile gap."

The "Missile Gap" Recedes

The national estimates on Soviet intentions and capabilities were produced on a quarterly schedule set in advance among the CIA, the Defense Department, and the NSC. One reason for this practice was so that the estimates could have an impact on the defense officials drafting the military budget for the following fiscal year, on the White House officials approving that budget, and so that the estimates could be used in Congress to justify the new budget presented in January of each year. The case of the fiscal 1961 budget was no different although the NIE was completed rather late in the budget cycle, December 1959.

At the time the NIE was approved by the USIB no one thought it would lead to a major dispute over Soviet missiles. But a dispute did ensue, beginning in January 1960 with a simple misunderstanding, and then mushrooming into a political controversy that lasted three months and involved Congress and numerous administration officials. This dispute would have further reverberations in the 1960 presidential campaign and helped to tie Eisenhower's successors into a defense program larger than they might have desired.

Almost before this dispute died down the Eisenhower administration had to confront the very thing it had feared most—revelation of one of its vital intelligence resources. This occurred when one of the U-2 aircraft crashed during an overflight of the Soviet Union. Loss of the plane ended the overflight program and would also have drastically reduced the available information on the Russians had not new intelligence resources become operational at about the same time.

The years 1960 and 1961 are in many ways a watershed period in the development of modern military capabilities and intelligence methods. The new "machine spies" provided a quantum jump in the information available to analysts. New intelligence organizations helped change the pattern of relationships in the intelligence community. Moreover, the very technology that was at issue in the "missile gap," the ICBM, was finally deployed by the Russians, further increasing the importance of timely intelligence on Soviet capabilities in this area.

The intelligence community exerted great effort to refine its estimates of Soviet capability. Photographs from the U-2 had identified the Russian nuclear test ranges at Semipalatinsk, Novaya Zemlya, and the weapons production facility near Alma-Ata; the antiballistic missile test site at Sary-Shagan; and the twin missile test centers at Kapustin Yar and Tyuratam. When CIA's Board of National Estimates met on Soviet matters there was an effort to bring different expertise to the data. Board chairman Sherman Kent encouraged BNE members to become experts on Soviet missiles. Executive secretary Howard Stoertz responded by focusing on this area, as did ONE officer R. Jack Smith. Kent also discussed tentative judgments to be included in estimates with military intelligence representatives or with officers from the Soviet Division of the clandestine services. The DDP's chief for Soviet intelligence even informally sat in on some meetings of the BNE. On other occasions the BNE meetings were attended by White House representatives, as when Kistiakowsky sat in for PSAC.

There were also methodological innovations in the estimates themselves. It was such an innovation that touched off the dispute of 1960. While preparing the national estimate in late 1959 the intelligence community decided to try to distinguish between different kinds of Soviet missile programs. The idea was to provide ranges of possible Russian ICBM inventories in the five-year projection that would reflect both an "orderly" Soviet development program and a "crash" program. Analysts conceded that the photo coverage of Russia from the U-2 was incomplete, but estimators reasoned that a Soviet "crash" could not escape detection by the U-2. The most likely explanation was thus that the Russians had an "orderly" effort under way. In the estimate the Soviets were still judged to have no operational ICBMs, but they were expected to have a small number (35) by mid-1960, then 140–200 in mid-1961, rising to 350–450 by mid-1963 (see Table I).

The new estimate was briefed to the NSC by Dulles on January 7, 1960. As science advisor George Kistiakowsky recorded, the message from the director of central intelligence "concludes that mid-1961 is the point of maximum threat because as of then we still won't have hardened missile bases and SAC will be vulnerable, too, but the threat is not catastrophic. In fact the missile gap doesn't look to be very serious."[35] Eisenhower seemed satisfied with the NIE, though he suspected that Soviet missile accuracies might be better than the five nautical miles of the estimate. But the President went ahead to approve a major increase in the U.S. ICBM program at the same NSC meeting.

That the "missile gap" charges were political dynamite was again illustrated on January twelfth, when the President held his weekly session with the Republican legislative leadership. Maryland Senator Thruston Morton asked Eisenhower what could be done about the fact that even small town constituents were becoming concerned over the image of U.S. military weakness. Eisenhower agreed to raise with Defense Secretary Thomas Gates and Joint Chiefs Chairman Twining the possibility of their making statements in congressional hearings on the budget to allay fears of a missile lag. Two days later, on the fourteenth, Eisenhower had Gates and DCI Allen Dulles present to the full cabinet a briefing that compared the budgeted military program with the reduced level of Soviet threat in the latest national estimate.

Gates and Twining were due shortly before the Senate Armed Services Committee for their presentation of the fiscal year 1961 budget. This was a fine opportunity for reassurances of the kind desired by Senator Morton, and Gates turned to this subject in his testimony of Tuesday, January nineteenth. The defense secretary told the committee that allegations of a three-to-one ICBM gap in favor of the Russians had been "based upon estimates of what the USSR could produce and was not an affirmative statement of fact." More importantly, "we do not now believe that the Soviet superiority in ICBMs will be as great as that previously estimated," although Gates did concede that at the moment

TABLE I. SOVIET ICBM DEPLOYMENT ESTIMATES 1958–1963

Estimate	Date	Mid-1959	Mid-1960	Mid-1961	Mid-1962	Mid-1963	Mid-1964
NIE 11-4-58	12/23/58	100*	100	500*	500	—	—
NIE 11-4-59	2/9/60	—	35	140–200	250–350	350–450	—
NIE 11-8-60	8/1/60						
Program A		—	30	150	270	400	—
Program B		—	35	200	450	NA	—
Program C		—	30	50	125	200	—
NIE 11-4-60	12/1/60	—	—	—	124–450	200–700	**
NIE 11-5-61	4/25/61	—	—	—	—	—	—
NIE 11-8-61	6/7/61	—	—	—	50–300	100–550	150–850***
NIE 11-4-61	1/10/62	—	—	—	35–100	100–250	150–450****
Supplement NIE	February 1963	—	—	—	—	120–250	175–450

*The estimate predicted that an inventory of 100 and 500 ICBMs would be attained at intervals of two years, but gave the earlier years in the case of a "crash" program.

**The Air Force also predicted 950 Soviet ICBMs for mid-1964 and 1,200 in 1965.

***Additional Air Force predictions were 1,150 Soviet ICBMs in 1965 and 1,450 in 1966.

****The estimate also presented the range of 250–800 Soviet ICBMs for mid-1967.

Source: Memo, McQuade-Nitze, "The Missile Gap Estimates," May 31, 1963 (declassified July 25, 1979) DDRS (78)-263(d).

the Russians might have a few rockets more than the U.S. In support of Gates the Department of Defense that day issued a transcript of his testimony before a House committee in which the defense secretary explained that there was a new type of intelligence estimate available which predicted what the Soviets "probably will do" in contrast to previous NIE predictions of what the Russians *could* do if they chose. The actual change in procedure involved measuring Soviet missiles "on their launchers" rather than in a general inventory. This was based on feeling that the Soviets had reached IOC with their SS-6 missile, that predicting the size of the deployed Soviet missile force was a useful intelligence exercise, and that the construction of operational launchers rather than simple hardware inventories was the best measure of Russian ICBM salvo capability. Gates characterized the new type estimate as one of "intentions."[36]

The wording proved to be unfortunate. There was an immediate storm of criticism of the defense secretary's presumption that he *knew* what the Russians *intended* to do. Even worse, it developed that Gates and the JCS Chairman presented slightly different estimates of Soviet capability to Congress, with resulting congressional suspicion that information was being withheld from Twining. General Twining himself reported to the President on January twenty-first that "with the exception of the public argument over intelligence based on intentions versus capabilities, his own appearance[s] and those of Mr. Gates had gone extremely well."[37] But Twining missed the point. The political storm centered precisely on his one exception. Many were concerned that the new estimate was only an excuse for minimizing the Soviet threat and a cloak for an inadequate defense policy.

At his press conference on January twenty-fifth President Eisenhower was asked by Chalmers Roberts whether he had had any part in the production of the new NIE and whether, as a military man, he agreed with estimates based on an enemy's intentions. Eisenhower replied that "our intelligence estimate is a very intricate and very complex thing, and you cannot take any one basis, any one channel of thought to make a proper estimate."[38] The next day Senator Stuart Symington charged that "the intelligence books have been juggled so that the budget books can be balanced."[39] The charge seemed to be supported by a January nineteenth speech made by the SAC boss, General Thomas S. Power, in which he claimed that a Soviet attack with a theoretical ninety-five-percent chance of eliminating SAC need be made with only three hundred missiles, and only half of those need be ICBMs. Power advocated an immediate and expensive airborne alert posture for his command.

Press reporting and congressional reactions put administration officials immediately on the defensive. Gates insisted before the House that there had been a significant change in the estimates:

> The intelligence information has improved so that it is now possible to have it more refined and better evaluated on what the Russian ICBM missile programs may be. Originally, it was only possible to estimate missile capability. There is now better information available from a variety of sources on a variety of subjects that are considered in reaching an intelligence estimate. There is obviously no information whatever on USSR intentions as to specific military or political policies or actions. Of course it is impossible to have such intelligence. What we have is a refined and better set of facts pertaining to the probable, or what the Soviet program may be.[40]

Allen Dulles, giving a speech before the Institute of Aeronautical Sciences in New York on January twenty-sixth, also maintained that he had been misunderstood. He claimed it to be standard operating procedure to shift to "probable programing, sometimes referred to as intentions" as more information became available and did not suggest any change in the intelligence approach to the problem.[41]

From the White House Eisenhower directed that an effort be made to acquaint journalists with the facts behind the new perception of Soviet missile strength. His special assistant for national security, Gordon Gray, held briefings with several reporters in the last week of January. In one such encounter on the twenty-seventh Gray told John Steele of Time-Life that the very phrase "missile gap" involved drawing a conclusion without examination of facts. When Steele wanted to understand how officials had been able to "downgrade" their intelligence estimates, Gray responded that

> there was no downgrading involved but that current estimates were based on available information and that the available information today was better than it was when the earlier estimates were made. I then sought to assure Mr. Steele that the current estimate came up from the intelligence community and in no way reflected any sort of a direction from the President or from anyone else.[42]

The national security advisor also recalled the "bomber gap" experience for Steele and suggested that there was a "universal tendency" on the part of military people and intelligence personnel to resolve any doubts conservatively, that is, in favor of judging the enemy to have a greater capability. Finally, Gray remarked that the public uproar concerned only the last two years in a five-year projection and that "no one seriously believes that there is much validity in a projection beyond three years." Such projections were "almost a matter of drawing lines on a chart."

However, the White House message was not reflected sympathetically in Steele's *Life* magazine article of February sixth or in a *Time* article with a February eighth cover date. Both followed the lead of General Power in advocating airborne alert for SAC bombers.

The Steele episode shows clearly the difficulty Eisenhower was having in getting support for nonalarmist views by the beginning of the 1960 election year. Gates's faux pas now opened the door to those who would take issue with administration defense policy. Among them was Senator Lyndon Johnson, preparing to make a bid for the Democratic presidential nomination, who said, "The new optimistic picture presented by Secretary Gates is based upon guessing what the Soviet leaders may be thinking. The missile gap cannot be eliminated by the mere stroke of a pen."[43] Johnson called new joint hearings on missiles and space programs and immediately sought testimony from Allen Dulles and other intelligence officials. Johnson wanted solid material from the CIA to settle the "missile gap" claims.

At closed session hearings the director of central intelligence was caught in a neat semantic trap by Missouri Senator Stuart Symington, who was as intent on a presidential bid as Johnson, and who had even less love for Eisenhower's steady state defense policy. One of the NIE projections credited the Soviets with a mid-1960 strength of thirty-five ICBMs, while SAC was going to have only a dozen of its own Atlas missiles operational by the same time. Administration officials had been saying that they could not subscribe to the belief that the Soviets retained a three-to-one superiority in ICBMs. Symington asked Dulles whether three-to-one was an accurate ratio. Allen Dulles refused to "speculate" on the grounds that CIA was not in the business of assessing American Forces and so could not compare programs. Symington then asked Dulles, for the record, to divide twelve into thirty-six and Dulles answered. The headline in the next morning's *New York Times* was that administration officials had "conceded" the Russians possessed a three to one advantage in ICBMs!

Senator Johnson's hearings opened with an appearance by the secretary of defense. Gates said he believed

> that the better evaluation of intelligence gave a different set of figures than were given under the less clarified possibilities and capabilities intelligence provided the year before. These gave a different set of possibilities for Soviet operational missiles.[44]

Gates further did not believe the Russians had sufficient missiles "to permit them to make any marginal decision to attack the United States" although both sides were approaching the relative position "where we can both attack each other and do great damage." General Thomas Power also came in from Offutt Air Base to give the SAC view. Surprisingly the general repeatedly asserted in response to questioning that he was in agreement with the NIE.

Air Force Intelligence came to the stand in the person of General James Walsh. Walsh revealed that USAF had dissented from the NIE due to its belief that the Soviets had a larger number of ICBMs than was projected in the estimate. He laid out the differences in response to a series of questions posed by committee counsel—most material of substance was deleted from the transcript. Walsh agreed under questioning that the figure of one hundred missile bases in Russia, a figure offered by the London-based International Institute of Strategic Studies, was about right," although the Air Force also believed the Soviets to be *capable* of producing even more ICBMs than Walsh himself thought they had deployed. Senator Thomas E. Martin (R-Iowa) initiated an interesting exchange on intelligence sources.

Martin asked, "General, do you have access to any intelligence information that is not available to Mr. Dulles's organization?"

"I have not," Walsh replied.

Then the follow-up: "Do you have access to all intelligence information to which they have access?"

The Air Force intelligence chief could only say, "I like to think so."[45]

Also damaging was the presentation of charts drawn up by the CIA showing projected missile strengths. This turned into a point of contention when JCS Chairman Twining was unable to answer questions based on these charts when he appeared before Johnson's committee. Moreover, Dulles's and Twining's charts differed. Twining was recalled before the Johnson committee to resolve the conflict between his own testimony and that of Allen Dulles. Twining's military staff assistant, L. P. Gray, maintained that all charts used in the JCS presentation were developed from the actual NIE figures in 1959. Twining had not seen the CIA chart that contradicted one of his own until after his testimony before both appropriations committees of Congress. Aside from the charts, however, the Joint Chiefs chairman was in agreement with the substance of the intelligence judgment: Soviet ICBMs were less threatening than had appeared to be the case in 1959. In Twining's view, "the cold-blooded figures do not present an accurate comparison of our overall military strength versus the Soviet Union." He emphasized that the Chiefs had nothing to do with formulation of the intelligence projections, "we just use what they, the CIA, give us.[46] The senators, whom Symington had led once again in the questioning, then determined to recall Dulles to the table.

The director of central intelligence did make some effort to clarify the confusion swirling around the estimates. The day before Twining's appearance Allen Dulles had sent Johnson a letter purporting to explain the differences, but this, too, was regarded as contradictory. Finally on February twenty-fifth Dulles came to Capitol Hill for five hours of closed session testimony which, in the end, still left the Senate confused. Senator Clifford P. Case (R-New Jersey) told reporters that the conflict over the NIE resulted from Dulles's attempt to incorporate material in his original Senate testimony that was not included in the national estimates. Dulles himself confirmed this at a luncheon on February twenty-eighth:

> Frankly I think I made a mistake. I took an estimate prepared for 1959 and one in the process of preparation and tried to put them on the same basis to simplify them. I extrapolated. The old estimate had little information on ICBMs but lots on IRBMs. In the old estimate we said we thought they would have a certain capability within a certain period of time. In the new estimate I took the median range of the old estimate. It was a reasonable extrapolation but one that had not been given to the Department of Defense before.[47]

Much like Dulles, the secretaries of state and defense were obliged to go on record in regard to the new national estimate. The State Department draft specified that

> in the case of the Soviet ICBM, the intelligence community last year did not undertake to estimate the number of ICBMs which the USSR would have in its operational units on any particular date, but merely the number it could make in certain periods of time after it had achieved an initial operational capability. Since last year, the intelligence community has received enough information about the Soviet missile program and about the other factors which would affect a Soviet decision regarding the actual production and deployment of missiles to enable it to attempt an estimate of the probable program. This estimate, as Mr. Dulles has said publicly, does not represent a downgrading of the Soviet missile system from last year.[48]

Similarly Secretary Gates made a presentation for the Defense Department when he appeared before the Johnson committee for the last time:

> Last year we had available to us the national intelligence estimate which gave us the numbers of operational ICBMs which the USSR could achieve or might achieve in various time periods. These were calculated to cover either of two possibilities: that the Soviets would pursue a vigorous but orderly ICBM program, and the other, that they would pursue a highly accelerated or "crash" program.

A year has now passed. Additional information has been acquired and further refinement has been accomplished. Considering the available evidence, we believe it is now well established that the USSR is not engaged in a crash program for ICBM development.[49]

It was Gates's firm conviction that "our deterrent and retaliatory position remains adequate to meet the threat today and in the years ahead." Conceding that General Twining had not seen Allen Dulles's infamous chart, Gates nevertheless insisted that the JCS were informed of all essential information regarding Soviet missile activities.

With the end of the joint hearings on ballistic missiles and space the public furor over the national estimates died down. President Eisenhower had gone to great lengths to defend his administration from charges of "juggling the intelligence books," and had even met personally with the USIB for the first time on record on February second. Senators Johnson and Symington achieved considerable media impact with their charges but both, it turned out, were defeated in their efforts to capture the Democratic nomination.

CHAPTER SEVEN
INTELLIGENCE RESOURCES IN THE LATE 1950s

While the 1960 political campaign was in full swing, with the "missile gap" charges unstilled, there occurred the celebrated "U-2 incident." This intelligence disaster put en end to the extremely valuable U-2 overflight program and complicated a further reassessment of the Soviet missile position then in progress within the intelligence community. The U-2 incident also disrupted the planned Paris summit conference of Eisenhower, Khrushchev, and the British and French leaders that had long been scheduled for mid-May 1960.

From the beginning of the overflight program the U.S. knew that the Russians were vitally interested in ending the U-2's domination of their airspace. No reply was ever made to the Soviets' secret diplomatic protest of July 1956, but early expectations had been that the U-2 would be able to elude Soviet air defenses for about two years. By that time, it was assumed, the Russians would have developed weapons capable of spanning the twenty thousand feet between the highest operating altitude of Soviet interceptor aircraft and that of the U-2 spy plane. In 1958 the Russians began to deploy massive numbers of a new surface-to-air missile (SAM) which was promptly dubbed the SA-2 Guideline by NATO authorities. Between 1955 and 1958 Soviet SAM strength had been concentrated in rings of air defense sites around Moscow, but with SA-1 missiles which lacked any high-altitude capability. The Soviets had shot SA-1 SAMs at the U-2's and attempted to climb fighters to the altitude of the U-2, but their planes stalled out in the thin air and the SA-1's had proved uncontrollable at U-2 heights. Now there was doubt about the altitude ceiling of the Guideline, which some feared could engage the U-2, and from about mid-1959 the Americans began planning U-2 missions so as to avoid known SA-2 sites.

The risks of flying over Russia were considerable and the White House maintained close control over the U-2 flights. More flights were proposed than were approved, and Eisenhower was personally aware of each succeeding series of flight "packages." The President maintained a generally cautious attitude, as illustrated by his cancellation of the U-2 flights while Premier Khrushchev visited the United States in September 1959. Following that state occasion the Russian leader invited President Eisenhower to visit the USSR, but both sides agreed first to a summit with British and French leaders. Given the earlier restraint, there is some question why an overflight was authorized just prior to the Paris summit. Missions for the U-2 were planned by a small staff of officers seconded from the Air Force and headed by Colonel Stanley Beerli (formerly 1010 Detachment commander at Incirlik). One flight of the 1960 program was carried out on April ninth. It is not entirely clear whether the next flight was part of the same series or was authorized separately. One version is that the flight was part of the regular quarterly series. A second explanation is that the April ninth flight had brought back disturbing evidence of new construction near Sverdlovsk which suggested a start on a first operational ICBM site, and the second U-2 was sent to take more photos of the area. Yet another story is that the Americans were alerted in April by the receipt of communications intelligence and agent reports that suggested the possibility of ICBM deployment near Plesetsk. According to the last two versions Bissell and Allen Dulles met with Eisenhower in mid-April to discuss the U-2 mission.

The secretary of state, Christian Herter, made the connection between the flight date and the Paris summit, scheduled for May fourteenth. Dulles was apparently told that the CIA might execute the flight at any time until two weeks before the summit. Months later the President would remark to his former advisor Sherman Adams, "When they brought me the plan for this particular flight, I approved it among several others within an intelligence policy already adopted. I had no thought of it having any possible bearing upon the summit or on my forthcoming trip to Moscow. Except for unforeseen circumstances it would not have had any."[1] The U-2 was scheduled to fly over both Sverdlovsk and Plesetsk. At Sverdlovsk the Soviets had Guideline SAM air defenses.

Allen Dulles apparently considered for a brief time sending the U-2 on May Day (May first), a Soviet holiday. Bissell, however, preferred not to press so close to the cutoff date. The orders to Colonel William M. Shelton, commanding 1010 Detachment, were to go as soon as weather permitted. Francis Gary Powers was one of the two most experienced

U-2 pilots in Turkey, veteran of twenty-seven missions since 1956. On April twenty-eighth the weather was good over most of Russia but Powers had not completed his preflight physical. The next day it snowed at Sverdlovsk. On the thirtieth there was cloud cover along much of the flight path. Francis Powers's U-2 flight was launched on May Day after all.

The flight initially went well. Another aircraft simulated a peripheral intelligence flight in order to divert air defenses. The specific aircraft Powers flew that day had a reputation for cranky performance. It was the same plane that had almost been destroyed in the emergency landing in Japan in 1959. When Powers was over Sverdlovsk and preparing for his photographic run, there was a loud noise, Powers recalls, which may or may not have been the explosion of a SAM missile. The U-2 lost power and fell out of the sky, and Francis Powers was captured along with the U-2's wreckage, its cameras intact and its strategic purpose clear. It is said that Khrushchev and other top Soviet leaders determined to bring the captured CIA pilot to Moscow as they stood above Lenin's Tomb watching the May Day parade go through Red Square.[2]

The first indication that something had gone wrong occurred when the plane became overdue at its destination, Bodø, Norway. There was breathless waiting at Incirlik for news of Powers's aircraft but hopes died after a few days. In Washington the U-2 loss was a major intelligence "flap" and Allen Dulles called the USIB into immediate session to confirm the contingency plan for a prepared story on the loss that would disguise the relationship between the airplane and the CIA. Officials were instructed to claim that the lost plane was a high-altitude weather research craft belonging to NASA.

Public reaction to loss of the plane was initially subdued because intelligence use of the U-2 was so secret. Only *The Washington Post* featured a news item reporting a NASA plane lost. Similarly the White House diary of George Kistiakowsky is silent on the incident until several days after. Even Kelly Johnson, designer of the U-2 at Lockheed, was not told of the downed CIA aircraft until Bissell informed him on May fourth. Then, on Thursday the fifth, before the Supreme Soviet, Premier Khrushchev revealed that a U.S. "bandit plane" had been shot down over Russia while engaged in espionage. This disclosure came while senior U.S. officials were participating in Operation Alert, a training exercise simulating a nuclear emergency in which Eisenhower and other policy makers were evacuated to an underground command post near Washington.

At relocation center "Crystal" the President held an impromptu session of the NSC. Only Joint Chiefs Chairman Nathan Twining, who had missed his helicopter, was absent. The NSC meeting was given a long comparative history of the U.S. and Soviet ICBM programs, with Herbert Scoville of OSI presenting the Russian side. The U-2 was discussed by a smaller group afterwards. Here the consensus was that some official statement would have to be made. Reportedly Thomas Gates was unhappy with the recommendation that the "cover" story ought to be maintained. Gates felt that the U.S. should not become involved in an "international lie." He was overruled. For good measure, however, the interagency 5412 Committee, which monitored all intelligence covert operations, recommended after meeting later that day that all provocative activities against Russia should be suspended forthwith. In the meantime the White House announced to reporters that a statement would be issued by the State Department and NASA.

The statement continued the "weather plane" cover story: the U-2 supposedly became lost in the course of a routine mission. When the decision on the cover story was made the U.S. already knew, from the reporting of Ambassador Llewellyn Thompson in Moscow, that the Soviets were holding Gary Powers and presumably interrogating him. Regardless of "cover" stories, the U-2 pilots themselves had standing orders to admit information that the Soviets would already know if they were ever interrogated. How Gary Powers might do under interrogation was an open question, and the Americans also did not know how much of the U-2 the Russians had taken. If they found the cameras, the NASA cover story lost credibility no matter what Powers told the Soviets.

Richard Bissell passed the news to the White House: the Russians had Powers. Still President Eisenhower tried to keep a lid on the U-2 affair. He even refused to inform congressmen on the grounds that "these congressional fellows will inevitably spill the beans."[3] How Eisenhower thought that secrecy of the U-2 could be preserved in this situation is still a mystery. Inevitably, on May seventh Khrushchev revealed that the Soviets were holding Powers and would try him for espionage. Even then high-level meetings at State and CIA split over the American response. The intelligence officials wanted to continue denying the Soviet allegations; State felt that some kind of admission was now necessary. Eisenhower sided with his intelligence officers.

Meanwhile public criticism mounted. Administration explanations that no such flight had been authorized over Russia, which followed the NASA cover story, only led to questions over whether President Eisenhower really had control over U.S. intelligence. Thus the official explanation backfired. By Monday, May ninth, the situation had become critical. Gates, Herter, and other officials gathered to decide on another public statement that the President could make. Charles E. Bohlen, am-

bassador in Moscow from 1953 to 1957, argued that the administration
should make no comment at all. The decision went against him. The
considerations are best put by Bohlen:

> I believe the reason Eisenhower decided to accept full responsibility for the
> U-2 was the fear that he would be criticized as a President who was not in
> charge, who did not know of the activities of his administration that could
> lead to nuclear war. There had been much criticism of Eisenhower as lack-
> ing the vigor and leadership of a president. He must have been conscious of
> these accusations. I still do not know how the situation could have been
> handled better. The bungling of the NASA release could have been avoided,
> but I think the results would have been very much the same. The downing
> of the plane and capture of the pilot made the problem insoluble.[4]

That afternoon Allen Dulles and Christian Herter met with eighteen
prominent congressional leaders to explain. Secretary of State Herter
told them "the government of the United States would be derelict in its
responsibilities if it did not, in the absence of Soviet cooperation, take
such measures as are possible unilaterally to lessen and to overcome the
dangers of surprise attack."[5]

At the White House on the afternoon of the ninth, Eisenhower led off
an NSC meeting with the statement that he did not want to hear *anything* about the U-2. Later Kistiakowsky talked to Gordon Gray about
the publicity value of publication of a few U-2 photos, but the President's military staff officer Goodpaster was not enthusiastic about the
possibilities. An order went forward to the 5412 Committee directing
termination of provocative intelligence operations. However, the press
release in which Eisenhower accepted responsibility for the U-2 left ambiguous the question of future overflights. Most of the press therefore
reported that the U.S. would continue to make reconnaissance flights
over Russia.

Public relations was only one problem of Eisenhower's U-2 fiasco.
The other was the Russian reaction and its effect on the Paris summit.
Almost immediately after the Russians shot down the U-2, CIA began
preparing an analysis of probable Soviet courses of action. At the NSC
on May ninth Deputy Director for Intelligence Robert Amory spoke for
the CIA while Allen Dulles was on Capitol Hill. The CIA Soviet analysts
opined that Khrushchev was engaged in posturing, building a position
on which he might fall back in the event the summit failed. Not to be
overly complacent, however, Eisenhower personally held a news conference on May eleventh and again accepted responsibility for the U-2 incident. The next day a strict order was issued that in the future all
intelligence operations which "threatened" the territory of a sovereign

state be cleared with the 5412 Committee. The same order had been issued in 1956, after Russian discovery of the Operation Gold tunnel into East Berlin, but apparently the U-2 was so sensitive that it had never been referred to the board that handled covert operations for the NSC.

On May fourteenth the presidential party left for France, arriving at Paris the next day. Eisenhower, making his courtesy visit to French President Charles De Gaulle, was told that the French had already asked the Soviets whether, under the circumstances, the summit should go on. The question had been posed by the French ambassador before Khrushchev left Moscow, and his coming to Paris at all was a hopeful sign in De Gaulle's view. Nevertheless, Khrushchev had already told De Gaulle that he insisted on an apology although he still did not understand why Eisenhower had admitted responsibility. De Gaulle's reply, that " 'that sort of thing is not done among responsible chiefs of government,' "[6] did not mollify the Russian. Khrushchev was clearly highly agitated.

The Paris summit formally convened on Monday, May sixteenth. As host De Gaulle chaired the meeting and gave the floor to Eisenhower for an opening statement. But Khrushchev interrupted and protested that he had requested to be first speaker. When he was asked to speak Khrushchev proceeded to read a long diatribe denouncing the U-2 overflights. The best riposte, according to one American eyewitness, was that of De Gaulle. At one point Khrushchev pointed at the ceiling and screamed, " 'I have been overflown,' " whereupon De Gaulle countered that France too had been overflown—by Soviet satellites. This startled the Soviet premier. When Khrushchev replied that the Soviet Union was innocent, De Gaulle asked how the Russians had gotten the photographs of the far side of the Moon which they had released after one of their Lunik shots.

"In that satellite we had cameras."

"Ah," remarked De Gaulle in a soft voice, "in *that* one you had cameras! Pray continue."[7]

Meanwhile President Eisenhower strove to control his emotions. When he rose to speak he referred to the U.S. statements of May ninth and eleventh, reiterated that overflights had been suspended and would not be resumed, but refused to extend a formal apology to Khrushchev. There the Paris summit essentially ended. Both sides' leaders left the Elysée Palace and traded charges at their respective press conferences, and Eisenhower returned to Washington on May twentieth. With the summit also ended hopes for a visit to the Soviet Union by the President.

Eisenhower returned to a chorus of criticism for ruining the summit with his U-2 mission. The President felt it ironic that the mistake which everyone knew would someday occur had come at such a crucial moment. Allen Dulles drew the conclusion that the hardest intelligence decisions are on terminating operations that are successful. Democrats, notably John Kennedy and Adlai Stevenson, got more ammunition to use against continued Republican leadership in their 1960 political campaign.

The U-2 incident shows that sensitive intelligence operations cannot ultimately be hidden and raises questions about the value of secrecy. There were certainly legitimate needs for secrecy in developing and using the U-2. Yet when the lack of knowledge on the part of low-level officials led to misstatements to the press in the 1960 incident, the costs of secrecy become more apparent. Moreover, if the U-2 had not been so closely held, bureaucratic resistance might have developed to the unfortunate timing of Gary Powers's flight. In the absence of secrecy there would have been less potential for public relations miscalculations by officials and less shock when the public learned that an American aircraft had been shot down over Russia. Finally, knowledge of the U-2's existence and capabilities had slowly been filtering out anyway, particularly after the 1959 Atsugi crash, and further efforts to preserve secrecy promised only diminishing returns. Most importantly, as George Kistiakowsky seemed to realize, revelation of the U-2's intelligence role might have helped defuse the intense "missile gap" debate by suggesting confidence that the U.S. in fact knew what the Soviets were doing with their ICBMs.

The worst losers in the U-2 business were the analysts of Soviet intelligence. With the loss of a single plane ended a collection program that had produced, according to Richard Helms in 1975, fully ninety percent of the hard data on Soviet military developments that was available to the intelligence community. This could have been an insuperable loss to American intelligence. That it was not was due to the vision and creativity of U.S. technological development and the appearance of new human intelligence resources, which provided a new basis for estimates of Soviet strategic developments. The new collection means can be said for a time to have transformed the intelligence picture of Russia.

The Revolution in Intelligence Resources

Much as the U-2 had provided a quantum leap in the information available to intelligence analysts, the new resources becoming available in the early 1960s went far beyond filling the gap left by the U-2.

One new source was the National Security Agency (NSA) which expanded its communications facilities worldwide, creating new NSA stations along the Soviet periphery. In the late 1950s important NSA electronic intelligence (ELINT) and communications intelligence (COMINT) facilities were built in the obvious places like Britain, West Germany, Turkey, and Japan. But NSA also established installations in less expected locations: there was a network of seven stations in Norway, and stations in Italy, Greece, and Ethiopia. Turkey became a virtual honeycomb of intelligence bases not only for NSA but for CIA and the armed services as well. An intelligence radar similar to those in Turkey, was begun in 1958 on one of the Aleutian Islands, to monitor the reentry of Soviet test missile launches. Director Joseph P. Burke of NSA's Production Division was reportedly instrumental in pushing for increased involvement in Soviet missiles intelligence.

In the mid-fifties the State Department approached the government of Pakistan about the possibility of establishing a "communications center" in that country. Arrangements were formalized in 1959 with a ten-year lease of a site near Peshawar, twenty miles from the Khyber Pass and a hundred and fifty from the Soviet border. By the time a news release reported the lease in July the construction of barracks was already under way. Peshawar became the base of the 6937th Communications Group of the Air Force Security Service. Its peak strength was three thousand U.S. personnel and several hundred local employees. Peshawar served as a convenient location with which to reduce the visibility of U-2 operations in Turkey (Gary Powers's U-2 flight was actually launched from there), and it collected communications intelligence on the Soviet ICBM center at Tyuratam, their antiballistic missile test site at Sary-Shagan, the atomic weapons test site at Semipalatinsk, and on Chinese activities at Lop Nor in Sinkiang province, where the Chinese atomic weapons program was conducted. Peshawar provided a "box seat" on an important range of activities:

> From here, tape recordings could be made of [Soviet] missile countdowns, military conversations, civilian radiotelephone communications, and other electronic emanations from Central Asia.[8]

The base was fully active by November 1960, when Rear Admiral Laurence H. Frost succeeded General Samford as director of the NSA. Later in the 1960s it was supplemented by listening posts in Iran, even closer to Tyuratam.

In the meantime the U.S. government had taken steps to tighten management over electronic intelligence. In September 1958 the old Communications Intelligence Board was merged with the IAC to form the USIB directly under Allen Dulles, although the secretary of defense retained direct control over NSA budget and operations. A separate NSC intelligence directive of 1958 made a formal distinction between COM-INT and ELINT. Allen Dulles followed up the directive on October twenty-first when he established permanent USIB subcommittees to govern both functions. When Peshawar and the other stations were completed the NSA was already operating smoothly within its new management framework.

A second major addition to intelligence resources resulted from a Soviet citizen's offer to spy for the United States. Colonel Oleg Penkovsky, a high official in the Chief Intelligence Directorate (GRU) of the Soviet Army, had become disillusioned. Contacting U.S. officials in Turkey in August 1960, Penkovsky expressed a willingness to give vital Soviet defense information to the United States. His offer was rejected at the time. Richard Bissell, who had risen to head the Directorate of Plans (CIA's clandestine services) in addition to running the U-2 program, had a low opinion of the value of agents and conventional espionage. There were also fears in CIA that the Penkovsky offer was really an attempt by the KGB to penetrate the CIA.

Later in 1960 Colonel Penkovsky made the same offer to the British secret service, who accepted, assigning Greville Wynne to collect Penkovsky's reports. They then offered this intelligence to the CIA, who this time accepted it with alacrity. The value of his reports was evident. The Directorate of Plans (DDP) worked very carefully with the Soviet agent. There were some delicate moments, as when Penkovsky insisted upon being given a British uniform and allowed to walk the London streets thus attired, regardless of any risk of discovery by the KGB. But for almost two years Penkovsky was quite prolific—he provided over five thousand documents of a highly classified nature in addition to personal evaluations on a wide range of topics.[9]

The third significant development was the evolution of an earth satellite that could perform the same photographic reconnaissance function as the U-2. There were no Soviet defenses against reconnaissance vehicles in orbit nor any possibility that such defenses would appear in the foreseeable future. Satellites would enable intelligence to increase the area of the Soviet land mass recorded on film and hence offered the possibility of showing exactly how many Russian ICBMs were in place, and would also provide a total profile of Soviet military capabilities other than ICBMs. The absence of atmosphere allowed even sharper pictures, as the camera would remain stationary. In short the satellite reconnaissance craft seemed to be an almost ideal mechanism, a true "machine spy."

Some of the earliest thinking on reconnaissance satellites in the United States was done at the Rand Corporation. A study in May 1946 envisioned an earth satellite at a cost of $150 million over a five-year period. In April 1951 another secret Rand study examined the utility of a satellite for reconnaissance. Three years later yet another Rand study was done on the potential of "an unconventional reconnaissance method," and described the required subsystem technologies in some detail, forecasting that a complete satellite system could take seven years to develop and cost $165 million. When the Killian Committee met in 1954–1955 the satellite proposal was among its recommendations.

Encouraged also by the Air Force Science Advisory Board and the CIA on March 16, 1955, the Air Force issued its "General Operational Requirement No. 80," which specified interest in a "strategic satellite system." After studying proposals from the aerospace industry the Air Force selected Lockheed, Martin Aircraft, and Radio Corporation of America (RCA) to perform year-long design studies on satellite components. On June 30, 1956, the Air Force informed Lockheed that it would be prime contractor for the satellite project, now known as the "advanced reconnaissance system." Personnel at Lockheed called the satellite effort Project Pied Piper. In keeping with the intense interservice rivalry of this period the Army also came up with its own proposal for a reconnaissance satellite using the Jupiter missile, which, it was claimed, would put spy satellites of five hundred pounds in space by 1959. The initial funding level for the Air Force program was only twelve million dollars. In the summer of 1957, however, substantial attention was given to future reconnaissance systems within the CIA, leading to high-level consideration of a funding increase. White House meetings with Allen Dulles and Richard Bissell in August apparently approved both an acceleration of Pied Piper and a follow-on aircraft to replace the U-2. During September the CIA approached the Pentagon and two months later the funding level was quadrupled. In the meantime the existence of Pied Piper was disclosed in the industry magazine *Aviation Week* on October 14, 1957.

The journalistic revelation led to concern over the secrecy of the reconnaissance satellite. The Soviet Sputnik launch had openly bared the Soviet ICBM threat, but the Pied Piper technology, based on an Atlas booster which had not yet achieved production status, could not fill the near-term need for a satellite. Eisenhower had only the U-2. He considered telling the nation of this plane to reassure it after Sputnik but ultimately rejected this idea. While the President had encouraged satellite development, for a near-term satellite there was only the Army proposal. The President's Board of Consultants on Foreign Intelligence Activities, including both Edwin Land of Polaroid and Jim Killian, then suggested to Eisenhower that he go to the Air Force for a booster, their planned Thor IRBM, and to CIA for the satellite. Allen Dulles was once again willing to provide money from his discretionary fund and extend the cloak of CIA secrecy over the reconnaissance development. The new program was called Corona and Richard Bissell directed it in addition to his duties as DDP. Eisenhower approved Corona in February 1958 amid high hopes: Bissell's deputy, the Air Force's General Shriever, told the 1958 Johnson subcommittee hearings that the U.S. would achieve a reconnaissance satellite using the Thor and a recoverable photographic capsule system by the spring of 1959.

While the original Pied Piper program was curtailed, stilling public speculation, and Corona sought a near-term satellite, the Air Force continued to seek a satellite of its own. Like Corona the Air Force Sentry program made use of the Lockheed upper stage called Agena; however it sought to exploit a different method of photographic transmission. One concept involved a television camera/tape recorder combination that would replay its stored images upon command from the ground. Another possibility was "live" transmission of the televised image. Sentry was only the beginning of a proliferation of satellite programs that provided massive management headaches for the Eisenhower administration. Before the end of 1958 there were programs to develop an early warning satellite that exploited spaceborne infrared techniques (Midas); to provide weather forecasting (Tiros); worldwide communications capability; navigational data for ships and planes; and geodesy, mapping, and magnetic field data for targeting offensive ballistic missiles.

The administration exerted some effort to bring these problems under control. As part of a major defense reorganization in 1958, Eisenhower created an Advanced Research Projects Agency (ARPA) under Roy L. Johnson to oversee Defense Department research and development. In mid-1958 Johnson was given control over all satellite programs and ARPA absorbed the budgets of these projects. Satellite programs had been budgeted at $152 million for fiscal 1959. Supplemental funding requested for ARPA in July 1958 included $186 million for Sentry and another $108 million for other space projects. At the same time, planning for fiscal 1960 called for an ARPA space budget of some $350 million *exclusive* of Sentry funds.

The concentration of development funds in ARPA had consequences opposite to those intended. While ARPA was able to concentrate some of the best personnel, it also made the ARPA budget a target for the armed services. More programs meant that the sponsoring service would be able to act as "executor" for a larger portion of ARPA's money. Thus the services increased their satellite proposals in the hopes of getting more money. Interservice competition was intensified rather than eliminated.

Meanwhile, the CIA's Corona program went forward very close to its schedule. A first satellite with an Agena-A upper stage and a Thor booster was ready for launching in January 1959. The test was to be made from the new U.S. missile facility at Vandenberg Air Force Base (formerly a Navy base called Point Arguello). A procedural error on the countdown on January twenty-first forced postponement of the launch into February, for which Eisenhower upbraided Bissell. A second launch failure occurred on February twenty-fifth. After the NSC meeting on the twenty-sixth the President started to ask Allen Dulles for explanations. Fortunately for the CIA, a third launch attempt on February twenty-eighth was successful in putting the satellite into orbit, and the CIA program acquired public exposure that was inevitable, given pieces of hardware flying in space. A cover was adopted—the satellites were publicly dubbed Discoverer and the program was described as scientific in nature.

Unfortunately there were innumerable things that could go wrong in a remote-controlled satellite and Discoverer entered a prolonged testing phase.

Discoverer 1 successfully achieved orbit but once in space it could not stabilize itself and continued spinning uselessly. Discoverer 2 was launched successfully on April 13, 1959, but a timing error on reentry meant that the film capsule fell off over northern Norway and there is speculation that it may have been recovered by the Russians. The next two shots failed to achieve orbit and Discoverer 5 failed when the capsule was mistakenly ejected farther into space. Failures continued to plague Discoverer into 1960. Among them were electronic malfunctions in the Agena spacecraft, radio beacon malfunctions in the capsule, failure of the capsule's parachute to open, premature engine shutdown, and failure to detect the reentry of the satellite's capsule. As Richard Bissell subsequently recalled,

It was a most heartbreaking business. If an airplane goes on a test flight and something malfunctions, and it gets back, the pilot can tell you about the malfunction, or you can look it over and find out. But in the case of a recce satellite, you fire the damn thing off and you've got some telemetry, and you never get it back. There is no pilot of course, and you've got no hardware, you never see it again. So you have to infer from telemetry what went wrong. Then you make a fix, and if it fails again you know you've inferred wrong. In the case of Corona it went on and on.[10]

Recurrent failures increased frustration in the administration. This was not only true of the CIA-Air Force satellite effort, but also of USAF's own Sentry satellite. In that case the developers were having quite a problem with their arrangements for imagery transmission. Eisenhower's civilian advisory group on intelligence, the PBCFIA, encouraged him to believe that both imagery transmission systems for overhead reconnaissance were overambitious for the technology attainable, a view which was supported by the PSAC. James Killian told the President on July 14, 1959, that "I have not seen evidence that [Sentry] has had the hard-boiled technical review to determine what is realistically possible," and also that the program might be too costly.[11]

As the Air Force continued Sentry development it changed the name in 1959 to SAMOS (for Satellite and Missile Observation System). In an exchange on August nineteenth Billings told George Kistiakowsky just how elaborate SAMOS really was:

In the satellite project SAMOS, there would be ten television channels to the ground and a library of information so complete that a general (LeMay?) sitting at his easy chair in the Pentagon, by just pressing a button will be able to see on a screen the complete display of current military activities televised from anywhere in the world.[12]

By contrast the Air Force was not optimistic about the film-capsule recovery technique used in Corona/Discoverer and even canceled their application of this type of imagery transmission system in the spring of 1959. Although the program was reinstated by high-level intervention its schedule had already fallen behind by so much that the earliest date at which the Air Force could field a recovery-type SAMOS using an Atlas-Agena booster was pushed ahead to 1961. Kistiakowsky noted in December, after a visit to General Shriever at the USAF Ballistic Missile Division (BMD), that the Air Force felt it was

suffering greatly from contradictory orders which they receive almost on a weekly schedule from Washington and which keep changing their program. BMD acts as if they were at the point of despair. They will clearly object to the PSAC recommendations because they believe that "readout" SAMOS is much more promising than "recovery" Samos.[13]

The organizational differences in the satellite area were so great that Eisenhower's ARPA device was ineffective in this area.

The bureaucratic mess finally moved the President in late 1959 to create a new organization to manage the satellite programs in intelligence. This was the National Reconnaissance Office (NRO) within the Office of the Secretary of the Air Force. The NRO was made subordinate to a panel composed of the Air Force secretary, the director of central intelligence, and the director of defense research and engineering. At the same time Discoverer, SAMOS, and other satellite programs were taken out of ARPA and returned to the Air Force. This meant that satellite proposals would compete with weapons proposals for USAF research and development dollars and so would restrain the multiplication of recommendations.

As organizations evolved the hardware was slowly perfected. In February 1960 came the first attempt to launch an Atlas-Agena booster combination with a Midas early warning satellite. By the end of March launching pads were being completed at Vandenberg for SAMOS. Congress added money to the fiscal 1961 budget for SAMOS ($83.8 million) bringing the total space budget that year to $427 million as of August. On August tenth, at last, the Discoverer 13 mission was a complete success although the Air Force publicly claimed it had carried no sensor equipment. Six days later Discoverer 14 was also successful and its film capsule was retrieved by the 6593rd Test Squadron flying C-130's out of Hawaii. Brigadier General Richard B. Curtain, who had directed satellite activities at Vandenberg, was brought back to Washington to head the SAMOS project office under Air Force Secretary James Douglas. Although SAMOS 1 failed to achieve orbit on October 1, 1960, it was clear that the U.S. now had the technologies necessary for a reconnaissance satellite. Even a successful SAMOS was only a question of time. Thus within three months of the abortive summit in Paris the United States had regained the reconnaissance capability lost when Gary Powers's U-2 went down over Sverdlovsk.

One additional factor remains to be mentioned that complemented the expanded overhead reconnaissance capability. This was in intelligence support. Intelligence requirements were planned by means of a committee process and implemented through what were called priority national intelligence objectives (PNIOs). Eisenhower revised the directive governing PNIOs on December 21, 1959, in a way that suggests the PNIO was becoming overburdened as a collection planning device:

> Although a given subject may be listed as a matter of priority, not every bit
> of information relating to it will be required with equal urgency and some

may be procurable by routine means. It is therefore incumbent upon research personnel to exercise discrimination in allocating analytical resources and in formulating information requirements so as to accord priority
only to those aspects of the listed subject which actually require a priority
research or collection effort.[14]

Satellite photography of sites in the Soviet Union was conducted according to missions planned, available weather reports, and the best local
timing for photographic conditions. The early flights were approved by
a procedure similar to that governing the U-2 overflight program.

The resulting photographs went to an organization that specialized in
developing and interpreting reconnaissance pictures. The CIA had had
a Photographic Intelligence Division since 1953, when Richard Bissell
brought in Art Lundahl to head a group of thirteen photo interpreters.
Lundahl had been with Naval Intelligence during the war and in 1945
he had gone to Anacostia with the Navy's division for what was then
called "photogrammetry," essentially imagery analysis. He had built up
a division within the Directorate of Intelligence by 1958, when it was
merged with a statistical analysis division from the Office of Current
Intelligence to form a Photographic Intelligence Center (PIC). In 1961
this was made a "service of common concern" conducted for the community by CIA and Lundahl's group became the National Photographic
Interpretation Center (NPIC).

Meanwhile increasing amounts of material were becoming available
to photo interpreters to aid them in identifying installations of various
sorts. There was a growing stock of photography on file from U-2 flights
and tourists in Russia. Modern manuals supplemented the traditional
stereoscope as a tool for photo interpretation. The Air Force included
picture scales for assessing size in its manuals on guided missile systems (AFM 200-62), airfield installations (AFM 200-40), atomic energy
installations (AFM 200-56), mechanical processing industries (AFM
200-59), and military installations (AFM 200-61). Most of these were
products of the 1956–1962 period.

By 1960 the essentials of a massive intelligence-collection and -inter-
pretation capability were in place. The effort had required considerable
time and expense; the scattered data available suggest that the overall
cost for reconnaissance satellites alone over 1957–1960 was in excess
of $1.3 billion. However, the high cost was amply repaid in the stream
of quality information that began to flow to intelligence analysts concentrating on substantive issues.

CHAPTER EIGHT
THE END OF THE MISSILE GAP

In January 1960, while the senators were dramatizing the discrepancies in testimony among Allen Dulles, Thomas Gates, and Nathan Twining in the ICBM dispute, there were further developments in Soviet missiles intelligence and *yet another* change in the projection of Soviet forces. While the national estimate based upon Soviet "intentions" was being formulated in the fall of 1959 there had been a strong Russian ICBM test program in progress. The Soviets were averaging an SS-6 launch every week. On September 13, 1959, the Soviets came up with another "space spectacular" when they were able to hit the moon with an 858.4-pound Lunik satellite. The booster used was the SS-6. In November Khrushchev claimed to a conference of journalists that Russia had "such a stock of rockets, such an amount of atomic and hydrogen warheads, that if they attack us we could wipe our potential enemies off the face of the earth."[1] In the same speech the Soviet leader claimed that a single plant in Russia had produced "250 rockets" in a year's time. In January 1960 there was another series of SS-6 shots into the Pacific. Tass claimed that one of these shots had fallen within 1.24 nautical miles of its target, exhibiting somewhat better accuracy than they had been credited with by the U.S. intelligence community. The series also included a satellite of "unknown but presumed Soviet" origin and several failures. The series was observed in the impact area by three Soviet ships and a "large concentration of [U.S.] naval intelligence forces." This notwithstanding, the nature of the Soviet test series remained a mystery. Herbert Scoville of CIA briefed Kistiakowsky at the White House on February third, information which Allen Dulles repeated to the NSC the following morning. On Thursday, February fifth, Eisenhower held a special restricted meeting on the U.S. reconnaissance satellite programs.

In the January SS-6 test series, which Kistiakowsky thought related to Soviet development of ablative nose-cones for their ICBMs, the successful shots were accompanied by a number of failures. Similarly the Lunik spectacular of 1959 had been preceded by several failures, and the ICBM test program in 1959 was accompanied by an undisclosed but significant number of poor performances. By January 1960 there was still no evidence of Soviet ICBM deployment beyond the Tyuratam test center. The SS-6 was extremely large and the difficulties entailed in servicing a large liquid-fueled missile led Army and Navy intelligence to believe it could only be employed along rail lines. None materialized and this led to a SNIE in February 1960, in which the Army's Major General John Willems and the Navy's Admiral Frost argued for a very small or no Soviet ICBM force. The BNE did not accept this contention but did agree that the Soviets probably would not equal the predictions previously made in a November NIE. The projection for mid-1961 in the February estimate was for thirty-five ICBMs, thirty-four percent of the December figure. This was the origin of the number on which Stuart Symington challenged Dulles and got his "three-to-one ratio" headline.

After the January 1960 test series there was a reorientation of the Soviet ICBM program. There were no further missile tests for an interval and then the Soviets introduced a brand-new ICBM prototype. Later it was learned that the commander of Soviet Strategic Rocket Forces, Marshal Mitrofan I. Nedelin, appointed in December 1959, had been killed along with several hundred other scientists and technicians in the explosion of a test missile during fueling in August 1960. It is not clear whether this accident was associated with an atomic-powered rocket, which some thought the Russians to be developing, or with a more conventional SS-6 ICBM. Nevertheless the accident was followed by an eight-month halt in the Soviet testing program.

This second hiatus in the Soviet ICBM program only gradually became apparent to U.S. intelligence, which meanwhile continued to refine its estimates on Soviet activity. In early 1960, looking ahead over the long term, the community began to prepare a national estimate on trends in Soviet capabilities for the period 1965 to 1970. Although direct evidence is scanty it is likely that the intelligence community at this time began to expect the appearance of a Soviet solid-fueled ICBM in either a hardened or mobile configuration, similar to Minuteman. The Russians might mix these rockets with the older SS-6's for a more flexible force. The 1965–1970 trends estimate, NIE 11-60, was approved by the USIB on April 12, 1960.

With the lack of renewed Soviet ICBM tests U.S. intelligence issued a special estimate in early August that generally confirmed the analysis

of the February NIE. Then the annual estimate on main trends in Soviet capabilities and policies, NIE 11-4-60, reiterated substantially the
same conclusions. By this time the U.S. had recovered at least four film
capsules from Corona reconnaissance satellites and thus NIE 11-4-60
was based upon somewhat more detailed information than the estimates
of previous years. For mid-1963 the NIE projected a force of two
hundred to seven hundred Soviet ICBMs, a much wider range than that
posted earlier in 1960. The lower end of the range represented a reduction in the projection for 1963. Perhaps CIA was now closer to the
Army-Navy contention of few or no Soviet missiles, but the Air Force
continued to insist on a high rate of Soviet deployment. Very probably
the halt in tests led some to suspect, as in 1959, that the Soviets were
now moving ahead to deployment. By the time NIE 11-4-60 passed the
USIB, on December 1, 1960, however, there was still no evidence of
SS-6 deployment although the Americans were assuming the Soviet
ICBM had achieved IOC.

Although the intelligence estimates steadily reduced the projected
magnitude of the Soviet ICBM effort, the "missile gap" controversy remained current. In January the press reported that Dulles thought the
Russians to be building ICBMs at two plants on a three-shift, round-
the-clock schedule. Defense analyst Henry A. Kissinger wrote in the
manuscript of his *The Necessity for Choice,* which was published in
January 1961, that the U.S. margin of survival had narrowed danger-
ously and that

> for all the heat of the controversy it is important to note that there is no
> dispute about the missile gap as such. It is generally admitted that from
> 1961 until at least 1964 the Soviet Union will possess more missiles than
> the United States.[2]

In another passage Kissinger explained the implications of the "fact" of
the missile gap by alluding to the long lead times necessary to develop
modern weapons so that "even should we change course immediately
we could narrow the gap rather than close it."[3] Kissinger also noted
General Thomas Power's alarming speech of January 1960 and pointed
out that it would be rash to maintain that the Soviets could not accumulate three hundred or five hundred missiles. Kissinger's views were
typical of those of many academic strategists of the time and he was
employed for several months as a consultant to the NSC of the new
administration.

John Kennedy was inaugurated President on January 20, 1961. With
fears concerning the adequacy of American defense efforts, JFK imme-

diately appointed a committee to review the fiscal 1962 budget submitted by Eisenhower just before his administration left office. Robert McNamara left his job as president of the Ford Motor Company to become secretary of defense. Roswell Gilpatric, McNamara's deputy, was a former defense official and both were very much interested in new management techniques. Such techniques had been McNamara's specialty at Ford and their application to defense issues had been advocated by analysts at Rand, most importantly in Charles J. Hitch's *Economics of Defense in the Nuclear Age,* which proposed a novel method of programing military budgets. Hitch, Alain C. Enthoven, Daniel Ellsberg, and others also came to the Pentagon with McNamara to apply "systems analysis," as it was called, within the Office of the Secretary of Defense (OSD). McNamara's "whiz kids" had their first exposure to the issues under Paul Nitze, who chaired the review of the fiscal 1962 budget.

Probably the most important question was the size of the planned U.S. ICBM force. Even before Kennedy came to office a total of about 1,100 ICBMs had been programed, including 450 Minuteman missiles funded in fiscal 1962 and 108 Titan large liquid-fueled ICBMs. Most U.S. ICBMs were to be placed in dispersed, hardened silos in an effort involving over twenty thousand workers in eighteen states at a cost of seven billion dollars. The solid-fuel Minuteman, which offered very high potential readiness rates, was now generally accepted, but how many of them to build was as yet undecided. Nitze and the Defense Department review panel favored a substantial force, as did the Joint Chiefs, who reportedly wanted some 1,600. SAC wanted 10,000. Some at the NSC wished to restrict the new missile to levels as low as 250. The issue clearly turned on the projected dimensions of the Soviet ICBM threat.

At the Pentagon, Secretary McNamara reviewed the available intelligence estimates. The most recent, NIE 11-4-60, still found no operational Soviet ICBM sites, although the numerical range it used to show Soviet strength implied current capability. During the transition between administrations McNamara examined this NIE, held extensive discussions with Thomas Gates, who refused to credit claims of a "missile gap," and also looked for himself at some of the photos of Russia. At his first "background," or off-the-record session with reporters at the Pentagon, on the evening of February 6, 1961, McNamara revealed his intention to use a five-year defense plan for programing the annual military budgets and spoke about the work of the defense task forces. Following the presentation McNamara was asked about the alleged "missile gap." He replied that he could find no signs of a Russian crash program on ICBMs and further that both sides had about the same small number of missiles in the field. According to several reporters

McNamara said explicitly that there was no "missile gap" and this was how the exchange was reported to President Kennedy, who had been so strident about closing the gap while he ran his 1960 campaign. Kennedy tried at first to claim that the press conference had not occurred and later that the defense secretary had been misunderstood.

The resolution of the Minuteman question, however, suggests that the "missile gap" was either nonexistent or not taken very seriously— rather, it was politics that mattered. McNamara's compromise position, under the JCS request by twenty-five percent, was for a twelve-hundred missile Minuteman force. He recommended to Kennedy only eight hundred on the grounds that, although the missiles were not really needed, that was the minimum amount with which they might get by Congress. Privately McNamara was saying to aides in 1961 that the total programed Minuteman force was not likely to exceed one thousand, even though the approved number between 1961 and 1963 fluctuated from eight hundred to thirteen hundred.

According to McNamara, the "missile gap" continued only because divergent opinions persisted within the intelligence community. One major, responsible for coordinating Army contributions to the national estimates, has recorded his thoughts on this "fascinating but grueling" assignment. The number ranges in the estimates were derived from examining "every scrap of evidence and every line of reasoning." While photographic evidence was good, there was not yet complete coverage of the Soviet land mass and other information was not conclusive, so that "good objective analysis was the key to success in this endeavor." In particular,

> the estimates laid out arguments concerning percentages of photographic coverage, possible Soviet rates of production for the big missiles, construction rates for launchers, and the timing of the test program for the SS-6.[4]

Some felt the NIEs were largely based not on the evidence itself but on what prejudices were brought to the evidence by analysts. General Willems of the Army and Rear Admiral Vernon L. Lowrence, director of naval intelligence, were in general agreement that the SS-6 was so large and unwieldy that it was unsuited for operational use as an ICBM. They also reasoned that, if deployed, the missile would have to be serviced by railroads, thus severely limiting possible ICBM sites. Since there were photos of a good portion of Soviet railroad rights-of-way, a strict reading of the evidence indicated zero as the most accurate projection of Soviet ICBM strength.

The Army-Navy position differed considerably from that of Major General James H. Walsh's Air Force intelligence branch. While in December 1960 the other services anticipated fifty SS-6s by mid-1961, Walsh's minimum projection remained at two hundred. In fact, some USAF officers argued that there was no basis on which to conclude that Soviet ICBM strength was *less than* two hundred. The Air Force projections soon became suspect in McNamara's OSD, however, as a result of two incidents that cast doubt upon USAF cooperation within the intelligence community. First a civilian analyst working for Walsh, Robert A. Kilmarx, presented the defense secretary with a briefing that exaggerated the evidence in a transparent fashion in order to support Air Force policies. Then, in March, McNamara was given another briefing at Offutt using figures that were not in the NIEs. It turned out that the briefers had used SAC's own intelligence figures.

In December 1960, at a conference for disarmament held in Moscow Jerome B. Wiesner and Walt W. Rostow, both of whom had been appointed to senior positions in the Kennedy administration, were taken aside by a Soviet Foreign Ministry official. He reminded them of the "missile gap" talk and suggested that, if the new administration went in for a massive rearmament campaign, it could not expect the Soviet Union to remain a passive spectator. Three months later the Russians resumed ICBM testing with the entirely new SS-7 missile, launched from Tyuratam into the Pacific. Testing continued at a rapid rate, suggesting that the SS-7 development program was already far advanced. There were also several space shots and, on April 12, 1961, the Soviets launched Yuri Gagarin in the first manned orbital spacecraft. The Russians continued to use the SS-6 in their space program although it was never again tested as an ICBM.

These recent events required a new intelligence interpretation. The BNE consequently went to work on an NIE covering Soviet capabilities in guided missiles and space vehicles which was approved by the USIB on April twenty-fifth. However, while it was being drafted, "agent in place" Oleg Penkovsky was asked for a report on Soviet rocketry. In response Penkovsky apparently furnished the CIA with three rolls of microfilm in May 1961 which provided a complete picture of the Soviet position. Included in the package was technical information on the deficiencies of the SS-6, an admission from official Soviet records that the program was " 'ten months and thirteen days' " behind schedule, and minutes of the Kremlin meetings that decided to scrap the SS-6 as an ICBM.[5] In addition the Americans succeeded in orbiting Samos 1 on January 31, 1961, and that satellite provided over one thousand photographs of interesting portions of Russia, requiring several months of analytic work before the resulting intelligence could be embodied in an estimate.

Thus very soon after the Penkovsky information came through BNE was obliged to do another national estimate, approved on June 7, 1961. Again the Air Force came in with a high projection—some three hundred Soviet ICBMs before midyear. For its part CIA halved its previous projection and now predicted only fifty to one hundred, with support from the Army and from the State Department's Bureau of Intelligence and Research (INR). Roger Hilsman, INR director for the new administration, accepted the Army argument on railroad servicing for the big ICBMs and concluded: "this behemoth was just too big, too bulky to serve as a practical weapon."[6]

Most interesting was the action of Admiral Lowrence and the Office of Naval Intelligence (ONI). The Navy people broke with their previous support of the Army position. Instead ONI revised its own projection of operational Soviet missiles down to the "nominal" level—ten or less. The ONI analysts argued that the Soviets had conducted fewer than twenty ICBM tests in the preceding two years, that fewer than half of these had impacted near the target, and that the Soviets had never conducted a salvo firing or a mass launch, necessary for a disabling attack against SAC.

The June estimate signaled the breakup of the old view that posited a minimum production rate for Soviet missiles. Intelligence analysts had begun to work not so much from Soviet "intentions" as with current data covering most or all of Russia. The conclusions of the June NIE were substantially reiterated in the annual estimate on the main trends in Soviet capabilities for 1961–1966, NIE 11-4-61, which was approved by the USIB on August twenty-fourth. This represented sort of a midpoint in the search for a new consensus in the intelligence community, which had already begun drafting another NIE on the strength and deployment of Soviet long-range ballistic missile forces. While this was in progress the political and military situation around Berlin became critical, causing the White House to request an emergency military assessment of Soviet capabilities in the context of the Berlin crisis. The resulting report from CIA is dated September 6, 1961, and is important for the précis it gives of the emerging intelligence consensus.

The "Current Status of Soviet and Satellite Military Forces and Indications of Military Intentions" was signed by the acting CIA Director, General Charles P. Cabell. With regard to the SS-7 tests the paper reported that

test firings began early this year, and thus far the firing program has been much more intensive but much less successful than the earlier program to develop a first-generation ICBM. . . . Based on the chronology and the degree of success to date, we are confident that neither [the SS-6 nor the SS-

7] will be operational as ICBM weapon systems during the coming autumn and winter.

This conclusion had implications for the projection of deployed Soviet missiles:

These estimates cover the span from "a few" to 125 as of mid-1961 and are presently under urgent review. Although there has to date been no formal change in the estimates of Soviet strength contained in NIE 11-8-61, we now believe that our present estimate of 50–100 operational ICBM launchers as of mid-1961 is probably too high.

In addition there was revision of the estimates of the "missile gap" period:

Our estimate was based on the belief that for several years the Soviets had engaged in a relatively steady though deliberately paced program to deploy first-generation ICBMs. On the basis of accumulating evidence of ICBM development and deployment we now believe that the Soviet leaders recognized the serious disadvantages of their extremely cumbersome first-generation system and proceeded to a vigorous development of a more suitable second-generation system. We now believe that they deliberately elected to deploy only a small force of first-generation ICBMs in 1960–1961 even though they had the capability to deploy ICBMs in considerably greater quantity.[7]

The CIA views in this memorandum, uncoordinated with those of other agencies at the time of their formulation, received support from the Army, ONI, and INR and were the consensus view in NIE 11-8/1-61, which reduced the projection of Soviet strength to fewer than thirty-five missiles. This national estimate was approved by the USIB on September 21, 1961.

Air Force authorities did not abandon their long-held views on Russian ICBMs without a last struggle, despite Penkovsky and the satellite photos. General Walsh's analysts had been over the missile evidence several times already in 1961. Since the evidence itself made it harder and harder to take the Soviet ICBM threat seriously, the Air Force's stubborn contentions won friends neither in McNamara's Pentagon nor in the White House. More than from the Air Force as a whole, the last go-round in the worn "missile gap" arguments came from SAC. The SAC commander had the primary mission of attacking the Soviet Union in case of war, and General Power was worried about the survivability of his bases. In a book written in 1959 (but not actually printed until five years later) Power argued that during my last years as commander in chief of the Strategic Air Command I could not escape the impression that the military threat is being underestimated and that, as a result, there is a growing tendency toward neglecting or disregarding some of the most ominous aspects of that threat.[8]

In the late summer of 1961 word of the SAC views evidently reached John Kennedy. The President, it might be said, sometimes looked for the dissenting "footnote" even harder than he considered the text of documents, and Kennedy ordered the intelligence community to report on the differences between its consensus view and that of SAC. A delegation of officials from CIA and the services were accordingly flown out to Offutt to meet with General Smith. Much as McNamara had been, the delegation was treated to a real "scare" briefing. Using aerial photographs of Titan bases in Utah, SAC demonstrated how effectively missiles could be hidden. Among the structures suspected as camouflage for ICBM sites were a Crimean War memorial and a medieval tower. Insisting that a percentage of missiles could be hidden, SAC declared there could be as many as one thousand Soviet ICBMs and that at least two hundred were emplaced.

This assessment was so far at variance with the available evidence it won no support, although there seems to have been something of a bureaucratic rearguard action. During Thanksgiving weekend, when the President was at Hyannisport, there were a final series of meetings on the fiscal 1963 defense budget and civil defense efforts. There the Air Force tried to make the case that Soviet ICBMs numbered between six hundred and eight hundred, but the weight of evidence was plainly against it and the issue, according to Kennedy intimate and historian Arthur Schlesinger, finally just withered away. On November twenty-sixth Secretary McNamara signed a directive designed to prevent services whose program requests were rejected from making direct approaches to Congress. This did not stop Chief of Staff General Curtis LeMay from using his independent contacts, but it did put the Air Force on notice it had better get on board.

There the "missile gap" ended for all practical purposes—four years of intense uncertainty, bitter dispute, and political maneuvering. In actual fact there *was* a "missile gap" which, if anything, favored the United States. Total U.S. cruise and ballistic missiles rose from 54 in April 1961 to 78 four months later. In addition the Navy had 80 sea-launched ballistic missiles (SLBMs) in five Polaris submarines and SAC had another 1,526 strategic bombers (571 B-52, 889 B-47 and 66 B-58). The Soviet Strategic Rocket Forces described by Penkovsky amounted to a few individual missiles, some quite powerful, but hardly a coherent force capable of a simultaneous disarming strike against U.S. retaliatory forces. There were also perhaps 120 Bear and 70 Bison heavy bombers and 1,100 Badger medium bombers, of which it was estimated that the Soviets would have been able to put 100–200 over the United States in an attack. The total was a substantial force, capable of devastating American cities, but it could not have disarmed U.S. forces. Calculations done for McNamara indicated that programed U.S. forces could have absorbed a full-scale Soviet attack and still would have been powerful enough, if targeted against Soviet cities, to kill over one hundred million people and destroy eighty percent of Soviet industry.[9]

The United States not only had huge strategic forces, but it was changing its doctrine and targeting policy for their use. Upon coming to office the Kennedy administration found that the war plan consisted of a single option—the President could order only a massive "spasm" attack which indiscriminately targeted the Soviet Union, China, and the Soviet satellites in Eastern Europe and the Far East. The Joint Chiefs believed such an attack would result in between 360 and 525 *million* fatalities worldwide. All the U.S. forces were configured to execute a massive-type attack. For example, the smallest unit of Minuteman missiles that could be ordered to fire was a squadron—but the Minuteman squadron contained fifty ICBMs and each missile carried over a megaton in nuclear explosive power. Kennedy and McNamara were both interested in gaining options other than massive attack; indeed the Kennedy strategy aimed at "flexible response" and the creation of a range of options. In March 1961 Secretary McNamara directed the Pentagon to examine possibilities for "counterforce" targeting of the Soviet military as an alternative to nuclear strikes on cities, and a device to allow "controlled response" to Soviet attack, thus presumably "limiting" nuclear war. Even though counterforce required more weapons, it seemed U.S. forces were large enough: in April 1961 there were 836 weapons in U.S. constant-alert forces alone, and this had risen to 2,657 by July 1964 (see Table II). The force was large enough to allow the United States to conduct a nuclear attack and still retain reserve forces for what the academic strategists called "intrawar bargaining."

As for the forces themselves the basic levels to which the U.S. would build were determined in the early period of the Kennedy administration. The Hickey Study done for the NSC recommended a level of 2,000–2,150 Minuteman missiles by 1971 and 42 to 47 Polaris fleet ballistic-missile submarines. The Department of Defense eventually approved 41 Polaris boats and this was the number built. The Minuteman issue dragged on somewhat longer but the number of ICBM warheads finally

TABLE II. WEAPONS AND MEGATONS IN THE SINGLE INTEGRATED OPERATIONS PLAN (SIOP) 1961–1964

	1 April 1961 Alert	1 April 1961 Non-Alert	15 July 1961 Alert	15 July 1961 Non-Alert	1 July 1962 Alert	1 July 1962 Non-Alert	1 July 1963 Alert	1 July 1963 Non-Alert	1 July 1964 Alert/Non-Alert
TOTAL WEAPONS:									
Aircraft	792	1185	1212	890	1381	886	1670	1117	1777/1201
Cruise Missile	4	23	0	0	0	0	0	0	0/0
ICBM	24	3	24	54	122	11	401	131	768/0
SLBM	16	16	32	48	48	48	64	48	112/80
TOTAL MEGATONS:									
Aircraft	1593	5213	2680	4024	2882	3964	3007	3339	4034/3582
Cruise Missile	15	87	0	0	0	0	0	0	0/0
ICBM	35	4	84	225	476	34	969	328	1681/0
SLBM	8	8	16	24	24	24	35	22	93/66

Note: These totals do not include forces assigned to Europe or the Pacific but incorporated into the SIOP. Such forces accounted for 262 weapons (149 MT) on 1 April 1961 and 370 weapons (173 MT) on 1 July 1964.

Source: "SIOP," dates above, summary lists (declassified May 31, 1977). LBJ Papers: National Security File: Agency File, box 11-12, folder "Dept. of Defense v.1."

deployed by the United States was precisely 2,150. The forces were also somewhat more flexible—after the fall of 1961 the U.S. did develop the procedures to selectively launch single missiles at any of a number of preprogramed targets.

In the meantime not only had the U.S. resolved the "missile gap" to its own satisfaction but the decision was made to tell the Russians we knew the gap to be false. It is believed that during the September 1961 crisis over Berlin, President Kennedy showed satellite pictures to Soviet Foreign Minister Andrei Gromyko with the implication that he knew how many missiles the Soviets had. The meeting took place on October sixth, about two weeks after the completion of NIE 11-8/1-61.

On Tuesday, October 10, 1961, four days after Kennedy's meeting with Gromyko, Deputy Secretary of Defense Roswell Gilpatric addressed the Business Council of Hot Springs, Virginia. Gilpatric told his audience that the United States had such a nuclear capability that it could deliver on the Soviet Union, in a retaliatory "second strike," at least the destruction that the Soviets might inflict by striking first. A Russian decision to go to war would therefore be an act of self-destruction on its part. This time the message was explicit. *Aviation Week,* which had delighted for many years in carrying articles that emphasized American military weakness, did not cover the Gilpatric speech at all.

Organizational Prospects and the Gap in Retrospect

One obvious point about the "missile gap" disputes was the way in which there had been such wide divergences among the military intelligence branches and the CIA. The SC divergences were clear even before the substantive issue of whether the Soviets had a lead in missiles was resolved. In the last two years there was widespread dissatisfaction within the Eisenhower administration about the behavior of military intelligence. At the Office of the Secretary of Defense intelligence aides to Thomas Gates felt the services seemed to be in business for themselves and ignored the needs of the defense secretary. Others were concerned that the Joint Intelligence Group, supposed to serve both the defense secretary and the Joint Chiefs, was largely ineffective. The White House was disturbed at Air Force stridency.

In the fall of 1959 the director of the Bureau of the Budget, Maurice Stans, had gone to President Eisenhower with a list of eighteen studies it wanted on different aspects of government. Two of these were on intelligence. Similarly, Secretary Gates in March 1960 mentioned to the

President a study of defense intelligence which he described as a huge conglomerate spending $1.5 to $2 billion annually. Eisenhower favored the proposals for studies of intelligence but little happened until after Gary Powers's U-2 was lost over Russia. Then the evident bungling of the NASA "cover story" almost begged for an investigation and resistance melted away. The Bureau of Budget, the President's Board of Consultants on Foreign Intelligence Activities (PBCFIA), the CIA, and the secretaries of state and defense agreed to conduct an interagency study under the aegis of the director of central intelligence. Allen Dulles selected CIA Inspector General Lyman D. Kirkpatrick to head the study group, with staff assistance from Herman Heggen of CIA and representation from the NSC, State, the Pentagon and the PBCFIA. The committee was called the Joint Study Group.

After holding some preliminary meetings the Joint Study Group spent the summer and fall of 1960 visiting installations and getting briefed on intelligence activities. There were trips to SAC and to CIA stations in Western Europe. As Kirkpatrick recalls, "We were exposed to some learned and some superficial discussions of the reliability of various different types of intelligence. We heard a *lot* of talk."[10] The study group was specifically directed to pay special attention to military intelligence.

The Kirkpatrick Report was submitted on December fifteenth. The study group had met ninety times since July tenth, and had held discussions with 320 individuals of fifty-one organizations. The resulting report cautioned about military domination of the intelligence process. It noted that the USIB had six military and only four "civilian" members, that the JIG had failed to provide a "focal point" for the secretary of defense or to coordinate service estimates, and that USIB had not formed any central management or intelligence requirements mechanism.

Among the forty-eight recommendations of the report were suggestions for a central requirements mechanism, for an interagency National Photographic Interpretation Center, and an expansion of the role of the JIG by requiring it to coordinate service intelligence estimates. At the same time it recommended that the armed services be limited to observer status on the USIB.

A number of these recommendations were embodied in new NSC intelligence directives that were approved by the outgoing administration on January 18, 1961, most importantly the formation of NPIC. The Kirkpatrick Report was also passed along to McNamara. The incoming secretary of defense was so impressed that he asked the Joint Chiefs for comments on the report within thirty days. McNamara felt that he was in the strange position of being responsible for the bulk of intelligence collection activity without having the means to control either collection or intelligence production programs. His encounters with Air Force intelligence early in 1961 convinced McNamara that stronger leadership was necessary in intelligence. McNamara decided to form a new organization, the Defense Intelligence Agency, in place of the JIG.

DIA was given responsibility for all Defense Department intelligence resources, for review and coordination of defense intelligence functions, for responding directly to priority requests from the USIB, and for satisfying the intelligence needs of the components of the Department of Defense. To accomplish these missions DIA would have a total of eleven directorates. McNamara appointed Lieutenant General Joseph Carroll to head DIA. Carroll was a Chicagoan, a former special agent for the FBI, and inspector general of the Air Force at the time of his appointment.

The choice of an Air Force officer for DIA proved to be fortunate in that it reduced some of the opposition that could have surfaced. Carroll threw himself into the work of building DIA from the ground up. Provision was made in the fiscal 1963 budget for a $2.8 million headquarters building but this appropriation failed to pass Congress. Carroll began by going separately to each service and drafting detailed joint plans for transferring responsibilities and capabilities to DIA. The agency officially opened in November 1961. Secretary McNamara conceded to the Senate that there were divergent views on whether DIA would result in a more effective intelligence capability, but he insisted that it would reduce duplication in military intelligence. Thus a major result of the "missile gap" was the formation of a new intelligence organization.

Wide divergences of opinion were possible, in part, because of the nature of evidence and of the analytical techniques used by intelligence officers. In the development of new types of weapons there is a natural progression, which inhibits availability of information. In a 1967 study this phenomenon was called the "information gap." In essence the "information gap" starts with knowledge of basic research, which is fairly accessible given the need of scientists to communicate their basic research findings. As basic research is applied to military programs, such as development of an ICBM, a cloak of secrecy is imposed and uncertainty inevitably rises. This trend is then reversed as a weapons system emerges from the design stage and begins testing, and then the data base improves consistently as the weapon moves through testing to production and deployment.

In the case of the Soviet ICBM, intelligence was well informed of Russian laboratory work by 1953. The Americans correctly foresaw the emergence of a Soviet IRBM in the 1955–1957 period. The national estimates correctly predicted the Sputnik some years before the event. Most importantly the 1955 NIE predicted a "nominal" Russian ICBM capability for 1960. In fact the Soviet Union deployed a "nominally" sized ICBM force that very year. Yet the national estimates that followed contained successively larger predictions for 1960 and were thus increasingly mistaken. Further, the NIEs predicted thousands of ICBMs, a notion that can only have resulted from extrapolation of previous experience—the predictions of Soviet medium- and intermediate-range missile production, simpler rockets whose production in such numbers was still possible.

The "information gap" intervened with the Soviets' inexplicable testing halts in 1958–1959 and then 1960–1961. The information was not false or useless but incomplete. Faced with this uncertainty the community agencies, formulating their contributions to the NIEs, had to surmise in order to cover missing data, making all such analyses subjective in nature. In this context organizational interests facilitated choice among competing interpretations of the evidence.

Sputnik, with its implication of a Soviet ICBM attack, forced the Americans to become conscious of the survivability of SAC. It was technically impossible even to warn SAC of a ballistic-missile attack before 1960. The Gaither Report's findings crystallized a way of thinking about the strategic balance in the missile age, and Khrushchev's ICBM boasts plunged the thinkers into a desperate effort to rectify weaknesses in U.S. nuclear forces before the operational reality of the Soviet missile.

The critical nature of the military situation made the national estimates that much more important. The checkered history of SS-6 testing then increased the ambiguity in the intelligence debate so that, because some ICBMs *had* been fired, the Air Force could claim the Russians would deploy before they had finished testing. Other intelligence agencies were then asked to answer a negative proposition: that there were *no* ICBM launching sites in the Soviet Union. This was an inherently impossible task given the limited capabilities of the intelligence collection systems then available.

Improved technical collection did not immediately end the "missile gap" claims. Part of the reason was related to the fact noted by Raymond Garthoff, that most estimates, particularly those sounding an alarm, become public to one degree or another.[11] The "missile gap" became a real issue in Congress and then in the country at large, with the effect that overt political considerations inhibited the drafting of a more accurate, less alarming intelligence estimate. In effect the more the political salience of the "missile gap" arguments, the more difficult to preserve objective intelligence estimating. The several effects of this chaotic situation are well put by Edgar Bottome in his own examination of the "missile gap": services could choose to support their own view rather than those in the NIEs; distinct ranges of figures for things like "crash" and "orderly" programs gave officials the option to choose either or become confused between them; and finally, it was left open to some administration figures to continue reliance on the earlier and more pessimistic national estimates.[12] For those outside the executive branch the situation was further complicated by hearsay, mixtures of fact and rumor, and the continued Air Force footnotes in the NIEs. The "missile gap" was not merely a sterile intelligence "dispute" but one involving the most important problems of the uneasy relationship between intelligence and politics.

CHAPTER NINE
MISSILES OF OCTOBER

In addition to its role in analyzing long-term military threats the intelligence community was responsible for predictions in situations of immediate crisis. As director of central intelligence Allen Dulles placed special emphasis on CIA's warning function, and continual attention was devoted to the matter. A community-wide Watch Committee had been set up in 1954 with staff provided by the CIA. The Watch Committee served to alert the NSC to emergency situations, and its original terms of reference made explicit mention of the putative Soviet threat. Within the committee there was repeated study of the "indicators" that might tip off an observer to imminent military action amid some concern that, in the nuclear age, traditional concepts of what constituted an "indicator" had become outmoded. This work was formalized by the establishment of an interagency National Indications Center in 1961 which replaced the Watch Committee.

Formation of the National Indications Center was only one of the changes made by the Kennedy administration. Kennedy also abolished Eisenhower's civilian intelligence panel (the PBCFIA) and continued the consolidation of the military intelligence units within DIA. On the other hand he retained Allen Dulles as chief of intelligence and the set of NSC Intelligence Directives promulgated by Eisenhower on January 18, 1961, remained in effect. It seemed the new administration was interested in streamlining but not in major reorganization per se.

This policy changed after a failure of massive proportions in April 1961 when a CIA covert operation miscarried in Cuba. Since the spring of 1960, when the Eisenhower NSC began to insist on weekly Cuba briefings and consider actions including military measures, pressure for acting against Cuban Premier Fidel Castro had mounted. By the fall CIA had come up with Operation Pluto to infiltrate parties of American-trained Cubans back into their Caribbean island to overthrow Castro. It was the largest covert operation that the Directorate of Plans (DDP) had organized to date; Richard Bissell and DDCI General Charles P. Cabell were working closely with the Pentagon. The Pluto plan mushroomed into a full-scale beach invasion to be made by a Cuban brigade with its own armor, and miniature navy and air force, using what struck Arthur Schlesinger as an "Anzio model." President Kennedy approved the invasion plan and issued National Security Action Memorandum (NSAM) 31 to implement it on March 11, 1961.

That the U.S. was backing anti-Castro forces was already an open secret among many in Latin America and the United States, and Kennedy's attempt to maintain secrecy while greatly expanding the scale of the operation led to mistakes when the Cubans attempted to storm ashore at the Bay of Pigs on April seventeenth. Everything possible went wrong. Preinvasion airstrikes were crippled by Kennedy's secrecy orders, and proved less successful than expected. The "cover story" was exposed when a Cuban exile B-26 landed at Miami and proved unconvincing in its role; Adlai Stevenson at the United Nations was publicly shown to have lied when he denied any U.S. involvement. Senator Barry Goldwater advised Kennedy to do anything necessary to make the invasion a success, but Kennedy was unwilling to go as far as American intervention. When the landing force went in, there were problems with offshore reefs that Bissell's planners had refused to credit in aerial photographs. The airfield at the Bay of Pigs proved to be serviceable though NPIC said it wasn't, so that no preparations had been made to use it. Several American- and British-made jets in the Castro air force sank the exiles' navy and ruled the air over their beachhead, and then Castro's army concentrated faster than anyone thought it could.

By Wednesday, April nineteenth, it was all over—1,114 survivors of the exiles' Brigade 2506 marched into captivity. The next day, Allen Dulles told Richard Nixon, was the worst of his life. Kennedy was upset that everyone, including CIA and the Joint Chiefs, had assured him the plan would work, some of them in writing. He was upset that no one had come forward to warn of the dangers, and that Richard Bissell had held the operations plans so tightly that many military and even White House officials apparently misunderstood both their complexity and their implication for the need for direct U.S. action.

Kennedy publicly accepted responsibility for the Bay of Pigs failure as Eisenhower had for the U-2 incident. But there was plenty of blame to be shared. By mid-1961 Kennedy had changed his Joint Chiefs of Staff and determined to fire Allen Dulles. Richard Bissell, who had been in line to replace Dulles, was not considered. From that day a search went forward for a new director of central intelligence. President Kennedy offered the job to Clark Clifford, who had helped draft the original CIA legislation in 1947. Clifford declined. Then it was offered to Fowler Hamilton, a New York lawyer with an interest in intelligence. Hamilton went instead to the Agency for International Development. There were suggestions made inside the intelligence community to appoint Richard Helms, Bissell's deputy, to head the agency. Eventually the job went to John A. McCone, former chairman of the AEC under Eisenhower, California shipping magnate, and Republican conservative. It was thought the McCone appointment might help defuse conservative opposition to the Kennedy administration. It is also said that McCone particularly impressed Kennedy with his knowledge of Soviet missiles intelligence gained while at the AEC. The appointment was announced when Kennedy presented a speech at the Naval War College on September 27, 1961.

McCone rapidly dispelled any doubts about his ability to assert authority in the CIA after Allen Dulles's long tenure. Dulles drove away from the change-of-command ceremony on November twenty-eighth in his specially equipped limousine, and McCone discovered that the retiring director would be allowed to retain the car. When an ordinary government auto turned up to drive him home, McCone gave orders that a limousine similar to Dulles's be provided for himself within twenty-four hours. McCone also called in the heads of the other intelligence agencies and told them that if they gave him cooperation, he would help make them more powerful than ever. Richard Bissell stayed on at DDP until February 1962 but McCone replaced all his deputy directors. Within the year most of the chiefs of division had been replaced as well. All together something less than two hundred CIA officers were quietly retired after the Bay of Pigs.

For his own part, President Kennedy reinstituted the civilian advisory panel on intelligence, which was now styled the President's Foreign Intelligence Advisory Board (PFIAB), and requested an investigation of the abortive operation. The NSC was also reorganized and an NSC Special Group began to monitor covert operations, succeeding the 5412 Committee which had done so for President Eisenhower.

Buildup to Crisis

Given Cuba's status as the first avowedly Communist nation in the Western Hemisphere, there was intense U.S. interest in Cuban activities. Action against Castro did not stop with the Bay of Pigs failure but rather assumed a new form. At an NSC meeting on April 22, 1961, John Kennedy insisted that the point now was not to dwell on failure but to move forward. The Pentagon was directed to examine the question of large-scale open enlistment of Cuban soldiers. Later the Joint Chiefs were told to update their contingency planning for an invasion of Cuba. The CIA was directed to undertake a program of covert political and economic measures against Cuba under the rubric of Operation Mongoose. For this purpose the CIA organized Task Force W in the Western Hemisphere Division of its Directorate of Plans. William K. Harvey, who had headed CIA's Berlin Station at the time of Operation Gold, was appointed to lead the task force.

Mongoose was a major covert operation, supervised by the NSC Special Group, which included McCone, Robert Kennedy, and General Maxwell Taylor, at that time the President's senior military advisor. Central control was maintained by a working group under Colonel Edward G. Lansdale, an Air Force officer noted for his role in covert operations in the Philippines and Viet Nam during the 1950s. Soon Harvey's Task Force W had created a CIA field station in Miami with a personnel strength of four hundred officers, two thousand agents, and a budget of $50 million. Task Force W linked up with anti-Castro Cuban groups and, with help from the Army, was soon training and arming Cubans for commando raids and sabotage missions against Castro's Cuba.

Monitoring the effectiveness of Operation Mongoose was up to the analysts of CIA Directorate of Intelligence (DDI), headed until 1962 by Robert Amory, and then by Ray Cline. The DDI probably came out looking best in the Bay of Pigs fiasco since it had never been convinced that a spontaneous uprising would overthrow Castro when the exile brigade landed in Cuba. In particular Sherman Kent's BNE had questioned the notion both in an SNIE in December 1960 and in memorandums to Dulles in January and March 1961, whether time was on the side of the U.S. plans for the invasion.

Within Ray Cline's directorate, which numbered perhaps twelve hundred analysts and spent $50 to $60 million annually, most of the intelligence interest in Cuba was centered at two offices. One was the Office of Current Intelligence, the other the Office of Economic Research. Both were examining the impact of American economic sanctions against Cuba, as well as the extent of Soviet foreign aid to the Castro government. Following the Bay of Pigs the Soviets began to expand their military aid to Castro, supplying Russian weapons in quantities, including forty jet fighters of older MIG models. By the beginning of 1962 most of the Cuban army had been reequipped with Soviet weapons. The community consensus in NIE 85-62 that March was that the

Soviets might soon give Cuba some jet light bombers known as IL-28's. These planes were outmoded, slow, and short ranged, but they were offensive weapons and could reach the United States from bases in Cuba. For the first time it seemed that the Caribbean island might pose a military threat.

At about this time one of Cline's analysts began to notice significant changes in the pattern of Soviet merchant shipping traffic. Ships that had been used to carry military equipment to Indonesia were being diverted to the Havana route, still loaded with military goods. No estimate was written based on this information, and a proposal for overhead photo coverage of Soviet merchant ships bound for Cuba was rejected. Nevertheless beginning in early 1962 the frequency of U-2 flights over Cuba increased.

Two decades after the event Premier Khrushchev's motivations in Cuba remain obscure. His decision was to emplace MRBM and IRBM missiles on the Caribbean island. Some sources suggest that the Soviet decision originated in an effort to break the deadlock over Berlin in Soviet favor, an outcome that had eluded Russian efforts in several previous attempts. Others believe the Russians were trying to balance the overwhelming U.S. advantage in strategic nuclear forces by means of a "quick fix" in which Soviet short-range missiles were put within striking distance of U.S. targets. Still others argue that the Soviet motive was to protect their Cuban client state from a repetition of the Bay of Pigs-type invasion.

Briefly the Soviet plan involved the installation of a number of units of long-range nuclear-tipped missiles on Cuban soil. These would be screened by a network of surface-to-air missile (SAM) sites, coast defense rocket installations, compact Soviet ground-troop battle groups, and an improved Cuban military furnished with more modern Soviet weapons. The missiles would be a combination of MRBM (eleven hundred nautical-mile range) and IRBM (twenty-two hundred nautical-mile range) delivery vehicles. The MRBMs had the virtue of being capable of rapid erection once site preparations had been completed, and would provide the Soviets with a nuclear capability during emplacement of the IRBMs, which required construction of concrete structures at the site. Missile deployment in Cuba would outflank the U.S. defense perimeter, which was oriented northwards against Russia over the Pole. It would also complicate the timing factor in any American-planned strike against Soviet nuclear forces by precluding the simultaneous elimination of units located both inside the Soviet Union and in Cuba. Further, the deployment roughly doubled the size of Soviet nuclear forces when measured in megatons targetable against the United States. These military factors made Cuba a potential blue chip in any Soviet bargaining with the U.S. government.

The Soviet plan was not only advantageous from a military standpoint but also related more directly to the protection of Cuba. After the Bay of Pigs, Khrushchev felt obliged to remind the U.S. that Cuba was under the protection of ICBMs based in Russia, but neither this nor the first wave of military aid had lessened the pressure being exerted on Cuba by the exile organizations and the Kennedy administration. While there is no data confirming Soviet claims of a new and larger exile "brigade" being organized to train in Nicaragua, U.S. economic sanctions greatly reduced Cuban trade while harassment of Cuba due to Mongoose covert operations was intensifying.

Indications of a change in Kremlin policy were initially limited to articles in the Soviet press, which suggested a more active stance on both Berlin and Cuba and an increased awareness of the dangers of war. There were also occasional statements from Khrushchev and Moscow gossip, such as the report that Chinese diplomats were pleased with the Russians for finding a striking, new way of handling Berlin. Nor could Soviet intentions be deduced from shipping activity in the first half of 1962 since there were few military shipments among the average of fifteen dry-goods ships that called monthly in Cuban ports. Some of the evidence was suggestive but none of it was conclusive.

Disturbing reports of Soviet activity began to accumulate in July. First Khrushchev canceled the military manpower cuts he had authorized in 1960 and approved an increase of several billion rubles in defense outlays. The replacement of Kiril S. Moskalenko at the head of the Strategic Rocket Forces also became known. There were press reports that the Russians had begun to harden their ICBMs by placing them in concrete bins. After a lull in early July, Soviet commerce with Cuba increased at a rapid rate, much of which was in military goods. Between July twenty-sixth and August eighth there were at least eight military shipments into Cuba. Some of them were going into Mariel, a small port on Cuba's north coast that had hardly been used in years and which is often not even shown on maps of Cuba. It was rumored that Mariel had been placed off limits to everyone but Russians.

Independently of the Americans, French intelligence began to receive reports alleging Soviet military activity through its still-existent agent networks in Cuba. Knowing that the French had agents, and disturbed about the reports CIA itself had been getting, John McCone went to the Washington chief of the SDECE (*Service de documentation extérieure et de contre-espionnage*), P. L. Thyraud de Vosjoli. McCone and de Vosjoli agreed that there was not enough information available and the French intelligence chief agreed to travel to Cuba and canvass his networks. De Vosjoli was aware of the Cuban penchant for exaggeration—in 1961 SDECE reports based on Cuban information projected two thousand to fifteen thousand Russians in Cuba at a time when the actual number was around seven hundred—and on his trip he found little to startle him:

> All the intelligence I collected showed that Russian missiles had been brought in. But it was the same old story. For years the Cubans had flooded all the intelligence services, embassies, and newspapers with tales of *cohetes,* as they called the missiles, supposedly hidden in numerous caves along the coast. . . . I suspected our Cuban friends of talking about something they hardly knew. . . . I was soon convinced that their imagination had been working again.[1]

The SDECE chief did get one report of a more serious nature, however, from a former noncommissioned officer with the French Army in Germany. The man sighted a rocket being carried on a multiwheel transporter, the missile being "bigger, much bigger" than any of the missiles he had seen with the U.S. Seventh Army in Europe. All of de Vosjoli's information was passed along to the CIA.

Not that U.S. intelligence did not have the same problem with "*cohetes*" as the French—Roger Hilsman notes that the file on claims of rockets in Cuba for *1959* was four inches thick. In the period of the buildup there were numerous aerial reconnaissance flights and fully fifteen hundred reports from agents or Cuban refugees, plus tabulations on Soviet-bloc shipping traffic. One analyst recalls two reports of big missiles at the time so much material was passing through his office that he was sending two classified wastepaper-basketsful to the shredder every day. These reports had little impact. Meanwhile the Soviet buildup accelerated with twelve additional military cargoes arriving between August eighth and twenty-fourth.

This Soviet activity provided the backdrop for the latest phase of Operation Mongoose. In early August there was secret discussion of an assassination attempt against Fidel Castro. On the eighth the NSC Special Group met to consider actions intended to result in a popular uprising within Cuba before October. Robert Kennedy and Maxwell Taylor were both among the most aggressive in the Special Group, but the NSC had to admit there was little probability of a revolt. General Taylor told the President on August twentieth that Castro could not be overthrown without direct U.S. intervention on the ground in Cuba. Two days later, however, the CIA continued covert Mongoose operations by contaminating the cargo of sugar aboard a freighter bound for Russia while the ship lay docked in San Juan, Puerto Rico.

Meanwhile in mid-August the DIA requested photo coverage designed to confirm the presence of SAM missiles. John McCone was even more concerned. He wrote a memo to Kennedy flatly stating that the Russians were building installations for offensive missiles in Cuba. A week later McCone reiterated his opinion at a meeting with Secretary of State Dean Rusk and Defense Secretary Robert McNamara. Neither accepted his hypothesis. Not one to be stopped, John McCone stated his suspicions again, directly to the President, at a meeting on August twenty-second held to consider the possible psychological impact of the introduction of Soviet offensive missiles into Cuba. However, Kennedy probably saw these beliefs as "the suspicions of a professional anticommunist."[2]

McCone proved unable to convince the President of his views. In fact he could not even sway the CIA on this matter. Sherman Kent of BNE insisted the director was speaking without foundation. As the Soviet buildup continued, however, Langley became more and more uncomfortable. There was a meeting of the Policy Planning Staff at the State Department on August twenty-first, which Ray Cline attended as the CIA representative. The group concluded that there might be "some convulsive effort" by the Soviets internationally. Chairman Walt W. Rostow ended the gathering by observing that the U.S. might be about to witness "the greatest act of risk-taking since the war." Ray Cline piped up to say, "Maybe we're seeing it right now in Cuba."[3]

The next day one of Cline's intelligence units, the Office of Current Intelligence, produced a report (No. 3047/62) called "Recent Soviet Military Aid to Cuba," which detailed developments since late July. The Soviet buildup included large quantities of transportation, communications, and electronic equipment. Over fifteen hundred passengers had arrived in Cuba under "security conditions" and an equal number with fanfare. Total Soviet-bloc personnel in Cuba now stood at five thousand. OCI also noted that a dozen refugees had independently reported on construction activities at two sites near Matanzas. Twenty military shipments had already arrived and another five ships were en route from ports in the Black Sea. Cline passed the OCI report along to the White House, where the impression was that something new and different *was* happening in Cuba, but Kennedy preferred to think it related to refurbishing of the Cuban air defense network.[4]

Two days later some of the material in the OCI report was given to the press in a background briefing by Roger Hilsman, from the State Department. The CIA inaugurated a special daily Cuba situation report under the codeword *Psalm*. A U-2 flight carried out on August twenty-ninth positively identified two SAM sites and raised possibilities about six other locations. Photos showed two SAM missiles already on launchers plus, at sea, missile-equipped patrol boats of the Komar class. The pictures were shown to President Kennedy on Friday, August thirty-first. That day Kennedy determined to issue an official warning to the Soviet Union regarding its buildup in Cuba.

Even while Kennedy was being apprised of the U-2 pictures showing Soviet SAMs going up, Senator Kenneth Keating (R-New York) rose on the Senate floor to make the first of ten speeches warning of Russian moves in Cuba. In this instance Keating claimed to have information on the landing, between August third and fifteenth, of twelve hundred men at Mariel who wore Soviet fatigue uniforms. The senator also said that observers had seen Soviet military convoys on Cuban roads, landing craft, and "cylindrical objects that had to be transported by two [railway] flat-cars."[5] If Keating's information was correct, and the senator insisted it was though he refused to divulge his sources (even to John McCone, a personal friend), the Kennedy administration might be charged not only with inactivity but with acquiescing to a violation of the Monroe Doctrine, which prohibits the introduction of foreign military forces into the Western Hemisphere.

Although Khrushchev gave Kennedy assurances, conveyed through Anatoli Dobrynin, his new ambassador in Washington, that Russia would do nothing to complicate the international situation prior to the November elections, these statements did not calm the waters of American politics. Both senior Republican congressional leaders, Senator Everett Dirksen (R-Illinois) and Representative Charles Halleck (R-Indiana), made Cuba statements on September seventh. Dirksen invoked the Monroe Doctrine and cited Soviet aid to Cuba as a violation of it. Over the next ten days six different congressional resolutions on Cuba were proposed, all of which favored an active U.S. role, implying criticism of Kennedy for not meeting the challenge. Hearings were held before the Senate Foreign Relations Committee on Monday, September seventeenth.

Senator Keating declared, "I can't believe that the building of this base one hundred miles from us is not a threat."

"Do you have information that makes you rather positive that the missile bases there now can be converted readily [into offensive missile installations]?" asked Senator John Sparkman.

"My information is they can," answered Keating.

Sparkman followed up, "I think a lot would depend on the convertibility of those missile bases." He had information that the SAMs could not be used offensively.

Keating insisted, "I think that is a very important point and my information is that they are readily convertible into launching facilities for intermediate-range missiles, not long-range missiles."[6]

Political pressure against the Kennedy administration was mounting. A certain amount of new raw information became available to intelligence early in September but nothing that could by itself reveal the Russians' ultimate intentions. There was another U-2 reconnaissance flight over central and western Cuba on the fifth which brought back pictures of a MIG-21 supersonic fighter parked in front of four shipping crates presumed to be additional MIG aircraft plus photos of more SAMs going into position. On September eighth a naval reconnaissance aircraft took photographs of the deck of the Soviet freighter *Omsk* which had been built with very large hatches for the timber trade. *Omsk* had vehicles on deck but the hatches were closed to conceal the cargo in the holds. That the ship was riding high in the water suggested the cargo was bulky but not heavy. It may have been that *Omsk* was carrying the first of the MRBMs destined for Cuba. The ship arrived in Cuba on the ninth, but bad weather the next day ruined the pictures taken by another U-2 overflight. On September eleventh President Kennedy ordered a doubling of U-2 flights so that Cuba would now be surveyed weekly.

Stepped up aerial reconnaissance posed something of a problem for the U.S. government at this stage. It happened that a U-2 had strayed over Russia's Sakhalien Island for nine minutes on August thirtieth due to a navigational error. Then, on September ninth, a Chinese Nationalist U-2 had been shot down over the mainland by SAM missiles. In view of the deployment of SAM defenses in Cuba the risks associated with the Cuban overflights were rapidly increasing. There was some consideration given to covering Cuba with peripheral flights that only occasionally "dipped into" Cuban airspace, avoiding violations by oblique photography.

While overflight alternatives were under consideration, Sherman Kent and the BNE were drafting an SNIE on Cuba. Through mid-September BNE labored, and came forth with SNIE 85-3-62, "The Military Buildup in Cuba," which summarized the evidence of Soviet arrivals and itemized the equipment known to have reached Cuba. For the first time in a national estimate, BNE gave explicit consideration to the McCone hypothesis that the Russians might be introducing long-range missiles, but it judged that

> The establishment on Cuban soil of a significant strike capability with
> [MRBM and IRBM] weapons would represent a sharp departure from Soviet
> practice, since such weapons have so far not been installed even in Satellite

territory. Serious problems of command and control would arise. There would also have to be a conspicuously larger number of Soviet personnel in Cuba, which, at least initially, would be a political liability in Latin America. The Soviets might think that the political effect of defying the U.S. by stationing Soviet nuclear striking power in so menacing a position would be worth a good deal if they could get away with it. However, they would almost certainly estimate that this could not be done without provoking a dangerous U.S. reaction.[7]

BNE warned that the U.S. should be especially careful for signs of such action but judged on balance that the Russians were not deploying offensive missiles. The estimate was approved by the USIB on September nineteenth. Interestingly enough, postmortems on the Cuban crisis concluded that the first shipment of missiles arrived on the eighth, was moved out of Havana by truck convoy at night from the ninth to the fourteenth of September, and that a second shipment reached Cuba on the fifteenth. Yet at the time USIB approved the estimate no dissents were appended.

Not all officials were satisfied with SNIE 85-3-62. Among those who were not was John McCone, abroad on his honeymoon and confined to needling Langley with cables, the so-called "honeymoon cables." One of these on September tenth had first suggested that BNE do the special estimate, but McCone wanted a firm statement that SAMs were being placed in Cuba to shield the arrival of long-range missiles. There were other cables on September seventh, thirteenth, sixteenth, and nineteenth. When the SNIE appeared, McCone cabled on the twentieth that it should be recalled and rewritten because BNE had not considered the factor of increased Soviet bargaining power that would follow from IRBMs successfully deployed in Cuba. McCone's deputy director, General Carter, considered the cable and its disagreement an internal CIA affair.

As September wore on, intelligence indications of offensive weapons began piling up at an alarming rate. A stunning report came from a Cuban accountant who was able to gauge the precise length of the missile dragged past his house. The man packed his bags and headed for Florida on September twelfth, and walked into the CIA office at Opa Locka eight days later, giving a detailed account of what could only be an MRBM. Other reports followed: night movement of truck convoys; activities associated with ballistic missiles in Pinar del Río on September eighteenth.

At the DIA, Colonel John Wright was examining pictures of the Cuban SAM sites and noticed that these formed a trapezoidal pattern such as was seen in certain SAM installations that protected missile bases in

Russia. Projecting the geometrical shape on a map of Cuba, Wright found it centered near the town of San Cristóbal in western Cuba. He went to General Joseph Carroll, who supported a request for immediate coverage by high-altitude reconnaissance. The CIA accepted this DIA proposal on September twenty-ninth, placing central and western Cuba on a list for coverage, and then placed a top priority on this requirement on the third of October.

The request for western Cuba coverage was reviewed by the Committee on Overhead Reconnaissance (COMOR), as well as by the NSC Special Group. Both meetings occurred on October fourth; COMOR approved aerial coverage of all of Cuba, which in practice meant western Cuba, which had not been overflown for some time. The NSC Special Group directed Colonel Ralph Steakley of the National Reconnaissance Office (NRO) to prepare recommendations for the use of remote-controlled drones rather than manned aircraft in the photo missions, and on the possible use of RF-101's or other jet photo planes for low- or medium-altitude missions, doubtless on the theory that these aircraft would be more survivable than the unmaneuverable U-2 in the Cuban SAM environment.

Before further action could be taken, eastern Cuba was covered twice more by U-2's, on the fifth and seventh of October. Another COMOR meeting on the ninth approved the flight plan for a U-2 to cover San Cristóbal where DIA suspected the presence of Soviet MRBMs. The NSC Special Group also met, rejected the use of drones or RF-101's, but directed NRO to use Air Force rather than CIA pilots for the U-2 flight. President Kennedy approved it on October tenth. Two pilots of SAC's 4080th Strategic Reconnaissance Wing were then familiarized with the CIA version of the U-2 which they would fly. The western-Cuba flight was delayed further due to bad weather, but it was rescheduled for Sunday, October fourteenth.

By this time the first concrete evidence of Soviet offensive weapons was available from DDI, mostly as the result of efforts by two analysts at OCI. According to one of them, Victor Marchetti, the OCI men had been innovating a method they called "crateology" for determining the contents of shipping crates the Russians used to import equipment in the buildup.[8] In the second week of October the director of naval intelligence, Rear Admiral Vernon L. Lowrence, produced deck cargo photographs taken by a destroyer on September twenty-eighth. Marchetti and his associate judged that the visible packing crates contained I1-28 Beagle bombers, whose introduction into Cuba had long been expected by intelligence.

As the daily "Psalm" report carried news of the I1-28's, Senator Keating made another of his "threat from Cuba" speeches on Capitol Hill. This time the senator not only claimed the presence of offensive weapons but specified there were six IRBM bases going up in Cuba. Keating asserted his information was "one hundred percent reliable." Again the Republican senator's assertions flew in the face of administration statements, in this case those of McGeorge Bundy before a congressional committee on October third. On October fourteenth Bundy reiterated in a television interview:

> I know there is no present evidence and I think there is no present likelihood that the Cuban government and the Soviet government would, in combination, attempt to install a major offensive capability.[9]

The planned U-2 flight over western Cuba was executed the same day that Bundy appeared on *Meet the Press*. The Air Force pilot detailed for the mission was Major Richard S. Heyser. Heyser made a landfall southwest of the Isla de Pinos and then flew north above the Cuban mainland. His photographic run over San Cristóbal lasted five minutes and was without incident. Heyser returned to base and his films were rushed to the NPIC for processing. Within twenty-four hours prints were available for analysis. The pictures revealed site preparations for offensive missiles, MRBMs, at San Cristóbal.

The information caused a flurry of activity around Washington late on Monday the fifteenth. First to hear was DDI Ray Cline, who in turn told General Carter and Roger Hilsman. Carter, deputy director of central intelligence was again filling in for McCone, now in California for a funeral. Carter called the director of DIA. General Carroll alerted officials at the Pentagon. Hilsman, as head of INR, informed Secretary Rusk. At about eight thirty that evening Ray Cline got through to McGeorge Bundy at home and told him, "It looks as though we've really got something." The pictures identified a launching pad, some buildings associated with ballistic missile bases, and even one MRBM on its trailer. Cline was assured that afternoon by CIA experts that what was visible represented a major investment in weapons and facilities. Intelligence officials agreed to an immediate USIB gathering for the afternoon of October sixteenth.

Early Tuesday morning the U-2 pictures were taken to the White House by Cline. In McGeorge Bundy's office CIA experts explained them to the assistant for national security and Robert Kennedy. Bundy then took the photographs to the President's bedroom, where Kennedy was reading the morning paper. His reaction was to order stepped-up aerial reconnaissance, including low-level missions. At the NSC later that morning Carter conducted the intelligence briefing using blown-up copies of the pictures. But this early evidence had to be taken on faith. Robert Kennedy recalls that

> I examined the pictures carefully, and what I saw appeared to be no more than the clearing of a field for a farm or the basement of a house. I was relieved to hear later that this was the same reaction of virtually everyone at the meeting, including President Kennedy. Even a few days later, when more work had taken place at the site, he remarked that it looked like a football field.[10]

Similarly McGeorge Bundy later said,

> The pictures upon which the photo interpreters drew that conclusion [that offensive missiles were being installed] would not have suggested to the ordinary collector of Kodak snapshots that anything remarkable was going on, and without a relation of confidence built up over time between photo interpreters relatively far in the bowels of the Agency, their seniors, and the President himself, I do not think that it would have been possible for the President on the first day of that crisis . . . to have been persuaded that he was dealing with a reality.[11]

The first projections were that it would be ten days before any of the MRBMs attained operational status.

This intelligence plunged the U.S. into the Cuban Missile Crisis, perhaps the closest the superpowers have come to war thus far in the nuclear age. Over the following days President Kennedy formed a more compact Executive Committee (EXCOM) of the NSC in order to fashion a response to the Cuban buildup. The EXCOM examined local and international risks entailed by a number of options. All the meetings began with briefings on the latest information by McCone or another CIA representative. Basically the options were resolved into three possible choices; blockade of Cuba, airstrike against the missiles, or invasion of the Caribbean island.

John McCone returned to Washington on October seventeenth and participated in all the subsequent EXCOM discussions. The CIA director's general reading of the international situation evidently convinced him that the Soviets would not react violently, either at Berlin or elsewhere. He reputedly favored an airstrike against the missile bases as the best way of removing the provocation. The extent to which he expressed these predilections is unclear, but this was a definite change from the practice of Allen Dulles, who would almost always defer to the secretary of state when asked his opinion on policy matters.

The central estimate staff at CIA was not so heavily drawn into crisis operations as the director. EXCOM did require several SNIEs during the period, to which the Board of National Estimates responded, but the protracted process of interagency coordination was largely avoided. With daily USIB meetings any problems of interpretation were rapidly resolved and it would not be surprising to find out that the USIB itself took a hand in some of the drafting work on the national estimates.

BNE sent forth SNIE 11-18-62 on October nineteenth, which held that it was possible but not likely that the missiles were intended as bargaining chips. BNE preferred to believe that Russia sought to demonstrate that the U.S. could not be safe even within its own hemisphere. The SNIE stated that the Soviets must have assumed that the missiles' presence would become public knowledge, implying that Khrushchev expected the U.S. to know the missiles were going into position. Use of force against the missiles would put the Soviets under pressure to retaliate, but BNE reasoned that the Soviets would not fire the missiles even if they became operational because they wished to avoid a general war. The result of confronting the Russians with U.S. knowledge of the MRBMs, was anticipated as follows:

> If the U.S. confronts Khrushchev with its knowledge of the MRBM deployment and presses for a withdrawal, we do not believe the Soviets would halt the deployment. Instead they would propose negotiations on the general question of foreign bases, claiming equal right to establish bases and assuring the U.S. of tight control over the missiles.[12]

The whole tone of this special estimate seems to encourage military action by minimizing the probable Soviet response to such an action and by observing that less forceful means would not be effective. This is so far at variance with the tone of the September nineteenth estimate that it is difficult to believe BNE drafted both. It is not known what McCone said to his estimators after returning from his honeymoon, but now, a month later, BNE apparently shared McCone's attitude.

Meanwhile aerial photography continued. Pictures on October seventeenth showed construction progress at San Cristóbal, revealed two new sites near Sagua la Grande for MRBMs, plus extensive construction for IRBMs at Remedios and Guanajay. At the MRBM sites some fuel trucks were also sighted. On October eighteenth the USIB-approved morning briefing of EXCOM predicted that the first of the MRBMs might be operational within eighteen hours. The pace of U-2 flights was raised to six or seven a day, with the 4080th Strategic Reconnaissance Wing making almost twenty sorties between October fourteenth and the twenty-second. At the time, however, Presidential advisor Theodore Sorensen was telling Kennedy that most of his advisors agreed the Cuban missiles did not add to the probability of a first strike against the U.S., would not reduce the impact of a U.S. first strike, and would not add significantly to available Soviet retaliatory forces following any American nuclear attack on the Soviet Union.

But SNIE 11-19-62, approved by the USIB on October twentieth, again provided implicit support for those favoring military action. The estimate laid out details on the Cuban sites: firm evidence indicated four MRBM sites, considered already operational. Two IRBM sites had been uncovered, one of which could become active within six weeks (the other would take eight to ten). Each site had four missile launchers and was believed to have been furnished with one reload missile. Reloading might take four to six hours for the MRBMs, six to eight hours for the IRBMs. The MRBMs already on the pads could be launched within eight hours of a Soviet decision to do so. Other equipment identified included twenty-two Il-28 bombers (one assembled, three uncrated, the remainder still packed), thirty-nine MIG-21 fighters (four still crated), and twenty-four identified SAM sites. The key judgment was contained in the estimate's twenty-second paragraph:

> We believe that the Soviets would be somewhat less likely to retaliate with military force in areas outside Cuba in response to speedy effective invasion than in response to more limited forms of military action against Cuba. We recognize that such an estimate cannot be made with very great assurance and do not rule out the possibility of Soviet retaliation outside Cuba in case of invasion. But we believe that a rapid occupation of Cuba would be more likely to make the Soviets pause in opening new theaters of conflict than limited action or action which drags out.[13]

The special estimate could not have been more alarming, or more supportive of the use of force. Given the contents of this and the special estimate of the preceding day it may be significant that Sherman Kent was sent to Paris on the twentieth to inform De Gaulle of the situation— senior officials may have thought that more cautious analysts were more useful out of town.

While McCone pushed for an airstrike, President Kennedy wavered between airstrike and blockade. The former option was ruled out after Air Force officers told Kennedy on the twenty-first that the absolute success of an airstrike could not be guaranteed.

On the twenty-second of October Kennedy delivered his speech and the world began to hold its breath. Twenty-two interceptors were airborne to guard against any rash actions from Cuba. The President declared that a missile launched from Cuba at any point in the hemisphere would be regarded as an attack by the Soviet Union on the United States and met with massive retaliation against Russia. He announced a "naval quarantine" of Cuba until the Soviets removed all offensive weapons from the island and left open the possibility of such further measures as invasion or airstrike.

As U.S. military preparations accelerated, intelligence found that Soviet construction activities were speeded up as well, with crews working through the night under the glare of floodlights. It became evident that the special estimates on the nineteenth and twentieth had slightly exaggerated the degree of combat readiness of the Soviet MRBMs. On October twenty-third the OCI reported six MRBM sites, totaling twenty-three launchers but thirty-three missiles. Only four of the sites were considered operational. The OCI report agreed with the SNIEs that none of the Soviet IRBM sites could be active before December first. However, for the first time, OCI expressed doubt as to whether any actual nuclear warheads were present with the Soviet missiles in Cuba.

Low-altitude reconnaissance missions over Cuba began on October twenty-third and supplemented the U-2 flights, which also continued at a high rate. Not even the loss of a U-2 to SAMs, on October twenty-seventh, when Major Rudolf Anderson of the 4080th Strategic Reconnaissance Wing went down over Cuba, could curtail the surveillance missions. The incident did bring tense moments at EXCOM, which, on October twenty-third, had considered the possibility of a U-2 loss and recommended in such a case that the SAM site responsible should be bombed. This recommendation was now forwarded but it was not carried out. From bases in Florida the Navy Light Photographic Squadron 62 and Marine Composite Reconnaissance Squadron Two carried out eighty missions of two to ten sorties each. In fact, from October twenty-second until November fifteenth, when low-level missions ended, the Air Force and Navy had carried out 162 of them. From the twenty-second until December sixth the Air Force also conducted 82 U-2 flights.

Some things were discovered from the low-level coverage that had not previously been known. Pictures taken on October twenty-fourth, combined with reinterpretation of older photos, enabled analysts to identify Soviet ground troop units. These were four twelve-hundred-man battle groups, quartered at four locations throughout Cuba, equipped with thirty-five to forty tanks each as well as infantry elements and Frog tactical missiles capable of using nuclear warheads. The photo interpreters were aided by the fact that the detachments in Cuba had built barracks adorned with the insignia of their parent formations in the Soviet Union. This information was distributed to American commanders on October thirtieth and would have been invaluable in an invasion.

The projection for Soviet manpower in Cuba was also revised to number some twenty-two thousand men.

The Soviet reaction to Kennedy's blockade ran the gamut from defiance to acceptance. Initially Khrushchev labeled the U.S. action as "piratical" and threatening to world peace. Ships believed to be loaded with the nuclear warheads needed by the Cuban missiles actually sailed from Black Sea ports at this time and were detected as they sailed through the Bosporus. On October twenty-fourth Soviet submarines in the Atlantic were observed accompanying their ships still en route. Later that day, however, the merchantmen were observed to stop in mid-ocean. One CIA office speculated the ships might turn back. Secretary Rusk commented, " 'We have been eyeball to eyeball, and I think the other fellow just blinked.' "[14] Some of the ships did return to Russia, presumably those with military shipments aboard. A Soviet tanker crossing the blockade line was stopped, and a freighter leased by the Russians was boarded by a party from two U.S. destroyers as she hove to 180 miles northeast of Nassau. The atmosphere at the National Indications Center was breathless as the interception was made, but the portents were good—*Pravda*'s headline that morning had read DO EVERYTHING TO PREVENT WAR. REASON MUST TRIUMPH! A subsequent summary from CIA's Office of Research and Reports confirmed that Russian freighters were returning to points of origin.

From the twenty-sixth to the twenty-eighth of October a settlement of sorts was reached, and a message broadcast over Radio Moscow stated that the missile sites would be dismantled and the missiles crated and returned to Russia. But the settlement was not without some moments of anxiety, several caused by the Americans themselves. In one incident an Alaska-based U-2 that was apparently engaged in a polar air sampling mission inadvertently strayed over Siberia. The pilot discovered his error after a few minutes, but not before both Soviet and U.S. fighter aircraft had been vectored to intercept the plane. The U-2 managed to reverse its course, rendezvous with the American planes over the Bering Strait, and return to base. But the Soviets moved for the first time in the crisis to place their air defense and ICBM forces on a maximum state of alert.

On October twenty-ninth in the Atlantic the U.S. destroyer *Cecil* picked up a sonar contact and began to track a Russian submarine. The Navy had orders to trail Soviet subs whenever they were detected, and half a dozen were harassed by sharp destroyers. But the *Cecil* contact was pursued aggressively for thirty-five hours of continuous stalking. The Soviet diesel submarine eventually had to come to the surface to recharge its air supply, and was then obliged to assume a course in conformity to the U.S. quarantine proclamation of October twenty-fourth.[15]

The Soviets are not known to have found out about a last incident, but it could have led to incredible complications if they had. The first reaction to the crisis of Operation Mongoose's Florida Task Force W was to field ten commando teams of six men each in Cuba. William Harvey thought they could serve to guide the U.S. invasion ashore and CIA headquarters at Langley evidently had no idea what was afoot. Three of the teams had already left for landing points on the north shore of Cuba when Robert Kennedy inadvertently learned of the operation through the anguished call of one of the "commandos," who wanted assurance that the cause was good. In consequence EXCOM halted all covert operations on October thirtieth, and Edward Lansdale was sent down to Miami to shut down Miami Station. It was incidents like these that prompted John F. Kennedy to remark, "There's always some poor sob who never gets the word!"

Aftermath

Intelligence was as important in verification of Soviet compliance with settlement of the Cuban crisis as it had been in the discovery of the Soviet missiles. By November second, the day on which Adlai Stevenson at the UN sent the Soviets a letter specifying what items of equipment were considered "offensive weapons" by the United States, the Kennedy administration was able to announce that Russian MRBMs were being repacked into shipping crates. That same day, however, there was an intelligence report that I1-28 bombers were still being assembled at two airfields in Cuba, and this was confirmed the following day by ORR. Earlier the President had stated that the bombers in Cuba did not affect the strategic balance; now in November he was convinced the U.S. could secure their removal as well. Robert Kennedy carried a proposal to Dobrynin that the U.S. would lift the quarantine if the Russians would agree to remove the I1-28's within thirty days. This action was opposed by the JCS, who argued to the President that the blockade must be maintained until the bombers were actually gone. The Chiefs also felt the United States should insist on the withdrawal of Soviet troops from Cuba.

Premier Khrushchev accepted the bomber proposal. On Robert Kennedy's birthday, November twentieth, Soviet ambassador Dobrynin brought him the Soviet reply. Within five days the NPIC was able to show pictures demonstrating that bombers at Holguín were being packed for shipment. By the twenty-ninth crates at both Holguín and San Julián airfields had begun their journey to ports of embarkation. Some left through the small port of Nuevitas. Pictures NPIC developed on December fifth showed that all the I1-28's were gone. More U-2 pictures, taken on January 20, 1963, showed the IRBM site at Remedios to be abandoned, its concrete structures dynamited into rubble. Other photographs a week later showed the same conditions at the former IRBM site near San Critóbal. In 1963 the United States removed the IRBM missiles it had stationed in Turkey. Operation Mongoose also ground to a halt.

This Cuban Missile Crisis is one of the most often analyzed episodes in American postwar history. Examination has led to postulates on risk taking, crisis management, bureaucratic politics, and government process. In the immediate aftermath the executive branch conducted postmortems with the Office of the President, the Department of Defense, and the intelligence community. Congress also made a study of intelligence on Cuba, and showed an active interest in the events of the crisis during the hearings on the fiscal 1964 military budget.

The main intelligence postmortem was ordered by McCone and carried out by an interagency group under Roger Hilsman. He later wrote that "for a while there was some uneasiness at the possibility of some real alley fighting developing" within the intelligence community.[16] Most contentious was the question of whether aerial photography might not have discovered the missiles sooner. But it was not difficult to show that no request for aerial coverage had ever been refused. Any delay caused by consideration of alternatives other than use of U-2's for manned overflights had been negligible. The secretary of state could not be charged with obstructing collection since both Rusk and the White House had been pressing for better information all along.

This question of photography was also a main focus of the congressional inquiry, which sought to establish whether a "photography gap" had existed with respect to Cuba. Reasoning from the fact that the San Cristóbal area had not been covered from August twenty-ninth until October fourteenth, several senators and representatives tried to prove that intelligence had allowed such a "gap" to develop. One introduced data showing Havana weather conditions to refute the argument that the weather had been too poor to fly during the last half of September. In a February 1963 appearance before the Senate Appropriations Committee, McNamara was extensively questioned to show that more detailed photo coverage might have revealed some site preparations at San Cristóbal as early as September tenth.

The main charges against intelligence were lodged by the Preparedness Investigating Subcommittee of the Senate's Armed Services Committee. Their report conceded that U.S. intelligence had done "a reasonably competent job . . . in acquiring and collecting intelligence information," but it lashed out at the analysts, noting that

> faulty evaluation and the predisposition of the intelligence community to the philosophical conviction that it would be incompatible with Soviet policy to introduce strategic weapons into Cuba resulted in intelligence judgments and evaluations that proved to be erroneous.

Further,

> in reaching their pre-October 14 negative judgment the intelligence analysts were strongly influenced by their judgment as to Soviet policy and indications that strategic missiles were being installed were not given proper weight by the intelligence community. A contributing factor to this was the tendency on the part of the intelligence people to discredit and downgrade reports of Cuban refugees and exiles.[17]

In 1964 the so-called "philosophical predisposition" was raised to the level of a theory of intelligence by Klaus Knorr, a Princeton political scientist and occasional consultant to intelligence, who had participated in one of the Cuba postmortems. Knorr's paper in an academic journal coined the term "behavioral surprise" to describe the situation in which prior expectations fail to apply to the facts.[18] Such a criticism is possible in the Cuban case because of the "notorious" SNIE of September 19, 1962, which, it will be recalled, concluded that the Russians would not deploy strategic missiles in Cuba. Although in hindsight this judgment was clearly mistaken, the real question is whether the conclusions in the special estimate were palpably wrong at the time the document was drafted.

It should be recalled that the BNE drew up the estimate in response to McCone's "honeymoon cables." At the time McCone was attempting to garner support for his own hypothesis that the Soviets were going to deploy offensive missiles. While the evidence was limited to sightings of SAMs, which did not seem related to defending any particular points in Cuba, McCone theorized that the Soviets sought to deny Cuban airspace to U.S. surveillance planes in order to conduct the next stage of their buildup in secrecy. Other analysts reasoned, however, that since it is an island, an area-defense of Cuba would be more feasible. In addition the Soviets had already provided SAM missiles to Iraq and Indonesia and, given the Bay of Pigs experience, Soviet arms, including SAMs, could have been intended to ensure that any future invasion of Cuba could only be conducted as a major military operation. The agent-reports that Congress accused intelligence of downgrading, and which might have made a difference in the September nineteenth estimate, had not yet arrived at Langley. It should be noted that the inaccuracy of the September SNIE led the analysts to err too far in the opposite direction in October, when they implicitly supported arguments for military action against Cuba.

As for the "philosophical conviction" that the Soviets would not deploy strategic nuclear weapons outside their borders, this probably was a prejudice held by U.S. intelligence. At the time of Cuba the intelligence community had just emerged from the "missile gap" phase with a general disposition toward avoiding overstatements of capability. During the gap period there had been recurrent claims of the presence of Soviet MRBM or IRBM missiles in satellite countries ranging from Poland to Albania. Some of these reports had such widespread circulation that they were accepted by public commentators, but none was ever proven true by intelligence. Until 1962 there was no instance in which the Soviets had, in fact, deployed strategic weapons outside Russia, even though Eastern European deployment might have improved their coverage of targets in NATO Europe. Nondeployment outside total Soviet control *must* have been an explicit tenet of Soviet policy, from which they deviated to deploy missiles in Cuba. Coupled with the lack of positive evidence for McCone's hypothesis or Keating's assertions, the U.S. analysts obviously had some grounds for their prejudice.

What about the downgrading of agent resources with which Congress charged intelligence? It is true that the Cuban exiles were by and large considered unreliable informants. The massive number of their reports and the large proportion that had proven to be without foundation seemed to indicate caution. Further, the problem was endemic not only to U.S. intelligence but also to those other organizations which worked with the Cubans, such as the French SDECE. Agent sources accounted for some important information but it appears that most of the Cuban-agent reports served only to increase the noise level through which analysts had to discern the accurate information. The CIA postmortem on the missile crisis established that of two hundred Cuban-agent reports bearing on the missiles specifically, only six had been accurate.

At the same time it should be noted that not all agents were regarded with the same degree of skepticism. Oleg Penkovsky was one agent who was considered highly reliable. In fact, photo interpreters were able to decide at an early stage that MRBM missiles were being installed at certain locations because they had a copy of the official Soviet MRBM field manual furnished by Penkovsky to U.S. intelligence. Unfortunately in the midst of the missile crisis Penkovsky and his British case officer, Greville Wynne, were arrested by Soviet security police in Moscow. Penkovsky was tried and executed, Wynne was imprisoned and later exchanged.

Perhaps the greatest excesses in the intelligence reporting on the Cuban crisis concerned not the September SNIE, which was mistaken, but the October special estimates, which favored intervention. Here it can be argued that the initial discovery of the missiles stampeded the intelligence community—BNE wanted to get back "on board" with McCone. In this instance the SNIEs would have significantly narrowed the options available to President Kennedy had not some of the EXCOM decision-makers fought strenuously against airstrike and other options that escalated immediately without providing a chance for the Russians to back down. Even with the close control that was exercised, escalation could have occurred at several points: when Major Anderson's U-2 was shot down or the other U-2 blundered over Siberia; when the Mongoose covert operators dispatched commando teams in the midst of crisis; or when naval incidents occurred in the North Atlantic. Fortunately escalation was avoided but it might have been, to adopt Dean Acheson's description of the crisis, a "homage to plain dumb luck."

The most ironic feature of the crisis is that the military threat might never have been there at all. If it is true that the nuclear warheads for the Soviet missiles were not dispatched until after mid-October, then the actual missiles in Cuba were useless as a strategic force. Once the blockade was in effect the warheads could not be gotten into the island. This calls attention to Soviet bungling in Cuba, which was substantial. In a plan that relied on deception to multiply Soviet nuclear forces, no efforts were made to camouflage or otherwise conceal the missile site preparations. Moreover, if McCone was correct that the Russians wanted a SAM network to deny Cuban airspace to U.S. surveillance, it is inexplicable why MRBM site preparations were begun at all before the SAM batteries were fully operational. And there was also enormous risk in the Soviet plan. One element of the September special estimate was quite correct from the U.S. standpoint—it was inconceivable that the Soviets could establish a major strategic capability in Cuba without provoking an American response. The Soviets apparently assumed there would not be one, a basic miscalculation which would cost Khrushchev his job two years later when the Cuban misadventure was used as justification to oust him.

On balance the intelligence community provided the Kennedy administration with enough warning of the Soviet missile deployment to allow it to elaborate an effective response. Whatever the difficulties associated with use of any particular information source all had been utilized in an effective fashion. Policy makers were successfully provided with daily observations on Soviet activity over a considerable period. Intelligence was also successful in monitoring the withdrawal of Soviet offensive weapons, providing the administration with assurances despite our inability to reach agreement with Castro on "on-site" inspection of the dismantling. Had the missiles been discovered sooner, the performance might have been brilliant, but as it was intelligence was creditable.

CHAPTER TEN
THREAT FROM DEFENSE

In the wake of the Cuban crisis both the U.S. and Russia moved toward some accommodation in arms control. The main accomplishment of this was signature of a Partial Nuclear Test Ban Treaty during 1963, an event which focused public attention for perhaps the first time upon yet another facet of the new military technology—ballistic missile defense (BMD). The question of the extent to which the Soviets might have developed or be deploying defenses against atomic attack was considered militarily significant by planners and by the intelligence community throughout the sixties and seventies. A number of theorists and public figures of the period thought that BMD would be the next major evolution of the strategic balance and did their best to ensure American primacy in this category of forces. Analysis of Soviet progress on missile defense was accordingly a primary component of intelligence reporting.

The underlying premises of BMD can be described briefly and are of some importance. First, under theories of deterrence, was the *threat* of using forces offensively to restrain the opponent from unleashing war. Defense could be accomplished by ICBM forces that successfully disarmed the opponent in a counterforce attack, called "damage limitation" in the jargon of the McNamara Pentagon. The alternative to counterforce was deterrence with second-strike forces to carry out retaliation against the opponent, "assured destruction" in the jargon. But an effective BMD could upset the "assured destruction" equation by eliminating attacking forces, reducing the scale of retaliation, conceivably even to "acceptable" levels. Thus the possibility of BMD was considered potentially destabilizing for the nuclear balance—either side, seeing its deterrent power eroded by BMD on the other side, might be tempted to attack preemptively while it still possessed some striking power. The key intelligence questions on BMD were: how effective a given antiballistic missile (ABM) system might be, and what degree of ABM deployment would be necessary to provide such a strategic benefit.

BMD was foreseen at a very early date. In 1955 the U.S. Army, which had charge of the American BMD effort, described the problem as being how to hit a bullet with another bullet. Bell Telephone Labs and the Army undertook studies after July 1955, focusing on the ICBM as the primary target for defenses. In early 1957 the Army ordered full-scale development of an ABM, the Nike-Zeus, and later that year the AEC completed feasibility studies on a warhead for the missile. Nike-Zeus was first flight-tested on August 26, 1959, but the system never reached production because the Eisenhower administration determined that it could be countered relatively easily. Nevertheless the existence of a U.S. ABM program and the wide interest in the possibilities for BMD gave the intelligence community a convenient point of departure for observing similar developments in Russia.

The first intimation that the Soviets also considered BMD feasible came even before Sputnik, in a September 1957 article that discussed radar detection of ICBMs in flight. That November the Soviet minister of defense Marshal Malinovsky, in a speech to Russian officers, stressed the need to give greater attention to antiair and antimissile defense. There are reports that in 1958 the Russians organized an independent component for defense against rockets within their Air Defense Troops, the Soviet service arm responsible for defense of home territory.

Apprised of U.S. developments and watching for indications of a Soviet BMD program, intelligence was initially unperturbed. The 1957 NIE concluded that the Soviets would not be capable of deploying an ABM before mid-1962 at the earliest. The Gaither Report projected some ABM capability on both the U.S. and Soviet sides by the middle of the period 1961–1975. In 1958, however, the U-2 brought back evidence of construction of primitive ABM radars at the Soviet test site of Sary-Shagan, which became the center for all Soviet BMD development testing. During a visit to the Soviet Union in 1959, Vice President Richard Nixon saw what were believed to be space-tracking radars close to Moscow. By late 1960 discussions at the NSC revealed some concern that the Soviets might achieve an operational ABM before the U.S. Shortly thereafter a national newsweekly reported that U.S. intelligence had received "positive evidence" that the Russians had an ABM, which they were working to perfect. In November 1960 a high Soviet officer claimed in an *Izvestia* article possession of a missile designed to intercept "offensive pilotless devices" at high altitudes.

The first year of the Kennedy administration brought new developments in Russian BMD. Most significant was the nuclear test series late in 1961 that ended a three-year-old testing moratorium. Five days into the series the Soviets fired a nuclear charge at high altitude over the Sary-Shagan experimental radar, undoubtedly to test the effect of nuclear-induced "blackout" phenomena on the radar's tracking ability. Reports were widespread but unconfirmed that this test had actually involved a live warhead on an ABM missile against an ICBM in flight. Three days later, on September 9, 1961, Premier Khrushchev expressed satisfaction with the Soviet BMD effort. At the twenty-second Party Congress that October, Marshal Malinovsky made a point of reporting that the problem of destroying ICBMs in flight had been solved.

Coupled with these reports was the disquietening news that deployment was proceeding as well. Clearing and site preparation work was found in the vicinity of Leningrad. The concrete foundation work was similar to the test beds at Sary-Shagan, and the location of the sites was placed squarely across the planned flight corridors of American ICBMs en route to points in European Russia. The Soviet development was called the Leningrad System by U.S. intelligence. Eventually about thirty launcher structures were observed and construction continued into 1962.

By all accounts Leningrad was a technological turkey, lacking sophistication as an ABM system. Freeman Dyson, a physicist working through the summer of 1962 for the Arms Control and Disarmament Agency, turned in a paper with an interesting prescription for coping with Leningrad:

> . . . summarizing what I had learned about the Soviet ABM system and recommending a sharp change in the official American response to it. In the past, I said, America reacted very stupidly to Soviet attempts at defense by bluff. We failed to understand that it is to our advantage to be facing a defense by bluff rather than a militarily real defense, even when the quality of our intelligence is not good enough to tell the difference. For example, in 1960 we enjoyed a superiority in offensive missiles while the Soviet Union concealed its weakness by maintaining a missile bluff. We then demolished the Soviet missile bluff as conspicuously as possible with public statements of the results of U-2 photography, and so forced the Soviet Union to replace its fictitious missile force with a real one. It would have been much wiser for us to have left the Soviet bluff intact.
>
> For the future I argued that the United States should strive by every means in its power to sustain and buttress the Soviet ABM bluff. We should try and discourage the American Secretary of Defense from making loud public statements of the Soviet system's ineffectiveness.[1]

This Dyson paper and another similar effort were filed and forgotten, victims of those in American politics who would have upbraided Mc-

Namara (and Kennedy) if the U.S. government had "let" the Russians be "ahead" in anything.

Intelligence about the Leningrad system was actually used in the Senate debate over ratification of the Partial Nuclear Test Ban Treaty in 1963, which prohibited all but underground nuclear blasts. The Test Ban was the product of the détente that followed confrontation in Cuba, negotiated by a U.S. team under Averell Harriman in Moscow that summer. Opposition to ratification was marshaled by Senators Strom Thurmond (D-South Carolina) and John C. Stennis (D-Mississippi), who were concerned that the Soviets would conspire to violate the test ban, using the results to gain a lead over the U.S. in BMD. The senators received some support from CIA Director John McCone, who as Eisenhower's chairman of the AEC had always opposed any cessation of nuclear testing. A national estimate on Soviet defensive forces had been produced in the midst of the Cuban crisis and was alarming on their ABM potential for 1967. McCone had testified to the Senate on the basis of this in May 1963, and during most of the summer a CIA analyst was temporarily attached to Senator Stennis's office to help make the case against the Test Ban Treaty. Thurmond, using information supplied by McCone, called the Senate into the first secret session of its history in order to argue that Leningrad was an operational ABM, that the Russians were ahead in this field, and that any test ban would hamper the U.S. effort to match and surpass the presumptive Soviet ABM lead.

Not even within the intelligence community was there total agreement with McCone on the test ban issue. Other senior CIA officials disagreed with his appraisal of the capabilities of the Leningrad system. Officials at the Departments of Defense and State, and the Arms Control and Disarmament Agency, doubted whether the Soviets would be able to prepare in advance a test program which would leave the U.S. with no time to restart its own atmospheric nuclear tests. Only strong intervention from the White House eventually stilled John McCone's objections to the Test Ban Treaty; President Kennedy formed a task force of senior national security officials to counter criticisms of the treaty before the Senate.

One of Kennedy's strongest supporters before Congress was, of course, Defense Secretary McNamara. In his August 1963 testimony McNamara declared that he did not believe Russia had tested "by full-scale high-altitude test" the vulnerability of an ICBM reentry vehicle to nuclear blast. He stated with confidence that U.S. strategic forces could reliably penetrate any existing Soviet ABM defenses. Kennedy had said earlier in August that developing an effective BMD appeared to be technically beyond the Russians and McNamara concurred with the President's assertion. He also felt the prohibition on nuclear explosions in the atmosphere or underwater provided by the treaty would prove to be readily verifiable. The Senate agreed with the administration and the Test Ban Treaty was ratified by a vote of eighty to nineteen on September 24, 1963.

On the specific question of Russian ABM progress there was some difference between McNamara's stance at the treaty hearings and the position of the intelligence community, as cited in his fiscal year 1964 classified posture statement presented in February. There the defense secretary observed that the Russians were known to be working on two different BMD systems. One of these was Leningrad which intelligence thought might have been designed against shorter range missiles like IRBMs. The second ABM had definitely been configured against all missile types and the estimates judged it might be deployed on a limited scale by mid-1968. The Russians themselves made it obvious how unnecessarily pessimistic the estimate had been; in 1963 they were observed to reorient their missile defense effort. Although they continued to make statements stressing the feasibility of their ABM, the Leningrad system was never deployed and the sites that had been built for it were eventually dismantled.

Tallinn and Galosh

The commander of the Troops of National Air Defense (PVO Strany) was replaced in 1962 by Marshal V. A. Sudets. In 1963 new construction was observed near Tallinn in the Soviet-controlled Baltic state of Estonia, as well as at some of the previously cleared Leningrad sites. Once again foundation work resembled structures at the Sary-Shagan test facility, but this time there was a further ambiguity— radars previously associated exclusively with aircraft tracking appeared at Sary-Shagan. The technology was dubbed the Tallinn system after the city where it had first been observed, but U.S. analysts faced the serious difficulty of deciding whether Tallinn was intended primarily against aircraft or missiles.

The advent of Tallinn corresponded to more activity near Moscow. North of the Soviet capital two large ABM-type radars were visible under construction. In the November military parade through Red Square the Soviets wheeled past a missile that looked like a high-altitude defensive weapon. This was promptly designated the SA-5 by NATO officials and called Griffon. Sites cleared for Griffon would subsequently reach from Riga on the Baltic to Archangel on the Arctic Ocean. Marshal S. S.

Biryuzov commented in February 1963 that Russia had successfully solved the problem of destroying rockets in flight. Later that year another senior Soviet officer asserted that the nation already possessed a BMD.

These developments could not pass unnoticed by U.S. intelligence. After the Cuban Missile Crisis John McCone had moved to strengthen CIA's capacity to handle scientific and technical information. In August 1963 he reorganized his Directorate for Research into a Directorate for Science and Technology (DDS&T). The CIA deputy director, Albert Wheelon, who headed the group, was also made chairman of the USIB subcommittees on guided missiles, scientific intelligence, and atomic energy. Wheelon moved in turn to form an office within DDS&T called the Foreign Military and Space Analysis Center. These DDS&T analysts would be important interpreters of the Soviet BMD.

On the military intelligence side contact between CIA and DIA at the working level was expanded by the formation in 1962 of a Joint Analysis Group (JAG) composed of analysts from CIA's offices of scientific intelligence and of research and reports, plus personnel from DIA. JAG was to provide regular reports on Soviet military strength called National Intelligence Projections for Planning (NIPPs). Unlike the NIE format, in which judgments were based on evidence or on reasonably confident assessments of probability, the NIPPs provided precise numbers of weapon systems, sometimes weapons not even off the drawing board, five or ten years into the future. Clearly the NIPPs and the Joint Intelligence Estimates for Planning (JIEPs), a similar type of report, were based on very little more than speculation. The Tallinn system and the JAG reports became a point of contention in the controversy over Soviet strategic defense forces in the 1960s.

The main question before the intelligence community in 1963 was how to explain abandonment of Leningrad and the sudden intensive work on Tallinn. Secretary McNamara, his director of defense research and engineering, and Army Intelligence under Major General Alva R. Fitch all felt it reasonable to conclude that Tallinn was an ABM system. The Soviets had made an abortive start in this direction; the abandonment of Leningrad suggested that they had something better in mind. At the same time the appearance of the American Minuteman and continued growth of the Polaris forces furnished the Soviets with ample motivation for missile defenses. The JAG 6-63 study consequently reasoned that the Soviets would continue their emphasis on defense over the next decade and would invest in defenses at a relatively constant rate, including both improvement of existing weapons and introduction of new ones.

The 1963 NIE concurred with this perception. Though there was some skepticism within CIA and the Navy, there was general agreement on a very high projection of the future Soviet ABM force based upon the extensive work observed on Tallinn. The NIE projection is said to have expected up to two thousand long-range ABM interceptors plus as many as six thousand to eight thousand shorter-range ABMs that would be used within the atmosphere, most likely Tallinn-type missiles such as Griffon and its follow-ons. McNamara outlined the NIE conclusions to Congress in his fiscal 1965 posture statement as follows:

> It now appears that the Soviets are deploying an antiballistic missile (ABM) system around Leningrad. They may be starting to deploy one around Moscow. We believe that this system probably would be effective against single missiles but would not be effective against ballistic missiles equipped with even elementary penetration aids.[2]

In their November 1964 parade the Soviets wheeled past some large cannisters with rocket engine nozzles protruding from the rear. Western analysts maintained this was the first appearance of another ABM missile, the Moscow deployment of which McNamara had spoken in February, which was now given the NATO designation Galosh. Some CIA analysts began to doubt that Griffon missiles associated with the Tallinn sites were really ballistic missile defenses, despite the fact that Soviet television had shown film that year of what purported to be a live SA-5 interception of a missile. At any rate Tallinn was growing to massive proportions whether or not it was an ABM. The complexes each had three batteries of six launchers each, arrayed around a single engagement radar. The system's flaw seemed to be the radar. Not only were there few radars, but the radar scanners were mechanically operated and evidently could track only one target at a time. All this suggested slow reaction time and marginal ability to meet a massive ICBM attack, tending to discount the missile defense value of the Tallinn line.

Other evidence seemed to support the opposite conclusion—the television pictures shown by the Soviets, for one thing. It was also true that the Soviets had installed Tallinn radars at Sary-Shagan, clouding the issue of whether Tallinn's radar was only for air defense use. These indications led Army and Air Force intelligence to conclude that Tallinn was part of a massive BMD effort by the Soviets. These services brought pressure on the DIA, which was accused of always concurring with CIA views. The evidence is not clear concerning the position of the Navy, with some sources contending that Rear Admiral Rufus L. Taylor refused to subscribe to this pessimistic interpretation while others hold that all the services were unanimous on Tallinn in the 1963–1965 period, enabling the Navy to press for greater funding for Polaris submarines.

In early 1964 Marshal Sudets of PVO Strany wrote in *Red Star* that Russia had created a reliable defense against both aircraft and missiles, a statement that seemed to allude to Tallinn. Then construction of the first of three ballistic missile early-warning radars began. Called Hen House, the radars were, like U.S. BMEWS, the size of several football fields and were located at Irkutsk, along the Barents Sea coast, and in the Baltic state of Latvia. Later there was site preparation work for a phased-array radar, called Dog House, near Moscow.

The Soviet ABM question was particularly important in the context of the budget preparations for fiscal year 1966. Here Secretary McNamara faced crucial choices: whether to fund engineering development of a multiple warhead reentry vehicle called MIRV, and what to do with the antiballistic missile Nike-X, which the Army wanted to deploy to protect American cities. MIRV would ensure penetration of any Soviet missile defense by saturating it with so many warheads that effective defense would be rendered impossible. Nike-X deployment would channel a share of the strategic-forces budget to the Army and would allow American generals to assert that the Soviets were not ahead on BMD.

There was also pressure on the USIB for more intelligence about Soviet BMD, and pressure by USIB on the community to generate additional information. The list of priority national intelligence objectives (PNIOs) was supplemented four times in 1964, with the last revision issued a month in advance during December. In NIE 11-4-64 and in a special estimate, intelligence found declining growth, declining overall investment, and rising consumer demand in the Soviet Union. This picture conflicted, however, with the evident, large Soviet outlay in BMD hardware, which could only be interpreted as Soviet determination to continue ABM at a high rate. But the evidence on Tallinn itself inclined McNamara to take a cautious stance. He spoke of "considerable uncertainty" in intelligence but drew the provisional conclusion that "evidence indicates that the [Tallinn] system may well have a capability against aerodynamic vehicles rather than ballistic missiles."[3] McNamara nevertheless decided to continue the MIRV program, although he refused to approve deployment of the Nike-X.

Almost simultaneously with the appearance of McNamara's statement, the February 1965 *Bulletin of the Atomic Scientists* carried an important article by General Nikolai Talensky, of the Soviet Academy of Sciences. Talensky argued that technically it was quite possible to "counterbalance the absolute weapons of attack" with equally absolute weapons of defense and that remaining problems could be solved through "creative human thinking" to which there were no limits. Talensky dismissed the Western view that ABM deployment would destabilize the nuclear balance:

> From the standpoint of strategy, powerful deterrent forces and an effective antimissile defense system, when taken together, substantially increase the stability of mutual deterrence, for any partial shifts in the qualitative and quantitative balance of these two component elements of mutual deterrence tend to be correspondingly compensated and equalized.

Moreover,

> the creation of an effective antimissile system enables the state to make its defenses dependent chiefly on its own possibilities, and not only on mutual deterrence, that is, the goodwill of the other side.[4]

Talensky's view was widely shared by other Soviet thinkers.

Throughout 1965 the actual pace of the Soviet BMD program remained unclear. Communist Party leader Leonid Brezhnev indicated in a July radio speech that Russia had achieved significant results and further developments expected shortly would greatly improve performance. Brezhnev's assertion was consistent with the 1964 edition of the standard work by Marshal Sokolovsky on military strategy, which declared that in principle a solution to the ABM's technical problems had been found. Brezhnev also stated that the ABM program would have to be managed properly, and in August 1965 there was a complete reorganization of the industrial ministries, including those engaged in missile and ABM research and development. Construction of Galosh facilities continued around Moscow, although no ABMs were installed. Progress on Tallinn proceeded at a slower rate.

At this time both CIA and DIA were arguing that the Soviet ABM would have negligible capabilities given that it was perceived to be less effective than Nike-X. (McNamara continued to refuse authorization for Nike-X on the grounds that it would be ineffective.) The Joint Analysis Group had been dissatisfied with the results of the 1964 NIE and now challenged this CIA-DIA view. JAG analysts saw any argument based on analogy to Nike-X as specious because it measured a *current* Soviet BMD effort against *future* foreseeable U.S. capabilities (MIRV); rather, arguments should pit current Soviet capability against current U.S. forces. JAG maintained that the Soviets could gain a momentary strategic advantage by deploying an admittedly inferior ABM, which would have some capability so long as the U.S. ICBM force was not equipped with penetration aids or MIRVs.

Although JAG's reading of Soviet ballistic missile defense did not gain wide credence, it reflected growing differences within the intelligence community on Soviet BMD. In 1965 General Carroll reversed the DIA position on Tallinn, now viewing it as a BMD. Secretary McNamara described the differences in his posture statement of January 1966 which went into Soviet ABMs in some detail. Here the Galosh missiles were associated with the missile defense complexes around Moscow and with the ABM radars being constructed. The judgment was that this was an exo-atmospheric[5] intercept system, which might achieve initial operating capability by late 1967, but more likely the following year. There would be a lag of another year or two before Galosh could successfully engage Polaris missiles. On Tallinn the posture statement was very carefully worded:

> We had at one time estimated that the Soviets were constructing an anti-missile defense system which might be operational at Leningrad as early as mid-1965 and at Moscow by mid-1967. However, numerous indications point to Soviet difficulties with this program. For example, there have been a series of changes and modifications to the ABM facilities and equipment at their test ranges, and activities at the deployment sites has [sic] been highly sporadic.
>   We had also previously judged that all these activities were primarily antimissile defense oriented. Currently the weight of the evidence suggests that two distinct programs are underway: (1) a probable antiballistic missile defense around Moscow and (2) a new defensive system being deployed across the northwest approaches to the Soviet Union.[6]

With regard to the second system, Tallinn, McNamara pointed out that available evidence did not permit confident judgment on whether construction at the four Tallinn complexes thus far discovered "could be for defense against ballistic missiles or aerodynamic vehicles or both."

Uncertainty in the intelligence community was compounded in 1966 by increased urgency. Acceleration of the Tallinn program was observed; the number of sites discovered increased to twenty-two, with several "farms" of launch complexes in a barrier line, as McNamara had said, "across the northwest approaches to the Soviet Union."

The dispute over Tallinn's purpose remained unresolved. One intelligence analyst confessed to *Newsweek* reporter Lloyd Norman that " 'to be perfectly honest, we don't know enough about the Soviet ABM to be sure what it is they are putting in the ground.' "[7] The CIA continued to insist that Tallinn was a surface-to-air missile (SAM) system. Against a high-altitude manned bomber the Tallinn would have been effective, but with its radars incapable of any "interesting ABM performance," the

SA-5 was not suitable to use in an ABM mode. CIA preferred, when projecting a future Soviet ABM, to predict a major increase in Galosh coverage. Naval Intelligence under Rear Admiral Eugene B. Fluckey supported this CIA interpretation while Army, Air Force, and DIA continued seeing Tallinn as a BMD system. Meanwhile the BNE was reported to have a growing suspicion that the Soviets had moved to actual deployment of ABM missiles, the last step necessary after construction of sites and radar infrastructures.

The 1966 NIE on Soviet defensive forces was drafted by the BNE in October and approved by the USIB on November seventeenth. The estimate concluded that Galosh would be effective against a limited attack of currently operational missiles on the Moscow area, but would be rendered less effective by advanced penetration systems (MIRV) or swamped by a heavy attack. The estimate also continued to maintain that Tallinn was a SAM rather than an ABM system and buttressed this contention with evidence that certain of the Tallinn complexes were located so that the Dog House and Hen House early-warning and missile-tracking radars could furnish them with no useful targeting data. It is not yet clear whether the NIE projected current deployment of Galosh and its major expansion—sources differ on this point. But footnotes were inserted by the Army, the Air Force, and DIA.

To the surprise of Robert McNamara, the Joint Chiefs used the estimate to recommend to President Lyndon B. Johnson the immediate deployment of Nike-X. Johnson met with McNamara, Deputy Secretary Cyrus Vance, JCS Chairman General Earle Wheeler, other JCS members, and Special Assistant for National Security Affairs Walt W. Rostow, at Austin, Texas, on December 6, 1966. The Chiefs drew attention to the intelligence on Soviet ABM and ICBM deployment and unanimously requested production funding for Nike-X to be placed around twenty-five American cities. McNamara and Vance opposed any such decision. The argument degenerated into an exchange over the meaning of nuclear superiority and parity. McNamara insisted that current intelligence on Soviet forces did not constitute grounds for the Nike-X, especially since U.S. systems already approved—specifically the Minuteman III and Poseidon MIRVed missiles—would override Soviet defenses anyway. No decision was taken immediately.

Later that same day McNamara delivered a strong statement to the press on why the contingencies envisioned by the Joint Chiefs were already covered in the defense budget. Some days later it became known that "influential officials" at both Defense and State questioned the estimate that Russia was proceeding with full-scale ABM deployment. The feeling was that Galosh might still be in the research and development stage and that the Soviet government might not yet have made a deployment decision on BMD.

The basic reason for McNamara's December 1966 news conference at Austin very possibly was that the defense secretary felt the Nike-X issue slipping away from him. BMD in the United States had picked up a constituency in the industry, the Pentagon, and Congress. The Joint Chiefs were not alone in pressing for deployment. There was some public criticism of the Department of Defense for "slowing" the U.S. ABM program. Congress began a practice of appropriating more than McNamara requested for ABM and the secretary, so far with LBJ's support, would refuse to spend the money. Of the Soviet ABM, Senator Strom Thurmond (R-South Carolina) had said,

> Assumptions of U.S. ability to penetrate Soviet ABM defenses are based on the *absence* of hard intelligence confirming a high performance capability for the Russian system.[8]

This carried the implication that McNamara worked on the basis of faulty intelligence information. Under the circumstances McNamara's justification for opposition to the Nike-X and the way it was presented would be crucial in the handling of this matter when the fiscal 1968 budget went to Congress in January 1967.

The annual posture statement went out on January 23, 1967. McNamara included unprecedented detail in his delineation of the Soviet ABM threat, perhaps to allay Senator Thurmond's fears over the adequacy of intelligence. McNamara described both the CIA and DIA positions but without attribution, and supplied additional data on the Soviet ABMs. The Galosh system complexes comprised sixteen missiles (two batteries of eight), each battery with a Try-Add triple unit engagement radar. Six complexes were then under construction, one was "dormant," and a total of eight would complete a ring defense of Moscow. Technical details on the Galosh missile showed it to be definitely an exo-atmospheric interceptor. Galosh might attain IOC in 1967 or early 1968 and reach full operational status with six complexes in 1970–1971.

On the Tallinn the statement noted a new appreciation that the SA-5 did not have any low-altitude capability. This negated its effectiveness against U.S. bombers, which had switched to a doctrine of low-altitude penetration in the early 1960s. It was precisely this, combined with the realization that widespread Tallinn deployment would be far less expensive than equivalent Galosh coverage, that had led the Joint Chiefs of

Staff to insist that Tallinn was an ABM. Another view, which was quoted approvingly by McNamara, was that in fact Tallinn was a SAM system originally designed to counter high-speed, high-altitude U.S. bombers of a type never deployed. McNamara's statement said,

> The pattern in which [Tallinn] is being deployed, the configuration of the sites and their equipment, and the apparent characteristics of the radars all lend credence to this view. . . . The local radars associated with the launchers appear to be of limited capability and would appear to need the support of the much larger but vulnerable Hen House radars if the system is expected to perform with a reasonable degree of effectiveness in the ABM role.[9]

The U.S. was reasonably certain that the Moscow ABM would be completed but without more evidence on Tallinn or Galosh deployment around cities other than Moscow, "we can only conjecture about the ultimate scale, effectiveness and cost of the Soviet ABM effort." McNamara nevertheless postulated that a "full scale deployment" would cost the Soviets twenty to twenty-five billion dollars. The defense secretary wished to emphasize that ABM was expensive for Russia, that his own prudent military planning had already assumed its deployment, and that Tallinn was not projected as an ABM by the Department of Defense.

McNamara's views were examined closely by the Congress, not all of whose members accepted his positions. Albert Gore, Democratic senator from Tennessee, told the press the Russians had ballistic missile defenses at Moscow and twenty-six other places, a figure that can only have been arrived at by counting Tallinn as an ABM. Strom Thurmond pressed Director of Defense Research and Engineering Dr. John Foster on Tallinn only to be told, "To our knowledge there is no operating [Soviet] ballistic missile defense system yet."[10] Senator Allen Ellender (D-Louisiana) interrogated McNamara closely on the preparation of national estimates and threat analyses.

On January twenty-eighth, appearing with McNamara before the Senate, JCS Chairman General Earle Wheeler was pressed to reveal his ideas on deployment of Nike-X. "Bus" Wheeler proceeded to state the grounds for the Joint Chiefs' recommendation to LBJ to deploy the ABM around twenty-five cities in a so-called "light" defense. What Wheeler did not say was that the Chiefs' "light" ABM defense would be the first step to thickened defense later on. Instead Wheeler told the Appropriations Committee of increased Soviet ICBM capability and of their ABM progress:

Should the Soviets come to believe that their ballistic missile defense, coupled with a nuclear attack on the United States, would limit damage to the
Soviet Union to a level acceptable to them, whatever that level is, our forces
would no longer deter, and the first principle of our security policy is
gone.[11]

Wheeler explicitly disagreed with the secretary of defense on Nike-X in
one of the most public confrontations between civilian leadership and
the military since the "bomber gap" and "missile gap" investigations
and the defense reorganization of 1958. Responding to the Joint Chiefs,
in 1967 the Congress again appropriated funds for Nike-X deployment
but Robert McNamara impounded the money.

As time passed, the Tallinn sites appeared more and more like other
Soviet SAM sites. Nuclear weapon handling facilities failed to appear at
the Tallinn complexes, ruling out the optimum "kill mechanism" an SA-
5 as an ABM might have used. Since Tallinn was clearly an endo-atmospheric weapon this observation led to the conclusion that it had
been designed to combat aircraft, not missiles. It was also notable that
no construction starts for Galosh sites other than at Moscow had appeared in several years' time. It thus became more difficult for the intelligence community to plausibly project a near-term large-scale Soviet
ABM in place.

In his last posture statement, that for fiscal 1969, Secretary Mc-
Namara stated that the majority in intelligence now believed that the
SA-5 had no ABM capability. On Galosh, McNamara pointed out that
there was no sign of the Soviets moving toward the type of defense felt
to be most feasible—a terminal defense within the atmosphere, in
which the earth's envelope of air could be used to screen out decoys
and chaff. For this the Russians would need, he thought, an interceptor
missile with an ultra-high rate of acceleration (technical journals called
this "hypersonic") like the American Sprint. If the Soviets were to begin
developing a Sprint-type missile, McNamara felt it unlikely the rocket
could be operational before 1973–1974, and the development would be
unmistakable to U.S. intelligence two years in advance.

SAM Upgrading

But the debate over Soviet ABM did not end. Instead the
ground shifted to a different technical issue, whether the Tallinn's SA-
5 missile could be "upgraded" to have an ABM capability. This issue

was at first most vehemently pressed not by an intelligence agency at all, but by the office of the Director of Defense Research and Engineering (DDR&E).

During the 1960s the DDR&E rose to a position of primacy in the Department of Defense. Eisenhower created DDR&E in the 1958 reorganization to unify management over R&D programs and Herbert York, the first DDR&E, had done a good deal to impose a DOD-wide perspective to research and development efforts. Robert McNamara's strong leadership at the Defense Department, gave the DDR&Es of the Kennedy and Johnson administrations a strong base with which to work. Dr. Harold Brown had consolidated the span of DDR&E functions; his successor Dr. John Foster expanded them. By 1968 Foster had imposed a rigid program-approval system in the Pentagon which included, at the first stage, "development concept papers," which justified weapons systems in terms of the threats they were intended to reduce as well as on other grounds. Because of its role in developing weapons systems, DDR&E had a potential interest in intelligence, as well as more direct involvement in managing research and development on intelligence collection systems. John Foster made explicit DDR&E intelligence interests when he seized on the Tallinn SAM issue.

Originally, Army G-2 under Major General William P. Yarborough had argued that the Tallinn SAM could be "upgraded" for use in BMD. Clearly if this was the case, the Soviets still had much work left to do. Foster admitted as much when he told a Senate committee in January 1967 that

[the Soviets] have got components there which we feel rather strongly are ballistic missile defense, are suitable for ballistic missile defense. The system is not completed.[12]

About eighteen months later, in September 1968, Foster confirmed to the same committee that the Tallinn had been built to combat high-altitude bombers and went off the record to warn of "upgrading" possibilities. Upgrading might be accomplished by Russian production of radars capable of multiple target tracking and computers with the capacity and programs for target discrimination and engagement guidance. All this was contingent upon whether the SA-5 missile itself was capable of "interesting ABM performance."

The problem of reaching consensus on Soviet ABM capability was exacerbated by the move toward SALT talks with the Russians. Antiballistic missiles would be a major category for limitation. Consequently the projected inventory of Soviet ABMs going into the negotiations was crucially affected by whether Tallinn was counted as a SAM or an ABM—if Tallinn was an ABM or could be "upgraded" to function as one, the Russians must be deemed to have a much larger force. The Joint Chiefs followed Foster and refused to go on record with any judgment that Tallinn could not be improved. The DIA, responsible to JCS for intelligence matters, took their cue from the Chiefs and asserted that the SA-5 did have some potential for upgrading. Army G-2 was entirely willing to subscribe to this analysis. The CIA, which had a full division of analysts focused on Soviet ABM, continued to hold that Tallinn was only a SAM and it also reduced its projection of a major Galosh expansion. At DOD, the office of International Security Affairs under Paul Warnke sided with the CIA while Foster at DDR&E went along with the JCS-DIA view.

During the Soviet-American discussions held to elaborate a SALT negotiating position in 1968 the Tallinn issue remained an open question. A working group chaired by an official of the office of International Security Affairs failed to resolve the differences in spite of over two hundred pages of written analysis on the question. The Tallinn disagreement was finally referred to a Committee of Principals where Secretary of State Dean Rusk made an effort to evolve a solution that would settle the issue. Rusk's proposal, which was accepted and included in the negotiating instructions for the U.S. delegation, was to raise the SA-5 with the Russians and either satisfy themselves that Tallinn was not an ABM or include the Griffon missiles in the treaty totals for agreement.

No actual arms limitation negotiations were carried out in 1968. The opening of talks was delayed, first by the Soviet invasion of Czechoslovakia and then by the American elections. In the interim the Soviets added another twenty Tallinn sites and brought twenty-five existing complexes to operational status. It fell to Clark M. Clifford to report on these developments to Congress in early 1969. Clifford had been appointed secretary of defense by LBJ after McNamara moved over to the World Bank. He had some background in intelligence as aide to Harry Truman in drafting the original National Security Act of 1947 and as a member and then chairman of the PFIAB in the 1960s. Clifford was convinced of the validity of the CIA interpretation of Soviet ABM. In his fiscal year 1970 posture statement, presented on January 13, 1969, Clifford included a detailed discussion on Tallinn:

> With the passage of another year and the acquisition of additional knowledge as to systems' characteristics, a majority of the intelligence community is more convinced than ever that the so-called "Tallinn" (SA-5) system is

designed against fast, high flying aerodynamic vehicles, rather than ballistic missiles, although the latter possibility cannot be excluded. . . . It is considered unlikely that the Soviets will modify the "Tallinn" system for an ABM role; modifications to give it such a capability would be very costly and would involve very difficult technical problems. For example, as presently configured these complexes are highly vulnerable to nuclear attack; it would require deployment of a totally new engagement radar and a higher-performance, high-acceleration missile to give the system an effective self-defense or terminal defense capability against missile attack.[13]

The defense secretary also noted that Galosh building had slowed, with the Soviets apparently abandoning two of the six complexes under construction. Three of eight Try-Add engagement radars were judged operational and IOC for the others was expected before 1970. Concerning the direction of Soviet BMD Clifford made this statement:

It may be that the Soviet leaders are reconsidering their entire ABM defense policy, or it may simply mean that they have found the current Galosh system excessively costly or technically inadequate and are developing a new and better ABM system. Activity at their main ABM test site indicates that research and development related to this problem is continuing.[14]

Whatever the Soviet intentions no Galosh missile had yet been placed in a silo. The Johnson administration left office a week after Clifford's statement. Shepherding the fiscal 1970 military budget through Congress became the task of Melvin R. Laird, Nixon's secretary of defense. Laird was well connected in Congress, having sat as a representative on the House Armed Services Committee. He was generally regarded as a moderate on Viet Nam policy but a "hawk" where the Soviet Union was concerned. This attitude was apparent in the supplementals Laird requested for fiscal 1970, the most notable of which was for deployment of an ABM system called Safeguard, designed to use Nike-X components to defend U.S. ICBM fields. However, the administration chose to justify this request with reference to Soviet ICBM forces, not their BMD effort. Questions of Soviet ABM activity were thus temporarily put aside.

Laird did reveal at press briefings that the Russians were developing a new version of the Galosh missile, termed ABM-2 in place of the old Galosh ABM-1. It would have the ability to coast in flight and restart its engine for increased range. Laird felt that research and development on the ABM-2 was the main reason why the Russians had thus far failed to expand Galosh to cover cities other than Moscow. Yet, in 1969, the Soviets finally installed the less sophisticated ABM-1 missiles in the Moscow complexes. Meanwhile John Foster, whom Laird had retained as DDR&E, remained concerned about Tallinn and told a House Foreign Relations Committee panel in August 1969 that some means had to be found to control "SAM upgrading." This concern reverberated through the Nixon administration. Soon there had been so much discussion of the issue at the NSC that a joke identified "Sam Upgrading" as the newest member of the NSC staff.

While Laird did not make Soviet ABM the main focus of his 1969 activities the revelation of a new Galosh interceptor did accentuate the threat from defense. Further, Laird's claim that the ABM-2 was a "third generation" ABM suggested that the Soviets were about to develop something even more advanced than the technology embodied in the U.S. Safeguard. The information conveyed a highly pessimistic view of Soviet developments which was contrary to the opinions of many in intelligence. The result was that a draft estimate then before the USIB was leaked to *The New York Times*. The NIE argued both that Galosh deployment was being slowed, not increased, and that even a fully manned Galosh system would hardly affect the strategic balance between the superpowers.

In his own first posture statement, that for fiscal 1971, Secretary Laird was more restrained in his description of Soviet BMD. Laird did claim that modifications to Galosh were then being developed and might become available as early as 1970. The new exo-atmospheric ABM-2 interceptor could be completed by 1974–1975. But Laird wrote that

> no evidence of development of a short range intercept system comparable to our Sprint has been noted, although the intelligence community believes that the Soviets recognize the desirability of supplementing their long-range system with a Sprint-type capability at some point in the future.[15]

Laird also conceded that evidence acquired in 1969 had reinforced the USIB judgment that Tallinn was unlikely to have any ABM utility at that time. The only Soviet ABMs were in the three Galosh sites that had been brought to operational status.

The restrained tone of Laird's statement did not mean that "SAM upgrading" had ceased to be a divisive issue, however. A memo issued by the NSC Verification Panel on December 30, 1969, posed questions of the strategic implications and verification problems of " 'possible upgrading of Soviet air defense missiles to give them ABM capabilities.' "[16] DDR&E still insisted that, in the absence of treaty provisions precluding Tallinn "upgrading," the U.S. should not accept any constraints on its MIRV program or curtail MIRV deployment. One service at this time was projecting as many as seven thousand to nine thousand Soviet ABMs within a few years while even the NIE carried a figure that was far greater than the number of ABMs actually deployed by the Russians. The possibility of "upgrading" was also used at an NSC meeting on March 25, 1970 when Laird, his deputy David Packard, and JCS Chairman Earle Wheeler justified their rejection of SALT bargaining positions on the basis of reference to it. The general status of Soviet ABM arose at the Verification Panel on August 9, 1971, when National Security Advisor Henry Kissinger asked Director of Central Intelligence Richard Helms whether the Russians might be induced to dismantle their Galosh. Helms's reply, which contrasts with the CIA view of marginal utility for Galosh, was that he did not think so.

During 1970 the Soviets activated their fourth Galosh site with sixteen more ABM-1 missiles. On February twenty-third, in an article hailed as the most authoritative Soviet statement on ABM since 1967, Defense Minister Marshal Andrei A. Grechko opined that Soviet ABMs could hit attacking missiles at any height or speed and at great distances from defense sites. In 1971 Laird announced that the Russians had resumed work on a fifth site in the Moscow ring but this complex was never activated. Eventually the ABM-2 interceptor replaced the older Galosh in the system but Soviet BMD has remained of strictly marginal value.

Rather than massive expansion the Soviets chose to limit ballistic missile defense under SALT. In 1972 the Russians signed an ABM treaty with the United States restricting themselves to two ABM groups, each with not more than one hundred interceptor missiles. In 1974 a further protocol to the 1972 treaty reduced the number of agreed ABM sites to one for each side. The four complexes in the Moscow network never deployed more than sixty-four ABM missiles, and even this level may have been subsequently reduced—in March 1980 the Soviets told the U.S. of their intention to dismantle two of the remaining Galosh complexes with thirty-two of the interceptor missiles. In regard to the Tallinn system, posture statements after fiscal 1973 dropped any reference to the "upgrading" question. The NATO designation for the SA-5 missile, Griffon, was also quietly changed to Gammon in order to rid the missile of identification with the earlier Tallinn dispute. For their part the Russians have continued to increase their SA-5 deployment at a rate of about one hundred launchers a year over 1970–1975 and then two hundred launchers in 1975–1976. Without an ABM rationale, and given the U.S. bomber doctrine of low-level penetration, against which the SA-5 has very little capability, the only apparent role for the Gammon is against U.S. SR-71 reconnaissance aircraft and high-flying Hound Dog air-to-surface missiles launched from SAC aircraft. Neither function would seem to require the approximately eighteen hundred SA-5 missiles thought to be in place. Thus doubts about "SAM upgrading" persist. From 1972–1975 there has been testing of a short-range interceptor missle, in conjunction with the SA-5 radar. Whether this is the SA-5, a modified SA-5, or a new "hypersonic" interceptor is not clear from the evidence available to the public. In addition there are reports of the development, beginning in 1974, of a "transportable" ABM radar called the X-3. Built around several trailers, the X-3 reportedly can be activated within several months, rather than the years needed to construct conventional, large radars. The system is also thought to incorporate computer technology more advanced than the Soviets were previously thought to possess. However the X-3 is also thought to be hampered by relatively low power output, which would limit its range and ability to discriminate real from decoy targets.

These indications point to a Soviet interest in actually "upgrading" the old Tallinn technology, although the fact remains that, even were the SA-5 Gammon to be "upgraded" with improved radars and computers, what the Soviets would then have would be an inferior ABM system purchased at substantial cost. The SA-5 could also be used as a base for deployment of a newer "hypersonic" interceptor missile, but again replacement of eighteen hundred SA-5 missiles would be tremendously expensive.

In 1978 the public version of the posture statement noted that Galosh was being maintained in partially operational status and that "advanced ABM systems" remained in development. There were press reports of an intense effort to design an ABM defense with large hypersonic interceptors, more accurate radars, and better command and control that would be capable of rapid activation in case of need. The Joint Chiefs also warned that the Soviets were improving their early warning and engagement radars and developing new missile system components. In 1980 there were reports of construction of a modern phased array radar near Moscow for tracking and engagement purposes, but still eighteen months from completion. The relevant national estimate, NIE 11-3-80, is reported to conclude that the Russians might be capable of deploying "a high quality thick bank of BMD systems" within a year of the time that their activity became unmistakable to U.S. intelligence.[17]

Whatever the case with present Soviet developments it is true that progress in BMD has not been rapid in either Russia or the United States. In over two decades of effort the Soviets have not been able to field an ABM of greater than marginal capability. The U.S. systems embodied in Nike-X, Sentinel, Safeguard, and the 1970s research and development program called Site Defense have been more advanced than the Russian but still incapable of fending off a ballistic attack. All ABM concepts based on missile interceptors have been susceptible to saturation by large-scale attacks, while there have also been crucial weaknesses in radar and data-handling capabilities.

The existence of this anachronistic Tallinn system alongside a slowly moving ABM effort created the basic area of ambiguity that confronted U.S. intelligence. If Tallinn was not an ABM it was not "rational." If it could be "upgraded" then perhaps it could be made "rational" and its costs transformed from a wasteful boondoggle for Soviet defense industries into a functional component of Soviet defenses. But those intelligence agencies that viewed Tallinn as an ABM were most directly interested in the matter. The Army was using the existence of Tallinn to argue for Nike-X. The Air Force would have the mission of penetrating the Tallinn defense in case of a war. DDR&E had the role of developing technology to counter such Soviet weapons.

For its part the CIA was the earliest to hold to a SAM projection for the Tallinn system. CIA was also fairly consistent in opposing the bleak interpretations made by some of the military services. But trying to prove the Tallinn had *no* ABM capability was a mistake. In the face of strong service interests, with MIRV and Nike-X hanging in the balance, a balanced approach was doubly difficult.

Some perplexing questions still remain. Why anyone believed there could be a Soviet "lead" in ABM is one, given the practical military ineffectiveness of all BMD schemes at that time. Another is why intelligence expected the expansion of Galosh projected across several NIEs, when that Soviet program proceeded at such a slow pace and was, in fact, curtailed even before it became operational. A final question, which may never be answered, concerns the Soviets themselves: why did they continue a strong Tallinn program for many years despite the apparent lack of rationale for such an air defense weapon? Moreover, once the U.S. debate on Tallinn became known to the Soviets it could be seen that deployment heightened U.S. fears. Why, under these circumstances, did the Soviets continue to field additional SA-5 missiles through the 1970s?

CHAPTER ELEVEN
INTELLIGENCE ORGANIZATION AND RESOURCES IN THE 1960s

The single most important trend in U.S. intelligence resources throughout the 1960s was the improvement and increasing sophistication of the technical collection programs, which burgeoned with new technologies and novel methodologies. Much as the U-2 had been the single major resource in the 1950s, now the satellites supplied important coverage of Russia. Satellites were useful for more than just taking pictures; their capabilities also included early warning, nuclear test monitoring, rapid communications and interception of others' communications, weather, mapping, and nuclear-strike planning.

Corona and SAMOS were only the first of a long series of reconnaissance satellites stretching to the present day. Three of them were orbited just during the Cuban crisis, in addition to the United States' first geodetic satellite, Anna, which collected magnetic field information necessary to missile targeting. In the earliest years, proud of its space accomplishments, the U.S. would routinely announce satellite launchings. The practice ended in 1964, and there would be little public discussion by officials of intelligence satellites for the next fifteen years.

By 1963–1964 the satellite programs were fully developed, with the U.S. engaged in a broad array of intelligence-related satellite activities. Two types of photographic satellites were developed, one for large-scale "area" surveillance, the other for special, high-resolution "close look" coverage. The number of launchings peaked as early as 1964, when the U.S. put thirty-eight intelligence-related satellites into space. Launching activity remained at this high level for several years, then dropped off, because the newer satellites achieved progressively lengthened lifetimes for each orbital vehicle—the average lifetime in 1966 was a week or two, a decade later it stood at fifty-seven days—and rather than one film capsule would carry a number of them.

On May 26, 1962, President Kennedy ordered Secretary of State Rusk to establish an interagency committee to review the political aspects of American policy on reconnaissance satellites. The Soviets were expected to demand prohibition of reconnaissance satellites in the United Nations and the administration needed to have a response. Thus came about the "NSAM 156 Committee," named after the NSC directive that had established it. The committee rapidly agreed on eighteen recommendations, but there was no agreement on an arms control proposal for a ban on "weapons of mass destruction" in outer space. The State Department and Arms Control and Disarmament Agency (ACDA) proposed the measure, but the Defense Department opposed any ban that was not part of "general and complete disarmament," which a decade of intermittent negotiations among the major powers had brought no closer. For its part the intelligence community feared that an international treaty on outer space might affect information collection.

In July President Kennedy ordered more detailed examination of a space weapons ban. This was still opposed by the Joint Chiefs and the Pentagon along with the CIA, represented by Deputy Director Herbert Scoville, and the National Reconnaissance Office under Joseph Charyk, undersecretary of the Air Force. In time, however, the Soviets developed their own photographic satellites and no longer wished a ban on them. A resolution banning "weapons of mass destruction" from outer space passed the United Nations General Assembly in 1963 and was converted into a treaty by President Johnson and the Soviets during 1967.

It will be recalled that in the Eisenhower administration the space-program proposals had multiplied quickly. Many of these were inherited by Kennedy, who also supported NASA with his promise that America would reach the moon within the decade. Kennedy attempted to regulate the space programs by delegating responsibility: NASA received control of all manned spacecraft, the Air Force all unmanned spacecraft. The National Reconnaissance Office (NRO) acted as executive agent for the Air Force in anything related to "special projects," as the reconnaissance satellites were called. DDR&E also had a role in "special projects" development, with an executive assistant for program management and membership on a committee with the secretary of the Air Force and the director of central intelligence, which issued guidance for intelligence research and development.

One early promising program was the Manned Orbital Laboratory (MOL) announced by Secretary McNamara in December 1963. This was to be a large spacecraft (or small space station) on which astronauts could live for extended periods. There were a number of possible military applications for MOL, among them identifying satellites in space, experiments on weaponry in space, tests of the accuracy achievable by orbital bombardment systems, and command and control of military operations in wartime. Intelligence uses were also legion. Photography was one. Another was "ferreting" out electronics intelligence (ELINT) transmissions, for which it was thought that MOL might be especially valuable since at the time separate satellites were required to identify sources and to intercept their transmissions. The CIA fought hard for control over MOL as a successor to the U-2. President Johnson approved MOL on August 28, 1965, but CIA was made to share it with the Air Force and other interested parties.

The prime contractor on the MOL program was McDonnell Douglas, which was to build five stations for a total of $1.5 billion. Martin Marietta had a supporting contract to develop a Titan III-M missile as booster for the satellite. Crew would be flown up aboard Gemini spacecraft. The MOL was expected to weigh twenty-five thousand pounds of which only five thousand pounds could be reconnaissance equipment. Planned weight grew as the Pentagon wanted more things on MOL—it attained thirty thousand pounds by the summer of 1966. Cost also inflated: to $2.2 billion by spring 1967 and $3 billion in 1969. The date for initial operating capability slipped as far ahead as 1970–1971. There was a standing joke that the only reason for MOL was to keep the Titan III-M on the boards, itself expected to cost another $2 billion. Finally it transpired that MOL's reconnaissance payload was exceeded by the third-generation satellites, while new "ferret" satellites appeared to take up its ELINT function. MOL never flew except in dummy form, and it was canceled on June 10, 1969, after $1.612 billion had already been spent on the program.

A more successful if equally expensive effort was the new satellite, originally the Low-Altitude Surveillance Platform (LASP). Advances in photographic technology made possible an "articulated" lens structure, which greatly increased focal length, and thus ground resolution.[1] New films and methods, including infrared and multispectral photography, similarly increased information obtained from pictures. LASP was developed as Program 647, given the nickname "Big Bird." Cost figures are classified still but must have been considerable, some claim billions. The first "Big Bird" was launched on June 16, 1971, by a Titan III-D and had an orbital lifetime of fifty-two days. By all accounts the satellite and its advanced version Key Hole have been highly successful. One launched in 1976 was in operation over three hundred days. In 1977, for the first time, two Key Hole satellites were launched at the same time, together with attachments for ELINT ferreting.

One rationale for satellite development was the vulnerability of manned reconnaissance aircraft and resulting danger to their crews. Indeed, between 1950 and May 1964 some twenty-six aircraft and 108 crewmen were lost on intelligence missions. But increased reliance on satellites did not eliminate the need for the aircraft. Rather, with area satellite coverage, planes took detailed pictures in much the same way as "close look" satellites. Planes also covered those areas deemed too difficult or expensive for satellite use. The U-2 remained in operation under SAC, while a half dozen of the planes were given to the Nationalist Chinese for coverage of mainland China. But the U-2 was supplemented by a new aircraft, one more capable of survival in hostile airspace. This plane's existence was revealed by President Johnson in a February 1964 news conference. Called the SR-71, it set a number of world speed and altitude records in May 1965.

The SR-71 concept originated in 1958. Intelligence officials could already foresee the obsolescence of the U-2, but were not yet sure that satellites could replace it. Bissell and Allen Dulles sought Eisenhower's approval for a follow-on aircraft and the President approved. Like the U-2, the SR-71 was a product of "Kelly" Johnson's Lockheed "Skunkworks" at Burbank. It was designed by Lockheed in conjunction with CIA's Development Projects Division and tested at Watertown Strip. The aerospace technology of the SR-71 was the same vintage as the B-70 bomber. It was a highly capable aircraft with a speed in excess of Mach 3, a ceiling of eighty thousand feet, and a substantial suite of electronic countermeasure equipment, eventually optimized against the SA-5 Gammon missile. The plane was initially called the A-11 and some thought was given to using it as an interceptor.

The first of the A-11's flew in April 1961. It was a twin-engine plane over twice as long as its wingspan and with a concave fuselage shape, mostly of titanium in order to withstand skin temperatures four hundred to five hundred degrees Fahrenheit. Each of its engines developed forty-two thousand pounds of thrust. Its speed was accomplished at the expense of range, a full fuel load being good for only about three hours at speed. There was a two-man crew made up of a pilot and a reconnaissance systems officer, each of whom typically would have had several thousand hours' flight-time before going into the SR-71 program. In its intelligence configuration the SR-71 was fitted with the best available cameras, ELINT receivers, and a novel technology called side-looking radar (SLAR), and recorders to store the information collected.

Titanium metal, used in constructing the SR-71, is difficult to machine and there were difficulties producing the aircraft. By early 1964 the CIA had taken delivery on several SR-71's and leased them back to Lockheed for further testing. Calling it Ox Cart in internal documents, the Joint Chiefs recommended deployment in planning for the fiscal 1966 budget. McNamara is said to have opposed it but he was overruled by President Johnson. It was after an NSC discussion in 1964 that LBJ first revealed the SR-71.

The advent of the SR-71 again called forth the long-standing CIA-Air Force differences over reconnaissance aircraft operations. The Air Force had been relegated to logistics support of the U-2 until it had gotten its own U-2 force. Now the Air Force wanted control of Ox Cart from the beginning. The conflict was resolved at the NSC level in 1967, and the Air Force won. About thirty-five SR-71 "Blackbird" aircraft were produced. They were assigned to SAC's 9th Strategic Reconnaissance Wing at Beale Air Force Base, California.

The planes are thought to have carried out missions over Southeast Asia, China, the Middle East, South Africa, and Cuba. One of Ox Cart's earliest missions was to photograph sites that were feared to be Red Chinese MRBMs going into position. Missions flown from British airbases as an aspect of Anglo-American cooperation received the code name Poppy, and SR-71's from the British base at Cyprus obtained important photo coverage in the 1967 and 1973 Middle East wars. The "Blackbird" is also thought to have been used to verify the presence of South African nuclear testing facilities in the Kalahari Desert in 1978.

Although Soviet airspace has been off limits to U.S. reconnaissance aircraft by presidential order since January 1961, it is likely that the SR-71's have conducted peripheral flights along Soviet borders. A defector from Russia who flew MIG-25's for the Soviet Air Force has commented upon how Soviet commanders resent their inability to combat the SR-71. Over eight hundred SAM missiles are reported to have been fired at SR-71's since the plane went into action but no "Blackbirds" are known to have been lost in action. Ox Cart has not been a panacea, however. The planes are difficult to maintain and expensive to operate. There have been operational losses, especially in the early years. Four SR-71's are known to have crashed by 1968 and overall losses by 1979 were reported at nine reconnaissance variants plus one of the YF-12 prototype aircraft. The "Blackbird" still works out of Beale Air Force Base. Since 1978 the United States has had a new reconnaissance aircraft under development, a modified and updated U-2R, which is expected to be optimized for ELINT rather than photographic missions.

.   .   .

The Navy has also been a major participant in intelligence collection. Naval aircraft participated in the peripheral flights along Soviet borders while ships were put in position to monitor the Russian ICBM tests. Another program in the early 1960s was the temporary use of warships for ELINT patrols off hostile coasts. Such cruises were made off Viet Nam, China, North Korea, and the Soviet Union. The destroyer cruises were called De Soto patrols, and generally involved outfitting the ships with extra detachments of communications personnel and equipment from the Naval Security Group, the Navy component of the NSA. At the time of the 1964 Gulf of Tonkin Incident, which marked a crucial escalation of the U.S. involvement in Viet Nam, the destroyers *Maddox* and *C. Turner Joy,* which claimed to have been attacked by North Vietnamese torpedo boats, were embarked on De Soto patrols.

Some naval officers opposed the De Soto patrols because they diverted combatant ships from other duties. The Tonkin Gulf Incident brought the end of the patrols. In the spring of 1965 Dr. Eugene B. Fubini, deputy to the DDR&E, recommended replacing temporary-duty warships with naval craft dedicated to ELINT interception. A start was made with the conversion of several Victory ships left over from World War II. Then three trawlers were converted at a cost of $10 million under the fiscal 1967 budget. One of the Victory-ship intelligence vessels, the U.S.S. *Liberty,* was bombed and badly damaged in the 1967 Middle East war. One of the trawlers, U.S.S. *Pueblo,* was captured in international waters off North Korea in January 1968. By 1968 the total number of U.S. servicemen killed in naval and aircraft incidents related to intelligence collection had risen to 225.

The Navy did not restrict itself to the use of surface vessels for intelligence missions. In operation Holystone, which was conducted from the early 1960s through the mid-1970s, nuclear-powered submarines of the "Sturgeon" class were fitted with additional NSA equipment and personnel. Missions were conducted along Soviet coasts and in territorial waters. Press accounts assert that Holystone produced much information of value to naval operations, allowed the U.S. to land agents on Soviet shores, and to tap telephone cables directly inside the Soviet naval base at Vladivostok. Holystone intelligence is also said to have included readouts of "various computer calculations and signals that the Russians put into effect before firing their long- and short-range submarine missile[s] on tests."[2]

The main difficulty with the Navy reconnaissance efforts was the risk to which participating ships and crews were exposed. Aside from the question of whether the Tonkin Gulf De Soto patrols had been intended to be deliberately provocative, the fact is that Brigadier General Steakley's National Reconnaissance Office (NRO) had rated the *Pueblo* cruise a "low risk" mission. In the *Liberty* incident messages complaining of harassment and mounting danger were not answered until after the ship had been attacked. Holystone involved a number of similar incidents. There was one in which a U.S. submarine attempted to surface in the middle of a Soviet naval task force; there were at least nine actual collisions between Holystone submarines and other ships; and on 110 occasions between 1965 and 1975 it is possible that Holystone submarines were detected by hostile ships. Despite this the military risk associated with the patrols was never rated as other than "low" by the Navy.

Under General Gordon Blake in the early 1960s, the NSA ground stations were supplemented by two new ones constructed in Iran in the 1960s, although the Peshawar base was lost in 1969 when the lease ran out and the Pakistani government refused to renew it. The Iranian stations, equipped with the latest over-the-horizon (OTH) radars, were effective replacements for Peshawar and furnished coverage of Soviet activity at Tyuratam. Plans for the Iranian stations mushroomed and under Project Ibex the U.S. contemplated increasing the number of installations from two to eleven at a cost of over one billion dollars. There was a struggle between CIA and the Air Force Security Service, which had operated Peshawar, over who would control the Iranian stations. The CIA won the battle and contracts went to Rockwell International in 1975 for construction, which proceeded under the "cover" of use by Iranian intelligence. But Ibex was quietly abandoned after the August 1976 murders of three Rockwell employees working on the project in Teheran. Other facilities operated by the services for NSA were located at Kagnew (Ethiopia) until 1970, Crete, Brindisi (Italy), Darmstadt and Berlinhof (West Germany), and Chicksands (Britain).

The NSA collected so much ELINT material from Naval intelligence, peripheral flight programs, the "ferret" ELINT satellites, and ground stations, that it could not process all of it even with the aid of large computers and skilled manpower. Already in the early 1960s there were boxcars on the tracks outside NSA headquarters filled with tapes that had not been analyzed, some in codes that had never been broken. In 1964 there was consideration given to dispensing with this—McCone's National Intelligence Programs Evaluation (NIPE) staff was not sure the material was worth the funds spent for storage. Eugene Fubini of DDR&E sided with the NSA belief that it was. A consultant study was done by a group under Richard Bissell, by now retired and working at the Institute for Defense Analysis. The results supported Fubini and the NSA, which continues to store unprocessed tape. Even by 1978 the total number of personnel within the intelligence community who specialize in computer analysis of the intercepted tapes numbered only about four thousand. There is still no alternative to storing materials that cannot immediately be processed. And the volume of such material must still be substantial.

While the NSA tried to cope with its masses of raw information, the DIA moved to establish itself within the intelligence community. DIA had been very effective in the Cuban crisis and its role was subsequently enhanced. The first active unit at DIA was a general Estimates Division. On November 2, 1962, McNamara directed General Carroll to take control of the Army Strategic Intelligence School and the Navy Intelligence School Postgraduate Department to form a Defense Intelligence School.[3] Shortly afterward DIA was given responsibility for all Pentagon mapping, geodesy, and vulnerability calculations. A further step followed on December first when the defense secretary issued his directive 5105.28, giving DIA general management authority for technical intelligence programs and the task of "analytical support" for the Office of the Secretary, the Joint Chiefs, and DDR&E. Under this order DIA would "provide a central point at which the technical intelligence findings of the services [could] be synthesized, reviewed, and evaluated . . . in accordance with priority needs such as missiles, space, and antisubmarine warfare."[4] Intelligence production facilities would be integrated in a new DIA Production Center, located at Arlington Hall from January 1, 1963. The merging of separate Army and Navy groups with the new division a month later essentially completed the formation of DIA, whose budget rose to $43 million in fiscal 1965.

Robert McNamara's intention in forming DIA was to make it more difficult for interested services to produce biased estimates and to limit duplication in intelligence. McNamara had closely followed the lines of the 1960 Kirkpatrick Report, and as DIA took over service intelligence units, manpower authorizations for the services themselves were cut by the corresponding number of slots. But the defense secretary could do nothing about personnel, which DIA still drew from the services, and officers being seconded to DIA were acutely aware that they would have to return to their parent branches after their assignment at DIA was completed. Thus the element of service interest remained. A former official has been quoted putting it this way: " 'DIA was born old; McNamara just gathered the drones and put them all in one building.' "[5] An additional weakness of the arrangement was that the secretary of defense allowed DIA to report to him not directly but through the JCS. No doubt this was a concession to the Chiefs, who lost their JIG on July 1, 1963, when DIA was fully operational, but it had the effect of putting the defense-wide agency back under command of the individual service chiefs, each of whom still had an intelligence branch in his own service.

It was intended that DIA represent all defense components on the USIB, eliminating the service branches' membership, although this was not done until 1963. On December twenty-first of that year John McCone recommended to the NSC that DIA be included on the Intelligence Board beginning on New Year's Day. McNamara concurred but, predictably, there was opposition from the Chiefs. General Maxwell Taylor, JCS Chairman, reported to the NSC on Christmas Eve that

> the individual Chiefs are not in favor of this action, preferring to keep their own intelligence officers as members of USIB. In their discussion yesterday they decided to note the action being taken and indicate to the Secretary of Defense that they may desire to reopen the matter after a reasonable trial period.[6]

Implementation was again delayed. Not until February 4, 1964, was McGeorge Bundy, Johnson's special assistant for national security, informed that the President had approved the action. McCone then approached General Carroll and the two agreed that some form of continued participation by the services on USIB might be appropriate. McCone wrote to Bundy on March third:

> I am arranging to have the intelligence chiefs of the military departments attend as observers those USIB meetings which are of particular interest to them collectively or individually. In addition they will retain the prerogative of expressing divergent or alternative views of particular significance, to be footnoted in such USIB documents as National Intelligence Estimates, Special National Intelligence Estimates, and the Watch Committee reports.[7]

When USIB issued its own document formalizing the changes on March sixteenth, the services were "invited and encouraged to attend as observers" without distinction as to subject. The services were also assured that they would retain full privileges on all USIB subcommittees, on which "no immediate changes will be made."[8] No changes were ever made. The military intelligence branches kept their place in the working apparatus of the intelligence community and retained their right to dissent on NIEs as well. As a result there was no effective reduction of the military role in intelligence, which had been the original aim of the Kirkpatrick Report.

Regulating all the intelligence resources and organizations was the system for planning and managing information acquisition, the Priority

National Intelligence Objectives (PNIOs). Analysts themselves often thought that too many were employed and too much activity was oriented solely to generating "intelligence requirements"; a better job could probably have been done by a few experienced men, working with the available data, and therefore aware of what was missing. Instead intelligence requirements were the object of repeated studies and reorganization efforts.

The basic directive governing PNIOs was revised on August 14, 1963. Whereas previously officials charged with collection were asked to exercise judgment in setting requirements despite the overall priority given to subjects, the 1963 directive specified priority treatment for "certain specific critical substantive problems within the general body of the intelligence required for policy planning."[9] These items would be given preference for allocation of research and collection resources and personnel. "Tasking" managers would determine which information was necessary to answer a given question, what was already available, what could come from routine collection, as well as what would warrant a priority collection effort. An effort was made to identify major areas of interest for a five-year future period.

In 1964 a revision of the directive made a connection between PNIO priorities and intelligence research and development programs. The basic PNIO directives were now supposed to guide budget requests and hardware procurement. Another revision issued on July 1, 1966, tried to step back from this, to reduce the impact of PNIO lists on U.S. programs by abandoning the five-year collection plans and identifying for priority treatment only "the most critical substantive problems which confront the intelligence community as a whole."[10] Two years later a further revision of the PNIO directive defined the intelligence objectives as "those fundamental questions affecting national survival which taken together constitute the most critical long-range substantive problems confronting the intelligence community as a whole."[11]

This indecision on intelligence requirements led to a study group formed in 1966 under CIA Inspector General Hugh Cunningham, when for several months selected intelligence officers examined collection procedures. In the December 1966 Cunningham Report the main conclusion was simply that U.S. intelligence collected *too much* information. A good deal of it was useful only to low-level analysts. Although intelligence officers were commended for looking out for that one last scrap of information that makes the others fall into place—that is to say, the "jigsaw theory" of intelligence—the resulting situation was one in which the glut of information clogged the machine. Finished reports were so numerous that policy makers could not know which way to turn. At the same time analysts were so deeply immersed in the daily cable traffic that they missed broad trends of development. Even computer storage and retrieval systems could do more harm than good, unless drastically higher standards were set concerning what information was worth keeping on file.

The Cunningham Report was a source of some controversy at CIA, where a senior executive group formed in early 1967 to review the report. It was composed of the deputy directors and chaired by Admiral Rufus Taylor, the deputy director of central intelligence. Taylor could not get the directorate heads to agree upon the programatic implications of the study, probably because they resented the report's critical tone. After several lengthy meetings they concluded that the report had only marginal utility for CIA, and it was not even passed along to the Pentagon. However, some action was taken on the problem of the glut of intelligence. Whereas ninety percent of collection requests had been approved in 1966, by 1968 only seventy-three percent received approval, and the volume of requests itself was almost halved.

CHAPTER TWELVE
THE SOVIET MISSILE BUILDUP

The basic weakness in Soviet strategic power was sharply demonstrated in the Cuban Missile Crisis. Only improved offensive nuclear forces could match the considerable American lead in numbers and quality of nuclear forces. The United States had a new system coming into operation, the Minuteman ICBM, of which there had been twenty at the time of Cuba. In dispersed silos and with solid fuel propulsion the Minuteman gave the U.S. nuclear arsenal a further qualitative boost and increased the number of U.S. forces able to maintain a day-to-day alert posture.

American intelligence examined the distribution of power that prevailed in the aftermath of the Cuban confrontation in a short paper on trends in the world situation that was prepared by analyst Willard Mathias at the BNE. Board Chairman Sherman Kent passed the uncoordinated paper, which was not an intelligence estimate, along to officials at the NSC in July 1964. One factor in the new situation was the hardened missile, much less vulnerable than previous ICBM types. As the paper pointed out, "In this age of mobile striking forces and hardened missile sites, it does not appear possible to build a military force capable of destroying an enemy's capabilities and simultaneously protecting oneself from unacceptable damage." The only "valid and rational" concept was deterrence. Insofar as Cuba was concerned,

the Cuban affair following upon the failure of other Soviet foreign policy initiatives of the past few years must have caused the Soviet leaders to become somewhat disillusioned about the utility of the strategic military power which they had striven so hard to acquire. To be sure, possession of this power contributed greatly to Soviet prestige and established the USSR in a position of strength far above that of any other nation except the U.S.

But the Soviets almost certainly believed that an intercontinental striking capability plus an arsenal of high-yield nuclear weapons would bring tangible benefits. . . . They must have expected to achieve at least a better bargaining position and a greater capacity to frighten or blackmail smaller powers into acceding to Soviet wishes. This has not occurred; moreover, the U.S. in response increased the tempo and size of its own arms program, thus confronting the USSR with the need to pursue still more costly programs if it was not to fall further behind. Thus while strategic military power has become substantial on both sides, it has not been particularly useful in the achievement of objectives beyond that of maintaining the strategic balance itself.[1]

Of course no one was more aware of Soviet nuclear inferiority vis-à-vis the United States than the Soviets themselves. As the agent Colonel Penkovsky observed, "Right now we have a certain number of missiles with nuclear warheads . . . but these are single missiles, not in mass production, and they are far from perfect." Indeed, "as far as launching a planned missile attack to destroy definite targets is concerned, we are not yet capable of doing it."[2] After Cuba Khrushchev for the first time made a definite claim as to the number of Soviet ICBMs—80 to 120. But the estimates in 1962 credited the Soviets with only 75 ICBMs and there are some who hold that the Russians had no more than four ICBMs at the time. If so it is little wonder that the Soviets backed down in the Cuban crisis. Clearly any plans they might have had in 1957 and 1958 to deploy 225 of the SS-7 ICBMs had gone unfulfilled.

The Soviets were alarmed at the inferiority of their nuclear force, and some sign of this was given to Freeman Dyson, a consultant for the ACDA, at the Pugwash conference in London in 1962:

In private conversations the Russians spoke to me in anguished tones, begging me to make the American government understand the urgency of the situation. They said that big decisions were soon to be made in the Soviet Union which would make the control of the arms race far more difficult. They gave me to understand that if there was to be any meaningful disarmament agreement in our lifetimes, it must be now or never. I have no doubt that they then knew that the tremendous buildup of Soviet offensive forces . . . was just about to begin.[3]

Disarmament did not result from the Cuban fiasco, only the Partial Test Ban Treaty. The Soviets moved to rectify their ICBM weakness on a broad front. Not only would there be more Soviet missiles, but, for the first time, the Soviets deployed missiles in dispersed, hardened silos. It is also the first time that Soviet missiles, using storable liquid fuels, were able to maintain a force posture such that at any moment there could be a high proportion of the ICBM force in an "alert" configuration.

By 1963 McNamara reported the presence of ninety-one Soviet ICBMs. Most of these were of the older SS-6 model, the original Soviet ICBM, which had been the object of the "missile gap" dispute. The SS-6 had a considerable payload, or "throw-weight" capability, and was believed to have a warhead yield of about five megatons. This missile was generally inaccurate, unreliable, and required substantial time to prepare for launching due to the need for fueling each time the missile was brought to alert status. Moreover, this ICBM was positioned aboveground, in the open, with several missiles at each launching site and little provision for protection. In the parlance of nuclear theory, the SS-6 was a "first strike" weapon because it could not survive an attack.

Given the deficiencies of the SS-6 Russia had substantial interest in a more capable ICBM. Testing of an SS-7 was observed in 1961. At that time there was still no evidence of "hardened" Soviet forces, prepared to withstand the blast, radiation, and electromagnetic effects of a deto-nated nuclear weapon. Hardened forces were the foundation of a secure retaliatory capability in the nuclear age. The Americans hardened every ballistic missile they deployed after the Atlas-F. Minuteman, with its solid fuel, and resulting high alert capacity and better reliability, estab-lished a new standard for nuclear forces. The Soviet Strategic Rocket Forces' SS-7, though newer, did not measure up to Minuteman stan-dards when deployment began in 1962. The Russians did build hard-ened sites for some of their SS-7's, but these were not single dispersed silos (like Minuteman). They were clusters of several ballistic missiles in "bin" type shelters. The rockets had first to be raised to an upright position and then fueled, a process that could take hours. Minuteman could be fired in minutes. Hanson Baldwin told readers of *The New York Times* that the Russian SRF was so vulnerable that single nuclear blasts on Soviet "cluster" sites could destroy up to eight of the ICBMs.

Secretary of Defense McNamara offered some comments on Soviet offensive developments in February 1963, along with his budget for fis-cal 1964. The statement reflected the Kennedy administration outlook in the immediate wake of the demonstration of strength in Cuba. McNamara pointed out that

> by and large, the latest estimates of Soviet strategic forces projected for mid-1967 in the latest National Intelligence Estimate (NIE) are of the same order as those we used last year in developing our five-year Strategic Retal-iatory Forces Program.[4]

The formulation is significant because McNamara used it repeatedly in posture statements during his tenure. Actually the projection up to the year 1967 had been reduced over the range used in 1962, because of a reduction in the number of SS-7's the U.S. expected would be operational by that time. In addition the Americans expected the number of Soviet missiles in "soft" aboveground emplacements to increase. The 1962 prediction was 100–150; now intelligence projected 150–250 "soft" Soviet ICBMs in mid-1967.

In his posture statement the secretary of defense noted some disagreements within the intelligence community. General Alva R. Fitch's Army analysts argued for a much smaller projection, expecting 250–425 Soviet ICBMs by mid-1967 rather than the community figure of 300–600. On the other side the Air Force under General Robert Breitweiser believed in a larger Soviet force of 700–800 ICBMs. McNamara reconciled the programmatic implications of the differing claims with an early use of his "greater-than-expected threat" device:

> In our analyses we have used the high end of the range of the latest National Intelligence Estimates as the median case, and the Air Force estimate as the "high" case. These figures were then extrapolated through mid-1968, allowing for a further increase of the number of fully hardened ICBMs to 200.[5]

"Fully hardened" ICBMs were those in the single, dispersed silos. Analysts felt the Soviets would deploy a new missile in dispersed silos as soon as they had the capability to do so. There was even some optimism among Pentagon officials, who believed that the Soviets would react to international crises in a more restrained way once they had achieved a hardened second-strike force, since this would presumably reduce any propensity for confrontation arising from the vulnerability of Russian strategic forces.

On the other hand, some officials, including McNamara, preferred to believe that the Russians would be better off not to try matching the U.S. strategic missile capability. SAC added over 400 Minuteman missiles to its force in 1963 (see Table III) and it was evident that only a very massive Soviet ICBM program could catch up with the United States in missile numbers, not to mention quality. Under the prevailing strategic balance, went the assumption, the Soviet leadership would be "rational" to choose an ICBM force sufficient to guarantee second-strike capability rather than suffer the diversion of a fairly large share of Soviet military expenditures. Expectation of a Soviet "minimum deterrent" caused these observers to anticipate only moderate expansion of the Soviet Strategic Rocket Forces and they believed that the SRF's military goal was parity with the United States. A cautious stance was also en-

TABLE III. HISTORICAL MISSILE FORCES 1960–1972

Year	United States ICBMs	ICBMs	Number Increase	Percent Increase	Soviet Union Innovation	SLBMs	Number Increase	Innovation
1960	18	10–35	—	—	—	15	—	—
1961	63	50	15	33	—	24	9	—
1962	294	75	25	33	SS-7	27	3	SSN-5
1963	424	91	15	6	SS-8	27	—	—
1964	834	190	99	110	—	27	—	—
1965	854	224	35	6.5	—	27	—	—
1966	904	292	68	43	SS-11	27	—	—
1967	1054	570	278	100	SS-9	27	—	SSN-6
1968	1054	858	288	50	—	43	16	—
1969	1054	1028	170	20	SS-13	120	77	—
1970	1054	1299	271	26	—	232	112	—
1971	1054	1513	214	16	SS-9M4	376	144	—
1972	1054	1527	13	1	—	440	64	—

This table includes only SLBM launchers mounted in deployable nuclear submarines; an additional 80 launchers for the SSN-5 were available on diesel submarines in 1960, decreasing to 60 by 1972 with the retirement of older boats. Figures compiled by the author from various sources.

couraged by previous "overestimation" that resulted from the mistaken U.S. perceptions of the "missile gap" period. The NIE projection of 300–600 SRF missiles in 1962 probably reflected this to some degree.

In 1963 the Strategic Rocket Forces continued to field additional SS-7 ICBMs in both soft and "coffin" bin-type sites. The rate of deployment allowed the Soviets to double their SRF in one year, building it to 188 ICBMs in April 1964. The number of missiles deployed rose from fifteen in 1962–1963 to almost one hundred the following year. The Soviets also introduced a new ICBM missile, the SS-8 Sasin.

In his congressional presentation of early 1964 McNamara gave a most detailed explication of his need for long-range projections on Soviet force levels and the accuracy he attributed to them. Secretary McNamara's posture statement of March 4, 1964, stated that

> we must plan our forces well in advance of the time when they will be needed and, indeed, must now project our programs at least five years ahead. For the same reason we must also project our estimates of the enemy's forces over at least the same period. These longer-range projections of enemy capabilities must necessarily be highly uncertain, particularly since they deal with a time period beyond the production and deployment leadtimes of enemy weapon systems. We are estimating capabilities and attempting to anticipate deployment decisions which our opponents, themselves, may not yet have made.[6]

To reinforce the assertion that estimates could be quite inaccurate, McNamara explicitly discussed the "missile gap" NIEs. He gave the figures for Soviet ICBMs at mid-1963 contained in each of the 1959, 1960, and 1961 national estimates, and then compared them with the count of Soviet ICBMs in mid-1963, namely 100. All the NIE projections for mid-1963 dwarfed the actual number and McNamara, noted that "these facts should be kept in mind as we discuss estimates for the 1967–1969 period." He went on to inform Congress that the new projection for mid-1967 was reduced from that he had given Congress in 1963. The intelligence community now believed there would be 325–525 Soviet ICBMs on-launcher. There would be no reload missiles and the Soviet bin-type launchers would still be clustered with three per site. Intelligence expected that by mid-1969 the Soviet force would grow to 400–700 ICBMs, each with a nuclear yield in the six- to thirteen-megaton range, and with most of the growth in new or improved ICBMs placed in hardened, dispersed silos. McNamara also observed that liquid-fueled missiles, upon which the Soviets had based their force, were much more expensive to maintain than solid-fuel missiles like Minuteman, and were more difficult to keep at operational readiness. He insisted that the U.S. maintained a great lead in instant-reaction forces, an assertion powerfully supported by the fact that *all* of the 768 ICBMs in the U.S. nuclear force on July 1, 1964, maintained an "alert" posture of readiness (see Table II). There was as yet no evidence of Soviet ICBM dispersal into hardened silos, of Soviet development of a solid-fueled missile. In addition the Soviet force was imperfectly hardened and large elements of it were still vulnerable to a first strike. To compensate the SRF deployed large nuclear warheads on their available missiles to maximize the megatonnage of their expected residual forces.

In the course of 1964 analysts began to see substantial shifts in the Soviet strategic forces program. The appointment of Marshal Nikolai I. Krylov as the new commander of the SRF was announced on May 31, 1963, Then the SS-8 Sasin missile was exhibited for the first time, along with other missiles like Galosh, Griffon, and an early Soviet submarine-launched ballistic missile, in the Moscow military parade of November 7, 1964. There were indications the Soviets were building early-warning radars, which would help improve the combat readiness of their ICBMs, and over forty excavations had been started for what would evidently be their first dispersed hardened silos. At the same time intelligence knew of an ICBM under development with great thrust and a comparatively large payload. These indications were disquieting, even though the actual increase in SRF missiles over 1964 was again under a hundred ICBMs, with 225 ICBMs projected for early 1965.

The Soviet program shifts were the subject of NIE 11-8-64. Yet despite concern expressed that the Soviets might "leapfrog ahead some time in the future," McNamara's 1965 posture statement remained unconcerned. He reiterated the formula that the new national estimates were "of the same order as those of last year," but there was a reduction in the projection for mid-1967 together with an increase of that for 1970. For the first time the Air Force projection partially overlapped the community-agreed range. Most significantly, the assessment of the SS-8 ICBM changed. Previously it had been thought this missile was designed for an extra-large-yield warhead. As seen in November 1964, however, the SS-8 emerged as nothing more than a parallel design for an ICBM similar to the SS-7—in essence "twin" development programs, as it were.

Robert McNamara met with the editors of *U. S. News and World Report* for an interview which was published in April 1965. The defense secretary conceded that Russia had the ability to catch up with the U.S. in numbers of ICBMs by 1970, but he felt it was not possible to foretell how the Soviets might change their plans. McNamara believed the Russians would not challenge the U.S. to a quantitative ICBM race, and stated that "there is no indication" the Soviets would do so. The secretary cited the reliability of his intelligence with the statement that "the possibility of error [in estimates] is materially less than it has been at many times in the past because of the improvement of our intelligence collection methods."[7] Meanwhile, the Russians' 1965 May Day parade included what was described as a solid-fuel ICBM along with an MRBM believed to be a mobile land-based missile. In a November article the SRF deputy commander, General Vladimir Tolubko, emphasized the advantages of mobile missiles:

> The presence of mobile roving intercontinental rocket complexes precludes the possibility of space and air reconnaissance. No one can know the area of locality of such launching ramps, which increases the survival capacity of our strategic means.[8]

A number of missile silos had been started for a large ICBM, while one of these missiles was used in a test (that failed) seeking to develop a "fractional orbital bombardment system." General Tolubko, in a Tass interview, commented upon this capability, saying that "even more powerful rockets, which can deliver nuclear warheads over ballistic as well as orbital trajectories and are capable of maneuvering on trajectory, are under development."[9] Soviet rocket boosters were capable of lofting such weapons, as was demonstrated when large Proton boosters were used to orbit scientific satellites during 1965. There was also the beginning of silo construction on a large scale. In a July speech to the graduating class of a Soviet military school, Communist Party Chairman Leonid I. Brezhnev argued that the United States underestimated Soviet missile power. Personnel in the SRF had risen to some 180,000, a substantial increase over 1964. New developments included the deployment of the first new SS-11 Sego missiles, a small ICBM about the size of the Minuteman, and the large SS-9 Scarp. The Soviets also began to use a liquid fuel that could be stored indefinitely aboard missiles, thus shortening the reaction time necessary to bring Soviet ICBM forces to operational readiness.

Given the increased pace of the missile program the elaboration of NIE 11-8-65 was an unusually important intelligence exercise. Vice Admiral William F. Raborn replaced John McCone as director of central intelligence in April 1965. Secretary McNamara pressed for a novel type of "net" estimate, one that would assess the Soviet and U.S. programs comparatively, or at least provide comparable figures for Soviet and American spending in specified budget categories. Some CIA officials believed that this assignment would exacerbate difficulties with DIA over supply of information to the CIA from the military agencies. Sherman Kent also opposed comparative military assessments on the grounds that CIA would be drawn into the debate over the size and adequacy of planned U.S. forces. But CIA did begin to create a method for projecting Soviet military spending more accurately with a team under Edward Proctor in its Office of Economic Research.

One of John McCone's last actions was to make certain clarifications in the work of USIB subcommittees. One of these related directly to the interpretation of Soviet guided missiles intelligence. On April 23, 1965, he issued a directive, which noted that "no complete separation of areas of interest is desirable or possible," and authorized all departments and agencies to "make such studies as [they] believe necessary to supplement intelligence obtainable from other departments and agencies." The community was enjoined to "develop special competence in those [missile] intelligence fields directly related to [their] primary departmental responsibilities."[10] The directive also established a revised charter for the Guided Missiles and Astronautics Intelligence Committee (GMAIC) under the USIB. This committee, with full participation from the services, supplied assessments of the technical characteristics of the Soviet ICBMs at issue in 1965.

Those formulating a national estimate in 1965 would have to make judgments on three Soviet ICBM programs plus the conjectured mobile missile. Confronted with the mass of technical evidence, significant differences emerged among the analysts in the community who specialized in assessments of Soviet strategic forces. The CIA reacted to the SS-11 by forecasting it would become the main Russian missile and it predicted 200–250 SS-11's for mid-1968. General Carroll's DIA argued that the Russians were more likely to emphasize their large SS-9 ICBM, which could be used for orbital bombardment and could more easily be equipped with mutliple reentry vehicles. DIA expected the overall number of Soviet missiles to increase somewhat more slowly than did the CIA, but it, too, expected rapid expansion of Soviet effective capability.

Secretary McNamara reported on these conclusions in early 1966. In his posture statement for fiscal 1967 McNamara acknowledged evidence of the small SS-11 and called it a major change in U.S. projections. He claimed to have some evidence that the SS-11 had been deployed in advance of the completion of its development cycle. On the other hand there was no sign of a solid-fueled missile. McNamara repeated his usual formulation that the threat was similar to that of previous years. He presented the projections for fiscal year 1967. Intelligence now expected 528–618 hardened ICBMs in mid-1968 and 760–1000 by mid-1971. "Soft" Soviet ICBMs would decrease from 146 to 20–80 by 1971 because the Soviets were expected to dismantle their obsolete SS-7 and SS-8 missiles. Finally, the Russians were also expected to have 25 mobile ICBMs.

The 1965 NIE and 1966 posture statement mark the beginning of a period in which intelligence failed to predict successfully the size of the Soviet SRF. (A glance at Table IV, and comparison with actual missile numbers for the Soviets given in Table III, will show the degree to which the FY 1967 projections, and other estimates before 1970, differ from the deployed Soviet inventory by those dates.) The gravity of the situation was soon apparent. Already a year later McNamara was saying that the rate of construction had been faster than anticipated on the SS-11. The pace of the Sego program even accelerated further, much as Minuteman had gained momentum in the early to mid-1960s. There were a hundred new SS-11's deployed in 1966–1967 and almost 300 in 1967–1968. Ultimately this missile alone would outnumber Minuteman when the SS-11 force peaked at 1,040 missiles in the early 1970s. Some 115 of the missiles were deployed in Soviet IRBM fields. By that time, combined with the other types of Soviet missiles, including the SS-7's and SS-8's, none of which was dismantled, the overall total of Soviet ICBMs far surpassed those deployed in the United States.

Intelligence analysts and defense officials were slowly struck by the size of the Soviet ICBM effort. Policy makers beat a hasty rhetorical retreat when Robert McNamara abandoned "damage limitation" as a strategic consideration, given the large size of the Soviet force. Also abandoned was the notion that the Soviets would content themselves with a second-strike "minimal deterrent." Between 1967 and 1969, analysts argued instead that the Russians had resolved to achieve parity with the United States and would build to match the number of American ICBMs. A later version of this was that the Soviets would like a slight numerical lead for prestige purposes but would not continue to expand their forces indefinitely. These assumptions were mistaken and the Soviet buildup continued until it was halted by SALT I in 1972.

Each year the intelligence projection of future Soviet ICBM strength was revised upwards. The 1968 posture statement predicted 818–910 missiles for mid-1969 and 1020–1241 for mid-1972 but it expected the Russians would completely dismantle their "soft" SS-7 and SS-8 ICBMs. The one posture statement produced by Clark Clifford, that for fiscal year 1970, projected a range of 1144–1221 Russian missiles in mid-1970 and 1098–1330 for mid-1972. The Clifford statement, given in 1969, likewise expected phasing out of the "soft" ICBMs and the deployment of 20–50 mobile ICBMs by 1972. These numerical esti-

TABLE IV. THE NATIONAL INTELLIGENCE ESTIMATES 1966–1970

Intercontinental Ballistic Missiles (ICBMs)

Year of Estimate	Projected strength (mid-year) 1967	1968	1969	1970	1971
1966	420–476	514–582	505–695	509–792	499–844
1967	423–484	670–764	805–1010	775–1027	805–1079
1968	536–566	848–924	946–1038	949–1154	939–1190
1969	570	858	1038–1112	1158–1207	1181–1270
1970	570	858	1028	1262–1312	1360–1439

Submarine-launched Ballistic Missiles (SLBMs)

Year of Estimate	1967	1968	1969	1970	1971
1966	24–30	24–42	24–78	24–114	30–138
1967	21	29	37–53	61–85	85–117
1968	24–27	43–46	75–94	123–158	187–238
1969	27	43	94–110	158–238	222–366
1970	27	43	110–126	184–248	296–376

The count on SLBMs includes only those missiles mounted in deployable nuclear submarines.

Source: Secretary of Defense Melvin Laird. Fiscal Year 1971 Classified Posture Statement, March 2, 1970, p. A-1.

mates were all exceeded by Soviet performance even though some expectations as to Soviet qualitative improvements, such as the prediction of a mobile ICBM, were not fulfilled.

The intelligence community has been roundly criticized for this period of underestimation of the Soviet offensive forces. These critiques were sanctioned by the Nixon administration, when Defense Secretary Melvin Laird mounted a frontal attack on the accuracy of estimates on Soviet forces, in 1970. Laird pointed out that

> the situation caused by the continuing rapid expansion of Soviet strategic offensive forces is a matter of serious concern. For some time, the Soviet forces which became operational in a given year have often exceeded the previous intelligence projections for that year.[11]

To back up his contention, Laird released the national estimate projections from 1966 through 1970. Laird confined his own predictions to the observation that there was now no consensus on what the maximum Soviet missile force would be, but that 1,300 ICBMs should be taken as the minimal projection of SRF inventory. The secretary of defense concluded by saying that if the Russians continued to deploy at current rates, by the mid-1970s they could have as many as 2,500 ICBMs.

The Soviet buildup continued in 1970 with the addition of 271 ICBMs, mostly SS-11's. It was one of the peak years of Soviet force growth, although by this time the Russian missile force was so large that the expansion showed only as a relatively small percentage increase. They possessed about 1,300 operational ICBMs and, in addition, they had begun a program of emplacing a number of SS-11's in SRF intermediate-range missile fields. These indications caused alarm within the Nixon administration. Army Chief of Staff General William C. Westmoreland stated that the Russians had all but closed the "missile gap." Nixon, in his 1970 foreign policy report to Congress, also expressed great concern over Soviet strength and apparent continued activity. The Soviet Union responded in March 1970 with denials that it sought nuclear superiority over the United States. Melvin Laird emphasized the estimate of $18 billion in outlays for the SRF in 1969 and gave little credence to the Russian disclaimers. CIA Director Richard Helms told Cyrus Sulzberger at about this time that the Soviets were carefully building up their military to be ahead of the U.S. in most respects by 1975. Secretary of State William Rogers voiced a similar opinion at a July press conference.

During a meeting of the NSC on August 19, 1970, discussion apparently focused on the strategic balance in 1970 and the ways in which this differed from the balance prevailing during the 1962 Cuban crisis. According to another participant, National Security Advisor Henry A. Kissinger was forced to admit that the Soviets were aiming for superiority, with arms limitation (SALT) if they could get it, but regardless of the outcome of talks. In the ensuing weeks various questions were raised as to the adequacy of the American nuclear deterrent and to the possibility that U.S. ICBMs in fixed sites were becoming vulnerable to a Russian first strike. Consideration was given to new targeting doctrines for U.S. nuclear forces, to the possibilities for various forms of "limited" nuclear options. In early 1970 the administration put before Congress the rhetorical "limited" options question of whether a U.S. president in a war situation should be confronted with the sole option of ordering massive attacks only.

Melvin Laird continued to take a very strident stand against the Soviet threat. In numerous speeches the secretary of defense warned of Soviet force increases. In July 1970, when the U.S. became aware of recent silo excavation starts in Russia, Laird used intelligence to good effect when he was able publicly to deny reports that the Soviet Union had halted its ICBM buildup since the start of strategic arms limitation talks (SALT) at Helsinki in 1969. Earlier Laird had asserted in a speech that Russia was quadrupling its missile megatonnage compared to 1965. Reporters at the Pentagon were shown films of Soviet multiple-warhead missile tests. Only in late December did the Department of Defense confirm that the Russians had indeed halted work on half the thirty-four silos that were under construction. Even then, Laird maintained that the intelligence warranted no slowdown of U.S. strategic programs, especially deployment of MIRVed land-based and sea-based missiles.

After performing a thorough critique of the CIA national estimates Melvin Laird made no use of these documents in formulating his fiscal year 1972 posture statement. Instead he relied on DIA for the threat assessments which enabled him to cite a high 1970 figure for Soviet missile strength—1,440—by including those SS-11's that were going into Soviet IRBM fields. While noting the slowdown in Soviet deployment, he maintained this might be only apparent and that the Soviets were really preparing to deploy a modified or new ICBM missile. He anticipated perhaps 125 new ICBMs by mid-1972. For his outyear projection Laird gave figures from the latest of the quarterly defense intelligence projections for planning (DIPPs) produced by DIA as successor to the old Joint Analysis Group (JAG). The DIPPs showed the Soviets might have 1381–1407 ICBMs by 1972, 1362–1490 in 1974, and 1302–1604 for 1976. Laird noted that the DIPP assumed the Soviets would phase out their older SS-7 and SS-8 missiles. Laird's pessimism was echoed by Nixon in his own 1971 foreign policy report, drafted under Kissinger at the NSC, which warned that apparent Soviet deployment halts were only pauses in preparation for new arms efforts.

Another Soviet development materialized in 1971, only days after release of Nixon's foreign policy report to Congress. Photographs showed a number of silo excavation starts in five clusters arcing across Russia from the Polish border to the Chinese frontier. They appeared in Soviet missile fields containing both SS-11 and SS-9 missiles, and evidently would be as large as those housing SS-9 missiles. There were several interpretations of the evidence: perhaps the new silos would be launchers for the expected new missile; they might simply provide increased hardening for existing silo-based missiles; or they might be used to house improved command and control facilities. In May 1971 Pentagon officials speculated that the holes were intended for two new types of missiles, but the Soviets did not test any new missiles in 1971, and one modified missile judged available to them that year was not deployed. In October the ambiguities of the situation were enhanced by the appearance of yet a third type of silo start, the excavation being more than four feet wider than the largest previously known (for the SS-9). The Soviets were also known to be enlarging two of the test launchers at their Tyuratam test facility. By July 1971 there were twenty-five excavation starts in Soviet SS-9 fields and another sixty-six in fields housing the SS-11.

CIA now found itself in an uncomfortable position. Bypassed by the secretary of defense, it was accused of having an "arms control bias" that led working analysts to minimize or discount Soviet activities. Indeed, in 1971 it was CIA analysts who argued that the new silo excavations were intended to increase hardening for existing Soviet ICBMs. An investigation of intelligence, ordered by President Nixon and made by a group under the direction of Office of Management and Budget Director James R. Schlesinger supported the "arms control bias" charge against CIA. Melvin Laird continued to find that the Soviet program "far outdistances" even the reports he had given Congress. Dr. John Foster, the DDR&E, believed that the new Soviet capabilities would make U.S. weapons obsolete, and that Minuteman would be vulnerable by the late 1970s. Air Force officials feared American capabilities had reached a "critical period."

As it happened there were new ICBM missiles involved in the Soviet silo starts. On April 22, 1972, the CIA informed interested offices in the executive that Russia might be about to test a new-type ICBM. By 1973 it was apparent that there were four new Soviet missiles in the testing stage. These were brought forward despite the SALT I agreement of May 1972 signed by Richard Nixon and Soviet Chairman Leonid Brezhnev, which froze the number of ICBM launchers at then-current levels. This SALT agreement effectively reduced the difficulty of estimating of Soviet force growth by ruling out any increase, although successful verification of SALT would eventually become an intelligence issue in its own right.

Assumptions and Performance

        In June 1974 came the beginning of even more widespread criticism of intelligence performance on the Soviet estimates of the 1960s. Noted nuclear theorist Albert Wohlstetter presented a paper to the California Arms Control Seminar rejecting traditional concepts of the arms race. Wohlstetter chose to shatter the generalization that nations in an arms race invariably exaggerate the strength of their opponents. By analyzing the estimates given in posture statements between

1963 and 1972 and comparing the projections with actual Soviet deployment as subsequently determined, he showed that the number of Soviet missiles deployed exceeded the projections in many cases where "predictions beyond the observable" could be culled from the documents.[12]

Wohlstetter found that "in spite of the myth of invariable U.S. overestimation, we systematically underestimated the number of vehicles the Russians would deploy" over a period much longer than that of the "missile gap."[13] Further, the size of the miscalculation allegedly grew throughout the decade even as the quality of U.S. intelligence collection programs improved. Intelligence performance measured in the posture statements was quite poor: in forty-nine of fifty-one cases the number of Soviet ICBMs exceeded the mid-range of the predictions and in forty-two of those cases the actual deployment also was greater than the "high" predictions. Numerous figures showed that ICBM predictions at mid-range averaged sixty-seven percent of actual Soviet deployments. The individual limitations of analysts were said to be compounded by the fact that tours of duty in intelligence were shorter than the prediction periods themselves.

The effect of the Wohlstetter critique was electrifying. The papers were printed in the journals *Strategic Review* and *Foreign Policy,* and reproduced as a pamphlet called "Legends of the Arms Race." The public criticisms were used to brand the CIA with a reputation for shoddy estimative work, and the critique was taken up by other analysts, notably William T. Lee and William R. Van Cleave. Most recently it was favorably cited by Henry Kissinger in a memoir of his government service from 1969 to 1973.

Wohlstetter's analysis was scathing in its scope and implications, and the general point must be conceded that the intelligence community failed to predict the extent of the Soviet missile buildup. But further analysis suggests that the critique is highly misleading. One recent examination of intelligence on Soviet forces warns of the dangers in examining intelligence production by means of statistical analysis of a set of figures rather than by reference to the evidence, assumptions, and arguments current in the community at the time of the estimate. Beyond the "power of consensus" and the "pressure of conformity" to which Wohlstetter objected, remains the fact that consensus failed to encompass all issues.[14] This effort to present the evidence and arguments current in the 1960s shows in some detail that intelligence disputes indeed make more sense in their context than the Wohlstetter critique suggests. It also confirms that violent disagreements raged on other issues while the community was supposedly "conforming" to national estimates on Soviet ICBMs. While the NIEs were wrong on missile numbers, it does not follow either that Soviet ICBMs were the most vital intelligence subject or that conclusions on overall intelligence effectiveness should be drawn from their methods of evaluating Soviet missiles.

An important point to be made about the 1960s NIEs is that the estimators were engaged in an inherently complex task. Robert McNamara did not tire of reiterating that intelligence was anticipating decisions that Soviet leaders might not yet have made. Naturally analysts had to make assumptions about Soviet actions. Statistical analysis of the NIE figures, as done by Wohlstetter, fails to allow for this. For example, year after year the estimates assumed that the Russians would dismantle the old SS-7's and SS-8's as modern silo-based missiles were emplaced. In reality the Soviets did not do so and these ICBMs were replaced by submarine-launched missiles in the mid-1970s. (This single difference between assumption and reality accounts for over two hundred ICBMs in the "underestimates" after 1966.) A similar assumption was made that the Soviets *would* deploy mobile ICBMs, which they did not do. Most telling is the statistical impact of assumptions about Soviet bomber forces, which actually did best in the Wohlstetter analysis, with the mid-range of the NIEs standing at ninety-one percent of actual Soviet forces. Here the assumption was that the bombers would suffer nominal operational attrition and that, because the Russians were not emphasizing bombers, no new production would take place. In actual fact, the inventory of the Soviet Long-Range Air Force changed not at all for a decade. Thus this entire intelligence "error" is accounted for by the single assumption that aircraft would not be replaced.

Statistical analysis of the national estimates is also limited to the study of quantitative issues. Completely neglected was the qualitative dimension of the arms race. Many would agree that it was precisely the qualitative advances of the 1960s that were most important in the evolution of the nuclear balance. In most qualitative cases intelligence "overestimated," that is, predicted the appearance of some weapons system before it actually materialized. In all cases in which the predictions were either "overestimates" or were accurate, there were no systematic underestimates of Soviet qualitative developments.

Secretaries of defense systematically sought to "hedge" against numerical underestimates through the "greater than expected threat" and the "force-plus options." It is possible that the NIEs were never expected to be too accurate *on the numbers*. The point was well made by Chairman of the Joint Chiefs Admiral Thomas Moorer on February 25, 1972. Moorer opened by saying that estimates are always subject to some degree of uncertainty. It is possible to project through a year or so, said Moorer, because intelligence usually has a good idea of the time lag between the start of a deployment and operational status for major weapon systems. Beyond that time the difficulty increases because both the number of units an opponent might actually start in a period and the goals toward which he is building are unknowns. Projections of up to five years in the future can only give good indications of the kinds of weapons that might appear, given adequate information on Soviet activity and the parallel developments in the U.S. Beyond five years all the NIEs can do is to postulate the kinds of programs that might be economically and technically feasible for the adversary and would be strategically desirable. The clear implication is that qualitative rather than quantitative predictions are the most important contribution of the estimates.

CHAPTER THIRTEEN
THE SOVIET MIRV

The most striking feature of the multiple independently targetable reentry vehicle (MIRV) was its great attraction for a wide range of defense planners. Conceptually a MIRV weapon involves the use of a single ICBM booster to loft a number of warheads, or reentry vehicles (RVs) at the same time. The RVs are carried aboard a single platform called a postboost vehicle which controls guidance and aiming for each of the RVs, and it releases them sequentially. Unlike a simple multiple warhead (MRV), the MIRV warheads can each be separately aimed at different targets that are widely separated. The United States was the first to develop MIRV and the justification for so doing lay in the possibility that Soviet ABM could conceivably threaten the viability of "Assured Destruction." If the Russians also developed MIRV, especially a MIRV with high accuracy, United States ICBM forces could become vulnerable even inside their hardened silos and measures would have to be taken to address this threat. Clearly, then, the possibility of Soviet MIRV development was a key intelligence question and a prime issue for those defense planners who must "hedge" against Soviet MIRV deployment. Detecting the emergence of a Soviet MIRV was principally a matter of carefully watching Soviet research and development of new and modified ICBMs, and for this the intelligence community had long been refining its methods and organizations.

It was John McCone who first determined to establish an entire directorate for scientific intelligence matters, including both analytical components and those responsible for research and development of intelligence technologies. In 1962 McCone formed the Directorate of Research (DDR), but the reorganization plan was soon stymied when the older directorates successfully retained control of components supposed to go to DDR under the plan. The Directorate of Intelligence, for example, retained OSI. In 1963 McCone made another effort to consolidate the scientific intelligence components. This was the formation of the Directorate for Science and Technology (DDS&T) under Albert Wheelon, which this time incorporated OSI.

"Bud" Wheelon was a brilliant young scientist who had served in the Office of Scientific Intelligence since the late 1950s. He came to CIA from the Thompson-Ramo-Wooldridge (now TRW) Corporation, which did much missile work for the Air Force. Wheelon was aggressive in creating capabilities for DDS&T, and he moved it into missile intelligence in 1964 by drawing upon OSI to form a Foreign Military Space Analysis Center within DDS&T. This included a Defensive Division which performed analyses of Soviet ABM, and an Offensive Division which interpreted ICBM programs. Bruce Clark, an analyst with the DDI's Office of Current Intelligence, who was quite interested in Soviet strategic forces, moved over to DDS&T to head the Defensive Division. Sidney Graybeal, a former B-29 pilot who was one of CIA's first analysts of missiles intelligence, took over the Offensive Division. As CIA's deputy director for science and technology, Albert Wheelon himself headed the Guided Missiles and Astronautics Intelligence Committee (GMAIC) and coordinated the community-wide effort in this area.

In 1967, with the support of many at CIA and that of Robert Mc-Namara, R. Jack Smith, the deputy director of intelligence, laid the groundwork for creation of a component specifically oriented toward space analysis. Edward Proctor's military economics group and the Offensive Division from DDS&T were joined in the Office of Strategic Research (OSR) under Bruce Clark. Later consolidation added DDS&T's Defensive Division as well. By 1968 Clark's OSR had a full division concentrating on military space analysis which, in practice, amounted principally to monitoring Soviet activity.

While the CIA improved its analytical capabilities on military-space developments, the Air Force was also intensely interested in this subject. Both USAF's Washington headquarters and the intelligence branch of SAC at Offutt made studies of Soviet missile potential. Technical analyses were at first the responsibility of the Air Technical Intelligence Center (ATIC) located at Wright-Patterson Air Force Base in Ohio. During 1961, when Major General Robert Breitweiser headed USAF intelligence, the ATIC group was assigned to the Air Force research and development organization, the Air Force Systems Command, thus becoming part of the Foreign Technologies Division of that command. In analyses of Soviet missile tests FTD had the primary responsibility for interpreting communications intercepted from the Soviet rocket boosters to their ground controls. During the 1960s FTD became the main vehicle for Air Force organizational expansion in intelligence. By 1972 the Air Force had thirty-three thousand personnel assigned to intelligence with a budget of $2.2 billion.

Military intelligence staffs were naturally apprehensive about the growth of CIA analytical capabilities in the military space area. Much as the services had tried to keep CIA out of military intelligence in the 1950s, in the 1960s there was an effort to push the CIA back from involvement in military space analysis. This effort was led by the Air Force and focused upon the GMAIC. The guided-missiles committee, at the apex of the community structure for space analysis since the "missile gap" days, still performed technical studies on Soviet missile characteristics as a contribution to the NIEs. The GMAIC included representatives from the services, DIA, NSA, the AEC, and CIA. GMAIC papers were coordinated in much the same fashion as the national estimates, although they did not serve the same function of informing policy makers. Rather GMAIC worked to inform the intelligence community itself.

Some Air Force people evidently felt that GMAIC was really a tool designed to achieve CIA dominance over the missiles subject area, and argued that this USIB subcommittee should be abolished. Officers pointed to the recently formed DIA and argued it could perform the same work, uncolored by the thinking of any one military service. The issue was resolved in Washington at a very high level with the decision to keep GMAIC and also allow CIA to stay in the missiles business; McCone's April 1965 directive on guided missiles intelligence production confirmed the responsibility of "all USIB agencies," and further enjoined GMAIC to foster, develop, and maintain a "community approach" to problems of guided missiles intelligence.

The primary data source for reports on both the numbers of Soviet missiles and on their qualitative characteristics was the Soviet test programs. For numerical purposes information obtained from them was used mainly to determine what new missiles were at the point of deployment and which others would become available over a given future period, typically five years. In qualitative prediction the test data was the primary raw information upon which forecasts of weapon system characteristics would be based.

Vital information was obtained from the telemetry output of individual Russian missile tests. Telemetry is the radio transmission and recording at remote ground stations of readouts from various measuring devices installed in key missile subsystems. These data were vital to Russian missile designers in discovering and correcting flaws in rocket performance. But telemetry signals were simple radio emissions and so could be recorded by U.S. intelligence at its ground stations in Iran, Turkey, and Pakistan, and by ships and aircraft along the missile's trajectory and point of impact. Telemetry gave indications of the fuel burn-rate of the missile, its in-flight attitude, and the amount of structural stress on missile components. In combination with photographic imagery of a missile showing its size and features, telemetry coverage could lead to conclusions regarding the thrust developed by a rocket, and therefore its payload and throw-weight. It could furnish intelligence regarding the in-flight stability of a missile along its ballistic trajectory, and therefore its accuracy and reliability. Compared with radar plots of missile tests telemetry could provide a very accurate picture of missile system performance.

American intelligence made a conscious effort to make use of the expertise acquired by firms involved in ICBM programs in the U.S., both by hiring aerospace engineers from the firms and by contracting studies out to them. One contractor, the Thompson-Ramo-Wooldridge Corporation, was given so much work in this area that it formed a telemetry analysis group in its space technology laboratory especially to work with the Air Force, and later CIA. Such contracting prevented excessive reliance upon in-house intelligence analysts who, because of their work, could not always keep up with the latest advances in missile design in the U.S., and thus might miss signs of similar progress by the Soviets.

Satellite photography complemented telemetry interception. Pictures could be compared with telemetry to check hypotheses about the weight and size of missiles. Views of new missiles on the test pad could indicate the imminence of a test, enabling U.S. intelligence to alert other collection systems to gather data. The volume of an ICBM could be calculated from pictures, supplying a corrective for suppositions about Soviet launch-weight, thrust, and payload. In addition photography could detect modifications made by the Soviets in their test facilities and range instrumentation and so provide long-range warning of the emergence of new missiles.

Another important data resource was the radar tracking carried on by the Americans' own ground stations. In the 1960s the Pentagon, using the Air Force as executive agents, developed a novel OTH radar matched with a dedicated antenna of the "dish" type. OTH radars could follow objects along the curvature of the earth and thus could monitor missile tests during their crucial early moments as well as at the instant when the launch booster released its single or multiple payload in space. Observing Soviet ICBM tests was one of the earliest applications of OTH radars and they were installed at two Iranian ground stations, called Takman I and Takman II. Another OTH radar, called Cobra Dane, was constructed in the United States on Shemya Island in the Aleutians, an ideal location to observe the fall of Soviet reentry vehicles on the Kamchatka Peninsula and in the Pacific Ocean.

When advance warning was available, the U.S. stationed aircraft and ships in the vicinity of the impact area. There is also some evidence that U.S. intelligence, using deep-sea retrieval techniques in an operation called Sand Dollar, was able to recover actual Soviet reentry vehicles that had fallen to the floor of the Pacific Ocean. In a successful clandestine operation, Ha/Brink, in Indonesia in the early and mid-1960s, the CIA was able to acquire actual samples of Soviet military hardware including the SA-2 SAM missile. Examination of the samples told analysts much about the state of the art in Soviet electronics and guidance gadgetry. With these data sources and a sophisticated analytical organization, U.S. intelligence nevertheless had an extremely difficult time attempting to divine the qualitative characteristics of Soviet missiles.

While the United States was becoming attracted to MIRV there appeared indications of yet another Soviet ICBM development program in 1964. Intelligence decided this would definitely be a large ICBM, and Secretary McNamara so reported in January 1965. The missile was identified as the SS-9 and it was given the NATO code name Scarp. It was expected to become operational that same year, emplaced in dispersed silos and armed with a single twelve to twenty-five megaton warhead. Soviet emphasis upon large missiles was further confirmed by the appearance of the SS-10 Scrag, an equivalent missile to the SS-9 which was canceled due to reliance on corrosive cryogenic fuels rather than the storable type of liquid fuel introduced with the Scarp. The Soviets also introduced their large Proton space booster in 1965.

Why did the Soviets continue to rely on the large rockets? By 1965 their nuclear weapons were far more efficient and with accuracy improvements, they did not require such large warheads. Yet the SS-9 had a gross weight of 450,000 pounds and a throw-weight of about 15,000. Among observers there were a number of competing hypotheses as to why the Soviets had again built a large ICBM. One theory held that the Russians wanted to loft very high-yield warheads, to compensate for their inaccuracy in attacks on hardened targets. A variant on this notion was that the SS-9's were specifically intended to attack U.S. launch control centers, each of which controlled ten of SAC's Minuteman missiles. Another hypothesis held that the large warheads were intended simply for "city busting," thus maximizing Soviet residual megatonnage that could be sent in retaliation if the U.S. ever launched a first strike on Russia. A variant on this was that as a big rocket, the SS-9 would play to Russian cultural affinity, connoting a solid or good deterrent. A third notion was that Scarp's large warhead was intended to provide a propaganda advantage, enabling the Russians to claim possession of the ultimate "terror" weapon. Yet another hypothesis was that the large payload of the SS-9 Scarp could be intended to maximize the feasibility of future MIRVing by Soviet missile designers who were aware of the possibilities but hampered by crude production facilities. A corollary to this last hypothesis was that the large missile would also maximize payload in the MIRVed missile force at some future time when this capability had been achieved.

In the face of this American uncertainty, the Scarp program went forward. Before the end of 1965 there were sixty-six SS-9 silos under construction. As the deployment proceeded, for the first time the 1965 NIE projected a Soviet MIRV as an impending threat for the 1971 to 1975 period, with deployment expected in 1970. Analysts at the time were working entirely from the theoretical knowledge of aerospace engineers since no one, the U.S. included, had yet succeeded in creating a MIRV.

The 1965 NIE was produced to support defense planning for fiscal year 1967. At the Pentagon budget planners projected a "greater-than-expected threat" force of several hundred highly accurate MIRVed SS-9's and an effective Soviet BMD. To "hedge" against this putative threat, Robert McNamara recommended in the conclusion of his draft presidential memorandum to Lyndon Johnson that Minuteman III and Poseidon MIRV be deployed. In its comments on McNamara's proposal the Bureau of the Budget chose to criticize the MIRV recommendation. It conceded that such military developments were conceivable, but underlined the fact that the posited threat was greater than that contained in the NIE and assumed a rapid and simultaneous deployment by the Soviets across two major areas of sophisticated technology. It then argued that aspects of the proposed MIRV program were not responsive to the postulated threat in any case. In appending covering remarks Spurgeon Keeny of the NSC staff agreed that the "greater-than-expected threat" in the draft presidential memorandum was the product of an "extremely crude analysis" in concluding that an unMIRVed American ICBM force could be disarmed. Keeny had been with the NSC when Dwight D. Eisenhower made the original decision to harden land-based missiles, and he had learned much about the difficulties inherent in mounting a disarming first strike. Nevertheless, Keeny maintained that the Bureau of the Budget criticisms were weak ones.[1] Lyndon Johnson approved U.S. MIRV deployment and language detailing the "greater-than-expected threat" was written into the fiscal 1967 posture statement, which McNamara sent to Congress in early 1966.

As McNamara pointed out, by 1967 there was still no evidence of an emergent Soviet MIRV capability. Instead the Russians achieved operational status in 1967 with the SS-9 Mod 2, a missile with very high nuclear yield. The indicators suggested that the yield was designed to compensate for inaccuracy in attacks against U.S. missile launch control centers. The Scarp missile depended upon radio command guidance from the ground until after burnout of its main booster stage, and radio antennas located at SS-9 launch centers were oriented so as to be associated with azimuths likely to generate trajectories that would impact on the Minuteman fields. Dr. Harold Brown, who was secretary of the Air Force at this time, would tell an audience much later that " 'the more than two hundred SS-9's were almost surely targeted against the one hundred Minuteman launch control complexes, two missiles to a complex for reliability.' "[2] In 1967 the Air Force began a program to provide extreme hardening for the launch control facilities in SAC.

For their part the Soviets began to modify the Scarp, although they did not, at first, aim toward a MIRV capability. In 1966 they began to test a Mod 3 version of the SS-9, which could deliver nuclear weapons using an orbital rather than a ballistic trajectory, the so-called "fractional orbital bombardment system" (FOBS). The FOBS version of the SS-9 became operational in 1969 and eighteen of these ICBMs were deployed in silos at Tyuratam, a sign that the missiles might need intensive servicing. Under the unratified SALT II Treaty, the Soviets agreed to dismantle these FOBS missiles and their launchers. The logical follow-on to FOBS, a *multiple* orbital bombardment system, essentially an earth satellite armed with a nuclear bomb, has never appeared in Soviet tests or known deployed hardware.

Robert McNamara announced the FOBS development in a meeting with the press in early November 1967. At the time McNamara was not overly concerned with the system. The additional guidance and propulsion machinery required for a FOBS used up valuable payload and forced a reduction in the nuclear yield of the warhead. Also, the complex flight path followed by a FOBS would inevitably reduce the accuracy of the warhead and make it next to useless as a counterforce weapon.

It has been postulated that design work for the SS-9 Mod 4 began as early as 1963–1964 and that the manufacture of long lead-time components must have begun no later than 1966. In 1963 the technical omega of missile design had been the simple multiple warhead (MRV), the "shotgun" warhead that was on Polaris A-3, although the MIRV concept had received mention in American technical literature. Then in 1967 two Soviet military writers published a book on selective targeting strategies, which might be open to the Soviets if they deployed multiple

warheads. For U.S. planning a good deal hinged upon whether the new
Soviet missile would be MRV or MIRV. In 1967 the United States officially acknowledged its MIRV programs, so there could no longer be
any doubt that the Soviets were aware of MIRV's potential. Moreover,
the U.S. decision in late 1967 in favor of Sentinel ABM deployment
would naturally press the Soviets in the direction of multiple-warhead
deployment, if only to saturate an American BMD. The question was,
how long had the Russians known about MIRV and were they working
on their own already? The MIRV question was the subject of an NIE in
late 1967 and the paper was said to conclude that the USSR was giving
top priority to the development of multiple warheads for its large
ICBMs, and would be able to attain operational capability with a MIRV
in five to seven years' time.

Concern slowly spread from the Pentagon to the attentive public.
Press coverage of NIEs on the Soviet MIRV was one result. In a mid-
1967 article defense writer Richard J. Whalen, noted that the Soviets

> are fast approaching a critical point in the development of their ICBM force.
> If their missiles are equipped with the advanced warheads and the more
> accurate guidance systems known to be within their technical ability, their
> force could quickly become a real threat to the hardened Minuteman mis-
> siles that are the backbone of the U.S. deterrent.[3]

Whalen also mentioned that the SS-9 could theoretically be fitted with
ten or more MIRV warheads and that only the time needed to install a
missile silo, typically about eighteen months, separated the United
States from such a threat. Another paper produced in September 1967
by a group of former military officers and defense officials saw things
equally starkly:

> Warhead design affects missile efficiency. The USSR has tended to rely
> upon warheads of greater size and yield than the United States, partly com-
> pensating for lower accuracy. The United States was able to obtain a better
> yield-to-weight ratio making for a smaller warhead and requiring less lifting
> capacity. Now as defensive [sic] systems improve and achieve more versatil-
> ity, the large warhead and great lift of Soviet missiles provide the room to
> incorporate multiple warheads and maneuverable warheads into a single of-
> fensive package. The Soviet Union may have provided itself, even though
> unwittingly, with a means of expanding its delivery capability without in-
> creasing the number of missile carriers.[4]

But Robert McNamara, in his fiscal 1969 posture statement, reiterated that there was still no evidence of an effort to install multiple warheads, with or without independent aiming capacity, on the SS-9. Yet

there were suspicions in intelligence that something was afoot. From January 1 through June 30, 1968, the United States maintained reconnaissance satellites over Russia for 117 of 181 days, including forty-one consecutive days in January and February when CIA thought an SS-9 test from Tyuratam was imminent. In fact, on August 28, 1968, the Soviets conducted the first test of their SS-9 Mod 4, a Scarp missile carrying three individual warheads. In the 1968 NIE the conclusion was that the SS-9 "triplet," as it was called, lacked independent aim capability and was therefore a MRV, not a MIRV. McNamara's successor, Secretary of Defense Clark Clifford, held to the MRV interpretation; in the fiscal year 1970 posture statement he noted that the four tests made of the triplet were indicative of MRV capability similar to the Polaris A-3.

Four months earlier Clifford had told a Senate hearing how much improved were U.S. intelligence capabilities over past years. He emphasized, "I should also like the record to show that the estimates that we now give of the Soviet nuclear and strategic strength is [sic] presented in such a manner that I accept it and I believe it."[5] At the time the 1968 NIE on Soviet forces was in draft form and contained a judgment that the SS-9 "triplet" was an MRV. There were no dissents at the time, and NIE 11-8-68 was approved by the USIB on October second.

Telemetry analysis on the four "triplet" tests since 1968 was of course the responsibility of the Air Force's FTD under Colonel George R. Weinbrenner. His Systems Division developed the thesis that the Mod 4 might possess some primitive MIRV characteristics. In particular, if the Russians could delay the separation of each reentry vehicle from the launching platform for seconds or fractions of a second, they could alter slightly the ballistic paths of each successive one. Although warheads could not be independently aimed in this fashion, if chosen targets were close enough together, the Scarp warhead could be a MIRV "functional equivalent."

As an intelligence unit attached to USAF's Systems Command, the FTD reported both to intelligence headquarters and to the Office of the DDR&E. Dr. John Foster remained DDR&E in the Nixon administration, one of the few Pentagon officials who stayed on at high levels. Foster had been active in intelligence disputes since his 1965 appointment, most notably in that over the Tallinn line and "SAM Upgrading," which some observers feel DDR&E "invented." Foster had already expressed some doubt about the multiple warhead SS-9, and he was receptive to the FTD arguments on the intelligence data.

In 1968 congressional testimony the DDR&E had argued that the job of the research and development community was to anticipate what an intelligent adversary would do in the future, given unlimited funds. Now, in the spring of 1969, Foster apparently felt that the separation of impact points the Soviets might achieve with the SS-9 Mod 4, the nuclear weapon's "footprint" as it was called, could exactly match the dispersion pattern of Minuteman silos. Concern was heightened by the fact, disclosed in early 1969 satellite photographs, that the Soviets had begun excavations for additional silos in a new SS-9 field. Melvin Laird apparently was convinced. The "footprint" argument also won some support from DIA and the Air Force. The military consensus became that the Sentinel ABM, an unpopular program which many sought to cancel, should be reoriented to defend Minuteman rather than to protect cities.

The results of the policy review were the subject of an NSC meeting on March 5, 1969. National Security Assistant Henry A. Kissinger saw the ABM as a weapon system in search of a rationale, and he argued strenuously against it. The Joint Chiefs of Staff, however, recommended ABM for the defense of land-based missiles, and President Nixon supported them. On March fourteenth Nixon held a press conference to make a formal announcement of his decision to deploy a phased ABM he called Safeguard, with successive stages designed to correspond to assessments of the threat to U.S. ICBMs. Nixon also directed his Foreign Intelligence Advisory Board to make an annual study of the level of threat to supplement the analysis in the NIEs. The ABM would use the same components that had been developed for Nike-X and for Sentinel but the site locations and radar characteristics and numbers would be slightly shifted. The Safeguard appropriation request went to the Congress as a supplement to the fiscal year 1970 budget.

In addition to the budget Capitol Hill was deliberating on whether the Nuclear Non-Proliferation Treaty should be ratified. All these matters required a formal presentation of Pentagon thinking and the spring of 1969 should be seen as a major postwar watershed of nuclear strategic doctrine.

One of the central inquiries of 1969 was that of the Senate Foreign Relations Committee into the military implications of antiballistic missiles (ABM). Early in these hearings a string of witnesses, who had been directors of research and development or science advisors to Presidents Eisenhower, Kennedy, and Johnson, attested to the technical deficiencies of the proposed ABM. They were supported by a number of academic analysts of political and military affairs, and built an impressive case against Safeguard. Evidently the radars and command-control provisions of ABM were the weak links in the system. The radars were much more vulnerable than the Minuteman system they were supposed to protect; they would have been blinded, in addition, shortly after the first nuclear detonations; there was also no guarantee that they could successfully discriminate between incoming warheads, debris, and decoys if the Russians chose to use them. Safeguard radar sites would become obvious targets for attack because their destruction would make useless all the interceptor ABMs under their control. At the same time it was not clear that the computers could work fast enough, with enough variables, to cope with an ABM engagement. Defense could probably still be saturated, and it would be less expensive for the Russians to add additional warheads than it would be for the U.S. to add defense.

Melvin Laird went before the Foreign Relations Committee in the third week of March, supported by a full retinue, including Deputy Secretary Packard and DDR&E Foster. Laird first cited the increased Soviet threat and alluded to the fact that SS-9's were being emplaced as recently as December 1968. On March nineteenth he also appeared before the Senate Armed Services Committee in support of the budget. There he referred to the SS-9's "tremendous warhead" and said the Soviets were testing multiple warheads for it. David Packard filled in details since, on the Defense Program Review Committee, Packard had examined the SS-9 threat:

> Essentially the conclusion I came to is this—that if you look at the *present* level of SS-9 missiles, and their continuing buildup of these missiles, the survival of our Minuteman force could be endangered.[6]

Packard concluded from the way the Soviets were testing multiple warheads for the SS-9 that "this is very likely a program aimed at destroying our missile silos."[7] General Earle Wheeler, still Chairman of the JCS, agreed that "new" intelligence could change the powers' relative strategic positions in the mid-1970s. Two days later Laird told a House committee that with the large throw-weight of the SS-9 the Soviets "are going for a first strike capability, there is no question about that."[8]

The DDR&E John Foster described a scenario, set in the mid-1970s, when the Russians would have 420 Scarp missiles with triplet warheads, a reliability of eighty percent, and an accuracy of .25 nautical miles CEP. Such a force was allegedly capable of destroying ninety-five percent of Minuteman, and the Pentagon was worried that if the Soviets could calculate they had a theoretical ninety-five percent chance of eliminating U.S. missiles, they would no longer be deterred from launching nuclear war. At various times in the spring and summer of 1969 Foster cited the SS-9 projection for the mid-1970s at four hundred to five hundred or up to six hundred. Laird used the four-to-five-hundred range in his own statements. The secretary of defense also declassified and released alarming technical information on the SS-9 in March, and again in April 1969. This threat was said to require Safeguard employment as soon as possible to defend the ICBMs.

The Pentagon presentation made no effort to describe some of the difficulties inherent in actually mounting such an attack. For one thing, the scenario provided only one warhead to attack each ICBM silo; thus the warheads had better be *very* reliable. The only possibility of compensating for misses lay in what is called "reprograming," which requires both sophisticated computer capability and "real time" intelligence. The assumption that the Soviets, whose computers lagged far behind those of the U.S., would have a reprograming capability by the mid-1970s was far-fetched.[9] In addition, the entire SS-9 force then in place and under construction would have to be replaced by the Mod 4, and the Scarp force would have to be expanded considerably.

Nevertheless, if the Soviets could develop such capable forces, nuclear theory offered no guarantee that deterrence could be preserved. This was recognized at the NSC. Henry Kissinger determined to investigate the SS-9 Mod 4 "functional equivalency" question and he formed an NSC working group on the MRV/MIRV issue. Lawrence Lynn was put in charge of the MIRV Panel.

At the NSC, examination of the 1968 national estimate did not clarify the basis of the disagreement. The NIE stated that Mod 4 was not a MIRV but did not discuss whether it was "functionally equivalent." The implication in NIE 11-8-68 was that the Scarp Mod 4 was not a counterforce weapon since the estimate explicitly concluded the Soviets were not seeking a first strike capability, a proposition explicitly contradicted by DDR&E. When Lynn attempted to examine these discrepancies with officials at CIA, some "reacted as if their professional integrity had been questioned, and as if close questioning by nonexperts was improper."[10] On April eighteenth Nixon noted at a press conference that "ever since the decision to deploy the ABM system called Sentinel in 1967, the intelligence estimates indicate that the Soviet capability with regard to their SS-9's, their nuclear missiles, [is] sixty percent higher than we thought then."[11]

While the NSC MIRV Panel reexamined the technical intelligence, the assertions of Secretary Laird and Dr. John Foster came under increasing criticism in Congress. A useful summary of the problems contained in the Foster scenario is a statement prepared by Dr. Carl Kaysen, who had been an NSC official during the Kennedy administration. In response to a question from Senator Stuart Symington (D-Missouri), Kaysen noted that Secretary Laird had used the annual posture statements and that

> to use these estimates of current and immediate future Soviet strength—which it neither revised nor disputed—to justify a threat in 1973 or 1974, administration spokesmen have simply projected a continued growth in numbers of Soviet missiles, especially the SS-9, at a high rate. Further, they have probably assumed, without explicitly so stating, that a substantial fraction of these would carry multiple, independently-aimable warheads, and also assumed, without any indication of supporting evidence, that these would be significantly more accurate than we now believe Soviet missiles to be.[12]

Kaysen thus noted discrepancies between the DOD testimony and the substance of intelligence previously included in the posture statements, especially that of Clark Clifford in January. The Senate was disturbed enough over these matters that in late April it queried the CIA about its position on the questions under discussion. Director of Central Intelligence Richard Helms replied on May seventh, confirming suspicions that there existed differences of opinion on the counterforce capability of the SS-9 triplet.

In a hearing before the Senate Armed Services Committee the next week, John Foster was challenged on his interpretation of the evidence. The DDR&E maintained that U.S. intelligence had generally agreed that the Russians would build a hundred or more of the large Scarps to ensure their second strike capability, and then large numbers of the SS-11 missiles to diversify their force and hedge against U.S. counterforce capability. However, contrary to expectations, after the advent of the SS-11 the Soviets continued installing additional SS-9's. Now Foster expected to see four hundred SS-9's by 1972 and some five hundred by 1975. While conceding that his scenario for disarming Minuteman assigned the Russians a rather high assumed accuracy, Foster insisted "I would like to say that I have no disagreements with the Central Intelligence Agency, nor has Secretary Packard or Secretary Laird." Yet, on May fourteenth, the DDR&E told the senators that "the continuing deployment of the large liquid-fueled SS-9 together with the development of new and more sophisticated reentry and targeting systems are consistent with the development of a first strike capability."[13]

This latest sally drew immediate fire from certain senators and from witnesses at the ABM hearings. Jerome Wiesner, former science advisor to Kennedy, charged that the administration was changing its intelligence predictions to suit its budgetary requests. There was even criticism from physicist Edward Teller of the nuclear weapons lab at

Livermore, who generally supported the Safeguard program. Senator Albert Gore (D-Tennessee) told reporters that "the National Intelligence Estimate does not concur with the statements made by Dr. Foster or by Mr. Laird." A reporter took Gore's comment to the Pentagon, where the spokesman

> at first said, "Mr. Laird's estimates are the National Intelligence Estimates." Later he amended this to say, "He uses the National Intelligence Estimates." Then he said he would have to check further after being informed that Senator Gore had said that Mr. Laird and Dr. Foster were "making statements that do not comport with the National Intelligence Estimates."[14]

When asked for his opinion, Committee Chairman J. William Fulbright (D-Arkansas) fully agreed with what Gore had said.

With the impending vote in Congress on Safeguard ABM appropriations, the White House considered it important to avoid any public expressions of disagreement between the Pentagon and CIA. Laird had already taken a public position, and he did not want his credibility challenged. At the CIA an estimate was being drafted, which was approved by the USIB on June 12, 1969. An intelligence memorandum was completed just in time for the NSC meeting on June thirteenth.

The memorandum contained the consensus judgment that, although the Soviet Union might be seeking more than strategic parity, it was not then striving for the capability to launch a first strike against the United States. Not only did the Soviets lack the intention, found the memo, but they also lacked the capability: the SS-9 triplet was found to be an MRV not functionally equivalent to MIRV and capable of hitting only a single aim point. This last feature provoked Kissinger to request that Helms make revisions, and so a fully coordinated estimate was returned to the CIA for rewrite. On June sixteenth Abbot Smith informed all holders of the estimate that it would be "editorially revised" by BNE to provide more discussion, pro and con, on the MIRV/MRV question.

As the CIA moved to rework its estimate, Laird presented an ABM statement before the Senate Appropriations Committee. He said that

> although we still have no conclusive evidence that these [Soviet] multiple reentry vehicles are independently aimed, the intelligence community considers it likely that the Soviets will go on with the development of MIRVs and install them on a new version of their SS-9 type ICBMs. Should they also greatly improve the accuracy of their smaller ICBMs, which the intelligence community considers possible, the survivability of our Minuteman force as presently deployed would be virtually nil by the mid- to late-1970s.[15]

It is noteworthy that Nixon himself now went so far as to refer to the SS-9's "footprint" and to make the functional-equivalent argument in a televised speech a couple of days later.

The Pentagon seemed to have drowned out the more cautious views on the SS-9, but at real political cost. An account of the contents of the national estimate leaked almost immediately to *The New York Times,* with the additional information that preliminary CIA analyses furnished Congress were very critical of the DOD position on the triplet. On Monday the twenty-third the Senate Foreign Relations Committee held a hearing with Laird and Richard Helms on intelligence and the ABM. Under stiff questioning from Fulbright, and Senators Symington, Gore, Frank Church (D-Idaho) and Clifford Case (R-New Jersey), Laird stuck to his contention of the "first strike" nature of the SS-9 Scarp, although he backed away somewhat from his previous claim that the Russian intention was to seek a disarming first strike capability. This was the core of an often stormy hearing. At one point Senator Symington remarked that "first strike capability is your ability to destroy the enemy and take as acceptable any losses he subsequently can give you."

Albert Gore then asked Laird, "What do you mean when you use that term first strike capability?"

"I mean the same thing."

Asked Symington, "Which is?"

Laird responded, "Which is that I want to be in a position where we can take a first blow and still retaliate, and I want the potential enemy to know that we can do that."

"Yes. But what is a first strike capability?" Gore asked.

"A first strike capability is a blow delivered against the United States—"

"That makes it impossible to retaliate," interjected Fulbright.

"Oh, no, not that makes it impossible to retaliate, but which makes it impossible to retaliate beyond any question of doubt."

"Let us have his definition," pursued Gore.

"No, a counterforce attack does not necessarily make it impossible to retaliate, Senator. [Deleted.] But my point is this: I want this country to be in a position where it can take a first strike, if that is what you want to call it, and that is what we usually have called it at our committee meetings."

The Senate majority leader, Mike Mansfield (D-Montana), then observed that Gore certainly knew what a first strike capability was and referred to "the old Nathan Bedford Forrest formula of getting there with the mostest the fustest or the fustest with the mostest."

"Yes, I understand Nathan Bedford Forrest," said Gore, "but I have not been able to find out from the Secretary yet whether he equates a first strike with a knockout blow or whether he does not, or whether he has taken the meaning today or the meaning—"

Laird tried to respond. "I want to be in a position—"

But Gore immediately cut him off. "I know what position you want to be in. I wish to know what you mean when you say the Soviets are 'going for a first strike capability.' " Fulbright agreed that he, too, was confused. Gore finished, "Do you mean they are going for a knockout blow capability?"

Laird replied that "I do not want them to ever be in a position where they have that choice."

Again Gore pressed his question. "Mr. Secretary, it is not the question of what you want. I want to know what you meant when you used that term."

Laird finally answered, "I meant a capability on the part of a potential enemy to destroy our retaliatory capability, our deterrent force in the United States to the point where it would no longer have an assured destruction capability. I could see no other purpose for the development and the continuing development of this SS-9 weapon.

"I had thought it was true that the SS-9 deployment would taper off. I accepted that. On many occasions when I sat on the other side of the table [as a representative], I remember perfectly well Secretary McNamara testifying before us that he thought the SS-9 deployment would taper off. It did not. [Deleted.].

"Senator Gore, it just seemed to me that this weapon was being developed to go after our Minuteman missile fields and was being deployed for that purpose, particularly when they went ahead with [deleted] tests on three warheads with five megatons each."

After Laird's testimony the senators were still confused about his use of the term "first strike capability." It had heretofore meant a disarming strike against *all* the adversary's nuclear forces, whereas Laird was using it purely with reference to the land-based missiles. They were also confused by the continued differences in interpretation between Laird and Richard Helms of CIA. It is impossible to detail the differences from the hearing record—as a security measure the entire Helms testimony was deleted from the published record of proceedings. In commenting on the hearings and deletions Fulbright remarked that

as the record now stands it leaves the impression that there have been no disagreements within the intelligence community as far as certain recent developments in Soviet weaponry are concerned. I feel that I had no choice but to agree to the deletions requested by the executive branch on the grounds of national security. But the fact of the matter is that there have been disagreements within the intelligence community on such recent developments, although all the testimony given at our June 23 meeting indicating such disagreements has been deleted.[16]

When the sanitized transcript was released on July 9, 1969, Fulbright also rose on the Senate floor to note that Secretary Laird had been forced to retreat from his hard line on Soviet intentions.

Within the administration the CIA was becoming increasingly embattled. Only two days later the JCS Chairman, "Bus" Wheeler, was criticizing intelligence prejudices on arms control to the NSC. Langley seemed to have little credibility within the executive. It is said that Henry Kissinger was furious with Helms for his testimony before the Senate. Evidently only his reputation in Congress for integrity, and the intervention of Senator Fulbright and others with Nixon in his behalf, preserved his position as DCI.[17] Laird, of course, stopped using CIA products, the national estimates, in his posture statements beginning the next January.

The attitude at the NSC is indicated by the formation of two panels in rapid succession to do studies on intelligence. The first had been the MIRV Panel, focused directly on the triplet dispute. This was only the precursor for the mechanism formed in the fall of 1969, the NSC Verification Panel, which became the main organ of defense decision-making in the Nixon and Ford administrations, dominated by Henry A. Kissinger. In Washington, Kissinger was in a position to mediate between CIA and DOD. While there is little doubt that the national security advisor was interested in the substance of the MIRV dispute, it is equally clear that the dispute helped the NSC establish an unprecedented degree of dominance in national security policy.

Officials at the Pentagon continued to assert that the SS-9 triplet was the functional equivalent of MIRV, and the development of such a weapon was consistent with seeking a first strike capability. The most striking example is the appearance of Dr. John Foster at a House subcommittee on August fifth. Foster told the group, which had convened to examine the diplomatic and strategic impact of MIRV, that the intelligence community prediction was for an operational Soviet MIRV by 1973. Forthrightly Foster declared

> I believe the evidence indicates that [the SS-9 triplet] is a MIRV. It doesn't prove without question that it is a MIRV, but to me, it very strongly indicates that it is a MIRV. I believe it is a MIRV.

Foster's view of the triplet intelligence dispute was, however, carefully worded:

I know there are individuals in the intelligence community who believe that it is a MIRV system the Soviets are testing. I don't know anyone who believes that they have completed their testing and would be satisfied with their present system.[18]

Following this heated eight-month dispute, a new NIE on Soviet strategic forces was in draft at ONE. Abbot Smith, who prided himself on maintaining expertise on all the subjects covered by NIEs, and Earl Barnes, ONE's expert on Soviet forces and a retired Air Force general, were mostly responsible for the product. They were able to achieve a community consensus, stated in the NIE, that the Russians were not seeking a first strike capability. The estimate was scheduled to go before the USIB on August twenty-eighth. The key paragraph read:

We believe that the Soviets recognize the enormous difficulties of any attempt to achieve strategic superiority of such order as to significantly alter the strategic balance. Consequently, we consider it highly unlikely that they will attempt within the period of this estimate to achieve a first strike capability, i.e., a capability to launch a surprise attack against the U.S. with assurance that the USSR would not itself receive damage it would regard as unacceptable. For one thing, the Soviets would almost certainly conclude that the cost of such an undertaking along with all their other military commitments would be prohibitive. More important, they almost certainly would consider it impossible to develop and deploy the combination of offensive and defensive forces necessary to counter successfully the various elements of U.S. strategic attack forces. Finally, even if such a project were economically and technically feasible the Soviets would almost certainly calculate that the U.S. would detect and match or overmatch their efforts.[19]

Clearly the draft text of the CIA estimate again flew in the faces of Laird and Foster and the statements of other senior Pentagon officials.

Severe pressure was brought to bear on Richard Helms to remove this judgment from the national estimate. An assistant to the secretary of defense apparently told Helms that the paragraph contradicted the public position of the secretary. In addition Eugene Fubini, now a member of DIA's science advisory committee, argued to a Helms associate that the judgment was inappropriate. As Helms recalled some years later,

On this issue of the first strike capability one of the things that occurred in connection with that was a battle royale over whether it was the agency's job to decide definitively whether the Soviet Union had its first strike capability or did not have a first strike capability. And this thing seemed so contentious that it seemed impossible to resolve.[20]

However, on September 4, 1969, Helms memoed the members of the USIB that the paragraph was being removed from the NIE. Helms has

said that when the director of central intelligence "clashes with the secretary of defense, he isn't a big enough fellow on the block."[21] In 1969
it was within Helms's prerogative to insist on the adoption of the national estimate as drafted, but instead he allowed the excision of this
judgment. Subsequently Thomas L. Hughes, outgoing director of the
State Department's Bureau of Intelligence and Research (INR), dissented from the NIE and reinserted the original paragraph as a footnote.

The Soviets Shift Direction

In 1969 the Soviets deployed over 100 new ICBMs, forty
Galosh ABMs, and several fleet ballistic missile submarines. Additional
ICBMs of the SS-11 class emplaced in the MRBM fields brought the
total closer to 170 for the year. A 1969 intelligence memorandum projected current Soviet strategic force spending at, in U.S. dollars, $6.5
billion for offensive weapons, $5.6 billion for ballistic missile defense,
and $14.2 billion for research and development (for all services). The
missile research-and-development program was reflected by seven tests
of the SS-9 triplet, one of the fractional orbital bombardment system
(the last Soviet FOBS test ever recorded), and seven of a new variant
on the SS-11 which carried penetration aids but was not a multiple warhead missile.

None of the Soviet activity presaged evolution of the SS-9 triplet into
a MIRV. The intelligence data still indicated RV release shortly after
booster burnout. The accuracies demonstrated by the Mod 4 did not
seem to improve, effectively diminishing any utility it might have had
in a counterforce attack. Tellingly, the Soviets even halted deployment
of the SS-9 in early 1970, partly as a signal of their willingness to proceed with SALT discussions, and also very probably because at that
time Soviet planners were reconsidering their force posture and making
the decision to deploy an actual MIRV warhead aboard a new generation of ballistic missiles. Some believe that engineering development of
the missiles must have started in 1969 and it is probable that program
decisions were made in the context of developing the Five-Year Plan
covering 1971–1975. The evidence, however, indicated that the SS-9
program was slowing down. In a policy statement of early March 1970,
the Soviet Union explicitly denied that it was seeking nuclear superiority over the United States.

Despite all indications, Melvin Laird reiterated essentially the same
threat characterization he had used in 1969. He professed to think that
if the Soviets continued their "accelerated" SS-9 program they might

threaten the Minuteman force even before 1974. In a speech on April 20, 1970, Laird pointed out that since 1966 the Soviets had quadrupled the nuclear megatonnage in their ICBMs and that the U.S. could be in a "second rate" position by the end of the decade. Four days later newsmen at the Pentagon were shown a newly declassified film of the reentry phase of an SS-9 test. The fifty-three-second film clearly showed the separation of reentry vehicles although the reporters could not tell from the film whether the RVs had been independently aimed. In June, before the NATO Nuclear Planning Group, Laird charged the Soviets with increasing the pace of their ICBM tests since the opening of SALT talks. In July, contradicting other senior administration officials, who had pointed out the halt in Soviet ICBM installation since August 1969, Laird declared that since the beginning of SALT the Russians had *continued* to deploy new ICBMs at a rate that would "dramatically increase" their strike forces. Finally, the first test of an MRV on the small Russian SS-11 Mod 3, in August, brought renewed charges from Laird on the momentum of Soviet testing. He now felt the claim of an operational Soviet MIRV by 1972 looked like "a very realistic projection."

One example of the impact of Laird's assertions in the U.S. is the threat assessment supplemental statement produced by the Fitzhugh Panel for the secretary of defense in September 1970. The Fitzhugh Panel was appointed the previous year to study defense organization, and this threat assessment was a spontaneous submission by seven members of the group. It concluded that

> our planners in the sixties assumed that if both superpowers had an adequate retaliatory capability neither would prepare for or risk a first strike. The evidence is now reasonably conclusive that the Soviet Union, rejecting this assumption, is deploying strategic weapons systems designed for a first strike capability. This evidence includes: (i) the continued Soviet production and deployment of ICBMs *after* having attained a clear numerical and megatonnage advantage; (ii) the emphasis on SS-9's designed as counterforce weapons capable of destroying U.S. hardened missile silos; (iii) the development of MRV with warheads also designed as counterforce weapons, and of MIRV by 1971–1972; (iv) the development of a fractional orbital missile which significantly minimizes warning time; (v) the construction of a [Yankee]-class atomic powered submarine SLBM launching fleet capable, with no effective warning, of destroying our national command centers and much of our B-52 bomber force; and (vi) the continued Soviet emphasis on strategic defense systems against both missiles and bombers—an emphasis without parallel in this country.
> The characteristics of these offensive and defensive weapons systems which the Soviets continue to expand, are consistent only with a preemp-

tive strike capability. Such a weapons mix and volume are not required for effective retaliation.[22]

In Laird's own fiscal year 1971 classified posture statement he postulated two possible Soviet approaches to force design. With a "Low Force Low Technology" program the Soviets could be expected to have 1,613 deliverable ICBM RVs by 1972, rising to 1,815 in 1974 and 1,986 two years later. Under the "High Force High Technology" crash program Laird projected some 1,822 RVs for 1972, 2,308 for 1974, and 3,053 for 1976.

At the end of July 1970 the Joint Chiefs were given their periodic briefing on the SAC by its chief, General Bruce Holloway. Working from the SIOP formulated by the Joint Strategic Target Planning Staff, Holloway told the Chiefs that, in a situation in which the U.S. absorbed a Soviet first strike, the available residual forces would then be insufficient to inflict damage upon the Soviet Union proportional to that sustained. This SAC conclusion challenged the conceptual basis of the doctrine of Assured Destruction, and the JCS elected to have the briefing repeated for the NSC. At an NSC meeting in mid-October officials again discussed whether the character of the Soviet missile buildup could be aimed at acquisition of a first strike capability. It is not surprising that the fourth round of SALT discussions, which began at Helsinki on November 2, 1970, found the United States and the Soviets farthest apart of any of the sessions on the terms of a potential arms agreement.

At the same time in Washington another high-level study was in progress on the survivability of American strategic forces. This had been ordered by the NSC's Defense Program Review Committee and was chaired by Gardiner Tucker, chief of DOD's Systems Analysis Office, who was also Laird's representative on the NSC Verification Panel. Evidently the study was not done on an interagency basis but was rather closely held within the Pentagon, and included only a "slight dissent" from the CIA. By projecting accuracies of .25 nautical-mile CEP for the SS-9 and .15 nautical mile for the SS-11, the study projected a threat to Minuteman by 1973–1974. The general theme of the vulnerability of land-based missiles to an SS-9 force was then taken up by the Navy, in a 1971 study recommending deployment of a fleet ballistic missile called the Trident. But the threat postulated in these studies was so implausible that the conclusions were widely criticized. The CIA, for example, argued that the Soviets lacked the material, and probably technical, resources to achieve the forces postulated. Others saw the parallel ICBM, SLBM, and bomber forces of the U.S. Triad as not so vulnerable as was claimed.[23]

.   .   .

For the Soviets 1971 was a peak year not only in terms of the number of new missiles deployed but, more importantly, for qualitative improvements. In about December of 1970 satellites detected new silo construction in both SS-9 and SS-11 missile fields, of which the Senate Armed Services Committee was briefed on March 4, 1971. Before intelligence received any indications that these were for an actual new missile, Senator Henry Jackson (D-Washington), who had not been present at the briefing but had probably been separately informed, claimed in a TV appearance three days later that there was "forbidding evidence" that the Soviets were deploying or were about to deploy a new generation of ICBMs at a rate of at least sixty to seventy annually. Jackson was criticized for the disclosure by Stuart Symington and William Proxmire, who observed that the discoveries were holes only: there was no evidence the Soviets had new missiles to put in them. John Foster also mentioned this silo construction in a March Senate hearing. Melvin Laird referred in April to the new intelligence "confirming the sobering fact that the Soviet Union is involved in a new—and apparently extensive—ICBM construction program."[24] By October Laird was saying that the pace of construction had far outdistanced even the projections he had given Congress in March.

In fact, the Soviets were not only increasing the hardness of their silos, as the CIA argued, but they were constructing harder launch control centers *and* they were preparing a new generation of ICBMs. There were four missiles involved. One was a follow-on to the SS-9 called the SS-18, or by its Soviet designation, the RS-20. Two other missiles, the SS-17 and SS-19, were parallel developments of a vehicle with, respectively, a quarter and a third of the throw-weight of the SS-18. The fourth ICBM was a small-payload missile, the SS-16, with great similarity to the Soviet solid-fuel SS-13, an unsuccessful parallel development to the SS-11 that had been curtailed after emplacement of only sixty rockets. On April 22, 1972, the CIA informed the NSC, the President, and other interested agencies that Russia was believed about to test some of the new missiles.

This occurred shortly before the U.S. and Russia agreed on the SALT I accords in Moscow during May 1972. When Secretary Laird appeared at the Senate Armed Services Committee to support ratification of SALT I, he claimed that the Soviets had indeed tested a MIRVed missile. But this was a misstatement. The test of the SS-18 Mod 1 showed only a large-yield single warhead missile. The Soviet MIRV was finally designed into the SS-18 Mod 2 and that, in turn, was not tested in flight before August 1973.

While the United States and Soviet Union focused on last-minute SALT negotiations, the great counterforce threat supposedly represented by the SS-9 seemed to recede. After over twenty flight tests since 1969, the Soviets still had not appreciably improved the accuracy of their triplet, which at 1.0 nautical-mile CEP was even worse than the single-warhead version of the Scarp. Without greater accuracy the counterforce potential of the triplet was considerably diminished. The Mod 4 was able to achieve only a slight variation in release times of its reentry vehicles. Another telemetry study, TRW's second, done in 1971, reversed the conclusions of the previous effort and stated that the triplet was not functionally equivalent to MIRV. On February 24, 1972, Melvin Laird conceded that the Russians "probably have not flight-tested MIRVed missiles thus far."[25]

Not only was Laird retreating from his previous stance, but so was John Foster. The DDR&E commented that the Soviets might "have canceled or curtailed the SS-9 triplet program." Most importantly, "analysis of the latest projections concerning Soviet missile growth rates and accuracy improvements indicates considerable variation in the time period in which our Minuteman forces would be seriously threatened."[26] Similarly, Admiral Thomas Moorer, who had replaced Wheeler as JCS Chairman, told the Senate that "regardless of whether the Soviets were, in fact, working on a MIRV, the Mod 4 has thus far failed to demonstrate the actual achievement of such a capability."[27] The posture statement for that year admitted that the Russians had stopped work on three SS-9 groups and slowed construction on two others.

When the Soviet MIRV was finally tested it was not on an SS-9 at all. Nor, when it was finally deployed for the first time in December 1974, was it even on the SS-9 follow-on. In fact, the SS-9 Mod 4 was never deployed by the Soviets. The first MIRVed missile was an SS-19. One hypothesis, advanced in 1973, explained that

the Soviet Union, up to now, appears to have been unable to master the gas-bearing inertial guidance technology [that made possible MIRVing of Minuteman III]. At any rate, analyses of Russia's missile and space activities have led to the conclusion that her guidance systems are several years behind those of the United States.[28]

At the SALT I ratification hearings in 1972 a long-time analyst of Soviet military affairs, Raymond Garthoff, was asked why he thought Russia had designed the SS-9. Garthoff's hunch was that "it could be that they saw it as more suitable as a candidate for MIRVing than the other missiles they had; since it has larger throw-weight, it would be easier to MIRV."[29] If so, the unsuccessful MIRVing of the SS-9, at a cost of $25–$30 million per missile, was a very expensive experiment for Russia. That the Soviets had to go to a whole new generation of ICBMs in order to incorporate MIRV technology is a telling indication of the actual strategic threat faced by the United States in 1969, when Laird and Foster waged their campaign on the SS-9 triplet.

In retrospect Garthoff's explanation of the SS-9 is entirely plausible. A Soviet MIRV was first projected by intelligence in 1965 precisely because the SS-9 had been detected at a time when U.S. analysts were becoming aware of the potential of MIRVed warheads. It was only logical that a large-payload ICBM would be the easiest to MIRV since it would impose minimum demands on Soviet skills in miniaturization, and would enable the Soviets to provide numerous on-board computer systems for RV release and guidance. This would be possible because the large throw-weight allowed the Soviets to add more RVs, or "fractionate" the payload, by accepting the use of smaller-yield nuclear weapons. The fact that the Russians ultimately proved unable to MIRV the Scarp was due to technical factors other than missile size and was, in 1965, in the realm of the unknowable. It is striking that, nevertheless, the initial judgment foresaw a Soviet MIRV in the 1970–1975 period— exactly on the mark, as the SS-19 Mod 1 achieved initial operating capability in 1974.

On balance the CIA performed admirably. Its early predictions were accurate, the agency showed a healthy suspicion that the Soviets were considering multiple-warhead development in 1967–1968, and also a healthy skepticism in 1969 and after on the Russian MIRV "functional equivalent" argument. Even Kissinger concedes CIA was right on this. When the real Soviet MIRV made its debut aboard a fourth generation of ICBMs, the CIA gave a full year's warning before the first tests, and three years of warning before the Soviet MIRV became operational. This actually improved upon McNamara's mid-sixties promise that the U.S. would be able to detect a Soviet MIRV two years in advance.

The director of defense research and engineering anticipated the Soviet MIRV by at least three years. Concomitant pressures to deploy a comparable U.S. MIRV then precluded any SALT agreement banning MIRVs, an option that could have been explored in 1969 but was not. Moreover, the U.S. decision to deploy MIRV must have figured in the Soviets' subsequent one to produce a new generation of ICBMs, including MIRVs. Within intelligence the dissension created by the MIRV debate, fostered by an office that was not even a formal part of the community, hampered objective observation of the new Soviet systems when the first indications were discovered in 1971.

In the words of one critic the secretary of defense

was able to surmount the obstacle of hard intelligence by using it to anchor
a base line of enemy present capability and then proceed to an extrapolation
based on a maximum possible exploitation of technology.[30]

Laird's stance supported DDR&E and the DIA, particularly after 1970
when he stopped using the NIEs for justifying the budget. The tone he
took in 1969 is known to have earned him twin admonitions from Richard Nixon in the form of copies of the President's inaugural address
with one passage underlined, "We cannot learn from one another until
we stop shouting at one another."[31]

Unfortunately, the MIRV case shows that being right does not necessarily convince the bureaucracy. Pessimistic views found free rein in
the Laird Pentagon. The intelligence debate of 1969 lost prestige for the
CIA at both the Pentagon and the White House, and helped the NSC
institutionalize control over the national security policy process.

CHAPTER FOURTEEN
MONITORING SALT

The possibility of bilateral agreements establishing limits on strategic weapons was an arms control initiative suggested by the United States in 1967. At that time President Johnson and Secretary McNamara preferred an agreement to the expenditure required for an ABM deployment. Soviet delay in responding to the initiative and then their invasion of Czechoslovakia precluded any immediate movement, but the intention to seek arms limits was passed along to the Nixon administration. Arms control and limitation then established itself as an area of major diplomatic activity for the next decade, ten years of Strategic Arms Limitation Talks (SALT).

Successful SALT agreements were an Olympian achievement in international relations: two nations in competition, with different priorities, philosophies, military traditions, and political systems agreed closely enough on certain military measures to sign a formal international accord. Despite the difficulties the possibilities for peace represented by SALT agreements were considerable and successive American administrations pursued arms limitation diplomacy. In the beginning the Johnson administration performed vital preparatory work that clarified the interests and needs of segments of the U.S. government. The freeze on offensive weapons deployment that eventually became part of the 1972 Interim Agreement had first been proposed as an element of general and complete disarmament by the Johnson administration in 1964. The multilateral Nuclear Non-Proliferation Treaty of 1968 also resulted from Johnson administration efforts. The Partial Test Ban Treaty, which moved the superpowers' nuclear tests underground, was concluded in 1963 while Kennedy was in the White House. As arms control measures accumulated, a program gradually evolved that defined permissible behavior by the powers.

The theoretical objectives of arms control are simply stated but difficult to achieve. With respect to strategic nuclear weapons, arms control seeks to reduce the danger of nuclear war, to reduce the destruction of war should it occur, and to reduce defense spending by saving money otherwise needed for new strategic weapons. Theorists also make a distinction between arms "control" and arms "limitation," in which the former consists of actual reduction and elimination of weapons while the latter implies only constraints on weapon characteristics, collateral systems, operating practices, or deployment patterns and scales.

Richard Nixon took office having used charges in his campaign that the Johnson administration had allowed the country to fall into a "security gap." At his first press conference Nixon answered a question on opening SALT talks by declaring his determination to "link" progress in one field of Soviet relations to their behavior in other areas and to the general status of American foreign relations. The doctrine of "linkage" and the apparent rejection of LBJ's defense policies suggested an aggressive administration without great interest in arms control. In practice, however, the United States did move to explore possibilities for arms agreements. The diplomacy was not smooth or rapid but the negotiations were formal and ongoing.

Once the SALT I agreements had been achieved, the administration oversold them to Congress and to the public, which led to a growing hostility toward the Soviets when Russia maintained the momentum of its weapons programs, particularly MIRV. Kissinger, being responsible for the SALT achievement, tried to avoid and delay the political problems attendant to his policy of "détente" by restricting knowledge of evidence that the Soviets were continuing some weapons developments. Ultimately there were allegations of a "cover-up" leveled at certain of Kissinger's actions, and fears of a deliberate Soviet deception. These contributed to rising dissatisfaction with Kissinger's performance as the national security advisor, and by then also as secretary of state. The intelligence community, due to its primary role in analyzing and monitoring Soviet compliance at the SALT agreements, was caught in the middle of these political currents.

Measures of SALT

The major exception to Nixon's appointments of loyal Republicans to his cabinet was Henry A. Kissinger as his national security advisor. Kissinger was a Harvard professor and policy advisor to Nelson Rockefeller, liberal Republican leader and Nixon opponent. However, Nixon had no real foreign policy expertise in his own inner circle and he required someone competent to run the NSC. The Kissinger appointment was also a concession both to liberal Republicans and academe. One of Kissinger's books, *Nuclear Weapons and Foreign Policy,* had been published in 1957 when Nixon was vice president, and a twenty-four page summary and extract had circulated in the Eisenhower White House. Nixon read this book, although it is not clear whether it was Andrew Goodpaster's digest or the full work he perused, and wrote in retrospect, "I knew that we were very much alike in our general outlook in that we shared a belief in the importance of isolating and influencing factors affecting worldwide balances of power."[1]

Nixon called Kissinger to his transition headquarters at New York's Hotel Pierre and, after describing some of his plans, asked Kissinger for advice on organizing the NSC. Foreign policy would be run from the White House, said Nixon, who felt that by ignoring the military the Johnson administration had not been given real options in crises. According to Kissinger,

> [Nixon] felt it imperative to exclude the CIA from the formulation of policy; it was staffed by Ivy League liberals who behind the façade of analytical objectivity were usually pushing their own preferences. They had always opposed him politically.[2]

This attitude is also reflected in the published work of White House chief of staff H. R. Haldeman, and Nixon himself notes, with an undertone of chagrin, how he was denied a CIA briefing prior to his 1967 visit to Russia and Western Europe.

Kissinger recommended an organization for the NSC that effectively reflected the staff system used in the Eisenhower administration, "weighted somewhat in favor of the State Department" by giving State chairmanship of some interdepartmental committees. It would be headed by an interdepartmental Senior Review Group that would review matters at the highest level and either require additional work or put them on the NSC agenda. Papers called National Security Study Memoranda (NSSMs) would constitute policy reviews while decisions would be handed down in parallel National Security Decision Memoranda (NSDMs). Of this series NSDM 2 laid down the NSC structure, excluding the director of central intelligence.

Nixon's hostility to the CIA has been noted; yet, when looking for a director of central intelligence, Nixon chose to retain Richard Helms, who had been serving since July 1966. Kissinger supported Helms despite his sense of Nixon's discomfiture because the national security advisor "thought it was dangerous to turn the CIA into a political plum whose Director would change with each new President."[3] When Nixon proposed to drop Helms from NSC meetings, Defense Secretary-designate Melvin Laird objected to the proposed scheme. He pointed out that the director of central intelligence was a statutory member of the NSC under the National Security Act of 1947 and that, without CIA on the council, the President would be vulnerable to criticism on major decisions taken without intelligence advice. Nixon agreed only to let Helms present factual briefings at the outset of meetings and was cold to him when he appeared at the NSC. On more than one occasion Nixon corrected the director factually or on pronunciation in the midst of CIA presentations. Until about mid-March 1969 Helms was obliged to leave the room after his briefing, but then "the situation became too embarrassing, too artificial, and too self-defeating to be sustained"[4] and Helms resumed regular NSC participation.

The sudden vulnerability of the CIA's status on the NSC was only one of a series of events that must have affected morale at Langley. Strong demands were made—on one occasion by John Ehrlichman acting for Nixon—to get documents on the Bay of Pigs fiasco that could undoubtedly be used against the agency in bureaucratic maneuvers. Another time the CIA was asked to violate its charter, which prohibits activities inside the United States, and organize surveillance of Nixon's brother. These pressures were in the background when the MIRV dispute climaxed in the mid-1969 questioning under oath of both Helms and Laird. At the same time another dispute raged over the possibilities for verification of prospective SALT agreements. This resulted from a formal interagency study, NSSM-28 on "SALT Criteria," ordered by Kissinger on March 13, 1969.

To understand the bureaucratic interplay over NSSM-28 it is necessary to bear in mind the administration's determination to control foreign policy from the White House, particularly important bilateral negotiations like SALT. For Nixon to "control" the SALT talks effectively meant the NSC would have to be preeminent among the government agencies involved—including not only the CIA and Pentagon, but also the State Department and the Arms Control and Disarmament Agency (ACDA), which were responsible for actual conduct of negotiations. Both participants and observers have noted that the internal deliberations on SALT alternatives were almost as complex as the negotiations with the Soviets.

The study memorandum requested by Kissinger required the SALT bureaucracy to derive a list of possible restraints that would be comprehensive and acceptable to the U.S. from both a military standpoint and that of "verification," or the ability of the United States to monitor Soviet compliance with SALT provisions. With statutory responsibility for arms control measures, ACDA led the NSSM-28 panel, but with only 156 total personnel this agency could do little more than coordinate the interagency paperwork. The head of ACDA, Gerard Smith, who also stood to be the chief of the SALT delegation, chose his deputy Philip Farley to chair the panel and urged rapid movement so as to begin negotiations as soon as possible. Many on the NSSM-28 panel were the same men who had worked on the Johnson administration SALT proposals in 1968, including Morton Halperin representing the NSC, Major General Royal B. Allison for the Joint Chiefs, and Ivan Selin, who represented Laird.

In April staff work on the SALT criteria suddenly slowed when the dispute over the SS-9 triplet cast doubt upon American ability to assess the characteristics of Soviet military hardware that would be the focus of SALT. At the same time CIA had been asked by the NSC to state the verifiability of each weapon limitation proposed in NSSM-28. Although one source reports that Helms initially did not want to have anything to do with verification, ACDA Director Gerard C. Smith recalls that in fact CIA was very confident about the possibilities for verification. Officers at Langley resented as "skulduggery" Kissinger's inquiry into the MIRV estimates with Lawrence Lynn's working group while NSC aides told reporters that Kissinger felt Richard Helms to have a vested interest in a SALT agreement that required extensive verification since this would increase the power of the CIA. Then the Joint Chiefs began "openly dragging their feet"[5] on the study memorandum.

The signs did not auger well for NSSM-28. When the first of the interagency options papers came before Kissinger he told associates that the possible combinations of such papers were mind-boggling and that it was not fair to ask the President to sort them all out. The bureaucracy was asked to come up with more formal measures that could be used as "building blocks" in the SALT negotiations. Eventually nine options emerged, embodied in a paper presented by ACDA to the NSC on June 25, 1969. Kissinger, over Richard Nixon's protestations, scheduled the President for a series of NSC meetings where SALT options were presented "so that directives could be issued with some plausibility on his authority."[6] Nixon was interested in the negotiations but bored with the details and was irritable and "glassy eyed" at the NSC meetings. During the meeting of June twenty-fifth the CIA presented its analysis that all the elements of SALT could be verified without much difficulty: Russian cheating would either be so minor as to have no impact on the strategic balance or else would have to be on such a scale that it could not escape detection. "Bus" Wheeler, speaking for the Joint Chiefs, commented harshly on the ACDA paper and was very blunt in his views on CIA treatment of the verification problem.

Such high-level criticism could not be ignored. Five days after the

NSC meeting, Gerard Smith sent Kissinger a memo in which ACDA recommended a special study of the verification problem by the NSC. This received support at the NSC staff level and was taken up by Kissinger. On July 21, 1969, an NSC Verification Panel was created. Chaired by Kissinger, it evolved from a study group into the focal point for SALT decision-making and intelligence monitoring. Ultimately the panel also supplanted the full NSC in the SALT area and became an instrument of Kissinger's control over the bureaucracy. As Gerard Smith later noted of Kissinger, "I must say that he had us all buffaloed."[7] The ACDA was isolated by creation of the NSC Verification Panel and would later be bypassed in the formal negotiations through Henry Kissinger's use of a "back channel" for direct communication with the Soviets through their ambassador in Washington, Anatoli Dobrynin. Even the Joint Chiefs became isolated at the Pentagon as the intervals between their direct contacts with Nixon lengthened perceptibly. Things got so bad that the Chiefs resorted to using a Navy yeoman who often accompanied Kissinger on diplomatic missions as a source of news. For its part the CIA was also neutralized. The foremost historian of SALT has noted that

> Kissinger would demand a more methodical and rigorous approach to verification and related issues. Rightly or wrongly, he found much of the earlier work lacking in rigor, and he, along with a few associates, placed the blame in large part on the CIA. For some time this agency would operate well out of the new Administration's favor, partly—perhaps mainly—because its work on SALT was thought to have lacked detachment.[8]

The new, more "rigorous" standards of verification were significant in that they excluded almost by definition a range of controls of great importance. The possible restraints thus lost were largely of the "qualitative" type, limits that would have reduced the military threat of a first strike by inhibiting Soviet MIRV development and accuracy improvements while leaving ICBM numbers untouched. With the exclusion of these less verifiable limits, which admittedly left unrestrained the technological area in which the U.S. enjoyed the largest lead, only "quantitative" limits on missile numbers were feasible. A decade later, when the Soviets had deployed a substantial MIRVed force and were gaining in accuracy to the point at which many feared an emergent first strike potential, it was much less possible to view with equanimity this early abandonment of the search for "qualitative" limits.

SALT negotiations finally began at Helsinki, Finland, on November 17, 1969. On May 26, 1972, President Nixon signed an ABM Treaty along with an Interim Agreement on the Limitation of Strategic Offen-

sive Arms. Henry Kissinger explained the agreements and their rationale in some detail to a gathering of interested congressmen at the White
House on June 15, 1972. He began by claiming that in the course of
formal ratification hearings the administration would demonstrate that
the agreements enabled the United States to maintain a defense posture
which "guarantees our security and protects our vital interests" while
at the same time contributing to "a more enduring structure of peace."
Kissinger spoke of the preparatory work that underlay SALT I. Addressing the pace of the Soviet ICBM buildup, Dr. Kissinger stated that

> as a result of decisions made in the 1960s, and not reversible within the
> time frame of the protected [sic] agreement, there would be a numerical
> gap against us in the two categories of land- and sea-based missile systems
> whether or not there was an agreement. Without an agreement the gap
> would steadily widen.[9]

After covering the substance of the agreements, Kissinger turned to the
ancillary inclusion of "agreed statements," "common understandings,"
and unilateral statements which had been appended to both agreements. The "agreed statements" were initiated by the SALT delegations
and the "common understandings" had not been formally initialed but
were points well understood by the sides. The so-called "unilateral interpretations" were intended "to make our position clear in instances where
we could not get total agreement." In answer to a question from Senator
John Sherman Cooper (R-Kentucky), Kissinger also stated that "there
are no secret understandings"[10] connected with the SALT agreements.

There followed an extensive series of hearings before the Foreign Relations and Armed Services committees of both houses of Congress. The
Joint Chiefs endorsed the SALT agreements provided several "assurances" were kept, namely that the U.S. would continue a broad range
of intelligence capabilities and operations to verify compliance, would
conduct an aggressive force modernization program, and would couple
this with a vigorous program of research and development. The ABM
Treaty was ratified by the Senate on August fourth. Senator Henry Jackson (D-Washington) offered an amendment to the enabling legislation
on the Interim Agreement specifying that future arms control agreements must be based upon equality of numbers for both sides. This
passed the Senate on September sixteenth. Nine days later the House
approved the Interim Agreement, as did the Senate on September 30,
1972. Instruments of ratification were exchanged between the United
States and Soviet Union at Washington on October 3, 1972, and the
SALT agreements entered into force.

The agreements achieved in 1972 were the start of a continuing process of SALT negotiations, and they became known as SALT I. After ratification the negotiators met to initiate discussions on a SALT II agreement. Precisely because SALT became a process, the record of Soviet compliance with SALT I became an important issue. In this respect it is important to note that in its endorsement of SALT I the Nixon administration chose to press to the limit the substance of the agreements, especially in its claim that the unilateral statements carried some weight in international law.

In the meantime the intelligence community geared up to verify Soviet compliance with SALT. Some preparations had already been made. On July 1, 1972, the intelligence community formed a Steering Group on Monitoring Strategic Arms Limitations chaired by the director of central intelligence. This group produced a quarterly report on the status of strategic forces with respect to the agreements, which was delivered to only twenty senior officials. Within CIA the main staff work was done by the Office of Strategic Research under E. Henry Knoche, who had worked with technical collection products since the U-2. In theory the SALT Steering Group would review the analyses from OSR and give notification of any instance in which Soviet compliance might be questionable. The NSC would then take up the issue and make the decision to have U.S. representatives at the Standing Consultative Commission in Geneva refer the question to Soviet delegates.

In practice, as in the case of the actual SALT negotiations, Henry Kissinger wished to retain control over subsequent verification discussions. His motives were undoubtedly related to the planned second round of SALT negotiations. On October 17, 1972, Kissinger called Helms to establish a formal procedure under which any instance where the CIA felt the Soviet Union to be in violation of any provision of SALT would be referred first to the NSC. According to Colonel Merritt of the NSC staff, " 'Dr. Kissinger wanted to avoid any written judgments to the effect that the Soviets have violated any of the SALT provisions . . . the judgment that a violation is considered to have occurred is one that will be made at the NSC level.' "[11] The result was that violation allegations would go to only seven officials. The President, the Secretary of State, ACDA, and the armed services chiefs of staff and their intelligence directors were not among them. But restrictions on the circulation of information were commonplace in intelligence work and this "compartmentation" was viewed as an essential security procedure. Edward Proctor, CIA's deputy director for intelligence from 1971 to 1976, for example, later saw nothing improper with the NSC-initiated "hold" procedure on SALT-related information.

Initially all went well. The U.S. government worked up a series of negotiating options for SALT II and began talks in November 1972. During these meetings Kissinger and Soviet Foreign Minister Andrei Gromyko signed a memorandum of understanding to regulate procedures of the Standing Consultative Commission. Ambassador U. Alexis Johnson was appointed to head the U.S. delegation to the SCC. The U.S. proposals for SALT II called for equal numbers of "delivery systems" (ICBMs, SLBMs, and bombers) plus a collateral limit on total force payload or throw-weight. This last provision was intended to achieve a qualitative restraint indirectly because a throw-weight constraint ceiling would inhibit the growth of Soviet nuclear forces in terms of the number of weapons on MIRVed platforms. For their part the Soviets wanted to include American nuclear forces based in Europe that were capable of striking Soviet territory, the so-called "forward based systems" (FBS). There was no immediate progress in the discussions. By April 1973 it was evident that a SALT II agreement could not be completed in time for the Brezhnev summit meeting at Washington scheduled for June 1973.

At the periodic SCC meeting on June seventh a Soviet official alluded to a point about SLBMs that none of the American delegates had ever heard of. U. Alexis Johnson cabled Washington that night to clarify the reference, which involved whether old diesel submarines of the Soviets' Golf class, armed with primitive SLBMs, counted against the SLBM ceilings contained in a protocol to the SALT Interim Agreement. Evidently some NSC staff analysts had found ambiguities in the protocol's definition of an SLBM missile that could be read in such a way as to allow the Soviet Union a ceiling of 1,020 SLBMs as against the 950 which American negotiators thought they had provided for in SALT I. What had actually happened was that a year before, on June 17, 1972, four days after the SALT agreements had been sent to Congress and two days after Kissinger told a congressional audience that there were no "secret agreements" in SALT, Kissinger had met through his "back channel" with Soviet Ambassador Dobrynin to clarify the SLBM protocol. Their agreement reaffirmed the 950 ceiling and was confirmed by Moscow, but the U.S. SALT delegation, not to mention Congress, learned of the fact only now, in 1973, eleven months later, and then from a *Soviet* diplomat. Intelligence discovered that for almost a year it had been unaware of a document that would have helped the community understand Soviet motivation for development of a new SLBM, the SSN-X-13. Kissinger claimed that the substance of his "back channel" agreement had been discussed at the NSC meeting of June 5, 1972, and contained in a memo on the nineteenth, but he has since conceded that "there was an interpretive statement that for some reason was not distributed to the bureaucracy . . . [but] why it was not distributed I cannot for the life of me remember now."[12] Kissinger aides later remarked that the clarification aide-mémoire, signed by Kissinger and Dobrynin on July twenty-fourth, had not been circulated because there was some question as to whether a presidential advisor had the statutory authority to sign such a document.

The effect of this revelation just a few weeks before the 1973 summit was to electrify the SALT bureaucracy and create further dissension in government. Furthermore, just as Brezhnev was due to arrive for the summit, intelligence discovered several excavations in Soviet ICBM fields that looked like silo starts. If this had been reported at the time there would have been pandemonium but instead the NSC suddenly clamped a "hold" on the information. Nixon handed the Soviets a note on June twenty-sixth about this subject during the conference. However, Secretary of State Rogers and ACDA were kept ignorant of the discovery. In fact the rigidity of the "hold" procedure was such that Rogers's deputy Kenneth Rush and the INR director Ray Cline did know of the report but could not tell their boss. This embarrassing situation culminated with a July thirteenth meeting at Langley among Edward Proctor, William Colby, and Deputy Director for Central Intelligence Vernon Walters, to discuss the director of central intelligence's responsibility to get from Kissinger "reasonable assurances" that President Nixon knew of the effects of keeping this information secret and still approved the restriction.

This information "hold" was terminated on August eighth. In the meantime Soviet silo starts continued until it appeared that a substantial program was in the offing. In addition the Soviets employed a novel technique in excavating, tunneling more or less straight downward rather than clearing a wide hole down to the desired depth and later repacking the surrounding earth. This "snail" technique made it more difficult to determine the volume of a given excavation since the "shadowgraphs" made with laser measurements from the U.S. satellites, and showing the depth of a hole, were more difficult to make with the narrow excavation brims. In any case Kissinger asked the Russians for an explanation of their activities and they replied that these "III-X" silos were to be launch control centers for their ICBMs, and that this would become clear as construction continued. At this early stage of construction, it is true, site preparations for a launch center or a missile launcher would be identical, thus constituting an "inherent ambiguity," as the Pentagon termed it in 1975.

First the CIA and later the intelligence community as a whole accepted the III-X silos as command control centers, although there has been some concern that these silos might be suited to rapid conversion to ICBM launchers. Some 150 III-X launch control centers were eventually dispersed throughout the Soviet ICBM complexes, and it became evident that no actual violation of the SALT I agreement had occurred.

The III-X silo question was only one of a series of indications that cast doubts upon Soviet motives.

Another was the belated appearance of the Soviet MIRV. By 1973, when the Soviets successfully MIRVed a modified SS-11, the U.S. had already been thinking of a third generation of guidance improvements, terminal guidance, in which the RV could correct its trajectory in the last moments before impact. It appeared that terminal guidance would make possible very high precision MIRVed warheads, and these would be ideal counterforce weapons. While disadvantaged on MIRV the Soviets still made one notable innovation. They perfected a method for ejecting an ICBM from its silo before ignition of the booster, in much the same way as an SLBM is fired. This had two important effects: it made feasible the concept of a reloadable ICBM (in a "hot" launch the silo must be refurbished before reuse), even though reloading would still take hours or more to accomplish; and it allowed the Soviets to put a larger volume (and throw-weight) ICBM in the same size silo. In August 1973 the Russians finally tested a real MIRV warhead and with it several new missiles. One missile, the SS-18, with sixteen thousand to twenty thousand pounds throw-weight, was even larger than the SS-9 it replaced. Two other missiles, the SS-19 and the SS-17, another Soviet parallel development program, replaced the SS-11. A third missile, the SS-16, was a low-accuracy but mobile ICBM.

One charge of SALT violation resulted from the size of the pair of fixed ICBMs. The SS-19 and SS-17 were both larger than the SS-11. In SALT I the United States made a great effort to put a limit on the Soviet "heavy" (large throw-weight) ICBMs, specifically, at that time, on the SS-9. The Soviets agreed not to convert "light" (SS-11) into "heavy" missiles and not to replace old SS-7 and -8 "heavy" ICBMs into "launchers for heavy ICBMs deployed after" 1964, and also accepted a limit of fifteen percent in the amount by which the size of missile silos could be increased. Melvin Laird told Congress that under these strictures the Soviets could not increase their missile size by more than about thirty percent. Kissinger told the congressmen that a "heavy" missile was defined as "anything with a volume significantly greater than the largest light ICBM now operational on either side." Such a definition would have limited the Soviets to about two thousand pounds of throw-weight in their "light" ICBMs, not the seven thousand pounds of the SS-19 or the four thousand pounds of the SS-17.

The constraint on silo improvements was made not in the agreement itself but in "Agreed Interpretation J" and in "Common Understanding A" to the Interim Agreement. These specified an augmentation limit of fifteen percent. Thus the U.S. understood that SALT I meant that the Russians could increase *either* the diameter or the depth of their silos, while the Soviets believed they could do both and did so in the silos designed for the SS-19 and SS-17 ICBMs. An increase of fifteen percent in both dimensions created silos that were fifty percent greater in total volume and the new missiles were forty to fifty percent larger than the SS-11. An additional weakness in SALT was that the definition of a so-called "heavy" missile existed only in a unilateral statement made by the U.S. on the day of the treaty signing.

In 1971 General Rockly Triantafellu's Air Force intelligence unit predicted that the SS-11 replacement missile would be larger than the original. The Soviets themselves confirmed this in early May 1972 when they told U.S. negotiators under Gerard Smith that two new missiles were under development to follow the SS-11 and that these were somewhat larger in volume. Throughout the negotiations the Soviets steadfastly refused to agree to any definition of "heavy" missiles and, according to officials of a later U.S. administration, explicitly said their refusal was due to the fact that the U.S.-proposed definition was in unacceptable conflict with their plans. Last-minute efforts by Kissinger and Nixon at the Moscow summit still failed to nail down a definition and the restrictions on the dimensions of possible silo modification were in fact an effort to compensate for this failure.

Consequently there were no treaty stipulations or common understandings to keep the Soviets from designating the SS-19 and SS-17 as "light" missiles. In addition intelligence discovered in 1972 that the follow-on missiles would in fact be larger than their predecessor. This became even more apparent when testing of the SS-19 began in 1973. The actual increase in volume—the SS-19 reached the midpoint in throw-weight between the SS-11 and the "heavy" SS-9—was disturbing, as were reports of the "cold launch" technique. In presenting the fiscal year 1975 military budget the secretary of defense, James Schlesinger, said of the Soviet MIRV that "while this development has been anticipated many years, the scope of the Soviet program as it has emerged is far more comprehensive than estimated even a year ago."[13] Efforts were undertaken in the SALT bureaucracy to confront the Soviets at the Standing Consultative Commission (SCC) and get explanations: at the State Department Seymour Weiss, chief of the Bureau of Political-Military Affairs (PMA), drafted a recommendation for SCC action; in March the deputy secretary of defense, William P. Clements, sent a memo to the NSC asking for a Verification Panel meeting on Soviet SALT compliance.

More evidence of Soviet SALT violations became known during and after the June 1974 summit at Moscow. One SALT information "hold" was imposed on June twenty-ninth, a second on July twenty-sixth, and two more on September eleventh and twenty-third. While the intelligence reports remain classified, speculation about their contents includes data on the SSN-8 SLBM (with range sufficient to reach the U.S. from Soviet home waters), increased accuracy for Soviet warheads, and, most suggestively, reports of a fifth generation of ICBM missiles in the design stage, going beyond even the SS-18 group. There were also numerous tests of the SA-5 radars, prohibited by the ABM Treaty—in fact twenty-four of them in 1974. Information held since June was not reflected in the SALT Steering Group intelligence report until September 1974. Two additional information "holds" were initiated on October eighth and twenty-second and were not lifted until December seventeenth. Possible subjects here were Soviet use of encryption to disguise the telemetry of SS-16's during tests and indications that sixty of the reputedly "landmobile" SS-16's had replaced the old SS-13's in the missile field at Teykovo.

SALT "holds" contributed to growing dissatisfaction with Henry Kissinger's leadership role. Not even the Vladivostok aide-mémoire, which provided a "framework" for a SALT II agreement and was the product of a late November summit between Brezhnev and President Ford, could restore Kissinger's luster. In December the long-awaited Verification Panel meeting on Soviet SALT compliance took place. Kissinger was able to get some support for *not* confronting the Soviets at the SCC based on the need to avoid compromising intelligence sources and methods. However, in January 1975 Defense Secretary Schlesinger reversed the Pentagon position on the security of intelligence sources, and a new decision was made to call a meeting of the SCC for February.

The senior U.S. delegate at the SCC, Sidney Graybeal, was ordered to present the SALT ambiguities to the Soviets and obtain a satisfactory reply. The U.S. had reviewed Soviet concealment efforts and decided they were only marginally important save for the question of telemetry encryption, but Kissinger and Schlesinger had both agreed that not even the word "telemetry" should be used in the SALT discussions. The questions raised at the SCC pertained to SA-5 radar testing, and the III-X silos, while the matter of the definition of a "light" ICBM was taken up directly by Kissinger and Andrei Gromyko in their discussions.

At the SCC the Soviets were responsive but firm. The III-X silos were identified as command control centers and the Americans accepted this explanation. The use of the SA-5 radar "in an ABM mode" was more difficult. The Soviets pointed out that the ABM Treaty did not prohibit non-ABM radars being used for range instrumentation in testing. They maintained the SA-5 radars were used for this purpose. This was plausible given that the radars faced the interior of the Soviet Union rather than the threat corridors from which any U.S. attack must come. The Russians went further, however, and halted this use of the SA-5 radars within seventeen days of the complaint. For their part the Soviets charged SALT violations as well. There were several allegations of U.S. concealment activities—covering ICBM silos with shelters that prevented reconnaissance satellites from surveying the silo and its contents. There were also charges that the United States had failed to dismantle older ICBM launchers that had been built in the era of the liquid-fueled Atlas ICBM.

The matter of the "light" ICBM was discussed several times but Kissinger could not get the Soviets to concede any questionable activity here. The impasse over the large throw-weights of the SS-17 and SS-19 was reflected in the failure to reach any new offensive limitation agreement at the 1974 Moscow summit and after. The U.S. offered two options for an agreement: either both sides would be allowed to MIRV an equal aggregate of throw-weight, or the U.S. should be allowed to MIRV more missiles than the Russians in compensation for the larger Soviet payloads. The Soviets rejected both alternatives.

In February 1975 *Aviation Week* disclosed a further instance of a possible Soviet SALT violation. This concerned a semimobile radar called X-3 which seemed suitable for ABM use. *Aviation Week* claimed that the same design team which had developed the SA-5 was working on the new radar. From then on charges of violations were more and more widespread in the press. Details on Soviet use of telemetry, SA-5 radars, and the III-X launch control centers were given in the *New Republic* in early June. In the July *Reader's Digest,* Melvin Laird charged that the Soviets had violated both the Interim Agreement and the ABM Treaty, and he repeated these charges in December with additional detail.

There was also great concern on Capitol Hill. Senator Henry Jackson called subcommittee hearings on Soviet compliance with the arms control agreements. The director of central intelligence, now William E. Colby, testified on February 20, 1975. A sanitized transcript of Colby's testimony was to have been issued but this was delayed many months and then quietly dropped. Secretary of Defense James R. Schlesinger also appeared on March sixth. Schlesinger dealt with the Soviet throw-weight gain, the III-X launch control centers, and the SA-5 radar testing. The evidence he gave showed that U.S. intelligence was well informed regarding Russian developments. One of Henry Jackson's main points that morning concerned the American government, however, and not the Soviet:

> I wish to emphasize that a significant part of the problem we face in assessing whether the Soviets are in compliance with the 1972 agreements is of our government's own making. By resorting to unilateral statements so-called as a device for building into the 1972 agreements limitations that could not be negotiated, the Nixon administration set the stage for the current drama of ambiguity and confusion.[14]

In the summer of 1973, in addition to his post as national security advisor, Henry Kissinger had been appointed secretary of state. As secretary Kissinger became responsible to Congress as well as to the President. Jackson asked for Kissinger testimony at his compliance hearings but the secretary of state remained too busy to appear. Although he avoided congressional appearances, Kissinger did not hesitate to defend his policies publicly. In answer to those who claimed that Soviet developments were giving them strategic superiority, Kissinger asked, "What in the name of God is strategic superiority? What is the significance of it, politically, militarily, operationally, at these levels of [missile] numbers? What do you do with it?"[15]

By the fall the press was saying that SALT II was eighty-five to ninety percent complete. But in the NSC meetings held in advance of Kissinger's negotiating sessions, Secretary Schlesinger still held back from full support of SALT while relations between Kissinger and the government bureaucracy deteriorated even further. On November 2, 1975, President Ford fired Schlesinger and also William Colby of CIA. At the same time Ford asked Kissinger to give up his post at the NSC. When he heard that Schlesinger had been fired, Major General Daniel O. Graham resigned from his post as director of the DIA.

In the wake of the "Sunday Massacre" it might have been expected that Kissinger's position was stronger than ever, particularly given the fact that his deputy, General Brent Scowcroft, succeeded him at the NSC. In fact events worked out quite differently. In an *Aviation Week* editorial of November 24, 1975, Robert Hotz charged that Ford and Kissinger engaged in "a deliberate policy of deception to conceal Soviet violations of both the letter and the spirit of the SALT agreements." Others believed that President Ford had not been told of questionable Soviet activities. A congressional committee then investigating the intelligence community, under the leadership of Representative Otis Pike

(D-New York), turned its attention to SALT and scheduled hearings for early December.

At the Pike Committee hearing on December second Admiral Elmo R. Zumwalt testified about Soviet violations of SALT. Zumwalt's information was relatively current since he had been chief of naval operations, thus a JCS member, until his retirement the previous June. The Pike Committee had also learned of the intelligence "holds" from documents provided in mid-November by the NSC and the intelligence community. Meanwhile Secretary Kissinger strongly defended his record on the SALT "holds" in a press conference of December ninth. He insisted that Ford was completely aware of the situation on Soviet compliance. There had been eleven NSC and forty Verification Panel meetings on SALT, four of them specifically on compliance, since the middle of 1973, each meeting beginning with a CIA briefing about the latest developments. The President had been briefed directly on compliance ten times, six of them during Ford's administration, and one NSC meeting had been completely given over to SALT ambiguities.

A key portion of Kissinger's reply followed his statement that all Verification Panel decisions on compliance had been unanimous. Dr. Kissinger then noted,

> The allegation that individuals or departments have held up consideration of compliance issues, have obscured consideration of compliance issues, have refused to deal with compliance issues, is a total falsehood.[16]

Kissinger proceeded to review for reporters some of the details of the "secret agreement" and of the alleged Soviet violations.

A week later the Pike Committee brought together an interesting cross section of witnesses: Ray Cline, old CIA hand and recent director of State's Bureau of Intelligence and Research; CIA deputy director for intelligence, Edward Proctor; and William Hyland, deputy to Henry Kissinger at the NSC. Cline described the SALT "holds" in great detail and commented in his prepared statement:

> A month is a long time for strategic intelligence about nuclear weapons to be suppressed if one conjectures that the USSR might be engaged in deception and actually planning an attack.[17]

Cline charged that the director of central intelligence, under the "hold" system, was demoted to a tertiary staff position in the national security bureaucracy.

William Hyland presented a defense of Kissinger, who, characteristically, refused to appear, and argued that a "hold" was not especially confidential. It was determined after the October 22, 1975, "hold," for example, that seventy-three persons within CIA alone had known of the information within one day, most of them the working-level analysts who had discovered the facts. Considering that substantial numbers in the Pentagon were also privy to "hold" information, Hyland put forward the figure of two hundred as the people "who got in on the ground floor." Ray Cline questioned why, if so many analysts knew of the withheld information, it was improper to inform the secretary of state (in reference to a 1973 case). Memos were quoted showing that a SALT monitoring report was published without the "hold" information. Hyland persisted with a firm "I know of no piece of information on this entire list that was completely withheld from [SCC members] or withheld from members of the Verification Panel."[18] Kissinger himself had said during his news conference that "there has been no case in which intelligence was not distributed in the quarterly intelligence publication that was concerned with the question of SALT monitoring."[19] Three years later a witness told a Senate Intelligence Committee hearing that a reasonable case could be made that perjury was committed that day before the Pike Committee.[20]

Meanwhile Admiral Zumwalt continued his charges that the SALT violation allegations had not been handled effectively. Zumwalt told a House committee on December fifteenth that

> I am saying there is data to support my judgment that the Soviet Union has violated the basic ABM Treaty, has violated the interim offensive agreement, and has violated in addition unilateral statements—all of them as they all were explained to the Congress. The nuances of the discussion of what these violations are have been used, in my judgment, by Secretary Kissinger to take our eye off the overriding fact that his own assurances have been violated. The nuances of differences have to do with, whether or not, calls a high probability of violation an ambiguity or whether you could prove in a court of law that it occurred.[21]

Zumwalt repeated these and similar charges in other hearings and in speeches and was prominently featured in *Aviation Week*.

In the midst of these cover-up allegations Kissinger was forced to cancel a planned trip to Moscow that was reportedly intended to finalize a SALT II agreement. Suddenly beyond all doubt loomed a real Soviet violation. Intelligence discovered in December 1975 that the Soviets had begun sea trials of four new Delta-class fleet ballistic-missile submarines. To remain within the SALT I limits this meant that they had also to dismantle fifty-one SS-7 and SS-8 ICBM launchers. In a particularly tough winter, Russian construction crews were unable to complete de-

mobilization of forty of the bin-type launchers. The United States raised
this question in the SCC in March 1976 and made a quiet diplomatic
protest in April. The Soviets explained their demolition difficulties and
asserted that the launchers had been rendered inoperative. Fortunately
this corresponded with the information of American intelligence. During May the Russians admitted the violation officially and the launchers
were dismantled.

It is interesting to note that in this one instance where the evidence
of violation was most concrete, the American delegates to the SCC reportedly had instructions to go slowly. NSDM 283 titled "SALT Contingency Planning" insisted that the U.S. commissioner

> should inform his counterpart that the U.S. government is not accusing or
> implying that the USSR is in violation with existing SALT agreements . . .
> [the issues] involve questions concerning compliance and related situations
> we consider ambiguous. The purpose of raising these issues is to resolve
> these questions, and, as necessary, to bring about corrective action.[22]

A clue to the American approach is furnished by a report on SALT verification published by the State Department in March. This document
noted several "dilemmas of response" which inhibit bringing allegations
of violation. The evidence must be sufficient to establish that a violation
has occurred; the security of the intelligence source must be considered
along with the magnitude of the suspected violation and the intentions
of the violator, with all action "carefully tailored not only to the facts of
the case but to the objectives of national policy."

> The central dilemma of response is the problem of ambiguous evidence. If
> we react to any evidence of violations no matter how ambiguous, we may
> put ourselves in the position of alleging violations which in fact never oc-
> curred. A false challenge may seem like a provocation; a large number of
> such challenges may needlessly undermine public confidence in an agree-
> ment, and can be expected to have a disruptive effect on our relations with
> the party challenged.[23]

Henry Kissinger was sincerely committed to SALT II but after 1975
his negotiating power was severely restricted. Illustrative of this change
was the fact that when Kissinger did reach Moscow in January 1976, a
representative of the Defense Department accompanied the negotiating
team for the first time. Nineteen seventy-six was an election year in
which "détente" became a forbidden word in a world of alleged Soviet
SALT violations, and American hostility over Soviet and Cuban moves
in Africa. No meaningful SALT exchanges were held after January. To

a great extent his failure was the product of his own policies. In his July 1979 testimony to the Senate on a SALT II Treaty signed by the succeeding administration, Kissinger admitted,

> We resorted to [unilateral statements] ourselves to perhaps an excessive degree in 1972, and in speaking to a group of congressmen in the White House at the time, I mentioned unilateral statements that we had made as a restraint on Soviet conduct. I think experience has shown that the unilateral statements that we made are not a restraint on Soviet conduct, that they do not bind the Soviet Union. And as a general proposition I would think it unwise to rely on them.[24]

Given ambiguities in the agreement the verification of SALT could only become more difficult. The matter of the size of "light" ICBMs is a case in point. The U.S. was aware in advance of the agreement that there would be new and larger fourth-generation Soviet ICBMs. Gerard C. Smith, who led the U.S. delegation at the SALT I talks recalls that

> at Helsinki we had been informally advised that while the Soviet Union would be deploying missiles of larger volume in SS-11 silos, they would not approach the halfway mark between an SS-11 and the admittedly heavy missile, the SS-9. I have seen no claims that the new Soviet missiles are greater in volume than this.[25]

Other observers argue equally passionately that the Soviets' intentions were more sinister. David S. Sullivan, a CIA analyst with the OSR, was fired after disclosing a highly classified CIA report to Senator Henry Jackson and his staff assistant Richard Perle, which concluded that the Soviets had deliberately deceived the U.S. on the size of the fourth-generation missiles.

In the ratification process of the SALT II Treaty, when it was finally achieved, the Senate Select Committee on Intelligence has had the primary role in ascertaining U.S. capacity to verify the agreements. For this purpose it was given extensive briefings, access to intelligence, and a special interagency report done by the director of central intelligence's SALT Steering Group. In this context the NSC also produced a report on SALT compliance, which is said to refer to eleven specific attempts by the Soviet Union to conceal aspects of its military programs extending back to 1966 and including such items as the building of dummy submarines and SAM sites, as well as the documented silo dismantling violation of 1976. In its own report the Senate Intelligence Committee concluded that the record on intelligence estimates has improved since 1970 "as a direct result of the improvements in the technical capabilities of United States reconnaissance systems."[26]

The Intelligence Committee also drew some conclusions about SALT I compliance and its relation to American diplomatic activity:

> It is clear from the SALT I record that intelligence of possible Soviet violation of the treaty was, in some cases and for a time, withheld from executive branch officials who had a need for such information. Lacking an oversight committee for intelligence matters, the Congress was not supplied the intelligence information on SALT monitoring.[27]

Most interesting of all is the case of David Sullivan, who, as he continued to reiterate his thesis of Soviet deception, seems more and more to have been drawn to the realization that perhaps not *only* Soviet motives needed monitoring in the SALT negotiations. In a 1979 paper Sullivan wrote:

> If, of course, Dr. Kissinger *did know* of the SS-19's large size in May 1972, as Assistant Secretary Slocombe claims, then Kissinger's 1972 and 1975 statements suggest that he not only misled Congress by incorrectly implying that the U.S. unilateral definition of a heavy ICBM would bind the Soviets, but he also knew in 1972 that the Soviets would later violate the U.S. heavy ICBM definition by deploying the SS-19. The issue thus could become the old Watergate question: What did Kissinger know and when did he know it? Mr. Slocombe's own analysis raises the unpleasant question of whether there was an attempt during SALT I to suppress critical intelligence information, a Watergate within Watergate, regarding the cover-up of bona fide national security issues. Slocombe's description of the SS-19 case therefore implies a much more serious criticism of Dr. Kissinger than that he was simply duped by the Soviets and that he incorrectly assured the Congress that the U.S. unilateral heavy ICBM definition was binding on the Soviets. Slocombe's analysis implies that Kissinger knowingly misrepresented U.S. knowledge of the SS-19 to the Congress in 1972 and again in 1975. Further, Slocombe's analysis could also imply that Kissinger suppressed information on the SS-19 in order to delay widespread recognition of the true facts.[28]

CHAPTER FIFTEEN
INTELLIGENCE ALARUM

Estimates of Soviet military spending were a product of McNamara's tenure at the Pentagon when, in order to have Soviet spending data to incorporate in systems analysis studies, the secretary of defense put substantial pressure on CIA to produce such estimates. McNamara's initiative was welcomed by some groups in CIA, particularly the analysts of the Office of Economic Reporting (OER), which had been working since the mid-fifties to create tools suitable for determining Soviet defense spending. Other analysts, including some in BNE, were less certain that the job could be accomplished effectively. However the use of explicit quantitative comparisons in systems analysis furnished a compelling rationale for improved economic reporting and CIA made an effort to develop better capabilities in this area.

There were several possible approaches to examining Soviet military spending. One was simply to take the ruble outlays reported by the Soviet budget each year and multiply this by some conversion rate from rubles to dollars. This was unacceptable because few analysts believed the announced figures for Soviet defense spending. Moreover, it was widely believed that the Soviet *definition* of "defense" in their budget was much different from the American, the Soviets excluding a host of items included in the U.S. defense budget. Among those things thought to be excluded are military education, medical care, retirement pensions, certain operating costs, research and development, and construction costs. Thus the Soviet announced annual figure, only a single line item in their state budget, hardly represented comprehensive coverage of the range of defense spending. The situation was further complicated by the fact that there was little agreement on what the actual ruble-dollar exchange ratio might be.

Another possible method of calculating Soviet defense spending was to take the announced ruble figures, within the Russian budget as a whole, and look for other unexplained "residuals" in the budget that might represent defense funds disguised within other categories. It was often claimed, for example, that "science" spending was substantially composed of outlays for military research and development. Yet a third method involved examining figures on actual output of Soviet industry and calculating the proportion of these diverted to servicing the Soviet "military-industrial complex."[1]

The method actually evolved by CIA was an amalgam of costing and modeling and was called the "building block" approach. Using the "building block" method, the CIA observed actual performance as far as possible by counting production of missiles, submarines, tanks, the number of divisions, manpower, and so on. These "observables" would then be evaluated in two ways: first intelligence would calculate how much the same array of material and manpower would cost the American economy to produce in dollars; then, as a check on Soviet figures and to assess the burden of military spending on the entire Soviet economy, CIA would calculate the cost of U.S. military factors in rubles as they would be produced in Russia. The parallel sets of figures gave what was thought to be more reasonable conversion factors for ruble-dollar exchange rates as well as giving a direct picture of Soviet military costs relative to American.

For several years the CIA continued to produce estimates on Soviet defense spending utilizing its "building block" method and alternately projecting in rubles and dollars. After the appointment of General Daniel O. Graham as deputy director for estimates at the DIA, however, military intelligence took an increased interest in reassessing the formulas under which CIA reached its economic conclusions. In the first instance DIA analysts challenged the costing methodology by which CIA economists established "prices" for weapons and equipment among the annual Soviet "observables." CIA was using the closest similar U.S. weapons systems in pricing Soviet weapons despite greater sophistication and capability of U.S. weapons generally. In measuring rubles no one really had a thorough understanding of pricing structures and price behavior in the Soviet economy. Beginning in 1970 DIA refused to use weapons costs and defense spending figures drawn from CIA estimates in its own intelligence products.

At the CIA, Richard Helms appointed an economist as deputy director for intelligence during 1971. Edward Proctor was a Harvard Ph.D. and one of the wave of young specialists brought in with Max Millikan in the early 1950s. With the Office of Research and Reports, predecessor to OER, Proctor had played an important role in creating the "building block" approach to projecting Soviet defense spending. As deputy director he initially defended CIA's use of the method, which came under criticism again in early 1972 during the drafting of a national estimate on Soviet defense spending from 1960 to 1971. Some criticized the NIE figures as implausibly low. These analysts pointed to the evidence of across-the-board Russian force building, including, in the strategic field, over sixteen hundred missiles of several types, a strong fleet ballistic-missile program, and substantial missile-defense and research-and-development outlays.

The budget arguments were pressed by analysts within both CIA and DIA, while advocates of the "building block" approach also cut across organizational lines. The materialization of a new generation of Soviet ICBMs, which occurred in 1972, tended to encourage the criticisms of the budget methodology. When Defense Secretary Schlesinger asserted a substantial Soviet spending lead in support of the fiscal year 1976 budget, new information became available to intelligence which cemented the conclusion that the Soviet spending exceeded American by far more than the twenty percent projected by CIA in January of 1975. There were unconfirmed reports that the information was obtained from defectors who had been Soviet economic planning officials as well as from a copy of a top-level Soviet document which gave real Soviet budget figures decided upon by the Politburo several years previously.[2]

Conservative critics of intelligence, including former CIA analyst William T. Lee, were already charging that the CIA method resulted in a figure that was only half of the "real" Russian outlay. The new evidence showed the hypotheses of critics like Lee to be closer to the actual Soviet figures than the "buidling block" method used by CIA. In the face of these developments Director of Central Intelligence William Colby formed a special study group of CIA and DIA analysts to revise the way Soviet spending figures were derived. In February 1976 CIA report SR 76-10053 revised upward the U.S. projections of Soviet spending. It was decided the Russians were putting up to forty percent more into defense than the United States, ten to fifteen percent of the Soviet GNP as compared to the six to eight percent projection of previous NIEs.

The revised budget estimates did *not* mean that the Soviets were stronger than before—the number of "observables" counted by intelligence did not change at all, but only the *cost* of these items to the Soviet economy and the burden of defense spending within that economy. Khrushchev, who had called Soviet defense industry "the metal-eaters," had promised that the Soviet economy would catch up to that of the United States by 1980. Instead, a Soviet economy projected at forty-seven percent of the size of the American in 1964 had risen to only about fifty-two percent of the U.S. GNP by Khrushchev's target date, while the defense sector continued to absorb a third of the annual machinery output of Russian industry. An October 1975 memorandum, from Andrew Marshall of the Pentagon's Net Evaluation Group, concluded that the budget controversy demonstrated that Soviet defense industry was only half as efficient as had been thought.[3]

The proportion of Soviet spending going to defense would have been academic except for the implications it carried for the U.S. estimate of Russia's basic intentions. If, in fact, the Soviets had been devoting such a large amount to defense for over a decade, then clearly the Soviets were far more bellicose than intelligence had believed. This judgment, coming on top of putative Soviet deception in SALT, and the general dissatisfaction with the quality of NIEs, led to a new critique of the NIEs.

The "B Team" Report

Henry Kissinger's dislike of "talmudic" national estimates was shared by others who considered that the CIA had failed to predict the scale of the Soviet missile buildup. Measures to correct the perceived difficulties began even before Gerald Ford became President. In particular, when James R. Schlesinger was director of central intelligence in early 1973 he instituted a number of changes designed to streamline U.S. intelligence, mainly a reduction in force of almost ten percent of CIA's eighteen thousand men and women under an early retirement program. This followed the withdrawal from Viet Nam and mainly affected the clandestine services and DDS&T's Office of Research and Development. When asked, Schlesinger is quoted as replying, " 'Ruthless? I'm just trying to clear the aisle so I can walk.' " Schlesinger also directed that, unless great detail was specifically requested, SALT estimates were not to exceed three pages, double spaced, in length.

Schlesinger was soon called away to head the Department of Defense and he was replaced by William E. Colby, a Southeast Asia veteran who had been deputy director to Schlesinger and had come up, like Helms, through CIA's clandestine services. Colby observed that because BNE opposed the Pentagon on a number of issues, Kissinger and Nixon had excluded CIA itself from some of their most sensitive dealings. BNE had become detrimental to CIA's organizational health; as Colby put it, "I was convinced that change was needed if their inclination toward fixed positions was not to lead to trouble."[4] The chairman of BNE, experienced analyst John Huizenga, resigned from CIA, and Colby dissolved the BNE in October 1973.

BNE was replaced with a new entity, called the National Intelligence Officer (NIO) system. Colby appointed senior intelligence analysts to monitor specific functional areas, like SALT, the Soviet Union, economic reporting, and regional affairs. The NIOs were individually responsible to the director and had no corporate identity. Each NIO retained only a minimal amount of staff support but he could rely on any office in the intelligence community to contribute to the drafting of national estimates until they were submitted to the USIB. Colby regarded USIB review as a sufficient "wise man" review for the NIEs (Huizenga feared that the NIE process would be compromised and come to reflect White House preferences).

In the meantime the President's Foreign Intelligence Advisory Board (PFIAB), a civilian "watchdog" group that oversaw intelligence for the President, became quite interested in reviewing NIEs. Since 1969 PFIAB had been making annual assessments of the strategic balance for Presidents Nixon and Ford, which were independent of the NIEs. PFIAB took a more conservative view in its annual assessments and was disturbed at the degree of divergence between its conclusions and those in the national estimates. In August 1975 PFIAB Chairman George W. Anderson, Jr., wrote to President Ford to propose that Ford direct the NSC to implement a "competitive analysis" of the intelligence on Soviet intentions and capabilities. Colby told Ford that he should wait to see the 1975 NIE before taking any action, since this estimate was being produced with the new formula and Colby himself was heavily involved in the drafting. This might meet the criticisms of the estimates. Ford followed Colby's recommendation but after the NIE was in circulation, in April 1976, PFIAB renewed its proposal for a "competitive" intelligence analysis.

Ford replaced Colby with George Bush in the "Sunday Massacre" of November 1975. Bush had no previous intelligence experience, being a Texas oil man, but he had been a congressman and U.S. ambassador to the United Nations in 1971–1972. He conceived his role as CIA director to be mainly a political one; he would form a buffer between the CIA and Congress after the big investigations that had been conducted, allowing intelligence to focus on its primary work of analyzing foreign developments. Secretary of Defense Donald Rumsfeld also appointed a new assistant secretary for intelligence, Robert F. Ellsworth, on 26 January 1976. Both Ellsworth and Bush accepted the PFIAB recommendation for a "competitive" intelligence analysis. President Ford and the NSC eventually directed that the experimental study be conducted.

While the PFIAB recommendation for "competitive" analysis was under consideration, the CIA proceeded as usual to formulate NIE 11-8-76 on Soviet intentions and capabilities. Under the NIO system the national estimate was scheduled early in 1976. It was the responsibility of Howard Stoertz, NIO for the Soviet Union. Stoertz was a senior CIA analyst who had long specialized on Soviet affairs and had been secretary to the BNE during the interagency debates of the "missile gap" period. Stoertz set up procedures for NIE 11-8-76 and work on the estimate had already begun when the "competitive" study was approved by the NSC. The group of analysts drafting the NIE were then titled the "A Team."

Against the A Team were arrayed a number of outside consultants organized into several panels. The form of the "competitive" study group was determined in consultations between Bush and William Hyland, the deputy to the National Security Advisor. The NSC-CIA contacts decided that there would be several separate reviews on technical issues, and one general review of whether the evidence cited in the national estimate would sustain conclusions other than those contained in the actual NIE. For the technical issues the NSC chose missile accuracy and bomber penetrability.

Bush and Hyland evidently also agreed that the competitive study groups, called the "B Team," would be composed of conservative critics who opposed CIA's "arms control bias." The individuals chosen for the B Team collectively possessed great government and intelligence experience. The group was headed by Richard E. Pipes, professor of Russian history at Harvard. Included in the B Team were General Daniel Graham, from DCI's Intelligence Community Staff; General John Vogt, former USAF chief of staff and commander in Southeast Asia; William R. Van Cleave, former SALT delegation member; and Thomas Wolfe, Rand Corporation analyst, former Air Force colonel and air attaché in Moscow during the "bomber gap"; Major General Jasper A. Welch, Jr., who headed USAF's component for systems analysis and simulation; Paul Wolfowitz, who represented the Arms Control and Disarmament Agency; Seymour Weiss from the State Department; and Paul Nitze, a service official who was a veteran of many previous consulting and interagency studies for government, including NSC-68 and the Gaither Report.

The B Team members mostly agreed that the United States was not taking Soviet military power seriously enough. When this group was asked to perform the competitive study the results were predictable—a scathing critique of U.S. intelligence failure to predict the scope of Soviet developments. In retrospect it has been asked why there was no "C Team," composed of analysts with views considerably more liberal than those of the intelligence community. Why the panel was so heavily weighted is still a mystery, and is even more inexplicable in the light of George Bush's exchange with Senator William Proxmire (D-Wisconsin) on May 24, 1976, in the course of annual CIA testimony to the Joint Economic Committee:

> PROXMIRE: One of the disclosures that concerns me most so far as the Church investigation is concerned is the evidence that the CIA tailored its reports on the Soviet MIRV program as a result of pressures applied by former Secretary of Defense Melvin Laird and the White House. Will you discuss that and state what steps have been taken to prevent a recurrence of that problem?
>
> BUSH: Mr. Chairman, I have stated that we would do everything we could inside our building and inside the community, to see that this did not happen. I have promulgated regulations since I have been director of central intelligence that were sent to the entire intelligence community.
> One of the most fundamental and principal of them, if not the first point, was I believe, that our estimates should come forward without regard for any existing budgets or programs. And I made this clear in my first comments to a group at CIA, the largest group that we could get to assemble. I have reiterated this at our staff meeting over and over again, and I am confident that the CIA analysts not only have the message but had it loud and clear before I came here. So, I think we have done administratively what is essential to see that estimates are protected from policy bias.[5]

However, Bush cooperated with Hyland to select the very strongly opinionated B Team and then largely divorced himself from the proceedings.

The B Team study of bomber penetrability focused on an examination of intelligence on Soviet low-level air defenses. Here the consultants showed that certain Soviet development programs had to be carefully watched, such as the SA-10 missile system, which might be designed to combat low-flying cruise missiles. The consensus on bomber penetrability, using low-altitude flight profiles, was that defense turns on the ability to detect incoming bombers at a distance sufficient to engage them and that the Soviet Union is unlikely to be able to field a "lookdown" radar able to distinguish bomber movement over land surfaces until the later 1980s.

On the subject of ICBM accuracies the B Team delved into the technical aspects of missile performance and guidance telemetry and emerged with novel conclusions. B Team members argued from the theoretical point that the accuracy of the Soviet missiles was essentially unknowable and that there was no evidence to support CIA's position that Soviet ICBMs were less accurate than U.S. ones. Indeed the B Team held it was possible that Russian missiles could be even more accurate than our own, which, if true, suggested that the U.S. land-based Minuteman missiles would become vulnerable in the near future. Some suspicions, such as those voiced by Navy Secretary J. William Middendorf in December 1976, that the Soviets were adapting their MIRVed warheads for terminal guidance from orbiting satellites, lent additional substance to this claim. This critique did not immediately change the intelligence-community consensus, but it is noteworthy that in 1977–1978 intelligence increased its projections for the accuracy of the Soviet SS-19 and SS-18 ICBMs.

In its overall study of whether the intelligence could justify interpretations other than those contained in the national estimates, the B Team panel monitoring the drafting of NIE 11-8-76 concluded that indeed a more ominous construction was possible. Here B Team members exceeded their mandate to study the current NIE by ranging back over all the examples of intelligence failures familiar to them from their government service rather than focusing on NIE 11-8-76. The B Team argued that the Soviet Union's ultimate intentions were to develop forces able to interfere with the free flow of ocean transport, to deny raw materials to the West, and to disrupt fuel supplies; it aimed for the projection of power on a global scale and strategic forces that would have a first-strike "war-winning" capability.

After the drafts of both the NIE and the B Team reports were completed, both groups gathered before PFIAB to argue their cases. B Team members cited the high levels of Soviet defense expenditure, the substantial Soviet investment in civil defense, research and development on BMD, and historical cases of intelligence failure to question CIA's interpretation. Representatives of CIA responded that the hard evidence did not permit such extrapolations, to be answered with exhortations to "get on board" or "become part of the team." Given the fact that the intelligence consensus subsequently came to embrace many of the points made by the B Team, opinions anonymously expressed by B Team members seem substantially correct. One felt that " 'we just licked them on a great number of points.' "[6] Another offered, " 'Sometimes we left them speechless. We had men of great prestige, some of them with memories going back twenty-five years or more, and they made devastating critiques of agency estimates." Richard Pipes himself thought that " 'if we made any impact on [the A Team] it was by force of argument.' "[7]

There is considerable confusion as to what actually was the impact of the B Team study on the NIE 11-8-76. Some B Team members professed to be highly pleased with the results, claiming to have turned the NIE "180 degrees" after it was returned for rewriting no fewer than three times. A congressional study of the B Team episode, however, has concluded that this view is incorrect.[8] In any case, NIE 11-8-76 went to the USIB for review on December 21. It did not go to George Bush for final approval until January 7, 1977. However, within four days of its USIB review, the national estimate had leaked to the press.

When the story of the B Team broke, the victors of the 1976 election were preparing their transition for the inauguration. The results of the B Team exercise were sent to President Carter for review. He dealt with this study by ordering an NSC study of his own, termed a Presidential Review Memorandum, on a net assessment of comparative Soviet and U.S. force postures. Carter ordered this study on February 18, 1977, and it eventually led to Presidential Decision Memorandum 18 plus follow-on analyses. In other words, the new administration did all it could to put the B Team episode behind it.

Paul Nitze for one had had experience with this kind of thing before. The Eisenhower administration had used similar tactics in dealing with the Gaither Report twenty years previous. Nitze did the same as Gaither members had done then: he took his campaign to the public. Together with like-minded citizens Eugene V. Rostow, David Packard, Richard V. Allen, and others, Nitze founded the Committee on the Present Danger with the declaration that the Soviet "drive for dominance" was the principal threat to world peace and that

> our country is in a period of danger, and the danger is increasing. Unless decisive steps are taken to alert the nation, and to change the course of its policy, our economic and military capability will become inadequate.[9]

Public knowledge of the B Team exercise led to widespread reactions from opinion makers and officials. Director of Central Intelligence Bush refused to comment on the conclusions during a television interview, but he remarked that outside challenges to NIEs seemed attractive and Bush considered recommending further "competitive" estimates to his successor. Some retired intelligence officials had sharp comments to make. Former DDI Ray Cline called the B Team group a "kangaroo court," while CIA's former deputy director for research, Herbert Scoville, charged that the integrity of the intelligence estimating process was being called into question. Carter's appointee for secretary of state, Cyrus Vance, rejected the notion that Russia had achieved or was achieving superiority but asserted that "general parity" prevailed. The day before Carter's inauguration, a *New York Times* editorial called the

B Team episode a "worst-case" assessment. A prominent Soviet expert on the United States, Georgi A. Arbatov, who was closely associated with Brezhnev, categorically rejected the implication that Soviet intentions were hostile, and presented evidence that the ICBM buildup since 1965 had been in response to a huge U.S. superiority in numbers of ICBMs and SLBMs. The controversy led the Senate Intelligence Committee to form a subcommittee to investigate the B Team's five-month study of intelligence.

Rumsfeld's view as secretary of defense is especially significant for its reflection of Pentagon thinking when the defense budget was submitted to Congress that January. He thought the B Team had done good work, and felt that the report only confirmed what he had been saying all year, that the United States had to act immediately to reverse "adverse trends" by increased defense spending. Rumsfeld warned in his posture statement for fiscal 1978 that "the Soviets give evidence of moving toward a fundamental shift in the 'correlation of forces' that would give them peacetime and crisis leverage over the United States." Even more telling, "emphasis in Soviet nuclear programs on quantitative superiority indicates concern for major warfighting potential," so much so that the trends "clearly are adverse to those who believe in freedom and self-determination."[10] Rumsfeld's defense budget request included funds for ICBM retargeting capability (Command Data Buffer), for a mobile ICBM, for cruise missiles, and for the first conversion of a Poseidon missile submarine to fire the Trident I submarine missile.

B Team members defended themselves against charges of bias in press conferences and letters to newspapers in early 1977. In July, Richard Pipes published an article giving his construction of Soviet strategic doctrine, which was very close to Nitze's view, and based on the elements of quantitative superiority and preemptive attack. According to Pipes, Soviet emphasis on defense through a civil shelter program and active missile defenses, plus a counterforce doctrine to eliminate U.S. nuclear forces, would give the Soviet Union a "war-winning strategy."[11]

In late 1978 the body of CIA analyst John S. Paisley was found in the Chesapeake Bay. Paisley had been CIA's coordinator for the B Team, responsible for furnishing classified information to the consultants during their study. He had also been deputy director of Langley's Office of Strategic Research (OSR), a member of the CIA-DIA study group on the Soviet military budget, and a friend of the Russian defector Yuri Nosenko. At the time of his disappearance, it is said, Paisley may have been working on an analysis for CIA of the leaks that brought the B Team report to public attention.[12] In the meantime the Senate had completed its inquiry. Senator Gary Hart (D-Colorado) wrote, "The correspondence about the exercise shows that the President's Foreign Intelligence Advisory Board (PFIAB) included members more interested in altering the conclusions of the national estimate than in improving its quality."[13] Already, in March 1977, President Carter had abolished PFIAB, to the consternation of a number of its members.

Even though the B Team and PFIAB receded into the past, many of their judgments increasingly became part of the consensus view. Intelligence estimates continued to show alarming trends. In regard to military spending, the CIA's 1977 unclassified report put the Soviet budget at thirty percent more than the American for the previous year, a total of $120 billion (in 1975 dollars). The January 1978 report reviewing 1977 put Russian military outlays that year at $140 billion (in 1977 dollars). Measuring the ruble budget in June 1978, CIA found that the Soviets' rate of increase was running at four to five percent annually and that they were spending twelve to thirteen percent of their GNP for defense. By 1980 Soviet spending was shown to be at some $165 billion in current dollars for the previous year. This was almost half as much again as American outlays.[14] It remains true, however, that Soviet industry and technology are less efficient than their American counterparts. One former ACDA analyst found that if the Soviet dollar amount is deflated according to these factors, it can still be seen to be less than or equal to our own military spending.[15]

It is possible to extract from the CIA's annual reports some specific observations with regard to the Soviet strategic forces. The Soviet air defense forces and SRF rank respectively fourth and last of the Soviet services in their shares of the defense spending "pie." The SRF expenditures, particularly, show a definite cyclical pattern related to deployment of the successive generations of ICBMs. Its share of the Soviet budget evidently stood at ten percent in 1967, fell to five percent in 1972, and then rose (with the SS-18 family missiles) to eight percent in 1977. Even so, Soviet spending on forces for intercontinental attack has represented a shrinking proportion of total outlays for strategic forces, from forty-five percent in 1975 to forty percent in 1977 and down to thirty-five percent in 1979. This is also reflected in the SRF manpower reduction during the period from about 375,000 to 300,000 in overall personnel. Moreover, the proportion by which Soviet spending in these categories exceeds American has been steadily eeclining, and U.S. outlays for SLBMs have exceeded Soviet since 1976.

A year before the B Team exercise CIA's basic outlook on the Soviet strategic threat was clearly stated in the director of central intelligence's "Perspectives on Intelligence," a five-year overview document:

The modernization program now under way will give the Soviets larger numbers of more accurate missile warheads, improved missile survivability, and greater operational flexibility. In their strategic offensive and defensive programs, research and development is aimed at unique applications of existing technologies and applications of advanced technology based on theoretical or technological breakthroughs. Given present and planned U.S. capabilities, we believe that the Soviets could not develop in the next five years a first-strike capability so overwhelming as to prevent substantial retaliation.[16]

The statement was penned very soon after the Russians emplaced their first MIRVed missile, an SS-19, in December 1974. Until that time NIEs continued to show that no Soviet counterforce threat would develop against Minuteman much before 1985.

The B Team began a reevaluation of that conclusion in subsequent national estimates. Carter's CIA director, Admiral Stansfield Turner, continued "competitive" estimating to the extent of contracting Rand Corporation for an early draft of the 1977 NIE, so that CIA could benefit from the experience of one of its analysts who had left Langley to go to Rand. Turner also endorsed the change instituted by George Bush in 1976 that eliminated the USIB and replaced it with an entity known as the National Foreign Intelligence Board (NFIB), which had the same functions but with the addition of Turner's deputy director for intelligence community staff as a member. In 1980 the United States Marine Corps was given observer status on NFIB, the first time the Marines have been included in national intelligence. In addition, CIA's analytical component, DDI, was replaced with a National Foreign Assessment Center (NFAC) of fifteen hundred professionals under Robert Bowie, a substantial portion of the three to five thousand analysts maintained by CIA, DIA, and NSA together.

In early 1978 President Carter issued a new executive order, number 12036, to regulate intelligence community organization. After a protracted struggle within the community, and four drafts of the order successively rejected by the White House, the new regime gave the director of central intelligence some additional power in the community but safeguarded the intelligence prerogatives of the secretary of defense. Turner received additional responsibilities for the consolidated intelligence community budget and for collection tasking of intelligence components. Within CIA Turner continued the trend toward reduction of intelligence manpower resulting from the end of hostilities in Southeast Asia. Already intelligence manpower had been reduced by thirty percent, now Turner directed two further reductions in force within CIA. These were mainly aimed at cutting the clandestine services. The DIA was reduced from seven thousand to forty-five hundred in manpower. Admiral Turner's intense interest in the national estimates led him to redraft NIEs himself or to ask the NIOs for changes in order to "fine-tune" the estimates. Overall the late 1970s witnessed a resurgence of military intelligence.

In 1974 the CIA believed that there was no near-term threat to Minuteman. In 1976 it was still agreed that Soviet accuracy improvements were no greater than anticipated. But this changed in the first years of the Carter administration, after the B Team's warning of 1976. By early 1979 the draft NIE being prepared at Langley's National Foreign Assessment Center projected a "drastic improvement" in Russian missile accuracy in the early 1980s, with more efficient guidance systems creating a possibility of disarming Minuteman in the mid-1980s.[17] The national estimate reportedly projected up to thirty-five hundred Soviet ICBMs by the mid-eighties in the absence of SALT, and there was some concern regarding about one thousand older ICBMs that the Soviets kept in storage after they were replaced by more modern missiles. Later that year CIA's national intelligence officer on the Soviet Union, Raymond McCrory, coordinated the 1980 national estimate. This recent NIE is said to conclude that by 1985 the Soviets could place eleven thousand warheads on their ICBMs and another five thousand on SLBMs, with a thousand more nuclear weapons on bombers. By 1990 the Russian inventory could be as high as twenty to thirty thousand. The national estimates on Soviet offensive and defensive forces completed in December 1980 are said to be some of the most extensive ever—over 350 pages—and to have very few dissenting footnotes from the CIA despite that agency's record of opposing very large force predictions. It remains to be seen if the Soviets will actually fulfill these predictions, but given such large forces it is not difficult to see how intelligence could expect a counterforce threat against Minuteman, even if theoretically such an attack would be difficult to plan and execute.

The new intelligence consensus can be seen to reflect growing general dissatisfaction with détente and accompanying doubt regarding the intentions of the Soviet Union. The process has been an inexorable swing from complacency to alarm, much as occurred following Sputnik.

Battles over Backfire

Ever since the Russians curtailed their procurement of Bison and Bear bombers in the late 1950s, some analysts had been expecting another round of bomber building. Intelligence thought this had occurred when signs of a Russian supersonic-bomber development program appeared. Predictions were made about two bomber aircraft, which intelligence called Bounder and Blinder. The year 1961 came and went without achievement of initial operating capability for either plane. Actually the Bounder was never deployed and the Blinder materialized only in 1963, but it was a medium jet bomber, not the heavy bomber expected by the Air Force. Nevertheless USAF continued to predict the appearance of a new Soviet heavy bomber, which led McNamara to note in 1964 that this view was not shared by CIA, DIA, or any of the other services.

Evidence accumulated slowly over the next five years. It was not until early 1969, when a large unidentified plane was photographed outside a plant at Kazan, that there was any hard intelligence to back up claims of Soviet bomber development. At the time the plane was described in appropriations hearings as a supersonic medium bomber. Even *Aviation Week* termed the plane an "intermediate-range bomber development." In his classified posture statement of early 1970 Melvin Laird noted the existence of the prototype aircraft for a "variable-geometry wing, supersonic dash bomber," with a combat radius of two thousand to twenty-seven hundred miles and initial operating capability projected for the 1974–1976 period. American authorities continued to monitor the development of this aircraft, which was given the designation Backfire. Congress was briefed on the plane in early 1971 and its existence was revealed to the public by *The New York Times* that September.[18]

The Backfire's engineering development proceeded apace, and the plane logged its first flight test during March 1970. The following year it was observed in testing and executing in-flight refueling from a Bison tanker at the Russian aircraft test center of Ramenskoye, east of Moscow. By early 1972 there were five Backfire prototype aircraft, all of which had been flown before the end of October. The Backfire is 131 feet long and 33 feet high, from the ground to the tip of its tail. It has a wingspan of 113 feet when its wings are extended for low speed operation, or eighty feet when they are swept back for supersonic flight. The plane is believed to have a gross weight of 285,000 pounds, and a payload of 20,000 pounds—two air-to-surface missiles, with tail-mounted automatic cannon directed by radar plus other electronic gear for defense. Backfire has a cruising speed of nine tenths of the speed of sound and a maximum speed of Mach 2.5. Actual production began in 1973 and a first operational unit was provided with eighteen of these aircraft a year later.

The Backfire is the latest in a long series of Soviet bombers from the Tupolev Design Bureau. The plane is something of a departure in the Soviet force structure as it is the first large bomber the Soviet Union has produced in almost two decades. In size Backfire lies between its immediate predecessor the Blinder (185,000 pounds gross weight) and the early heavy bombers (350,000 pounds gross weight), about eighty percent the size of the old Bison and Bear bombers, but less than sixty percent as large in gross weight as the U.S. B-52's currently in flight. In aircraft payload there is clearly no comparison—the Boeing B-52 has an advantage of 350 percent.

In Washington, the intelligence opinion on the Russian long range air forces, "SuSAC" as they called it, was that their medium bombers would not figure prominently in any air attack on the United States. This was concluded for a variety of reasons, ranging from the limited payloads of the planes to the difficulty of preparing staging bases and the meager self-defense capabilities. General Triantafellu's Air Force Intelligence dissented from this view.

The Air Force argued that Backfire could be used for intercontinental attack and should be considered capable of that in the national estimates. Triantafellu won his point in 1971, after getting support from the DIA for the intercontinental attack hypothesis. At Langley, Richard Helms did not believe the issue of a Soviet medium bomber was terribly important, and CIA compromised in a unanimous NIE judgment that the Backfire had the range for bombing missions against the United States. Unanimity was short lived, however. The CIA and other USIB agencies soon broke with the consensus. Basing itself on different estimates of manufacturing techniques, CIA argued that the Backfire's range was not as great as had been thought. The argument was good enough to convince the Air Force officer who was DIA's main analyst on Backfire, and in 1973 when General Daniel Graham was head at DIA that organization once again sided with CIA against the Air Force intelligence judgment. The new consensus viewed Backfire as a peripheral attack weapon.

Only a few months later the intelligence issue on Backfire was revived by the actual deployment of the plane with operational Russian air units. It turned out that the Tu-22M was being jointly procured by the Soviet naval air force and the long-range aviation component of the air force. In James R. Schlesinger's fiscal 1975 posture statement, the Air Force position received some support:

> The question of the range and primary mission of the Backfire has yet to be fully resolved. It now appears that the latest model will have a greater range than estimated for the earlier model. This factor, combined with its known refueling capability, would seem to indicate that the Backfire could be used as an intercontinental as well as a peripheral bomber, the role for which it appears best suited.[19]

Schlesinger's assertion provided important support for the Air Force whose intelligence chief, Major General George J. Keegan, who had replaced Triantafellu in 1972, had been developing the hypothesis that a new model of the plane called the Backfire-B was the longer-ranged bomber that should remove all doubts as to the plane's intercontinental function.

Through 1974 and 1975 the Russians produced additional aircraft and occasionally mentioned plans for new bombers even beyond Backfire. The majority opinion in intelligence was still that Backfire was designed for the "peripheral attack" mission. The CIA's military budget estimates found that about fifteen percent of Russian spending for strategic forces was going for the peripheral attack mission and in 1975 it put the Tu-22M production rate at one to one and a half per month, figures with which DIA was in agreement. The constant bickering over this plane led William Colby to decide in 1975 that he would attempt to "adjudicate" the intelligence dispute. The decision was taken to ask for a consultant study by aeronautical engineers who would estimate the Russian plane's capabilities based on the available information and hopefully resolve the range dispute once and for all.

During this same period the Backfire bomber became an issue of importance to SALT negotiators as well. Evidently, in the mid-sixties certain specialists in the Soviet Academy of Sciences proposed that an arms control agreement be sought that provided for the ending of bomber production on both sides. This was consistent with the steady reduction in strength of bomber forces in SAC which, with the introduction of the ICBM, had fallen from 142 squadrons in 1960 to 65 in 1965 (and would be further reduced to 26 squadrons by 1976). From the Soviet viewpoint such an agreement would have the effect of reducing the large advantage of SAC in numbers of bombers relative to Russian long-range aviation. Evidently the Soviet General Staff was alarmed by American plans for a new bomber, the FB-111, however, and rejected the notion of constraints on bombers as a valid objective for strategic arms limitation.[20] Strangely enough, there are a number of design similarities between the FB-111 and the Backfire bomber, both of which use swing-wings, are capable of supersonic "dash" tactics, and can carry the cruise missile. The Backfire is a much larger aircraft, about three times as large as the FB-111, but the latter can carry more weight in armament. The Backfire has greater range, but the Americans have a much more favorable ratio of air tankers to operational aircraft.

While SALT II talks focused on establishing limits on the numbers of MIRVed missiles on both sides, the Backfire became operational by mid-1974. That fall Kissinger and the Russians accomplished a "conceptual breakthrough" in the arms negotiations at Vladivostok and agreed on common upper limits for both MIRVs and total nuclear delivery vehicles. The Americans wanted to avoid any provisions that restricted air-craft and missile forces stationed in NATO Europe, including the FB-111 which could conceivably strike targets in the Soviet Union in case of war. For this reason the Soviets had a strong case to exclude also a "peripheral attack" weapons system like the Backfire. If, on the other hand, Backfire was seen as an intercontinental bomber, it would have to be counted in the common upper limit of twenty-four hundred set at Vladivostok. Kissinger's critics charge that he "gave away" the Backfire even before the Vladivostok meeting, and there is some evidence that he told reporters at the time that Backfire was specifically excluded in the Vladivostok accord.

The exclusion of Backfire at Vladivostok did not meet approval in the U.S. bureaucracy. Schlesinger and the Joint Chiefs strongly opposed any exclusion of Backfire, evidently reasoning that they could inhibit the buildup of this Soviet weapons system. This position was approved by the NSC Verification Panel so that when specialists convened at Geneva in January 1975 to work out the details of the Vladivostok accord, the U.S. delegation had been instructed to insist on the inclusion of Backfire. This action irritated the Soviets who both insisted that the Tu-22M was not a "strategic" weapon and also proceeded to reopen the issue of counting bombers equipped with cruise missiles. The acrimonious Backfire and cruise missile issues prevented the conclusion of a SALT agreement in 1975 and have bedeviled the arms talks ever since.

Gerald Ford wanted to resolve this question in a way that the military would accept, and he felt that he might be able to do so in another personal meeting with Brezhnev. This opportunity arose in August 1975, when the conference on security and cooperation in Europe met at Helsinki. Although this conference is generally known for its agreement on human rights, SALT was an important subject for bilateral discussions between the United States and Soviet Union. When the status of the Backfire bomber was raised, Leonid Brezhnev insisted that the plane was not an intercontinental bomber and described the Tu-22M's characteristics. Brezhnev's figures did not tally with the ones the Air Force had given to President Ford, and Ford pointed this out to the Soviet leader.

"Well, Mr. General Secretary, here is what our people tell me that Backfire can do."

Brezhnev was so struck with the differences between his official Soviet figures on Backfire performance and those presented by Ford from U.S. intelligence that he asked for an immediate recess to confer with Russian military leaders in the hall. After about ten minutes of murmured conversation the Soviet delegation returned to the table.

"Our figures are right. We know what the plane can do. Your figures are wrong," said Brezhnev.

Ford replied, "I have to depend on the information given me. Our people have been right in most instances in the past. I have to use our figures in negotiating with you."

It was clear that the Helsinki SALT discussions were at an impasse. Ford recalls that "we looked each other in the eye. Neither of us was going to give ground."[21] After returning to Washington, Kissinger strove to get approval within the administration for some formula that would salvage the SALT II Treaty before the 1976 elections. First the secretary of state managed to get agreement on a proposal that the Vladivostok ceiling for the Russians could be raised by about four hundred, in return for which the Tu-22M would be counted in the totals. The Soviets rejected that solution in September 1975. Kissinger redoubled his efforts within the Ford administration, insisting on the development of a new negotiating position, and he succeeded in getting the NSC to agree on a new approach. This time a certain number of Backfires—275—would be allowed above the Soviets' upper limit, but in return the Russians would have to abandon their effort to secure some provision restraining U.S. cruise missiles. Dr. Kissinger presented this package to Soviet Foreign Minister Gromyko in meetings at New York and Washington on September 18–20 at which time the press was being told that the SALT treaty was eighty-five to ninety percent finished.

The Soviets showed some interest in the American bargaining position—at least they did not reject it out of hand—and so a Kissinger mission to Moscow was set for January 1976. However, criticisms of Kissinger multiplied during this period and a new leadership in the Department of Defense, under Donald Rumsfeld, was more inclined to view Backfire with alarm. The result was to force changes in the U.S. position at the NSC. Several meetings were held at the White House, "intensive" ones according to President Ford, culminating on January 13, 1976, when the NSC discussed four options. Rumsfeld and the Joint Chiefs favored an option under which all Backfire bombers would be counted against the ceiling, while the U.S. agreed to ban submarine-launched cruise missiles and to count its bombers carrying cruise missiles as MIRV carriers. In the discussion Kissinger cited recent intelligence reports containing the results of consultant studies of Backfire aircraft performance. These reduced the projection of the Tu-22M's range, with the implication that the Backfire would be even less effective if committed to a strategic mission. General George Brown, Chairman JCS, retorted that the Backfire, even with reduced range, could hit targets all over the United States. Rumsfeld maintained that an agreement without some provision for Backfire would never get Senate ratification.

Kissinger's instructions from the NSC were to offer a variant on the option preferred by the Pentagon. The number of Backfires then in service would be exempted and future Backfires would count under the Vladivostok ceilings. The Americans would accept the limitations on their forces suggested by DOD. Kissinger warned that the Russians were likely to reject this package, and he had been furnished by the NSC with a fall-back SALT package he could offer. This was the separate Backfire ceiling proposal, of 275, with a reduction of ten percent in the overall ceiling of 2,400. Kissinger carried these proposals to Moscow, after giving a précis of them to Soviet Ambassador Dobrynin in Washington for advance notification. The Americans landed at Moscow's Vnukovo Airport in minus-ten-degree-Fahrenheit temperatures but with a warm reception from the Russians. The lead story in *Pravda* the previous day asserted that the Soviet Union was "full of determination to do everything that depends on it so that a solution might be found for the problem of limiting strategic offensive weapons and halting the arms race." Meanwhile, Kissinger's delegation for the first time included a Pentagon representative, Dr. James P. Wade, chief of the DOD SALT Task Force, who had his own channel of communications to Washington.

Predictably the Soviets rejected Kissinger's first option. Their alternative offer was a reduction of 100 in the Vladivostok upper ceiling in exchange for letting the Backfire bomber "run free." The Soviet chief of staff, Marshal Nikolai V. Ogarkov, was called into the room to present a Soviet briefing on Backfire performance to support the contention that the Tu-22M should not be construed as a strategic bomber. The Americans rejected the Russian offer of a minor reduction and Kissinger put forward his fall-back package, in which Brezhnev and Gromyko showed considerable interest. The Russians went back to the Politburo for a late-night session on January twenty-first and made a new offer to Kissinger the next morning. All profess to have been very excited with the possibilities for an agreement, but Kissinger had first to carry the Russian proposal back to Washington, and there Rumsfeld and the Joint Chiefs rejected it. The Americans finally agreed to send Dobrynin a different offer, which was to put the intractable cruise-missile and Backfire issues into a separate package for continued negotiation and sign a treaty embodying whatever else had been agreed on. The Soviets rejected this offer as well, in March 1976, because collateral constraints would apply to Backfire while the separate discussions on it proceeded. This ended the chance for SALT in 1976.

After all these delicate SALT negotiations, the situation was further complicated by a second flap over the Backfire intelligence. This resulted from cooperation between Kissinger and the CIA and from the studies of Backfire performance that had been ordered. Director of Central Intelligence Colby recalls:

> I found myself increasingly supporting Kissinger's efforts to keep the *process* of *détente* moving ahead with the comparatively cooperative Russian leadership then in power, and increasingly impatient with the Pentagon's insistence that all concessions be made by the Soviets. Thus, I used intelligence to try to expand the subject under debate from narrow weapons counts to the politics of overall Soviet policy.[22]

So Colby was in practical alliance with Kissinger when he "adjudicated" the dispute over the Backfire's range.

Various American aerospace firms plus the British Royal Air Force and British industry were asked by Colby to study Backfire performance. The prime contractor for the Backfire study was McDonnell Douglas Aircraft in St. Louis. Neither McDonnell Douglas nor the other contributors were eligible to receive actual national estimates or special estimates. So the information contained in NIEs and SNIEs was furnished to them without attribution. Given this arrangement it appears that McDonnell Douglas had access to accurate but incomplete intelligence on the Tu-22M and the conclusions of the St. Louis study were that the Backfire had a range of between thirty-five hundred and five thousand miles. At about the same time, however, the DIA gave its own information to other McDonnell Douglas engineers in California and their results estimated a range of forty-five hundred to six thousand miles for Backfire. The CIA produced an analytical study supporting the St. Louis conclusions while British opinions tended to support the California study. In late 1976 the CIA was accused by *Aviation Week* of slanting the information it had given to McDonnell Douglas at the instigation of Kissinger.[23]

The U.S. intelligence consensus shifted by degrees to view the longer range as Backfire's real capability. This had the additional effect of reinforcing the long-standing Air Force claim that the Tu-22M was an intercontinental bomber. One CIA official has been quoted as saying, "We now know the Air Force was right about the Backfire's range, but it is not clear in my mind that it had enough evidence to make the conclusions as early as they were made."[24] Competing claims surrounding this plane's performance, which included assertions as extreme as the claim that Backfire had 108 percent of the range of the B-52, were gradually resolved in favor of the conclusion that Backfire's range is substantial but not commensurate with that of a plane specifically designed to be a strategic bomber. It is thought that the Backfire was somewhat "overde-signed" for its role as a "peripheral attack" plane so that the Russians found themselves with a more capable aircraft than they had expected. Today public sources commonly credit the Backfire with an unrefueled range of fifty-two hundred and a combat radius of twenty-six hundred nautical miles.

At the time that the Backfire helped to compromise the Ford admin-istration's Salt negotiations and the dispute over the plane's capabilities divided the intelligence community, there were only about twenty-five Backfires in service in the Soviet air forces. There was an increase in production from the Kazan plant, which built the airframes and assem-bled the completed aircraft. In 1976 the CIA increased its projection of Backfire production rates to between two and two and a half per month, making twenty-four to thirty new planes each year. In operations with the Soviet naval air force, Backfire flew North Atlantic maritime recon-naissance from a base at Murmansk. The planes were also sighted at a base in the Soviet Far East, Anadyr, on the Bering Sea. The United States kept itself well informed on Backfire operations due to standing orders for the National Security Agency that required all "SuSAC" flights reported at six-hour intervals.

The January 1977 defense posture statement issued by Donald Rums-feld just before the Carter inauguration noted that "we continue to be-lieve the Backfire has an intercontinental capability given certain flight profiles. Use of its inflight refueling capability would assure interconti-nental ranges, and its performance is likely to be improved with time."[25] This evaluation has remained fairly consistent, with Rumsfeld's succes-sor, Dr. Harold Brown, noting in 1978 that "we believe that the primary purpose of the Backfire is to perform peripheral attack, theater, and na-val missions although it has some intercontinental capability, and can reach portions of the United States on one-way, high-altitude, unre-fueled missions."[26] In 1980 Dr. Brown noted relatively more concern for the maritime use of Backfire than for its limited intercontinental capability: Brown believed that the Backfire force could develop into a greater threat to shipping on the sea-lanes than the long-vaunted Soviet submarine force.

With such intense concern over Backfire the Carter administration faced the same problem of providing for the Tu-22M at SALT as had Ford. In approaching SALT, however, the Carter administration recog-nized that all efforts to include the Backfire within the actual treaty limits had failed. Accordingly, attention began to focus on parallel pro-visions that could be formulated, or so-called "collateral constraints," a notion that had been popular in academic arms-control circles since late

1975. There were numerous actual limitations that could fit within the rubric of "collateral constraints." These included limits on annual production, on equipment such as that for midair refueling, on armament, on where the planes might be based, and on the size and capacity of the Soviets' air tanker force. Many of these restrictions, and combinations of them, would reduce the intercontinental threat posed by the Backfire and were worth exploring since Brezhnev himself suggested the possibility of "collateral" provisions in January 1976.

The Backfire issue was raised in Washington meetings with Gromyko in September 1977. Once again the Soviets offered their own set of performance figures[27] and also mentioned measures they would take to see that Backfire did not become a strategic bomber. These were viewed as insufficient by the Carter administration, which assigned Leslie Gelb of the State Department to negotiate the matter with Alexander Bessmertnykh of the Soviet Foreign Ministry. The Russians repeatedly refused to consider basing restrictions, although refueling and production limits were more acceptable to them. The State Department leadership, Secretary of State Cyrus R. Vance, Paul Warnke at the Arms Control and Disarmament Agency, and Gelb, who ran the Bureau of Political-Military Affairs, were sympathetic because they felt that basing restrictions in an arms agreement would have little real effect. The Joint Chiefs of Staff (JCS) for a long time insisted on Backfire basing restrictions, but in mid-1978 they softened their stand after realizing that the precedent set might allow the Soviets to impose basing restrictions on future U.S. weapons systems in further SALT negotiations.

A different method to deal with the Backfire was to "count or counter," as JCS Chairman General David Jones suggested in 1978. This revolved around enhancing the air defense network that the Americans had built to counter the bomber threat of the 1950s. The McNamara Pentagon had allowed air defenses to atrophy, reasoning that if defense against missiles was not provided, then air defense against bombers was just a waste of money. Fighter interceptor squadrons controlled by NORAD declined from sixty-five in 1960 to thirty-nine in 1965. Later this basic argument was modified, if only to force the Soviets to spend some money on manned aircraft if they chose to retain a bomber attack capability. The early warning radars available to NORAD were reduced from over 350 in 1962 to 131 in 1970. Manpower in NORAD fell from 123,000 to 66,700 and the Army substantially reduced its force of Nike-Hercules surface-to-air missiles. A further policy decision in 1974 had eliminated Nike-Hercules altogether and set NORAD fighter interceptor strength at twelve squadrons, half from the active Air Force, the rest from the Air Force reserve.

In 1976 there was renewed interest in strengthening NORAD as a result of the Backfire threat and Rumsfeld planned to reequip NORAD interceptor squadrons with the very advanced F-15 fighter. By 1978, thinking of problems with air defense of NATO Europe, Brown recommended to President Carter that U.S.-based F-15's be made available for deployment to Europe in a crisis. It was in this context that the JCS advocated countering Backfire with an expanded NORAD. Studies of the proposal, however, showed that a major NORAD expansion would be extremely costly and this option was ultimately rejected.

At the NSC, staff assistant David Aaron proposed an "up-sized" and more powerfully engined FB-111 as "our own Backfire." The idea was novel enough that NSC special assistant Zbigniew Brzezinski brought Carter into the Special Coordinating Committee meeting where the option was under discussion. Carter liked the idea and the Joint Chiefs also supported it as an alternative to NORAD expansion. At a September 1978 SALT meeting in Washington, Carter told Gromyko that the United States reserved the right to deploy a comparable bomber. It was on this basis that the Backfire issue was settled in SALT II. The Russians agreed to "collateral constraints" on Backfire production and refueling, while the Americans hinted at "our own Backfire." The SALT discussions went on to other matters and progress was sufficient to schedule a Carter-Brezhnev summit for May 1979 in Geneva to sign the SALT II Treaty.

The numbers of Backfire bombers actually in the Soviet inventory continued to increase during the SALT discussions. By 1980 there were over one hundred Tu-22Ms in the active forces. These were split between the Soviet Navy and Air Force and, of the latter service's planes, forty are based in European Russia and another nineteen in the Soviet military districts bordering on the Middle East. In the summer of 1978 a second plant was found to be under construction alongside the Backfire production line at Kazan. If associated with Backfire production the plant could roughly double Russian capacity to build the aircraft. From the Air Force there were reports that some Tu-22M's were being used as tankers to extend the range of the others, but there was no evidence of the new tanker aircraft (dedicated solely to refueling) expected since 1974 or of the new strategic bomber to which the Russians occasionally allude. From DIA came a report that at Cienfuegos in Cuba there was construction activity possibly intended to make a runway long enough to land Backfire aircraft. With the fields at Holguín and San Julián, this would be the third base in Cuba able to accommodate the plane, and DIA hazarded a prediction that the Soviets might deploy a detachment of Backfires to Cuba. Finally, over the last months of 1978, the Russians held at least eight tests of a new cruise missile out to ranges of 750 nautical miles and some of these weapons were launched from Backfires.

The indications that the Backfire might be used to launch longer-range cruise missiles led the Pentagon to abandon a last-ditch effort to exclude conventionally armed cruise missiles from limitation under SALT. Pending the summit, however, Backfire remained on the formal list of heavy bombers the U.S. submitted for inclusion in the agreement. At Vienna the last SALT exchange on the Backfire was most probably related to the indications of additional plant capacity in Kazan. On June 16, 1979, by prearrangement, Brezhnev read a statement into the SALT record:

> The Soviet side informs the U.S. side that the Soviet Tu-22M airplane,
> called Backfire in the U.S.A., is a medium-range bomber and that it does
> not intend to give this airplane the capability of operating at intercontinen-
> tal distances. In this connection, the Soviet side states that it will not in-
> crease the radius of action of this airplane in such a way as to enable it to
> strike targets on the territory of the U.S.A. Nor does it intend to give [Back-
> fire] such a capability in any other manner, including by in-flight refueling.
> At the same time, the Soviet side states that it will not increase the produc-
> tion rate of this airplane as compared to the present rate.[28]

The Americans came equipped with their own statement that aug-mented the Soviet assurances, including a limit on the annual produc-tion rate to thirty aircraft. Carter read the key portions of the statement and then asked for confirmation of the production rate, in a departure from the agreed scenario. Gromyko responded that no answer to the question was required. Uncomfortable hours followed as the U.S. dele-gation sought some Russian expression other than "noncontradiction" of Carter's assertion. On the seventeenth Carter returned to the attack, delivering a "table-pounding" oration about his good faith in negotiating SALT, the preordained character of the agreed Backfire exchange, and the possibility that the Soviets could risk the entire SALT treaty if they reneged. Gromyko maintained that it was the Americans who were changing the arrangements on Backfire. Finally, Brezhnev threw up his hands and intervened in the discussion. He confirmed the figure thirty and concluded, "There, another Soviet concession." With the "collateral constraints" in place the SALT II Treaty was signed. Two months later Russian Premier Alexei Kosygin confirmed the arrangement to a visit-ing U.S. congressional group. He remarked, "The Soviet Union has made a treaty, the world knows it, the Western press knows it. You can ask the people in the street. If we build more than thirty Backfires, we vio-late the treaty." Back at Vienna a senior U.S. official had told *Newsweek*, "In the end we got exactly what we wanted."[29]

CHAPTER SIXTEEN
SALT II

Through most of the SALT negotiations there had been no question that intelligence could monitor compliance with the agreements. Some doubts occurred following the affairs of Kissinger's "secret understanding" on SLBM replacement, the SALT information "holds," and particularly the B Team episode, which called into question the objectivity of the NIEs. Brezhnev could complain in turn about the biases of American "hawks," as he did in his Tula speech before the Carter inaugural:

> Intelligence agencies, military staffs, and all sorts of institutes draw up bulky reports and treatises that interpret in a most arbitrary way the policy of the Soviet Union and its measures to strengthen its defense capability.

The Soviet leader insisted that

> the allegations that the Soviet Union is going beyond what it needs for its national defense, that it is trying to attain superiority in weapons in order to deal "the first blow," are absurd and totally unfounded . . . the Soviet Union has always been and remains strongly opposed to such concepts. Our efforts are directed precisely at averting the first strike and the second strike, indeed at averting nuclear war in general.[1]

But no Soviet statement could erase the threat imputed by American analysts from Soviet defense spending, civil defense efforts, allegations of "warfighting" strategy in Soviet military doctrine, and above all from the Soviet MIRV program with its massive SS-18 and highly capable SS-19 ICBMs.

The most important characteristics of MIRVed missiles from the standpoint of predicting future Soviet strengths were the launch-weight and throw-weight of the missiles; their manner of propulsion; and the number, accuracy, and explosive power of the warheads embodied in each type. Information on these characteristics was almost wholly the result of detailed observation of the Soviet tests by U.S. intelligence collection systems. SALT II, with its limits on the "fractionation" of missile throw-weight and on the size of missiles and their replacements, made intelligence on Soviet (and American) weapons development all the more important due to the attempt to limit qualitative aspects of the strategic forces of both sides.

Ideally Soviet missiles were monitored at the instant of takeoff from their experimental centers by U.S. ground listening stations run by the NSA and its service components. The mid-flight trajectory would be observed by radars from both the Aleutian Islands and the Middle East, along with ship-borne and airborne instruments along the missile flight path and at its point of impact. The whole process was facilitated by the fact that due to international maritime regulations, whenever a Soviet test missile was planned to land at sea, usually in the Pacific north of Midway Island, the Soviet Union issued advance warnings for merchant shipping to stay clear of the area. Such warnings also obviously enabled U.S. intelligence to prepare for the tests.

As has already been described, the most important data received from Soviet tests were the telemetry signals the missile radioed back about the performance of its components. Successful exploitation of telemetry intelligence required two things: first, that the missile's signals actually be received by U.S. stations; and second, that the U.S. would be able to determine which component was being measured by the signals on each telemetry channel. In the 1970s, however, both the reception and the interpretation of telemetry were to be complicated by new events. First the Soviets took measures to make their telemetry signals less accessible to foreign intelligence. Basically the Russians designed new telemetry transmitters that encrypted the flight test data before radioing it back to earth. Even if the Americans intercepted the signals, NSA specialists would have to break down the encrypted telemetry to its original form before CIA or the Air Force's Foreign Technology Division could actually attempt to analyze the missile's flight performance. The Soviets began using the encrypted telemetry method in tests of their intermediate range SS-20 missile during 1974. At the SCC the United States at one point raised the issue of "test range concealment" but the evidence is unclear whether these discussions included telemetry. It is known that U.S. negotiators under instructions from the State and Defense departments avoided all mention of telemetry in SALT meetings until July 1976, when the Soviets themselves raised the question.

After Carter came into office, U.S. delegates in SALT plenary meetings at Geneva once again raised the issue of telemetry. In the third paragraph of Article V of the SALT I Interim Agreement, both sides promised "not to use deliberate concealment measures which impede verification by national technical means."[2] At Geneva, Paul Warnke and Ralph Earle sought Soviet concurrence that the phrase "deliberate concealment measures" included methods of transmitting telemetry information. The Russians initially maintained that the prohibition did not apply to "current" test practices, but by September 1977 they had agreed in principle to refrain from using telemetry concealment in any way that would prevent adequate verification of SALT II.

At the CIA, Stansfield Turner and his deputy director for the National Foreign Assessment Center (NFAC had replaced the old Directorate of Intelligence after Carter entered office), Robert Bowie, now began to argue that the treaty should contain an absolute prohibition on the use of encrypted telemetry. Vance and Warnke realized that such a measure was "non-negotiable" and argued that the Soviets would never agree to it. In NSC meetings Brzezinski sided with Turner in an effort to have SALT II incorporate some explicit treatment of this subject. As a consequence Warnke again raised "deliberate concealment" in a lunch with Soviet chief delegate Vladimir Semenov during December, and the following day Earle presented a statement both orally and in writing that the U.S. interpretation of "deliberate concealment" extended to encryption of telemetry as well.

The Soviet response was noncommittal; Semenov emphasized that any doubtful case could always be taken to the SCC. Then, on July 29, 1978, the Soviets launched an SS-18 ICBM and encrypted its telemetry readouts, both from the booster, which had been done before, and, for the first time, from the reentry vehicles. Stansfield Turner was furious and many in intelligence thought that the Soviets were probing to discover exactly how much the United States knew about Soviet telemetry practice. In his account of SALT II, Strobe Talbott of *Time* magazine speculates that the Russians may have had three purposes: concealment of some specific improvement until after the new treaty could take effect; establishment of what the Soviets considered a permissible level of test encryption; and a probe of U.S. monitoring capability.[3]

Through the fall there were periodic exchanges on encryption in the ongoing Geneva technical discussions. As a treaty appeared to be very close, many people expected the announcement of a SALT summit conference between Presidents Carter and Brezhnev. On December twenty-first and twenty-second Cyrus Vance met with Gromyko again at Geneva.

As the diplomats gathered at Geneva, the Russians conducted a second flight test of the SS-18 from Tyuratam on December twenty-first, with telemetry encrypted. Unlike earlier tests of this missile the Mod 4 carried ten reentry vehicles and made two additional simulated releases of reentry vehicles that were not carried by the missile. Previously the Mod 4 had carried nine warheads and made a single simulated release—the "fractionation" limit of SALT II specifically allowed ten reentry vehicles for the SS-18 because of this configuration of the Mod 4. This was far fewer than the thirty to forty warheads which a missile with the throw-weight of the SS-18 was technically capable of lifting, but if reports from the December twenty-first test were correct, then the Soviets evidently intended a substantial increase.

Vance was informed of the test by the CIA representative in Geneva. Meeting with Gromyko the secretary of state raised the July flight test of the SS-18 as an example of prohibited encryption: the United States must be able to monitor all tests to ensure that new missiles fit within SALT parameters and old missiles had not received excessive modifications. The two sides developed a "common understanding" to SALT II, which included telemetry's relationship to verification. In these discussions Vance did not mention his knowledge of the previous day's ICBM test for fear of divulging how quickly American intelligence could furnish a preliminary analysis of a foreign missile flight. In any case, with his own statements to Gromyko as well as lower level exchanges, the Americans thought they were very close to final agreement on SALT II.

A cable reporting progress was sent to Washington over Vance's signature on the evening of December twenty-second. There Brzezinski convened a meeting in his White House office with Stansfield Turner, Harold Brown, David Aaron, Warren Christopher, the undersecretary of state, and Spurgeon Keeny, deputy director of ACDA. Turner was unhappy without a total encryption ban in the treaty, which the Soviets had already rejected in October. In any case he felt that the Vance-Gromyko understanding was a half-measure at best because the SALT treaty would explicitly permit certain types of encryption not related to SALT verification per se. After meeting through much of the night Turner was induced to agree that he could "live with" the treaty if Vance could get Gromyko to affirm that telemetry encryption like that in the July twenty-ninth flight test was impermissible. Vance strongly objected to these instructions to raise the Mod 4 test issue a second time but he was overruled by President Carter.

As directed Vance raised the SS-18 test again, to the consternation of the Soviet delegation. The Soviets did not reply directly but they subsequently reopened other issues the sides had considered settled. All chance of a summit announcement passed for the moment. On February 14, 1979, Soviet permanent SALT delegate Anatoli Karpov stated that the agreed common understanding was adequate to cover any telemetry case which might arise. Early in 1979 the Soviets also carried out another SS-18 flight test in which four simulated releases were made in addition to dispensing the package of warheads.

As late as the NSC meeting of March 5, 1979, Stansfield Turner was still pressing for a total encryption ban. Resolution of the issue finally required an exchange of correspondence between Brezhnev and Carter plus a note from Vance. In early April the Soviets replied that the issue was considered settled on the basis of this exchange. In the SALT II Treaty common understandings appended to Article XV prohibited measures designed at concealing the association of ICBMs and their launchers during testing as well as the stricture that "neither party shall engage in deliberate denial of telemetric information, such as through the use of telemetry encryption, whenever such denial impedes verification of compliance with the provisions of the Treaty."[4]

Encryption is a moot point if United States collection systems are not first able to record flight path, telemetry readout, and other significant indicators of weapons system test performance. A chain of interception stations had been established by the U.S. along the southern periphery of Russia in the 1950s and '60s. These provided access to data from the Soviet missile test centers at Kapustin Yar and Tyuratam, the "cosmodrome" of Baikonur, and the SAM and AMB test facilities of Sary-Shagan and Emba. Moreover, the reception of signals by more than one station enabled NSA to triangulate the bearings on foreign radio emissions to determine the precise locations of Soviet headquarters and installations.

In 1969 the United States refused to convert its ten-year agreement with Pakistan into a treaty and the agreement lapsed, forcing the closing of the monitoring station at Peshawar. At the time this was an acceptable loss due to the fact that new U.S. facilities had been built at Diyarbakir, in Turkey, and at Klarabad and Kabkan, in Iran. However, the Turkish stations were closed in August 1975 as a result of the severance of military relations that followed the Turkish invasion of Cyprus. This left the intelligence stations in Iran which were, however, among the most modern and the best situated of the stations in relation to their intelligence-collection targets. Operated by a unit of the Air Force Security Service called "Detachment 5," the Iranian stations alone could assure excellent collection of the telemetry from a Soviet missile test. The Soviets were interested in the bases and made periodic aerial reconnaissance missions over them, as well as playing constant electronic tricks to fool the receivers. Philip McCabe, a CIA contract employee, remembers, "They were interested in our equipment, in our antennas, because we were always getting new experimental antennas and other equipment. From the size and shape of our antennas they could figure out what we were looking for and what frequencies we were monitoring."[5]

When the Shah was forced to flee Iran in late 1978, the United States became aware of the danger to sensitive intelligence collection facilities posed by widespread Iranian civil disorder. In February the listening post at Klarabad was evacuated, followed by the one at Kabkan on March 1, 1979.

Intelligence officials realized at once the possible consequences with respect to monitoring Soviet military programs. Robert Bowie appeared before the House International Affairs Committee in executive session on January eighteenth to announce that one of the Iranian stations was being closed and that there could be difficulties if the other site was also lost. When, by early March, there was nothing left at the second site either, except for the large dish-shaped receiving antenna, there could be little doubt that monitoring the Soviets would be more difficult, at least in terms of receiving their telemetry.

As part of a plan to ensure Senate ratification of SALT II, the President had given strong assurances that U.S. verification capabilities were adequate. Against the recommendations of both the Pentagon and the CIA, in a September 1978 speech, President Carter officially revealed for the first time that American "photographic satellites" watched Russia constantly.[6] At the time the satellites had been only part of the more extensive network. After Klarabad was abandoned the President gave further assurances in a mid-January press conference and the intelligence community mobilized to study how to replace the Iran stations. Then after the loss of Kabkan in March, unnamed "well-placed officials" were privately telling reporters that the U.S. could not compensate for the loss of the Iranian stations for some time—according to Senator Henry Jackson for at least two years. Senator John Glenn (D-Ohio), who had made SALT verification one of his special concerns, stated that "I'm not satisfied as of now that we can get by other means what we got out of Iran."[7] Henry Jackson followed with a pessimistic speech in Houston on March eighth in which he claimed that loss of the Iranian stations had done "irreparable harm" to the United States: "However much some may seek to minimize the impact of the loss of the Iranian facilities on our ability to monitor Soviet compliance with SALT II, the fact is that we now find ourselves unable to learn whether crucial developments prohibited by SALT are actually taking place."[8]

The United States had felt so confident about its capabilities to monitor Soviet missile tests that in preparation of both the 1978 and 1979 budgets Admiral Turner eliminated $200 million in funds for new satellites expressly designed to receive Soviet telemetry transmissions. Despite this budget-cutting, U.S. intelligence already had developed such a satellite, Rhyolite, at a TRW Corporation plant in California. Moreover, as a result of rapprochement with Turkey, in October 1978, the U.S. resumed operation of its intelligence ground stations in Turkey, including Diyarbakir. In 1979 Chinese officials hinted at willingness to allow the U.S. access to information jointly collected on the Soviets, resulting in a secret agreement early the following year; U.S. equipment and advice were given on two ground stations in Xinjiang Province. Actually, the Iranian loss did not impair American ability to observe the mid-course and terminal entry portions of Soviet missile tests, which include the maneuvers performed by a MIRV "bus" to release a series of individual reentry vehicles towards different targets. U.S. facilities at Bodø and elsewhere in Norway still provided for full observation of Soviet testing from Plesetsk, and may have provided limited capability for south Russia as well. Finally, U.S. infrared Early Warning Satellites also detected any missile launch in Soviet territory, usually within about ninety seconds of launching, allowing the infrared monitors to provide course-tracking information and calculation of Soviet missile flight corridors and aiming points.[9]

Despite these known capabilities of U.S. intelligence collection systems, Secretary of State Vance concluded that Senate approval of SALT II would not be forthcoming in the absence of special attention to verification issues. Consequently the Carter administration introduced a new option for aerial collection of missile-launch telemetry. The plan involved a modification of the U-2 called the TR-1, then being flight-tested at Nellis Air Force Base in Nevada. The TR-1 had been developed to collect electronic intelligence for NATO and was equipped with a thousand-foot radio antenna which it could dangle in the air stream behind it. The plan was to use warnings of Soviet missile tests to fly such planes over the Black Sea at an altitude where they could pick up the signals from Tyuratam. This plan encountered difficulty when Turkey, which any such ELINT flights would have to traverse in order to reach the Black Sea, indicated that it might feel obliged to request Soviet assent anytime the U.S. wanted to make intelligence flights over Turkey.

Stansfield Turner evidently led a Senate group to the conclusion that the U.S. intelligence resources could only be fully regenerated a year before SALT II was scheduled to run out, that is in 1984. In response Secretary of Defense Harold Brown commented that while it might be true that all facilities could not be replaced until 1983 or 1984, it would take only about one year to improve collection systems sufficiently to ensure adequate verification of SALT II. Within two months, in June 1979, the Carter administration had evolved a new plan that avoided use of Turkish airspace by improving the ground station in Norway and developing a satellite called Chalet that would be specifically dedicated to interception of missile telemetry.

One source that could have helped resolve doubts arising from the technical intelligence was information from agents and defectors, HUMINT in the jargon. The mass of intelligence from the technical collection programs has tended to overshadow this traditional espionage method, although it is also true that modern security methods have made the work of the spy more dangerous. In a 1969 speech Clark Clifford had remarked that " 'penetration is a practical impossibility today through use of the human agent.' "[10]

Nevertheless efforts were made in this area. In 1970 General Donald Bennett, then head of DIA, proposed a USIB committee for direction of human-intelligence collection. This was resisted by DDP, with the result that an intelligence community ad hoc task force formed to study espionage needs. After a year's examination the task force recommended in favor of the DIA proposal. In July 1974 a USIB subcommittee was formed in this area and began to issue a current-intelligence reporting list for espionage guidance. Although the military made some use of these lists the CIA's personnel in the Directorate of Operations (DDO), were told the lists were for reference only. In 1975 CIA Director William Colby then established the position of national intelligence officer for special activities to assist him in making use of DDO and other resources to fill critical gaps in knowledge, as well as to help break down barriers between the clandestine services and technical collectors and analysts.

That more should be done about human intelligence was the conclusion of another report by the PFIAB, submitted in December 1976. It argued that the U.S. could no longer count on the technical collection systems in view of rapid Soviet scientific progress in all areas. The board also argued that human sources were even more important in providing information about intentions and that, given Soviet efforts to conceal strategic programs, agents were a corrective and complement to technical collection. Although the board itself suspended activities, some of the ideas it expressed in this report were not ignored, and Stansfield Turner attempted in 1977 to show senior NSC officials what human intelligence could do for them. In an early 1978 interview Admiral Turner said, "Rather than finding that increased technical capabilities diminish your human intelligence requirements, it's just the opposite. The more intelligence you have from technical sources, the more intentions you want to know . . . and you go to the human to find the intentions."[11]

Despite such interest some argued that the United States was no longer able to satisfy its human intelligence needs. For one thing, large parts of the Soviet Union were off limits to U.S. personnel. However, valuable material on SALT and on the Soviet economy was brought by defectors. In addition there were a number of "agents in place" in the 1960s and 1970s. Three of these were code-named Igor, Top Hat, and Fedora and supplied the Americans with counterintelligence material. Another Soviet source was a Foreign Ministry official named Vladimir Sakharov who subsequently defected to the West. Arkady N. Shevchenko, a senior Soviet official at the United Nations and protégé of Gromyko, cooperated with the U.S. for several years before his own 1978 defection. A Rumanian diplomat who defected in 1980, Nicholae I. Horodinca, third secretary of the Rumanian embassy, provided material on Soviet attempts to gain intelligence in the United States which helped lead authorities to David H. Barnett, a former officer in DDP who has now been convicted of spying for the Russians.

The most important U.S. espionage resource was a Foreign Ministry official whose code name has variously been reported as Trigon and Trianon. The official, Anatoly N. Filatov, was recruited by the CIA in the early 1970s. The Soviet press later reported that he spied for the Americans between February 1974 and his arrest in 1977. Filatov provided copies of classified Soviet cable traffic including material bearing on SALT. One cable (since reported to have disappeared from CIA files) purported to be an account of a discussion between Soviet Ambassador Dobrynin and Henry Kissinger on April 11, 1977, in which Kissinger is quoted as making highly disparaging remarks about the quality of the Carter administration leadership and its "comprehensive package" proposal. Kissinger has denied the substance of the allegations, and there is also an interpretation that this cable was a KGB "disinformation" effort to sow dissension in the U.S. It has been alleged that the KGB was alerted to Filatov's efforts through the inadvertent disclosure of certain nuclear weapons information by NSC staff aide David Aaron at a Washington reception. This has also been denied, and investigations by the CIA and Justice Department hold Aaron blameless in the Trigon affair. The only facts known so far with confidence in this case are that Filatov's CIA case officer, Martha Peterson, was arrested in Moscow and expelled from the Soviet Union in 1977, and that Filatov himself was sentenced to death on July 14, 1978. It has since been reported that Filatov's sentence was commuted to fifteen years' imprisonment and that he is still an inmate of the Soviet Gulag system.

One additional point of interest bearing on this espionage case has to do with the United States' system of information classification. Above the "top secret" category of classification are the "code word" categories, for instance Trigon. But the highest level is "blue line" intelligence, so called because such reports have a blue line drawn down one side of the page. The nuclear weapons information that supposedly led to Trigon's exposure, and certain other information that has been reported in the press, such as disclosures of a possible nuclear weapons test off South Africa, were such "blue line" reports. In September 1980 it was announced that a new top category of secret information, called Royal, was to be created. This information is to be restricted to no more than a couple of dozen senior officials and less than ten members of Congress. As an example of what kinds of information would be classified as Royal, officials said that reports of an "agent in place" in the Soviet Politburo, if intelligence had such a source, would be so classified.

On the road to ratification, the SALT II Treaty went first to the Senate Foreign Relations Committee, which had the major responsibility in recommending adoption, amendment, or rejection to the full Senate. The Intelligence Committee also made a detailed study of the verification aspects of SALT and the Armed Services Committee examined its impact on the U.S. military posture. Secretaries Vance and Harold Brown began the long parade of witnesses pro and con when they testified to the Foreign Relations Committee on July ninth and tenth. Vance presented the basic terms of SALT II and maintained that the agreement would aid in U.S. strategic force modernization and slow the momentum of Soviet strategic programs. With respect to verification the secretary of state pointed out that there were restrictions on encryption for the first time; that (also for the first time) the Soviets had agreed to exchange information on those strategic forces constrained under the agreement; that favorable counting rules had been adopted; and that difficult-to-verify mobile ICBM systems had been banned. Vance said:

> Let me emphasize that with or without SALT, we must have the best possible information about Soviet strategic programs. Our security depends on it. Without SALT, there would be nothing to prevent the Soviets from concealing their strategic programs. Thus the treaty's verification provisions have an independent value for our national security, quite apart from their role in enforcement of the treaty.[12]

Secretary Brown concurred in most of Vance's statements and focused on demonstrating that nothing in SALT II weakened the U.S. national security, and that "the Soviets cannot gain a military advantage by concealed actions that violate the agreement."

For their part the JCS also testified in support of the SALT II Treaty. Concerned senators pressed the Chiefs very hard for any indication of differences between their own position and that of the administration. General David C. Jones, JCS Chairman, conceded disquiet over the Soviets' preservation of their heavy ICBMs where the United States had no equivalent, and also revealed that JCS had consistently recommended the inclusion of Backfire under the SALT II delivery vehicle ceilings. Jones maintained that other constraints had been achieved in lieu of these, specifically the "fractionation" limit in the case of the SS-18 and the separate Soviet assurances on the Backfire. The Joint Chiefs believed that SALT II must be approved "with a full understanding that we will be required to undertake a series of important strategic modernization programs in order to maintain strategic parity within the limits agreed upon."[13] Thus like the Joint Chiefs of 1972, who wanted "assurances" along with SALT I, the JCS of 1980 required a vigorous weapons program alongside the arms limitation agreement. This included production of the cruise missile, which by 1979 was undergoing flight-testing, plus the development and deployment of a new, mobile, land-based ICBM called the MX, which would have greater accuracy and the same number of warheads as the Soviet SS-18.

The Senate was treated to a far more outspoken demonstration of military dissatisfaction on July twelfth when the former JCS SALT representative, Lieutenant General Edward Rowny, appeared at the Foreign Relations Committee. Rowny had been involved with SALT since 1973 and had met with Soviet delegates some 385 times before his resignation in June 1979, which he had submitted in order to be able to oppose SALT II ratification. Rowny asserted that the SALT verification provisions were insufficient, the "fractionation" limits meaningless, and that the treaty was not equitable because it allowed the SS-18 and the Backfire for the Russians.

Throughout the negotiating period of SALT II the Committee on the Present Danger issued papers and held press conferences highly critical of the Carter administration's SALT efforts. In 1979 the committee joined with the conservative American Security Council to form a Coalition for Peace Through Strength. Even before the Vienna summit the group issued a report condemning SALT II as not being equitable, not verifiable, and not acceptable to the United States. It stated that *"parity* is a condition which not only cannot be precisely determined, it is a condition that places the United States at a significant disadvantage."[14] Paul Nitze appeared with Rowny at the Foreign Relations Committee. General Graham and Eugene Rostow also testified in opposition to SALT II, while Graham put out a book, *Shall America Be Defended?*, condemning the American nuclear doctrine of mutual assured destruction, warning of the Soviet military buildup, and identifying SALT II as "the acme of MADness." It was a well-organized and funded public-relations campaign.

In the Senate hearings, former arms-control officials U. Alexis Johnson, Paul C. Warnke, and Gerard Smith supported SALT II. Citizen advocates like Richard J. Barnet of the Institute for Policy Studies and Jeremy J. Stone of the Federation of American Scientists argued that SALT II did not go far enough in capping the arms race but nevertheless recommended ratification. Some former officials split in their preferences. Admiral Thomas Moorer, former JCS Chairman, and Admiral Elmo Zumwalt told Senator Frank Church's committee that SALT II was militarily dangerous and politically unsound. Former National Security Agency chief and CINCPAC Admiral Noel Gayler; SAC commander General Russell E. Dougherty, and retired CINCLANT Admiral Isaac C. Kidd recommended adoption.

Henry Kissinger's testimony of July 31 indicated surprisingly lukewarm support, especially given that eighty percent of SALT was the result of his own negotiating skill. He recommended ratification only if the treaty were coupled with a defense buildup with five percent real growth in the military budget. Although administration officials subsequently professed satisfaction with Kissinger's "support," an exchange that occurred between Kissinger and Senator Paul Sarbanes (D-Maryland) better illustrates the delicate balance of Kissinger's position.

Sarbanes asked the former secretary of state, "Would you have closed on this treaty? Would you have signed off on it?"

"This is a very difficult question to answer. I have continuously expressed my reservations about the protocol, for example, in all my discussions with administration officials. . . . I am not here to criticize the signing of the treaty. I am addressing the question of the context in which ratification should take place."

Senator Sarbanes did not accept this reply and pressed Kissinger further. "I understand that, but assuming those clarifications you mentioned had been negotiated, would you have signed the treaty and presented it to the Senate for our consideration?"

Kissinger said, "Well, you see, in any administration in which I served, I would have opposed the unilateral changes in our defense program that took place since 1976, and therefore I would expect that the treaty come up under conditions of the military environment different from the ones that now exist. So it is very hard for me to answer the question in the abstract of what I would have done if I would have signed this."[15]

While the open hearings continued before the Foreign Relations Committee, the Select Committee on Intelligence held closed hearings and studies on verification over a four-month period. Witnesses included Ray McCrory, CIA's National Intelligence Officer for SALT, and Stansfield Turner. The intelligence committee met in a closely guarded caucus room inside the dome of the Capitol Building. The room had been built in the 1940s for an earlier, equally secret committee, the Joint Committee on Atomic Energy. The senators put great effort into producing a balanced report on verification, both in a long and detailed classified version and in a public release distributed on October 5, 1979. They concluded that U.S. intelligence capabilities had improved since 1970 "as a direct consequence of improvements in the technical capabilities of the United States reconnaissance systems and in the intelligence community's analysis of that data." The report noted that monitoring requirements had been given high priority in negotiating the SALT II Treaty. The central conclusion was that

> under current Soviet practices, most counting provisions can be monitored with high or high-moderate confidence. Monitoring qualitative limitations on weapons systems is a far more difficult task and is dependent on the collective capability of a large number of systems. In general, these qualitative limitations present some problems but most can, on balance, be monitored with high to moderate confidence. There are some provisions of the treaty which can be monitored with only a low level of confidence.[16]

Nevertheless the Intelligence Committee warned that intelligence capabilities could be "degraded" by different Soviet practices or by intentional deception, although this was limited by the treaty, and "the Committee finds that the SALT II Treaty enhances the ability of the United States to monitor those components of Soviet strategic weapons forces [sic] which are subject to the limitations of the Treaty."[17]

With the verification report in hand, the Senate Foreign Relations Committee began voting on its recommendations for the treaty. Verification changes were rejected by nine to six, incorporation of Soviet diesel submarines capable of carrying missiles by ten to five, Backfire incorporation by nine to six. Three "clarifications" were adopted. The overall treaty was passed by a nine to six vote on November ninth, when the SALT II Treaty was forwarded to the full Senate with the recommendation that it be ratified.

However, the SALT II Treaty never reached the Senate floor. Majority Leader Senator Robert Byrd (D-West Virginia) delayed bringing the floor debate, doubting that he had the two-thirds vote necessary to pass a motion of advice and consent. Thanksgiving passed. Then, in December

1979, the Soviet Union sent combat troops into Afghanistan. Some called the action the most aggressive Soviet move since World War II and chances for SALT II appeared dimmer than ever. In January 1980 President Carter affirmed that he would not seek ratification while the Soviets continued their occupation of Afghanistan. This diplomatic stance continued through the summer of 1980. Under the Reagan administration there is clearly no possibility of ratification of the SALT II Treaty as written. Consequently the Soviet Union seems to be exhibiting some interest in revision and modification of the treaty in the interest of maintaining the SALT process. To a high-level delegation of conservative former officials, including General Brent Scowcroft, who had been Gerald Ford's last NSC advisor, the Soviets said that the U.S. should suggest the changes it felt necessary. Illinois Republican Senator Charles Percy, incoming chairman of the Senate Foreign Relations Committee, told the Soviets during a visit in November 1980 that a SALT treaty negotiated by the Reagan administration will have a sure passage through Congress. Percy met with top Soviet officials including Brezhnev, Defense Minister Dimitri Ustinov, and Chief of Staff Marshal Nikolai V. Ogarkov in late November. Both Brezhnev and Ustinov, according to Percy, asserted "very strongly" that the Soviet Union would never make a first strike against the United States and reiterated that the motivation behind the Soviet military buildup has been to "catch up" with the United States.

Of major importance in the SALT II debate and throughout the history of arms limitation agreements between the United States and the Soviet Union has been the fear of a conspiracy to exceed treaty limits in pursuit of strategic superiority in nuclear weapons. The concept of a policy of deliberate violation became known as "breakout" in the SALT jargon. Breakout notions were rooted in the possibility that real superiority was attainable under conditions of nuclear plenty, a point that has been under debate among American strategic thinkers for a very long time. Fears of arms agreement violation prevented international agreements on surprise attack and nuclear testing in the late 1950s. Important technical arguments that agreements could be verified within an acceptable margin, such as those presented by a civilian panel in the Woods Hole Summer Study of 1962, did not prevent the resurgence of the "breakout" issue in ratification of the 1963 Partial Nuclear Test Ban Treaty. "Breakout" fears were also responsible for the verification study NSSM-28, ordered by the Nixon administration in 1969. At that time officials at CIA and the Arms Control and Disarmament Agency generally believed in the tenets of "assured destruction" and that the nuclear "balance of terror" was stable, unable to be upset by changes in the numbers or types of nuclear weapons on both sides, even changes of hundreds of weapons. Consequently, went this reasoning, any Soviet cheating at SALT that was substantial enough to convey strategic advantage would also have to be carried out on so large a scale that it could not be concealed.

A different view, often encountered in the 1970s, and formalized in Jimmy Carter's 1980 Presidential Decision Memorandum 59, argued that options for waging a limited strategic war were important. Proponents of this view tended to argue that violations could be hidden from SALT's "national technical means" of verification. A sophisticated and conservative critic of arms control, Edward Luttwak, has made the point succinctly:

> In retrospect it seems clear that the advent of satellite observation in the 1960s did not truly abolish strategic secrecy, thus assuring the information needed for arms control forever after; satellites merely opened a temporary window in the wall of secrecy because of the sheer coincidence that the weapons of the 1960s happened to be large and easily identifiable.[18]

Still Luttwak was misleading in his contentions about technical intelligence capabilities. When he wrote this, in the 1970s, large weapons like missiles were still the mainstay of strategic power, while satellites could detect objects down to inches in size.

In negotiation and ratification of SALT II the intelligence was good enough on both sides for negotiators to debate specific cases of alleged violations and deceptions. That such a debate could occur at all suggests that no real "breakout" would be possible. Nevertheless, attention must be given to military developments that might offer strategic advantage if pursued by the Soviet Union.

One way is by making their missiles impossible to find; another is by seeking "assured" survival through defense. Both possibilities had figured in the negotiations leading up to the SALT II Treaty. Both were resolved in some way in that treaty. On balance, neither would overturn the strategic balance in the absence of other military developments. U.S. military authorities remained concerned with regard to both possibilities, however.

Already in 1970 the Arms Control and Disarmament Agency commissioned studies to determine whether the numbers of mobile missiles could be verified solely by use of the machine spies, or "national technical means." One of the United States' "unilateral statements" given at SALT I warned that any Soviet deployment of a mobile ICBM would be construed as a breach of the spirit and letter of the interim offensive agreement. The statement was given despite the prevailing U.S. opinion among experts that mobile ICBMs could be counted within broad ranges, but with considerably less confidence than could ICBMs. At the time of Vladivostok, Kissinger told the press that mobiles could be counted to within about twenty-five percent of their real number, using only U.S. intelligence capabilities.

Soviet commander Marshal Andrei Grechko had mentioned the development of mobile missiles as early as 1967. In early 1968 McNamara cited "good evidence" of a Soviet mobile with characteristics similar to the SS-11 and expected 250–300 of this type, with a hundred of them in the mobile configuration, by mid-1972. The Soviets were actually developing a mobile missile, which they termed the RS-14 (NATO designation: SS-16), but this missile did not materialize until 1975. Still no evidence appeared of Soviet deployment of this missile. Instead the Russians fielded another version, the SS-20, as a mobile intermediate-range MIRVed system—the Soviet missile booster had two stages instead of three and a triplet warhead rather than the single and highly inaccurate weapon mounted in the SS-16. It was first deployed against China and later facing Western Europe as a new theater nuclear weapon.

Still there was no SS-16. Admiral Zumwalt, Paul Nitze, and others on occasion maintained that the Russians had produced the extra components (principally booster third-stages) necessary to convert the SS-20's to SS-16's and were stockpiling them, giving themselves the capability to deploy new ICBMs in a matter of days. Despite such fears there was no Soviet deployment and only one flight test after 1975. In contrast the United States was developing a mobile ICBM, the MX, which would become a highly accurate "silo buster" weapon in the 1980s. In 1977 the Soviet Union first offered to forego mobile deployment of the SS-16 and later to ban mobile ICBM deployment on both sides as part of SALT II. This was eventually included in the SALT II protocol. In the treaty the Soviets also agreed not to stockpile components for mobile missiles such as third-stage boosters for the SS-16 ICBM. The Pentagon's SALT Task Force chief, Walter Slocombe, reported in 1979 that there was some possibility that the Soviets were deploying a very limited number of SS-16's as replacements for fixed-silo SS-13 ICBMs but that there was no evidence of its deployment as a mobile system.

Another "breakout" fear centered on the question of stockpiling more generally. Could the Russians accumulate extra ICBMs and then reload their silos after firing? Much was made of the technique developed by the Soviets for "cold launch" of ICBMs, which would leave silos sufficiently intact to handle reloads, especially in the context of the late-seventies intelligence consensus that the Soviets had accumulated a stockpile of over one thousand older or surplus ICBMs. This was perfectly in accordance with the SALT agreements, which limited weapon *launchers* rather than weapons themselves. Indeed, the United States in 1975 maintained a stockpile of 324 surplus Minuteman ICBMs. Such missiles were used for reliability testing on both sides.

The "cold launch" capability applies to only two Soviet missiles, the SS-17 and the "heavy" SS-18 ICBMs. The former program ended after about 150 conversions of SS-11 launchers while the number of SS-18's stood at over 200 in 1979 and could build up to replace the entire force of 308 SS-9's. Even with these combined forces only a third of Russia's 1,398 ICBM silos could be reloaded, but not with older missiles from the stockpile, given the modifications made in the silos when the SS-17's and SS-18's themselves were emplaced. In any case, reloading could not be accomplished instantaneously and certainly not in less than the time-to-target of even a relatively slow penetrating bomber or cruise missile. In addition the SALT II Treaty prohibited the existence of stockpiles or reloading equipment at the same locations as ICBM silos, imposing a further delay in any attempts to reload ICBM silos. Thus stockpiling and reloading must be considered of marginal military effectiveness as part of any SALT "breakout."

Yet a third kind of "breakout" scenario involving offensive forces centered on whether the Soviets might multiply their warheads by exceeding MIRV limits. Theoretically they could secretly replace single-warhead missiles with visually indistinguishable MIRVed ones. The counting "rule" for MIRVed missiles within SALT had been a point of difference in the negotiations for several years. It was resolved by the Soviet concession at Helsinki in 1975 which allowed that once any missile had been tested as a MIRV, all missiles of that type would be counted as MIRVs. Difficulties in the practical application of this rule are illustrated by a case that arose during the Carter administration.

In the Ukraine there were two Soviet missile fields, Deraznya and Pervomaisk, in which MIRVed SS-19's were intermixed with SS-11's in much the same way as the Soviets had mixed SS-11 ICBMs with intermediate-range missiles in the early 1970s. At the NSC in the summer of 1977 there were disputes over the bases of Deraznya and Pervomaisk, where evidently only sixty of the 180 launchers actually contained MIRVed SS-19's. Harold Brown and Admiral Stansfield Turner favored counting *all* missiles in the two Soviet fields as MIRVed whether they were SS-19's or not. Others argued that the Soviets should be required to provide "functionally related observable differences," which would make it possible to distinguish MIRVed from unMIRVed missiles. At first it was thought there might be such an observable difference because of certain dome-shaped antennae associated with SS-19 silos, but later it was discovered that unMIRVed SS-19's also possessed such antennae. Intelligence eventually learned that the only dependable difference it could detect was a special transporter on which MIRVed SS-19's were carried to silos in which they were emplaced. This was not satisfactory for day-to-day monitoring of SS-19 force levels. Eventually the "tough" counting rule was accepted by the Soviets as part of SALT II despite the unMIRVed character of the SS-11's at the Ukrainian bases and the possibility, recognized by U.S. intelligence, that some of those SS-11's may actually be aimed at Chinese rather than American targets. Ironically, when the 1980 Olympics were held in the Soviet Union, the Olympic Flame that symbolizes peace entered the country at Deraznya, where the Russians had located powerful engines of destruction.

Some fears of a Soviet "breakout" were based on defensive rather than offensive weapons technology. Far more threatening than the BMD systems of the 1960s and '70s, is the notion of an "exotic" ABM that depends on scientific principles other than interception by a missile object. The most promising technologies in this area utilize the principles of high-energy particle physics to create beams of directed energy which, given sufficient power levels, could destroy or incapacitate nuclear warheads. The 1968 edition of Marshal Sokolovsky's book *Military Strategy* already contained some passages that cited interest in directed-energy beams for ABM defense. Through the 1970s there has been substantial Soviet research in particle physics, and there have been claims in the Western press that the Soviet directed-energy weapons project is as large as the U.S. "Manhattan Project" during World War II, including an investment of three billion dollars over ten years. According to the press reports the Soviet program has involved extensive facilities at Semipalatinsk, Sarova, Azgir, and at the Kurchatov Institute at Moscow, as well as a number of electron-beam propagation experiments carried out aboard manned and unmanned spacecraft. The scientific effort is supposedly directed by Dr. Y. P. Velikhov of the Kurchatov Institute.

The U.S. obtained information in bits and pieces throughout the 1970s. Some of it was from the satellites. Some was from the Soviet space program and observing its Cosmos and Salyut flights. Other information came from cultural exchange programs between American and Soviet scientists, in particular from a series of seminars by Soviet physicist Leonid I. Rudakov in the United States in July 1975. Moreover, the U.S. had its own high-energy laser programs with which to compare perceptions of Soviet progress.

The chief of Air Force intelligence, Major General George Keegan, became convinced in the mid-1970s that the Russians were engaged in developing a directed-energy beam weapon. This notion was rejected by the Atomic Energy Intelligence Committee of the National Foreign Intelligence Board, the intelligence community's central clearinghouse for this substantive area. But Keegan then acquired a team of talented young physicists, one of whom provided a report to the Air Force, which documented suspicions that the Semipalatinsk facility was being used for directed-energy weapons development.

The Air Force contention brought dissent both from other physicists and other intelligence agencies. Almost two dozen alternative hypotheses were suggested for the use of the Semipalatinsk site. A number of specialists believed that the Soviets could not possibly have brought together the number of subcomponent technologies necessary for a directed-energy beam at the site without U.S. knowledge of the fact. A munitions panel of the Air Force Science Advisory Board meeting at Lawrence Livermore also rejected technical hypotheses offered by the Air Force concerning how such a beam weapon would derive and store its power, and project it over distance. Keegan's physics team was able to develop evidence to refute all objections, however, and in 1975 the general disclosed his findings to William Colby, who directed a formal interagency intelligence study on the matter. The report on beam weapons was completed in time for Kissinger to be informed, shortly before his 1976 Moscow trip, that a facility of questionable application existed at Semipalatinsk.

Keegan retired in January 1977, subsequently aligning himself with Nitze, Dan Graham, and others in the Coalition for Peace Through Strength. The intelligence community continued to doubt the Air Force thesis and in June 1977 Admiral Turner told a congressional hearing that

> we have analyzed the particle beam weapon in particular in some detail. It is our belief that the component technologies that would be required to build that sort of capability are not advanced enough in the Soviet Union to give them the prospect of being anywhere close to developing such a weapon. Most of the evidence adduced to the contrary is based on the assumption that a particular facility in the Soviet Union is dedicated to this purpose, and additional assumptions about their state of technology. We think all of these assumptions are questionable. Further, we don't see signs of those efforts required for pulling this thing together.[19]

Subsequently the United States achieved important progress in its own directed-energy programs and began to feel that other such efforts were more feasible. In May 1980 an NIE reported that there is evidence of a Soviet project to develop a space-based laser weapon with antisatellite functions and that this might be effective against low-orbit U.S. satellites, including the machine spies.

At this time it is not clear that all the scientific and logistic difficulties of creating directed-energy weapons can be solved in the near future.[20] Nor is it necessarily the case that the Soviets will achieve this type of weapons capability before the United States. Both countries have strong directed-energy weapons programs. Indeed, in some aspects of beam tracking and aiming technique, and in lasers as opposed to proton beams, the U.S. appears to be more advanced. What is true is that beam weapons represent part of a further generation of weapons technology and the superpowers are poised for the leap to another round of the arms race.

Further fears about Soviet military activities were raised by an incident that occurred in Sverdlovsk during April 1979. According to press reports that first surfaced in West Germany, Sverdlovsk was hit by a sudden and severe epidemic of anthrax fever, in which between two hundred and one thousand persons died over a six-week period. Press reports attributed the outbreak to a mishap at a Soviet germ warfare plant outside the city. The Soviets themselves maintain that the disease was caused by improper handling of meats and denounced press reports as "impudent slander." In 1980 a Soviet journal reported that two persons in Sverdlovsk were tried and convicted of selling meat, pushing an infected cow carcass down an unused mine shaft and thus contaminating ground water, and giving infected meat to relatives. At the time the newspaper *Vecherni Sverdlovsk* published several articles about anthrax, which is called the "Siberian ulcer" in Russia.

The United States and 111 other nations are signatories to a 1975 treaty which bans the production and stockpiling of bacteriological weapons. As nearly as it can be pieced together, the Soviet incident began at a facility called "Military Compound 19" sometime between April fourth and sixth, in the Chakalov district. A loud explosion was heard by residents near the laboratory. According to these accounts the blast released the anthrax bacilli called strain "I-21." Its effects were reportedly reduced because the prevailing wind at the time was blowing away from the city and a late spring cold wave reduced the virulence of the germs. According to these reports there were several hundred fatalities in the first few days, and afterward deaths continued at a rate of thirty to forty a day into mid-May. Many victims came from the village of Kashino, eighteen miles southwest of the city. There are unconfirmed rumors that a Soviet general officer commanding the facility committed suicide following the first casualties. The plant itself was sprayed inside and outside with decontaminants, and large areas around it were graded and covered with asphalt. In addition, Sverdlovsk residents were mobilized for the cleanup and the topsoil was removed from fields in the path of the infestation. Moreover the streets of Kashino were also paved with asphalt, which is an unusual luxury for a Soviet rural village.

Initial reports of the Sverdlovsk incident were picked up from the West German newspaper *Bild Zeitung* of Hamburg, a sensationalist tabloid, and printed in the U.S. by the Foreign Broadcast Information Service, a component of CIA. The agency itself provided the Carter administration with an intelligence report on the subject on April 4, 1980, a couple of weeks after the United States officially raised the issue with the Soviets as a possible violation of the germ warfare convention. By June the Carter administration had raised the matter a second time. The Soviets have continued to maintain that the anthrax outbreak was related to natural causes.

U.S. intelligence has observed continuing progress by the Soviets in developing their strategic forces. Soviet accuracy improvements have come more rapidly than expected. Where it was first believed that Minuteman might become vulnerable only in the late 1980s, by 1979 the time of danger was considered to be the mid-1980s, and in 1980 it was cited as the early- to mid-1980s. Intelligence data in 1980 are said to indicate that Minuteman is either vulnerable now or soon will be.

American observers still fear the first strike. Those former "B Team" members who went to work for the Reagan campaign spoke of the threat often and loudly. It has been foreseen for some time that land-based missiles would become vulnerable. The United States, however, maintains only one third of its throw-weight and a quarter of its warheads on land-based missiles. By contrast the Soviet Union maintains almost three quarters of both its total warheads and its total throw-weight on ICBM missiles. Despite their extreme hardening, the Soviet missiles will also lose their survivability, but if the Russians lost all these they would be much closer to being disarmed than would the U.S. under equivalent circumstances. Moreover, this is true *whether or not* the United States deploys advanced precision attack systems like MX and Trident II, as admitted in this passage from the Fiscal Year 1980 Arms Control Impact Statements:

> It is possible that even with MX the Soviets may already perceive a growth potential for a Minuteman hard-target threat to their silo-based ICBM force from present and possible improvements to Minuteman. If so, Soviet planners would have to hedge against a potential US threat of retrofitting the Mk-12A on all [Minuteman] IIIs, the NS-20 guidance set on [Minuteman] IIs and a [deleted] accuracy for the NS-20, the design goal. The Soviets could possess only a [deleted] percent survivability for their ICBMs by 1982 using the above postulation. If they believe that their silos are softer than

we estimate, their assessment could be as low as [deleted] percent. Thus it
is possible that the Soviets would be little affected by what they would per-
ceive as only a marginally increased hard-target threat posed by the MX.[21]

Despite the deletions it is clear that if the vastly increased warhead
numbers of MX increased Soviet vulnerability only "marginally," then
the theoretical survivability of their ICBM force must be very low indeed. In fact the Soviets have said as much. During the 1974 summit
their military presented a briefing to U.S. officials of the projected U.S.
threat to their missiles that reputedly left Americans with their mouths
agape.

The military consequences are that the 1980s will witness the transition to a strategic balance under which there will be *mutual* first strike
threats. Either opponent launching first could conceivably gain a degree
of strategic advantage over the adversary. A more unstable strategic
"balance" can hardly be imagined.

The dangers of war arising accidentally in such conditions would rise
dramatically. This story of the Soviet estimate began by recounting how
false alarms led to nuclear alerts and the danger of war. Such false
alarms are not rare. In the eighteen months beginning in January 1979,
for instance, United States alarm systems alone generated a total of 147
"major" and 3,703 lesser false indications. Under mutual first strike
threat conditions military commanders need only make *one* mistaken
interpretation before the request for authority to make a preemptive nuclear strike becomes a reality. What is the role of intelligence in these
very dangerous times?

CHAPTER SEVENTEEN
CENTRAL INTELLIGENCE AND THE ARMS RACE

Whether arms control in any form can endure through superpower hostility is still an open question. Whether a policy of confrontation will lead to nuclear war is also unknown. The historical precedents are not encouraging. But whatever the chances for peace it is clear that United States intelligence authorities will have a key role in predicting international behavior. The prospects for arms control will be critically affected by intelligence coverage of forces restrained by treaties. In turn, perceptions of negotiators are to a large extent conditioned by the accuracy and objectivity of intelligence information.

The odd tangle between national policy and intelligence is a subject which former intelligence officials are reluctant to discuss, partly because intelligence can get in the way of policy, as illustrated in the intelligence-informed tabling of SALT II ratification. The topic is also sensitive because former officials, in both intelligence and from the State and Defense departments, and the White House, may be fearful of the charge of conducting "policy *without* intelligence," as Kissinger's endeavors were once described by Ray Cline, his own chief of Intelligence and Research.

Intelligence has often been excluded from policy discussions, and some members of the intelligence community have been reticent about influencing policy. But vigorous advocates also have insisted upon presenting their views: In 1962 the voice of John McCone from CIA was among those recommending the use of force to remove Soviet missile bases from that Caribbean island. More recently, CIA's Admiral Stansfield Turner exercised a policy role at certain crucial points in the negotiation of SALT II. Conclusions on the role of the intelligence community in postwar U.S. policy must remain tentative, for there is much that is unknown and which will not be declassified for many years. Nevertheless, some attempt must be made to grapple with the issue of policy versus intelligence.

Ideally, intelligence informs policy. Through intelligence, decisions can be made on the basis of reasonably accurate and objective knowledge of existing conditions. Clearly good intelligence contributes to good policy. Unfortunately, intelligence not only informs policy but restricts the range of policy choices as well. This may mean in practice that only uninteresting or counterproductive choices are available to the President when the decision has to be made. Because of the orderly progression of the bureaucracy from threat analysis to weapons development to engineering development and then deployment, mistaken intelligence may dictate requirements for worthless weapons or suggest impractical military strategies by seeming to make other weapons or other strategies irrelevant to the discussion. During the Missile Gap period, it will be recalled, President Eisenhower was under intense pressure to approve major accelerations in the U.S. missile program as a result of false Air Force reports that the Russians already had numerous ICBMs. The options chosen by Eisenhower had the effect of delaying ICBM deployment until the appearance of the new generation of Minuteman ICBMs while approving a size missile program (1,100 ICBMs) that enabled Kennedy to go full speed on deployment, with the result that the real "missile gap" faced the Soviet Union and not the United States. Today it is commonly conceded that the large lead which the U.S. had in ICBMs was the main factor in the Russians' decision to build a missile force greater in numbers than that of the U.S.

Intelligence information also conditions the public debate over national security policy. Most information, particularly if it is of an alarming nature, generally reaches the public in more or less watered-down fashion within six months to a year of its appearance at the intelligence-community level. Such information normally appears in a scattered and desultory way and because, by and large, the public is not really equipped to evaluate it, it usually helps to create or to further reinforce a hostile image of the adversary. The intelligence dispute over the Backfire bomber resulted in such a changed perception. As the general image became more hostile and the specific claims as to the Backfire's performance became progressively more extreme, a point was reached at which legislators, who are public representatives after all, were insisting that such a powerful weapon had to be included within the arms limitation treaty.

Through seven presidential administrations since the formation of the CIA, no easy interaction between "policy and intelligence" has yet appeared. The best measure would seem to be the presentation of accurate and objective intelligence but, since 1947, this has proved to be an elusive objective. Especially in the area of intelligence on strategic nuclear forces, attaining objectivity has proven even more difficult than it has been on other subjects.

The U.S. has repeatedly tried to create independent intelligence authorities as part of the search for objective intelligence. The NIEs have been *national* precisely because they have transcended the parochial interests of the individual intelligence agencies. Since 1947 there have been many experiments in drafting estimates as well as two distinct organizations responsible for NIEs and three governing boards supervising the intelligence community as a whole. In the mid-1950s the Intelligence Advisory Board lacked jurisdiction over the National Security Agency. Interestingly enough, however, the greatest expansion in NSA activities occurred only after the agency's inclusion in the United States Intelligence Board in 1958. Significantly this expansion proceeded concurrently with intense interest in Soviet missile and space activities, which was generated by the "missile gap" perceptions of Soviet capability.

The USIB always retained the prerogative of rejecting NIEs brought before it. Nevertheless for many years the task of actually drafting the national estimates was delegated to the Board of National Estimates and its subsidiary Office of National Estimates. The most important attribute of ONE was that it was an *office,* an institution, albeit within the CIA. This meant that an individual analyst drafting an estimate was at least insulated to some degree from partisan pressures applied by service interests and others within the Department of Defense. During his tenure in office Henry Kissinger led a campaign to dismantle the Board of National Estimates and was successful when, in 1973, the Board was abolished and replaced by what is known as the National Intelligence Officer system. Unfortunately the single NIO is inherently more susceptible to manipulation than the corporate BNE had been. The SALT "hold" items, the Backfire case, the B Team episode, and the intelligence differences on Soviet directed-energy weapons development all involved certain manipulations of the NIO system and do not encourage confidence with respect to this new system.

To support his criticisms of national estimates by ONE Kissinger charged that the papers were bland and like "talmudic documents." Unfortunately he was right. The price of "central," or generally approved, intelligence, was that individual differences in opinion were often submerged in an NIE by agreeing upon sufficiently ambiguous language to incorporate all views. One result of such an estimates process was a paper with a large amount of general knowledge—almost nothing the Soviets could do would surprise *all* the intelligence agencies. On the other hand such consensus NIEs were also likely to be of little value to the White House policymaker confronted with a specific question or option. Kissinger wanted intelligence to be more relevant and, under the NIO system, it has been. Under the law, intelligence is responsible specifically only to the President and presidents have made frequent use of their powers to reorganize intelligence as they wish. It is therefore significant that despite widespread intelligence organizational changes made by the Carter administration, nothing was done to move away from the mechanism of the NIO system begun under Nixon, or the National Foreign Intelligence Board, which replaced the USIB during the Ford administration. Having to choose between corporate integrity or policy relevancy in intelligence seems to leave responsible government on the horns of a dilemma.

As far as the actual collection of information is concerned it is clear that a massive amount of data flows through the intelligence community. One might even suspect that intelligence is collected too well, that with all the data analysts are swamped among a veritable flood of ambiguous but suggestive indicators. Neither the original intelligence requirements system (PNIOs) nor its successor (KIQs) have proven to be very effective in day-to-day collection guidance. Many former analysts have been concerned that the process for generating intelligence requirements is overbureaucratized and insufficiently informed about the real gaps in information which confront intelligence analysts.

Even with all the information, with a carefully coordinated mechanism for national estimates, and with an efficient organization for intelligence analysis, there have been numerous disputes over the nature and strength of Soviet strategic forces, as this study has shown in great detail. During the last decade conservative critics have repeatedly charged that U.S. intelligence systematically "underestimates" Soviet strength. These arguments have contributed to political demands for "unleashing the CIA" in the expectation that unrestricted central intelligence can avoid the systematic errors attributed to the national estimates.

The story of the Soviet estimates clearly includes numerous cases of both "underestimates" and overestimates." Intelligence underestimated the pace of the Russian ICBM buildup in the late sixties and that of Soviet SLBM construction in the 1970s. There were evidently underestimates of Soviet achievements in missile accuracy in the late seventies and it has been admitted that there was a substantial underestimate of the size of the Soviet defense budget. On the other hand there have been overestimates such as those of Soviet bomber forces and initial deployment of ICBMs in the 1950s. The 1960s underestimates do not "dwarf" the "missile gap" in size or duration: the bomber gap dispute raged for three years, the "missile gap" overestimates for five. Intelligence underestimated the pace of Russian missile emplacement only between 1967 and 1972. During that same period there were other overestimates: of Soviet MIRV capability; of the appearance of a mobile ICBM; of the ballistic missile defense capacity of the Tallinn SAM; of the appearance of a new Soviet penetrating bomber; and of the amount of defense goods purchased by the "defense ruble." Those who charge systematic underestimating draw their conclusions from only one category of intelligence and assemble their proof from a purely quantitative analysis.

Representative Les Aspin (D-Wisconsin) is chairman of the Oversight Subcommittee of the House Select Committee on Intelligence. Aspin finds a number of factors account for mistaken intelligence.[1] Among these are preconceived notions, "mirror-imaging," misjudgment of Soviet strategic priorities, political and bureaucratic pressure, spurious learning, and a failure to use Soviet sources. Preconceived notions were clearly involved in the Cuban Missile Crisis and later in the judgment that because the Soviets emphasize defense they would immediately expand their ABM to cover the entire Soviet Union. The effects of bureaucratic and political pressure are endemic and have often been observed at work in this study. With misjudgment of Soviet strategic priorities Aspin accounts for the 1960s underestimates of Soviet ICBM numbers, pointing out that intelligence considered the Soviets would focus on quality over quantity, rapidly deploy MIRV, and emplace large defenses. As for spurious learning, the community overcompensates for its errors rather than correcting the methods that produced them so that, again, the 1960s underestimates occurred as a reaction to the exaggerations of the "missile gap."

It is important to note that intelligence disputes occurred *because* of the possession of suggestive information and not in a vacuum caused by a total lack of information. Intelligence information was concrete and useful enough in most cases for bureaucrats to fight over its dissemination or interpretation. A review of the major disputes shows that key pieces of information on Soviet weapon performance reached intelligence *before* the deployment of those weapons in almost all cases.

Several of the Soviet estimates, among which are the Cuban ones, raise the direct question of intentions. Why did the Soviets put missiles in Cuba after all? Why did they build to precisely 1,513 ICBMs? Why do the Soviets continue civil defense, air defense, or strategic defense programs so vigorously? Is their MIRVed missile force intended to pose a threat to our Minuteman land-based missiles? Do the Russians intend to deploy a generation of energy-based ABM weapons? These and myriad other questions require not only analysis of real capabilities, but postulation of adversary intentions. The question of capabilities versus intentions is the thorniest of conceptual problems because intentions are in the realm of the unknowable, even more so in a closed society like that of the Soviet Union. Russia has historically maintained large military forces. Large forces today do not necessarily indicate an intention to seek war with the United States, although they may. The evidence is ambiguous once again.

Intentions may themselves be inchoate in the mind of the opponent. Or they may be imperfectly thought out, irrational, or only partially formulated. Furthermore, the observer's perceptions of them are conditioned by his own assumptions and preexisting beliefs as well as, in the military, a measure of service bureaucratic interests. Many years ago Secretary McNamara conceded that intelligence had to make projections even in advance of Soviet decisions on the programs in question.

Many would agree that drafting intelligence estimates is similar to assembling a jigsaw puzzle, insofar as conceptual process is concerned. Indeed, the puzzle analogy was made by the 1966 Cunningham Report, which warned that the necessity for sifting through all the information gathered could make it increasingly difficult to find the missing pieces. Even if information is found, its reliability must be established beyond the shadow of a doubt and, despite the "real" reliability of data, analysts from other organizations with specific and possibly conflicting interests must become convinced of the fact, which may be quite difficult if colleagues are "victims of groupthink."[2] Moreover, the entire exercise must be accomplished under conditions where intelligence is under considerable pressure to deliver daily "current" intelligence as opposed to long-range and carefully conceived estimates. Estimates themselves may be intended for any of several different purposes that entail different uses of information in the elaboration of conclusions.

Consideration of the problems of intelligence analysis leads to a healthy notion of the limitations on estimates, both conceptual and evidentiary. This study has shown that in case after case the main elements of evidence were collected successfully and the main lines of argument were laid out in detail by analysts, often years before the final resolution of the specific substantive matter under discussion. But no matter how good the information collected, how unambiguous it may be, and no matter how rigorous estimating procedures may be, and regardless of whether an intelligence community can eliminate its biases and bureaucratic interests, there remains a residual uncertainty in even the best intelligence estimates. This is discomfiting, to be sure.

Both the United States and the Soviet Union are at the brink of a new round of arms competition which promises to be very expensive and potentially very destructive. In the absence of arms control and with mutual hostility between the superpowers the military competition will intensify and may explode into military conflagration, with incalculable consequences for all mankind. The United States is currently deploying a new submarine-launched ballistic missile, the Trident C4, with an associated submarine as well as in older Poseidon boats. The new missile has equivalent accuracy and greater range (or greater accuracy at equivalent range) than the Poseidon. Land-based Minuteman III missiles with improved warheads and a "real-time" retargeting capability have substantial counterforce capability against Soviet land-based missiles which represent seventy-five percent of the throw-weight in the Russian nuclear arsenal. Under development are a new land-based missile, the MX, with more warheads and even greater accuracy given a generation of maneuverable reentry vehicles (MARV) which will make the MX equivalent to the Soviet SS-18 in hard target "kill capability." Nuclear-tipped cruise missiles now under development will be mounted aboard bombers in large numbers, further increasing the arsenal. At the same time the advent of "terminal guidance," in which satellites will aid delivery vehicles in course corrections during the last moments of flight, promises pinpoint accuracies from half a world away in addition to eliminating the accuracy differences between land-based and sea-based missiles (land-based missiles have traditionally been preferred because of their greater accuracy). There is also work proceeding rapidly on the development of a laser directed-energy weapon for ballistic-missile defense and other applications.

The Soviet Union evidently is also pursuing a directed-energy beam weapon, as has been already discussed. A new generation of ballistic missiles is under development, presumably with pinpoint accuracies as well (it is still unknown whether the present SS-18 family of Soviet missiles can improve its accuracy to this extent). The Soviets have continued to spend substantial amounts annually on air defense, missile defense, and civil defense. Currently the Soviets have also begun to deploy their first MIRVed SLBM missile, the SSN-18, and also deployed a satellite inspector/destructor system with some degree of capability against low-orbit objects in space such as reconnaissance and navigation satellites.

With land-based missile forces on both sides vulnerable to a first strike plus a plethora of highly capable weapons on both sides, the incentive for either in a nuclear confrontation would be to preempt, that is, launch land-based missiles before they can be destroyed in their silos or shelters. The command and control requirements for a force posture able to execute a preemptive response are such that both superpowers would have to assume hair-trigger stances. This is particularly true if a policy of "launch on warning," which some have advocated, is adopted. The danger of an accidental nuclear war then rises precipitously. Alarming failures have occurred in the networks that warn of a nuclear attack, such as SAC's mistaken alerts in December 1979 and June 1980, the latter of which was reputedly caused by one forty-six-cent microchip circuit which failed. These examples should serve as salutary reminders of what can go wrong with hair-trigger postures.

A complementary weakness of the present strategic balance is that it is becoming increasingly unstable. Nuclear strategies have traditionally been predicated upon the fact that there were no effective ways to defend against atomic attack. Beam energy weapons in combination with a new generation of very high speed computers may change the terms of the offense-defense equation. The advent of ultra-high-precision warheads and new sensors may enable a superpower to target sea-based as well as land-based forces, being thus enabled to wholly disarm the opponent rather than merely being restricted to disarming land-based missiles and nonalert bombers. Alternatively, a combination of civil defense capability, missile defense, and hard-target forces may lead the adversary to the (delusionary) notion that nuclear war could be fought at an acceptable toll in human destruction.

The strategic balance of the 1980s could be extremely volatile. A revolutionary weapons breakthrough by either side could convince the opponent that the innovator was on the verge of achieving real strategic superiority. The opponent might then be tempted to avert inferiority by launching an immediate war. Hair-trigger force postures under these circumstances could serve to encourage a decision for war by helping to give statesmen the confidence that they will actually be able to plan and execute a thermonuclear strike. Even if pressures for war were averted in the case of a technological breakthrough, there would at the least be a "Sputnik" effect in which the opposing superpower would redouble its efforts at a military buildup in order to close whatever "gap" had developed.

It is intelligence which must bring in the first notice of a Soviet technological breakthrough. In this connection it is comforting that the main outlines of Soviet technical development have long been known in advance, even if analysts could not agree on precise details or future trends. On the other hand it is disturbing to realize that what knowledge there is is continually subject to the doubt embodied in residual uncertainty. The beginning of wisdom, however, lies in the realization that one must go beyond intelligence to cope with the problems of the arms race.

AFTERWORD (1986)

A new administration has been elected and returned to office in the five years since this book was written. During the Reagan administration there have been changes in intelligence personnel, certain modifications of organization, increases in the sophistication of collection means, and growth in the national intelligence program budget. It is appropriate now to assess intelligence analytical performance under the Reagan administration, to survey the further evolution of substantive disputes and the continuing persistence of management issues. The following review of the issues illustrates the continuing quandary that faces analysts, managers, and consumers who concern themselves with the quality of intelligence information.

Intelligence Management

Ronald Reagan entered office following a political campaign in which he had spoken out against poor intelligence and committed himself to improvement of the system. Reagan's selection as Director of Central Intelligence (DCI), William J. Casey, seemed a step in that direction. Casey had had intelligence experience with the OSS in Europe during World War II. Accorded a respectful hearing by the Senate confirmation committee, the DCI-designate declared his primary objective would be to improve the intelligence product.

Casey had the ear of the President; he managed Ronald Reagan's 1980 campaign and shared a common vision with the man who became President. Casey and Caspar Weinberger had been personal advisors to Reagan, members of the so-called "Kitchen Cabinet." Now Casey would be DCI, and Weinberger the Secretary of Defense. In bureaucratic terms Casey cut a wide swath through the Reagan administration, with a DCI involved in policy to an unprecedented degree. In Reagan's first year he spent more hours with the Director of Central Intelligence than had any other President.

Within the CIA, Casey presided over a new reorganization effort. His commitment to work on the intelligence product was reflected in his action on the National Intelligence Council (NIC), a collegial grouping of the NIOs that had been formed by Admiral Stansfield Turner in the final year of the Carter administration. Previously the NIC had been under the supervision of the Director of National Foreign Assessments, Robert Bowie. Casey brought the NIC into his own office and appointed Henry S. Rowen to chair the council. Since the NIC controlled the terms of reference and drafting of estimates, Casey was assuming a much more direct role. Whereas Bowie had been regarded as a liberal, Rowen, though one of the McNamara "whiz kids" and a past president of RAND, has been closely associated with Albert Wohlstetter for many years and is regarded as a conservative very much in the mold of Casey himself.

The National Intelligence Council has undergone changes. The problem of limited staff support for the NIOs led to formation of an analytical group even before the Reagan administration. Senior analysts are drawn from the entire intelligence community for a staff of about fifteen in 1984. There are more NIOs without portfolio who can take over management of a draft estimate on a contingency basis. In fact the council has a larger size altogether, with seventeen NIOs currently assigned, including an NIO for Deception added in 1983. With a place in the DCI's office, a corporate board, and an analytical staff, it should be noted that the NIO system resumed some of the characteristics of the earlier ONE/BNE organization.

There also have been changes in personnel. Arnold Horelick, Turner's NIO for Soviet Affairs, left the CIA to direct Soviet studies for RAND's Social Sciences Division. Since January 1983 the Soviet NIO has been Fritz Ermarth, yet another veteran of RAND, as well as of the Northrup Corporation and earlier work at CIA. Ermarth had previously received a National Intelligence Medal for his analyses of Russia.

Reorganization also affected the larger intelligence component of the CIA. Under Turner this had been styled the National Foreign Assessment Center (NFAC) and had emphasized functional analyses, as against a regional pattern of organization. Casey's reorganization abolished NFAC, recreating the Directorate of Intelligence (DDI) with its shift toward a regional pattern of organization. Among the NFAC offices eliminated were the Office of Economic Research, the Office of Political Analysis, and the Office of Strategic Research. It was argued that the recrudescence of the regional office system, with elimination of the functional bureaus, would allow the consolidation of analysts with expertise in particular nations. For example the Soviet analysts were consolidated into a single Office of Soviet Analysis (OSA).

The reversion to a regional organization is sometimes credited to Casey's first DDI, John McMahon, who came over from the agency's operations side. McMahon, however, opposed Casey's initiative to move the NIC out of DDI and into the DCI's office. Casey later promoted McMahon to become Deputy Director of Central Intelligence, replacing him at DDI with Robert M. Gates. Interestingly enough, Casey then moved the National Intelligence Council back to DDI and made Gates the chairman. Currently the DDI continues to supervise the work of the NIOs.

Certain developments should be perceived as evolutionary, resulting from trends already evident in community practice. The DDI has retained NFAC's senior review panel, with the task of making retrospective appraisals of the accuracy of previously published intelligence estimates and reports. The academic outreach program has assumed even greater importance, with up to a hundred academic authorities working as consultants and reviewing the drafts of reports. There is also a sort of government outreach effort, in which officials of other federal agencies are asked to comment on prospective intelligence reports.

Intelligence analysts are themselves being asked to seek outside training. Those who lack Ph.D.s are encouraged to complete their degrees, while others are encouraged to attend academic or substantive conferences. According to George V. Lauder, CIA's director of Public Affairs, during 1984 some twelve hundred analysts attended almost five hundred different conferences. Many agency personnel presented papers or acted as commentators at these gatherings.[1]

Some changes have also occurred at the level of the National Foreign Intelligence Board (NFIB). As the Carter administration's successor to the U.S. Intelligence Board (USIB), the board continued to range the full gamut of intelligence community issues. Casey has restricted the NFIB to approvals of estimates and operations. Budgetary issues are now handled separately by a National Foreign Intelligence Council, an equal status group with identical membership. The DCI has also added his own deputy director (the DDCI) to these committees as the particular representative of CIA, freeing himself to act as arbitrator among the community agencies.

Supported by Casey, President Reagan has taken several actions in the intelligence area. One of the first was to recreate the President's Foreign Intelligence Advisory Board (PFIAB) as a channel for personal advice. Of the nineteen members initially appointed, many held views like Reagan's and only five had had previous experience advising a President on intelligence. Reagan also issued a new executive order to govern the basic duties and limitations for intelligence, which loosened many of the restrictions set during the 1970s. Other signs of Reagan's continued regard for intelligence include approval of rapidly increasing intelligence community budgets and of a new annex building for the CIA at Langley, on which construction began in 1983. Components like the Office of Soviet Analysis can yet anticipate a return to the headquarters compound.

Like Turner, Casey continues to play an active role in the formulation of NIEs, SNIEs and other reports. The DCI does not hesitate to demand that estimates be redrafted to his specifications. Production of these reports has increased as well: whereas in 1980 only about a dozen NIEs were published, the 1984 figure was three times as high, among a total of more than seven hundred long-term research assessments.[2]

Although the current DCI has involved himself in NSC policymaking far more than has been traditional, and although Casey has spent much time demonstrating an abiding interest in covert operations, his interventions on estimates have been keenly felt by analysts. Press reports indicate intervention with estimates on terrorism and on Latin American issues. During 1984 there were two resignations by CIA analysts who felt accuracy was being given short shrift, including the unprecedented resignation of a National Intelligence Officer. While there are no data as yet regarding DCI intervention on Soviet estimates, former CIA analysts have expressed concern over a general politicization of estimates and over what intervention on estimates may portend for morale of CIA estimators.[3]

Congressional oversight has had its least impact on analytical issues. Relatively few congressmen take the time to read the estimates, and so many legislators are not familiar with the intelligence product. The House and Senate intelligence committees have been confronted with a series of far more controversial issues, ranging from burgeoning budgets to covert operations against Nicaragua, to allegations of Soviet violations of arms control agreements. Focus has shifted by topic, with limited staff support, drawn by the political events of the day. Central America estimates are one topic that did receive detailed examination, in 1983. The NIO resignation in 1984 later centered precisely over an estimate in this area. It is significant that the intelligence community was able to avoid a committee hearing on this matter.

According to its 1983 and 1984 report, the Select Committee on Intelligence of the Senate conducted inquiries into perhaps a dozen areas other than the Soviet space program, including such heated questions as the CIA's mining campaign and psychological warfare manuals in Nicaragua, terrorism, the KAL 007 incident, and Freedom of Information legislation. On analysis, the committee reports, it had supported additional analytical personnel at various agencies and recommended increased use of competitive analysis, much like the B Team report, which the Senate committee specifically cites as an illustration. Lack of human intelligence, and counterespionage are raised as continuing problem areas in collection.[4]

Skilled analysts, increased outside review, and vigilant oversight have in no way diminished the potential for intelligence disputes. A review of official reporting on recent strategic force developments provides further evidence of both the inevitability of residual uncertainty, and the differing perspectives of intelligence agencies.

Recent Substantive Issues

Secretary Caspar Weinberger's FY 1986 Defense Department annual report credits the Russians with 8,000 warheads on ballistic missiles alone. The Reagan administration has also declassified some conclusions of NIE 11-3/8-85 in the political struggle over Congressional approval of the 1986 budget. This material was briefed by DDI Robert Gates in late June 1985; according to the presentation, if SALT II constraints held until mid-1990, there could be something over 15,000 Soviet warheads in 1994 while, under the worst case of buildup outside SALT, Russian deployments could reach as high as 21,000. There are unconfirmed reports that DIA dissented from this estimate in favor of even higher projections.

What is significant about these numbers is the comparison of perceptions in 1985 and those of 1979-1980. Harold Brown's last public posture statement, FY 1982, gave the Soviets 7,000 weapons aboard both missiles and bombers. At that time, NIEs were predicting up to 16,000 warheads by the late 1980s and 20,000–30,000 in the 1990s. Thus the newer estimates delay until 1994 the anticipated date of the Soviets' arrival at the 15,000 level, while the projection barely attains, under the worst case, the Soviet numbers expected in 1980. This suggests either that SALT could be working after all, or that the 1980 figures reported were drawn starkly in order to influence SALT II ratification.[5]

A very significant dispute, also revealed in the summer of 1985, concerns Soviet ICBM accuracy. It will be recalled that, swayed by the B Team's pessimistic assessment, the 1977 NIE had revised the prediction for the accuracy of the SS-19 and SS-18 missiles to a level that suggested a near-term counterforce threat against Minuteman. During the 1980 electoral campaign Reagan used this prediction to argue that the U.S. faced a "window of vulnerability," necessitating immediate force improvements including the MX missile and B-1 bomber. Strategic force analysts spoke of how the Soviets would be able to use their SS-19s to wipe out

American ICBMs while retaining the SS-18s as a reserve force to preclude retaliation.

According to press reports, in a section to which the Defense Intelligence Agency dissented, NIE 11-3/8-85 argues that the Soviet SS-19 has failed to demonstrate the predicted high accuracy. The accuracy estimate was again revised, this time from the previous .12 nautical miles to a projected Circular Error Probable (CEP) of about .21 nm. Although this accuracy loss does not sound too serious at first glance, standard missile effectiveness calculations indicate that, against Minuteman silos hardened to withstand blast overpressures of 2,000 pounds per square inch, the single-shot kill probability of the SS-19 declines from about .8 to only about .36, a level which virtually disqualifies the SS-19 as a counterforce weapon.[6]

Not much is heard these days about the Backfire bomber, one of the most intense intelligence disputes of the 1970s. The Reagan administration may have suppressed debate on the issue of the plane's capabilities. Backfire is now commonly shown as being capable of attacking the U.S. In what represents a subtle distinction, maps printed in Secretary Weinberger's annual threat handbooks, *Soviet Military Power*, display Backfire's range from Arctic staging bases. The operating airbases, also shown, are far to the south of the staging fields.[7]

Another Backfire development concerns its production rate, set at thirty per year at the 1979 Vienna summit. The press reports an unspecified intelligence projection that carries Backfire production at thirty-three aircraft in 1981 and 1984, and thirty-two for the years 1980, 1982, and 1983. Yet unclassified figures furnished Congress by both CIA and DIA show production at the constant rate of thirty a year, while bomber production is not known to have been raised as a SALT compliance issue. It is worth noting that the annual *Military Balance* series, published by the International Institute of Strategic Studies, cites Soviet inventories of 130 Backfires in 1980 and 235 in 1985, an average increase of 21 bombers a year. If agreed production ceilings *have* been exceeded, especially by the small number of twelve aircraft over five years, this detection in itself demonstrates a continued capability for verification by national technical means. Most recently DIA has finally revised downwards its own estimate of Backfire's range.[8]

The Backfire issue has largely disappeared. It has been overshadowed by the appearance of a real Soviet heavy bomber as well as by continuing research and development of long range cruise missiles. During the 1970s Soviet military commentators scoffed at American claims on Backfire, saying that they did not need Backfire as a counter to a B-1, that they could have their own B-1. It is indeed the case that Backfire has not been operated in the role of a strategic aircraft, rather, in exercises it has supported fleet operations, amphibious landings, and ground combat forces. Meanwhile the new Soviet bomber was in fact sighted on the ground at Ramenskoye in 1981 and *Aviation Week* even printed a photograph of what was purported to be this aircraft in its issue of December 14, 1981, claiming the plane would attain its Initial Operating Capability (IOC) in 1982.

In this case again, American intelligence had effectively anticipated the development. At Kazan in 1978 a factory was discovered under construction, near the plant that produces the Backfire. Earlier that year both the Secretary of Defense and the Joint Chiefs had spoken of a modern heavy bomber that might appear in the early 1980s. Harold Brown reported in early 1979 that the first prototype aircraft could be rolled out in the near future and said in his last posture statement in 1981 that the aircraft had been expected for several years. When the plane did materialize it was tentatively called the RAM-P. The NATO nomenclature Blackjack was assigned to this bomber the following year.

Blackjack did not in fact become operational in 1982. Prototypes of the bomber engaged in flight testing, and at the beginning of 1983 Congressional sources reported they expected that Soviet Long Range Aviation would receive its first operational aircraft in 1987. The Defense Intelligence Agency and the CIA are said to agree that fifty to seventy-five Blackjacks may be available by 1990. Other Defense Department projections given Congress foresee production of slightly over forty aircraft by then, twenty-seven of them in 1988-1990.[9]

Cruise missiles are the most recent Soviet force improvement and are potentially as troublesome for the U.S. as was the U.S. deployment of cruise technologies for the Soviets. Although there have been cruise missiles in the Russian forces for many years, the older systems were unsophisticated and intended primarily for short-range or naval attack purposes. The new cruise missiles incorporate Soviet-style terrain contour matching and have ranges similar to their American counterparts. Insofar as bombers are concerned, Soviet aircraft including both Backfire and Blackjack will be capable of carrying the AS-X-15, which is thought to have a range of three thousand km. The air-launched missiles are also being tested on a new variant of the Tu-95 Bear, with new production of strike versions of that bomber for the first time in over fifteen years. Some estimates expect that as many as sixty-nine of the Bear H variants may be built. The Soviets also have submarine- and ground-launched cruise models, the SSN-X-21 and the SSC-X-4, which may already be operational. In 1984 Moscow officially announced testing of cruise missiles, and in October of that year, deployment aboard submarines and bombers.

The existence of these modern cruise missile programs was revealed by U.S. officials in 1979, but it is not yet possible to fill in the intelligence background of what the Americans knew about the Russian programs.[10]

Air defenses were a special area of concern in the 1976 B-Team study, and both air and strategic defenses have remained controversial since. Soviet air defenses remain robust, although the number of interceptor aircraft is decreasing as more sophisticated planes are introduced. Deployment of the SA-5 Tallinn system continues, and for the first time some of these missiles have been exported, in this case to Syria. Again, air defense was reportedly a particular focus of the 1984 NIE.

Substantive disputes regarding air defense topics center on the rate of increase in the sophistication of defense systems. Contingent with its own reliance on tactics of low-altitude penetration by bombers and cruise missiles, the American interest in predictions of the date at which Soviet defenses will be fully capable has sharpened. Robert Hufstuttler, formerly chief of OSR, then the first director of the consolidated OSA cannot have endeared himself to the military authorities when, in late 1981, he told a Senate defense appropriations subcommittee that the cruise-missile armed B-52 would be as effective as the B-1 bomber against the Soviet defenses expected in the 1980s. Pentagon official T. K. Jones attempted to discredit the CIA analysis by claiming their assessments were based on radar signature data from the older more detectable B-1A rather than the modified B-1B requested by the Reagan administration.

The range and design of the Soviet SA-10 surface to air missile also appear to have been a subject of dispute. There have been claims that this missile has an unprecedented range for a SAM and also that it has capability against cruise missiles. Currently the Russians are developing an equally or even more sophisticated SA-X-12. Some think these systems, now credited with ranges of about one hundred km, may have capabilities against tactical ballistic missiles as well. The SA-10 was operational at forty sites in 1984, with four missiles per launcher and 350 launchers, according to the Defense Department publication *Soviet Military Power*. This source also expects that a mobile SA-10 could be operational by 1985.

Another vital issue is whether the Soviets have arrived at the combination of airborne avionics, electronics, and "hunter-killer" technologies necessary for a so-called "look down-shoot down" capability, that is, the ability to detect and engage bombers and cruise missiles flying at low altitude and shielded by the ground returns of the terrain they traverse. The latest generation of Soviet interceptor aircraft is credited with this capability, so that the issue has resolved itself into the rate of production of these aircraft. By the latter part of this decade, the Department of

Defense expects that the newer planes will form the backbone of *PVO Strany*. In addition, Soviet defenses are being supplemented by an airborne warning and control system, the IL-76 Mainstay, which greatly extends the flexibility of the Soviet "look down-shoot down" capability. The Pentagon report credits the Russians with producing four IL-76s by 1984 plus a capacity to build perhaps five additional ones each year.[11]

Linked to air defense, in particular in the Soviet *PVO*, is ballistic missile defense. SALT "breakout" fears in the late 1970s centered on a potential rapid deployment of ABMs by the Russians. No such event has occurred. The Soviets *have* evidently completed the development of a hypersonic acceleration interceptor missile for defense inside the atmosphere. The Moscow ABM, formerly containing only Galosh missiles, is being reinforced with the endoatmospheric interceptors plus new battle management radars. The Moscow system, which during the era of detente never attained the strength allowed by the ABM Treaty, is being built up to the full one hundred-interceptor level.

Still controversial is the potential of directed energy weapons. Early skepticism gave way in 1980 to intelligence community recognition of a Soviet program. Then, in March 1983 Reagan himself christened exotic technologies like laser as a possible solution to the nuclear dilemma, inaugurating a "Strategic Defense Initiative," more popularly called "Star Wars." Many American directed energy programs were consolidated under a new department-wide Strategic Defense Initiative Organization (SDIO). With both sides moving in this direction, it is not surprising that the intelligence estimates predict missile defense, through means of directed energy beams, to be an attainable military technology.

Such disputes as persist in the NIEs no doubt focus more on the pace and success of Soviet efforts than on the fact of them. The official view is given by Paul Nitze, an arms negotiator in the first Reagan administration and White House special advisor on arms control in the second. At a June 1985 conference on Soviet-American affairs, Nitze declared that the Soviet directed energy program was broad, employing over ten thousand scientists and engineers, working on all the several techniques recognized as technically promising by the U.S. Nitze asserted that the Soviets have made breakthroughs in power generation, including a rocket-powered generator and that ground-based laser anti-satellite facilities have been experimentally activated by the Russians at Sary Shagan—all this on top of the prediction that the Moscow ABM improvements will be complete by 1987.

Nitze's worst-case is that Soviet operational deployment of the ground-based lasers could begin almost immediately and reach IOC by the end of the 1980s. Meanwhile Soviet space-based lasers could be available for anti-satellite applications by the mid-1990s. A particle beam missile defense would take longer—"tests" foreseen before the year 2000, with kinetic energy weapons such as electromagnetic railguns possible by the mid-1990s.[12]

The question is whether such projected dates are at all feasible or realistic, even for the $26 billion that reports expect the Russians will spend between 1985 and 1989. There are two formidable barriers preventing the attainment of a "star wars" defense. Only one of them is the design and construction of hardware, on which the intelligence reporting seems to be focused. Beyond the obstacles of physics and computer capacity or speed looms the overarching problem of software, of the computer programming that drives the system. Not only is the programming a key element in overall success, in particular for a large-scale missile defense, but from the intelligence standpoint that element is the *least* visible portion of an ABM effort. A second problem of the missile defense estimates is that the intelligence community is being asked to predict much farther into the future—decades as opposed to two-, or three-, or even five-year intervals, which we have already discovered have their methodological weaknesses.

Arms Treaty Compliance

The extent to which SALT compliance became an obstacle for arms agreements was demonstrated in the SALT II ratification debate. Although legislative action on the treaty halted in response to the Soviet intervention in Afghanistan, it was clear by 1980 that there was considerable concern over Soviet compliance on arms agreements regardless of the substantive merits of the assorted charges. Recent accounts make even clearer the degree to which flaws in the back channel negotiation of SALT I prejudiced compliance with those agreements. In retrospect this careless diplomatic work appears even more damaging to American national interests.[13]

Ronald Reagan entered office after a campaign that disparaged the SALT regime. His administration made big changes in this arms area, even changing the acronym SALT to START (Strategic Arms Reduction Talks) in order to accent arms reduction. Kenneth Adelman, an ideologue of the anti-SALT Republicans, was given charge of ACDA, while such SALT opponents as Richard Perle and Paul Nitze received senior posts in the administration. Indeed, as deputy secretary for policy, Perle soon evolved into one of the more powerful players in the arms control bureaucracy.

In his campaign, Reagan made public statements that seemed to accept the arguments of those who charged the Soviets with systematic SALT violations. Reagan showed a clear sensitivity to Senate fears of loopholes in the SALT II Treaty, which has never been submitted for ratification, although the superpowers continue to observe its provisions. In office Reagan made verifiability a key criteria, perhaps *the* key criteria, for judging arms control proposals, sometimes to the exclusion of basic questions of whether arms restraints are desirable or necessary.[14]

Despite his grave concern with verifiability, Reagan for a long time failed to use the verification machinery established by the SALT regime. In March 1981, the first regularly scheduled session of the Standing Consultative Commission (SCC) of the new administration was postponed. Officials expected a strong push on SALT violations, but the bureaucracy has yet to agree on a list of ambiguities sufficiently serious as to merit SCC review.

The commission met in Geneva in May 1981. The American delegation was headed by Ambassador Richard Ellis, newly retired as chief of SAC. Ellis' most serious objections were to Soviet encryption of test telemetry, an issue that remains in contention to this day. On a lesser level was the SCC delegation's presentation on the continued presence of racks of rusting fuel tanks, some of them converted to grain storage silos, at the Soviet missile sites dismantled in the 1970s, to make way for additional SLBM submarines. It is reported that the Soviets found this charge difficult to take seriously.

For twenty months after this Geneva session the U.S. reduced its participation in the SCC. No compliance questions were referred to the SCC. The U.S. considered ending the written reports on U.S. force levels required under SALT II, which would have violated the agreement. In 1982, when the second five-year bilateral review of the ABM Treaty was to be made in the SCC, an effort occurred within the bureaucracy to transfer the review conference to some other forum.

Instead of quiet diplomacy, fears about Soviet compliance and charges of violations of agreements have figured prominently. Some of the most often used charges trace their origins to the flawed negotiation of SALT I. When an NIE completed in 1982 concluded that there had not, as yet, been any Soviet violation of the SALT II Treaty, the drumfire speculation on evasions only increased.

A major speculation in 1982 centered on whether the Russians had moved to field their SS-16 as a mobile missile, a mode of deployment prohibited under an annex to SALT II. There had been claims of the production of this missile since the mid-1970s, but the SS-16's testing record was poor. The Carter administration's estimate had been that the

SS-16 was not in the field as a mobile. At the most it might have been active in fixed silos at the old SS-13 site near Plesetsk. According to press reports the 1982 NIE continued to reject the estimate of mobile deployment on the SS-16.

Concrete compliance issues emerged in 1983. One concerned a new generation of Soviet ICBMs that may soon attain IOC. SALT II permitted each side to deploy one new missile. In October 1982 the Russians began testing a missile, which NATO dubbed the SS-X-24. A large rocket, similar in size to the American MX, the SS-X-24 was the Soviets' "new" missile. Then, in February 1983, Russian scientists at Plesetsk conducted the first test of a different ICBM, much smaller and evidently intended to be mobile. The Soviets claimed that this was a modification of an existing missile, which was allowed by SALT II under certain tight restrictions. Reports conflict as to whether the SS-X-25 is in fact the same size as the SS-16 or somewhat larger. This question cannot be resolved from information currently in the public domain.

Another serious compliance issue is one that heightens the fears of those who worry about "breakout" from the ABM Treaty. In 1983 U.S. intelligence discovered indications of construction of a sophisticated radar at Abalakovo, near Krasnoyarsk in Central Asia. Located fairly close to certain ICBM fields, the Soviet radar, some observers charge, may be intended for battle management in a surged ballistic missile defense. The Soviets claim this radar is for space tracking purposes and thus not limited by the ABM Treaty.

The radar and missile questions, and the continuing dispute over telemetry encryption, led the U.S. back to the SCC in late September 1983 for a special SCC session requested by the U.S. two months earlier. The session continued for several weeks, during which the Soviets furnished General Ellis with the explanations given above. None of the issues has been resolved. The most recent edition of *Soviet Military Power* expects SS-24 activation by late 1986 with the mobile ICBM to follow. Defense Department projections credit the Soviets with the capacity to produce about 140 mobile ICBMs by 1990, plus enough SS-24s to replace their entire MIRVed ICBM inventory.

These events were in train while new SALT verification studies progressed. In December 1983 the General Advisory Committee (GAC) to ACDA completed a 300-page study of compliance. The State Department itself reported to Congress in early 1984 and again in February 1985, while an interagency study is to report on the effects of continuing SALT limits by the date on which the SALT II Treaty would have expired, in October 1985. So far the State reports have been ambiguous while that of GAC positively excoriates the Russians. Much like the B Team, the

GAC had been given a decidedly conservative cast, while its study reportedly began with a laundry list of charges assembled by David Sullivan, dismissed from the CIA under Turner, for leaking intelligence material in order to oppose SALT. The tenor of the GAC final report is given by the observation that each of the Soviet actions resolved by the SCC during earlier administrations is listed here as a sure "violation." This report must be seen as a manifestation of the compliance controversy, not as a study that rose above it.

The diplomatic framework of the SCC successfully resolved issues in the 1970s, when the compliance debate was less vituperative, and has failed to do so in the 1980s, when the administration "committed" to compliance is in power. Influenced by the verification debate of this period, the effort to seek arms control has virtually ground to a halt. Indeed the most significant potential violations have emerged precisely as efforts to reach agreements have slowed. To put it another way, by rejecting agreement, the U.S. risks destroying Soviet incentives to observe existing limitations.

All this places the Reagan administration on the horns of a dilemma. Securing an arms control agreement, which is held to be a major objective for the second Reagan term, will require a step back from the harsh rhetoric of SALT "violation," yet such a step in turn would divide the President from his conservative political supporters. Reagan has had some understanding of this problem all along: even while denouncing the Soviet Union as an "evil empire" in the first years of his administration, he never flatly accused the Russians of SALT violations.

Ronald Reagan has tried to keep to a narrow middle ground. His public statements veer from accusation to denial. In March 1983, for instance, President Reagan remarked "there have been increasingly serious grounds for questioning compliance with the arms control agreements that have already been signed." Similarly the President's covering letter on one of the State verification reports to Congress stated that "there is cause for serious concern" about Soviet behavior on observance of arms agreements. But at his formal press conference of April 22, 1983, to the contrary, Reagan declared, "it is difficult to establish, and have hard and fast evidence, that a treaty has been violated." Moreover, President Reagan's letter accompanying release of the GAC's pessimistic verification report specifically noted that neither conclusions nor methodology of the study had been approved by either the White House or any other agency of the U.S. Government.[15]

Treaty compliance issues, it appears, have been used vigorously in the larger political debate over the desirability of Soviet-American relations.

At the same time, after acting to bypass the SCC, it was somewhat un-reasonable for the Reagan administration to expect that the SCC could function effectively to remedy questions posed at the 1983 special session. The Geneva meetings tokened a new nadir for verification effectiveness.

In more than a decade of debate over loopholes and alleged violations, the U.S. has yet to venture a choice on the more basic question: should agreements aim for real controls or for perfect verification? There is no political consensus on the larger issues, but the administration may be becoming more sensitive on the matter in its second term, as achieving some agreement with the Russians becomes more attractive to Reagan strategists. In a recent piece in *Foreign Affairs*, ACDA chief Kenneth Adelman acknowledged that "tough choices must be made between high-confidence verifiability and strategic significance." By the same token, the verification issue will linger until political consensus is achieved on the goals of arms control and the necessity for trust in the nuclear era.[16]

There has already been too much heat and not enough light in the verification controversy. In the process the danger has grown of the superpowers' losing sight of their shared interest in avoiding war and eliminating the arms race. Residual uncertainty pervades arms control monitoring as it does all forms of intelligence analysis, and even if perfect information were achieved, it does not follow that recipients would believe the reports. For this reason verification should never be taken as the central feature of agreements on arms control. Only the political will to reach and enforce agreements, on both sides, can make arms reduction a reality.

Soviet Defense Spending

A suitable microcosm that illustrates the continuing co-nundrum of intelligence analysis is the question of the level of Soviet defense spending. It may be recalled that this issue roused controversy in the mid-1970s. The CIA's "building block" costing model came under attack, and the estimate of Russian military spending doubled. Everyone ignored Soviet spokesmen who denied the annual four to five percent increases being claimed.

Under the Reagan administration the Defense Intelligence Agency initially took the lead in reports on Soviet military spending. An annual threat assessment, to which the DIA is a main contributor, *Soviet Military Power* replaced the yearly budget estimates published by the CIA. Spon-sored by the Secretary of Defense, the series became the administration's main public exposition of its view of the Soviet threat. DIA also spear-headed the government view in its appearances before the Joint Economic Committee (JEC) of Congress.

Ironically, both sides might have been correct in the Soviet spending debate—*retrospectively* Russian spending, especially procurement, rose very rapidly in the period 1966–1975 but then fell off. *Soviet Military Power* attributes the decline to the cyclical nature of military procurement and the rise in American defense spending. DIA representatives never-theless repeated the projection of four percent growth in both their 1981 and 1982 presentations to the JEC.

Observations of Soviet performance by the CIA have led to rather dif-ferent conclusions. A 1983 study by the OSA reported that the estimated dollar cost of Russian defense activities had risen at slightly less than two percent annually since 1976. Then, in 1984 JEC testimony, DDI Robert Gates not only confirmed the lower projection, but made the additional point that Soviet spending for their Strategic Rocket Forces and air defense had *declined* in absolute terms since 1977. These trends existed despite the projection, Gates testified, that the Soviets' rate of investment in general industry had maintained the four percent rate since 1981.[17] These figures suggest Soviet defense spending may be rising at only half the pace of expenditures in the economy as a whole, a judgment that would have definite implications for American defense spending. In releasing the testimony, Senator William Proxmire commented, "It is time for Washington to take official notice that Soviet military procure-ment has been stagnant for the past seven years and to stop acting like nothing has happened."[18]

The Defense Intelligence Agency continues to counter that Soviet pro-curement is rising at five to eight percent, faster than overall defense expenditure. Both agencies deny that they have any fundamental disa-greements on the economic intelligence within the community. It is true that both CIA and DIA continue to project the GNP burden of Soviet defense spending at thirteen to fourteen percent since 1965.

Methodology used by the CIA for its dollar cost estimates has been subjected to vigorous scrutiny, the DIA's methods are classified. When it turned up such different results, moreover, the CIA performed a sen-sitivity check of its results and discovered that the projections for many major Soviet procurement programs would have to have been "substan-tially in error" to raise procurement growth to pre-1976 levels. It may yet result that the net effect of the Soviet military spending debate is to double projections in the 1970s and halve them in the 80s. While this is an overdramatization, in effect there has been an information gap between the entry of data into the system and a revision of the community consensus. This suggests the proposition that, at any time, the estimate will be wrong. Again residual uncertainty operates.

Chemical Weapons

One issue of substance on which the intelligence community has largely been in agreement may serve as an illustration of the uncertainty imposed by limited scientific knowledge. This is the case of "Yellow Rain," the alleged use of poisonous trichothecenes by Soviets or their allies in Laos, Cambodia, and Afghanistan. The consensus has largely been that the Soviets are using such chemical weapons, a charge officially levelled by then-Secretary of State Alexander Haig in a September 1981 speech before the Berlin Press Association.

The charge was supported by State Department press releases, and in appearances by aides Walter J. Stoessel, Jr. and Richard Burt. In November 1981 Burt followed up with the claim that the evidence amounted to the proverbial "smoking gun," which turned out to be a captured Soviet gas mask with chemical traces on it. It is reported that a 1982 NIE confirmed the chemical attacks. That March, Secretary Weinberger was asked to provide evidence for his charge of Soviet chemical use in Afghanistan, but was unable to produce any documents on the subject. A crash effort by the executive, declassifying much intelligence information, produced a State Department report to Congress within a few weeks. An updated version was released by Secretary of State George P. Shultz in November 1982.[19]

Given the concern about chemical weapons sparked by the 1980 incident in Sverdlovsk, the charges of chemical attacks in Southeast Asia and Afghanistan were explosive. The problems were the limited evidence available and the imperfection of knowledge. In its reports the State Department had identified much of its evidence and made scientific arguments regarding the toxicity of various amounts of chemicals. Critics probed both the evidence and the theories. Interview evidence from Laos was found to be quite fragmentary, conflicting on some points, and perhaps orchestrated by individuals in the refugee camps.[20] On the technical evidence, some of the samples did not demonstrate required levels of toxicity when retested at other laboratories.

The "Yellow Rain" charges were serious enough that some of America's foremost experts were drawn into the debate. At the University of Minnesota, Dr. Chester J. Mirocha tested samples for the government, while, from Harvard, biochemist Matthew S. Meselson raised initial doubts about the limited evidence. Meselson went on to look into the question in some detail and discovered that toxic chemicals the Russians were alleged to be using were also produced and excreted by overpollinated bees, which are common in Southeast Asia. The "bee theory" Meselson propounded remains under debate; most recently the Harvard professor has introduced additional evidence supporting the natural occurrence of trichothecene chemicals in the amounts found by government experts.[21]

Another problem with the chemical warfare charge is that weapons of this type would be inherently inefficient, even in comparison to standard Soviet chemical munitions. This point was raised by Saul Hormats, who directed the development of chemical weapons for the U.S. Army before 1973. Hormats shows that it would require thousands of *tons* of the alleged agent to gas single villages when six shells from a battery of Soviet 122mm guns could destroy the same target with mere high explosives. Thus mycotoxin warfare might not make military sense.[22]

Both the "bee theory" and the military argument have been officially denied by the U.S. government, which buttresses its own conclusions with claims that British, French, and Canadian studies corroborate the results. For various political reasons, however, these countries have not openly taken sides in the controversy. The issue is of such sensitivity that an objective study also cannot be expected from the United Nations.

If nothing else, the "Yellow Rain" debate is likely to increase our scientific knowledge of bee behavior and pollination. Studies disputing the allegations of chemical attack are accumulating, while the U.S. government has presented no fresh evidence since 1982, which may be related to the fact that two investigators from the United States embassy in Thailand, who gathered most of the data used in the government analyses, were routinely transferred the following year. It is interesting that Alexander Haig, who spared the Soviets no criticism in his early memoir of the Reagan administration, chooses to cite his West Berlin speech only in another context, and does not raise the "Yellow Rain" charges at all.[23]

Espionage Developments

A topic that has aroused increasing interest in the United States over the past several years is espionage. In particular the breakup of a ring of Navy spies in early 1985 has caused great concern over possible security breaches. In view of the multiplying espionage cases, as well as the intelligence community's own concerns on Soviet HUMINT in the 1970s, it is worth reviewing espionage developments over the past few years.

In the summer of 1985, more persons were being prosecuted for espionage than at any time in American history. Fears for the adequacy of counterintelligence have been expressed, along with objections to the large number of Soviet bloc officials, currently more than two thousand, up to forty percent of whom may be intelligence agents, allowed to reside in the United States. The death penalty may well be reinstituted for espionage cases, while access to classified information is being cut back and counterintelligence strengthened.

The Defense Intelligence Agency (DIA) did a retrospective analysis at the request of Senator Sam Nunn (D-Georgia), which found that money replaced ideology as an American's reasons for spying. Over the preceding decade five spies had been CIA employees, three Air Force, three in the Navy, and one each in the Army, DIA, and the USIA. Of these only the spy at the Information Agency, who had little access to highly classified information, could really be classed as an ideological agent.[24]

Such conclusions are reinforced by the most recent case, the breakup of the Walker spy ring in the Navy. Retired chief petty officer John A. Walker was arrested on espionage charges in May 1985; investigation soon led authorities to charge his son Michael and his brother Arthur, along with Navy friend Jerry A. Whitworth, of acting in concert with Walker. All had been or were still active in the Navy, Arthur Walker as an officer. John Walker had been spying since the 1960s, the others, in particular his son, more recently. Through them it is believed that the Soviets received a good deal of information on ship movements, amphibious capabilities, communications procedures, and code key lists.

The Walker case has generated considerable concern on the last item. Fears have been expressed that Navy codes were broken, and some Air Force and somewhat fewer Army messages compromised as well. In fact, the affair may prove less damaging than believed. Code material to which the Walkers and Whitworth would have had access would necessarily be limited. The code keys change very frequently, sometimes from message to message. Communications procedure information from the Walker ring could have been more significant. It seems unlikely that the code revelations of the Walker group could be more serious than the early 1960s material compromised by Joseph Helmich, who worked for the Army branch of NSA in Paris at that time, and was indicted for espionage in 1981.

An aspect of the Walker case more closely related to strategic forces is the service of John Walker and Jerry Whitworth aboard Polaris missile submarines. Communications procedures that could have been divulged here include format information on the emergency action messages that release the fleet ballistic missile force. Still, Walker's experience dated from before the SLBM MIRV era, while procedures have been evolving continuously. Insofar as intelligence estimates are concerned, these documents are almost never sent through communications channels and are unlikely to have been divulged. From the Walker ring the Russians may have gleaned knowledge useful to their antisubmarine warfare research, and perhaps to tactical warning of attack, but not much else.

Of rather more concern to the CIA from the espionage standpoint are several other cases developed in recent years. One is that of Karl F. Koecher, a Czech immigrant who worked as a contract translator for the CIA. Koecher was arrested in November 1984 on charges of having passed to Czechoslovak intelligence whatever information, assessments, and personnel identifications he came across between February 1973 and August 1975. Koecher is currently awaiting trial and claims he was working for the CIA as a double agent in these dealings. Also of significance are the cases of William H. Bell and James Harper, Jr., aviation industry employees who gave material to Polish intelligence concerning radars, Minuteman missiles, and ballistic missile defense, among other items.

At least two cases involved spies who were foiled before the damage was done. In late 1976 a package was dropped over the wall surrounding a Soviet residence in Washington. Russian diplomats, fearing that the package contained a bomb, called in the police. Authorities instead found a photocopied CIA telephone directory, eight other documents, and a promise of more in exchange for money. Former CIA officer Edwin G. Moore was arrested in connection with this episode and is currently serving a fifteen-year prison sentence. In another instance, in May 1981 a SAC missile control officer, Lieutenant Christopher M. Cooke, was arrested after three visits to the Soviet embassy in his effort to initiate an espionage relationship. Prosecution of Cooke was waived in exchange for full cooperation with the Air Force investigation of the affair.

On the other side of the ledger are American intelligence gains from Soviet bloc defectors and agents. The recent attention given to espionage cases in the U.S. has obscured this facet of American intelligence resources. In fact, since the HUMINT discussions of the 1970s, the intelligence community has benefited from an enlarged stream of defectors as well as, according to the Soviet press, actual spies.

First, the Soviet bloc crisis over trade unions in Poland, specifically "Solidarity," produced an intelligence windfall for the U.S. Polish defectors since the end of 1981 have included their ambassador to Tokyo, a senior diplomat assigned to Washington, and a colonel of the Polish intelligence service who may have worked for the CIA even before his defection. A later bloc defector is Milan Svec, Czech deputy chief of mission in Washington, who came over in May 1985.

The Russians themselves have not been immune. One important defection in late 1979, revealed only more recently, was that of KGB Major Stanislav Levchenko, who had worked in Japan under journalistic cover. Another KGB major, Vladimir A. Kuzichkin, chief of the illegal networks in Iran, went to the British in June 1982. Just two months later Sevim Gueraibekov, a Soviet political scientist, fled a conference at Rio de Janeiro and received asylum in the United States.

In addition to the celebrated Shevchenko affair there have been two more recent defections of Soviets working for the United Nations: Nikolai Polyanski from the Paris offices of UNESCO in 1981; and, Vladimir V. Yakimetz, from the United Nations Secretariat in New York during 1983. An important recent defector, a major of Soviet military intelligence (the GRU), is Sergei Bokane, the Russians' deputy chief in Athens, who defected in May 1985 and is reportedly being jointly debriefed by the Americans and British. One last defector certainly merits mention. Identified only as "Grishin," this individual fled to Turkey and received American asylum in late 1983. The chief of staff of the Soviets' Transcaucasian Military District, Lieutenant General Grishin is the highest ranking Russian officer known to have defected to the West.

Meanwhile, in late 1981 *Izvestia* reported the arrest on charges of espionage for the Americans of Y. A. Kapustin, whose profession and employment were not identified other than to say he worked at a "Moscow enterprise." The previous year Russian engineer B. Nilov was also convicted on charges of spying for the U.S., allegedly having been recruited in Algiers as far back as 1974.

What is clear from all this is that there have been victories by both sides in the espionage competition, not by any means has the information flow been all in the direction of the Russians. While the Walker affair proved damaging to the U.S., Soviet General Grishin held a far more sensitive post, and his documents and debriefing undoubtedly constitute a massive security breach for the Russians. On the American side, from the standpoint of national intelligence estimates, at least, it does not appear that any of the known spies could have compromised this information. The Soviets may, but probably do not, have access to the most important documents.

A final point should be made regarding intelligence analysis. In the furor occasioned by the Walker affair and other espionage revelations, the general response seems to be taking the direction of classifying information even more tightly and of reducing the numbers of persons holding security clearances and thus access to the information. While a certain amount of this is justified, we should not be blind to the risk entailed. Since intelligence depends on the imagination and creativity of analysts looking at information, restricting access also means that fewer analytical eyes will be allowed to focus on the key indicators. There is a danger that intelligence analysis will suffer as a result, a danger that so far has not been brought out in any of the discussions of the subject.

Managing Intelligence Collection

Amid espionage furors and substantive disputes on the data, technological progress continues its inexorable advance. New nuclear weapons, new delivery means, even new categories of weapons challenge intelligence analysts. Imagination is necessary not only to interpret the data but even to conceive of what data needs collection. As it has been frequently in the past, the machinery for generating collection requirements was reorganized by the Reagan administration.

Only in the 1970s, under the Carter administration, did the DCI, through an intelligence tasking center, assume a direct role in the implementation of requirements. With the PNIOs collection was mostly managed by the Pentagon. In the KIQ system initiated by William Colby, the National Intelligence Officers were to arrange response strategies with the collection agencies. This system was never fully accepted, however. The Key Intelligence Questions were perceived as merely adding another layer to departmental requirements. Several agencies are reported to have responded to KIQs only where these fit with their own collection plans, while the DCI had no enforcement means of ensuring KIQs were met.

William Casey dealt with the organizational problem in March 1983 with his establishment of the Intelligence Producers Council. This is chaired by the DDCI and comprises senior officials of the NFIB agencies excepting FBI and the DOE. The council now draws up "National Intelligence Topics" (NITs), which have replaced the KIQs as community collection guides. The hope seems to be that by incorporating the collecting agencies into the requirement process, their responsiveness can be ensured.

What is significant in the NIT system is the decline of the analyst's role. While KIQs may have met resistance, the National Intelligence Officers (NIOs) setting them were at least in touch with analysts and had some awareness of the most gaping holes in the data base. The replacement of the NIOs by an NFIB-level interagency committee shifts control of the requirements process in the direction of the collectors.

Although it is possible the NIT system may work, historically it has been the case that when collectors dominated the intelligence requirements process, it has been research and development goals rather than information gaps that have determined many of the requirements set.

A further point is suggested by DCI Casey's management initiative. His establishment of an NFIB-level board illustrates his decentralization of control in some areas in order to devote himself to main areas of interest. Thus, while Casey works closely with covert operators, intelligence requirements, estimates, the NIOs and budgets have increasingly been given to interagency boards. This decentralization has proliferated the number of NFIB-level committees, and may end by diluting the community control achieved so painfully by the DCI since the early 1970s, strengthening the relative positions of the Defense Department intelligence agencies.

Conclusion

Continuing evolution of arms control compliance issues, space militarization analysis, and the search for evidence of revolutionary weapons breakthroughs are likely to figure as intelligence questions in the later 1980s. The record of the past continues to provide confidence that the main lines of Soviet development will be visible given existing intelligence means. What is less clear is whether, in a new strategic era of mutual first-strike threats, existing organizations can provide accurate intelligence estimates.

Some former CIA analysts argue that the degree of politicization of intelligence under the Reagan administration outweighs the institutional reforms in estimative organizations. There is evidence to support this view, although it does not come from the specific substantive area of Soviet force analysis. The military agencies retain their pessimistic views, which with some exceptions have been in the ascendant over the past decade, although the CIA has been regaining its credibility. The jury remains out on this question.

Estimative organization has resumed some of the characteristics of the BNE/ONE structure and other reforms have indeed been carried out. Competitive analysis is probably the most favored current reform. As the B Team experience illustrates, however, competitive analyses can too easily be transformed into witch hunts aimed at dissenting analysts. Competitive analysis also suggests a need for even more analysts, although this may not be possible within budget priorities and may encounter the problem of the recent interest in reducing access to information and numbers of security clearances. Poorly managed competitive analysis may lead to alternative estimates *each* of which is inadequate.

The military competition between the superpowers has crossed the brink on which it stood in 1980. Weapons then on the drawing boards are now entering testing or are even at the point of deployment. A further generation of new weapons is behind them. Although knowledge can never be perfect, accurate intelligence is as important as ever. Estimates with "spin" curry political favor with incumbents but damage long term national interests. Incumbents still fail to comprehend that the resolution of the arms race lies not in intelligence to support programs, but in the political will to achieve accommodation with competitors.

APPENDIX

ACRONYMS

ABM	Antiballistic missile	COMINT	Communications Intelligence
ACDA	Arms Control and Disarmament Agency	COMOR	Committee on Overhead Reconnaissance (1960–1967)
ACSI	Assistant Chief of Staff, Intelligence (Army and Air Force)	DCI	Director of Central Intelligence
AEC	Atomic Energy Commission	DCID	Director of Central Intelligence Directive
AFOATS	Air Force Operational Atmospheric Testing Squadron	DDCI	Deputy Director of Central Intelligence
AGER	Navy electronic intelligence ship designator	DDI	Deputy Director for Intelligence
ARPA	Advanced Research Projects Agency	DDO	Deputy Director for Operations (1973–)
A-2	Air Force Intelligence (1940s and 1950s)	DDP	Deputy Director for Plans (1947–1973)
ATIC	Air Technical Intelligence Center	DDR	Deputy Director for Research (1962–1963)
BMD	Ballistic Missile Defense	DDR&E	Director of Defense Research and Engineering (1958–1977)
BMD	Ballistic Missile Division (USAF)	DDS&T	Deputy Director for Science and Technology (1963–)
BMEWS	Ballistic Missile Early Warning System	DEW	Distant Early Warning
BNE	Board of National Estimates (1950–1973)	DIA	Defense Intelligence Agency (1961–)
CEP	Circular Error Probable	DIPP	Defense Intelligence Projection for Planning (1970–)
CIA	Central Intelligence Agency		
CIG	Central Intelligence Group	DOD	Department of Defense
CINCLANT	Commander in Chief Atlantic (unified and specified command, 1942–)	DPM	Draft Presidential Memorandum (DOD submission to White House, 1961–1969)
CINCPAC	Commander in Chief Pacific (unified and specified command, 1942–)	ELINT	Electronics Intelligence
		ESV	Earth Satellite Vehicle

EXCOM	Executive Committee of the National Security Council (1962–1963)	MRBM	Medium Range Ballistic Missile
FBI	Federal Bureau of Investigation	MRV	Multiple Reentry Vehicle
		NACA	National Advisory Committee on Aeronautics (1918–1958)
FBS	Forward Based Systems		
FOBS	Fractional Orbital Bombardment System	NASA	National Aeronautics and Space Administration (1958–)
GIRD	Group for the Study of Jet Propulsion (Soviet)	NATO	North Atlantic Treaty Organization (1950–)
GMIC	Guided Missiles Intelligence Committee	NFAC	National Foreign Assessment Center
GMAIC	Guided Missiles and Astronautics Intelligence Committee	NFIB	National Foreign Intelligence Board (1977–)
G-2	Army Intelligence	NIE	National Intelligence Estimate
HUMINT	Human Intelligence (Espionage)	NIO	National Intelligence Officer
IAC	Intelligence Advisory Committee (1947–1958)	NIPE	National Intelligence Program Evaluation (1963–1973)
ICBM	Intercontinental Ballistic Missile	NIPPs	National Intelligence Projections for Planning (1962–1970)
INR	Bureau of Intelligence and Research, Department of State	NORAD	North American Aerospace Defense Command
IOC	Initial Operating Capability	NPIC	National Photographic Interpretation Center (1961–)
IRBM	Intermediate Range Ballistic Missile	NRO	National Reconnaissance Office (1959–)
JAG	Joint Analysis Group, CIA-DIA (1962–1970)	NSA	National Security Agency (1952–)
JCS	Joint Chiefs of Staff		
JIEPs	Joint Intelligence Estimates for Planning (1961–1970)	NSAM	National Security Action Memorandum (1961–1969)
JIG	Joint Intelligence Group		
KIQ	Key Intelligence Question (1973–)	NSC	National Security Council
		NSDM	National Security Decision Memorandum (1969–1977)
LASP	Low-Altitude Surveillance Platform		
MARV	Maneuverable Reentry Vehicle	NSSM	National Security Study Memorandum (1969–1977)
MIRV	Multiple Independently Targetable Reentry Vehicle	OCI	Office of Current Intelligence
MIT	Massachusetts Institute of Technology	OER	Office of Economic Research (1967–)
MOL	Manned Orbital Laboratory		

ONE	Office of National Estimates (1950–1973)	RV	Reentry Vehicle
		SAC	Strategic Air Command
ONI	Office of Naval Intelligence	SALT	Strategic Arms Limitation Talks
OPC	Office of Policy Coordination (1948–1952)		
		SAM	Surface-to-Air Missile
ORE	Office of Research and Evaluation (1946–1947)	SCC	SALT Standing Consultative Commission (1972–)
	Office of Reports and Estimates (1947–1955)	SDECE	*Service de Documentation extérieure et de contre-espionnage* (French intelligence organization)
ORR	Office of Research and Reports (1955–1967)		
OSD	Office of the Secretary of Defense	SIOP	Single Integrated Operation Plan
OSI	Office of Scientific Intelligence	SLBM	Sea-launched Ballistic Missile
OSO	Office of Special Operations (1948–1952)	SNIE	Special National Intelligence Estimate (1950–)
OSR	Office of Strategic Research (1967–)	SRF	Soviet Strategic Rocket Forces
OSS	Office of Strategic Services (1941–1945)	SRP	Security Resources Panel (Gaither Committee)
OTH	Over the Horizon		
PBCFIA	President's Board of Consultants on Foreign Intelligence Activities (1956–1961)	SUSAC	Soviet Union Strategic Air Command
		TRW	Thompson-Ramo-Wooldridge Corporation
PFIAB	President's Foreign Intelligence Advisory Board (1961–1977)	UK	United Kingdom
		U.S.	United States
PIC	Photographic Intelligence Center (1958–1961)	USAF	United States Air Force
		USCIB	United States Communications Intelligence Board (1949–1958)
PNIO	Priority National Intelligence Objective (1954–1973)		
PSAC	President's Science Advisory Committee (1957–1970)	USIB	United States Intelligence Board (1958–1977)
RCA	Radio Corporation of America	USSR	Union of Soviet Socialist Republics

NOTES

FREQUENTLY USED ABBREVIATIONS IN NOTES

ACWD — Ann Whitman Diary (at Eisenhower Library)

ACWF — Ann Whitman File (contains DDE Diaries)

AP — Administration Papers (Eisenhower Library)

AWST — *Aviation Week and Space Technology* (periodical)

CS — Cabinet Series Papers (Eisenhower Library)

DAQP — Donald A. Quarles Papers (Eisenhower Library)

DDE Diaries — Eisenhower Diary Series (Eisenhower Library)

DDEL — Dwight D. Eisenhower Library, National Archives

DDRS — Declassified Documents Reference Service (microfiche collection)

FRUS — *Foreign Relations of the United States* (State Department annual documents series)

GERP — George E. Reedy Papers (Johnson Library)

GPO — Government Printing Office

LBJL — Lyndon Baines Johnson Library, National Archives

NA — National Archives and Reference Service

NSF:AF — National Security File: Agency File (Johnson Library)

NSF:CF — National Security File: Country File (Johnson Library)

NSF:NSCF — National Security File: NSC Staff File (Johnson Library)

NYT — *New York Times* (daily newspaper)

OF — Official File (Eisenhower Library)

OSANS — Papers of the Office of the Special Assistant for National Security Affairs (Eisenhower Library)

PCU — Project Clean-Up Papers (Eisenhower Library)

PSAC — President's Science Advisory Committee

RG — Records Group (National Archives identification system)

SP — Senate Papers (Johnson Library)

USC — United States Congress

USPSAC — U.S. President's Science Advisory Committee Papers (Eisenhower Library)

VPSF — Vice Presidential Security File (Johnson Library)

WHCOF — White House Central Office File (Johnson Library)

WHO — White House Office

WP — *Washington Post* (daily newspaper)

CHAPTER ONE: THE SOVIET INTELLIGENCE MISSION

1) William R. Corson, *The Armies of Ignorance*. New York: Dial Press, 1977, quoted p. 274.

2) The OSS Research & Analysis Branch might have found accommodating atmosphere at State but instead it slowly atrophied. The State Department's regional bureaus opposed intrusions by the intelligence group and the secretary of state evinced little interest in R&A activities. Morale among the former OSS researchers, many of whom had returned to other professional and academic jobs, was finally broken in 1947. Then, in an early "loyalty program" case, the former deputy director of the OSS Presentation Branch, Carl Marzani, was convicted on charges of disloyalty and concealing his membership in the Communist Party.

3) USC. Ninty-fourth Congress, Second Session. Senate: Select Committee to Study Governmental Operations with Respect to Intelligence Activities (hereafter cited as Church Committee). *Final Report: Book IV: Detailed Staff Reports on Foreign and Military Intelligence* (hereafter cited as Karalekas). Washington: GPO, 1976, quoted p. 13. (hereafter congressional sessions will be specified number of Congress/number of session).

4) Karalekas, p. 15.

5) Ladislas Farago, *War of Wits*. New York: Paperback Library, 1954, p. 81.

6) In connection with the Hitler-Molotov discussions it is worth noting that these have often been cited as evidence of Soviet intentions in the postwar world. At the present time, for example, it is asserted that Molotov claimed the states in the direction of the Persian Gulf for the Soviet sphere of influence. This is said to be the historical foundation for alleged Soviet motivations in Afghanistan and desire for a warm-water port or Iranian oil beyond that country. In fact, however, it was *German* representatives who suggested to the Soviets in the Hitler-Molotov discussions that the Russians would be better off orienting their aggressive ambitions in the direction of the Gulf. The evidence suggests that the German recommendation was part of an effort to deflect the Soviets from their traditional interest in the Dardanelles, the Turkish straits that are Russia's exit from the Black Sea. Thus attempts to argue that Soviet interest in reaching the Persian Gulf date from 1940 are distortions of fact. See Adam B. Ulam, *Expansion and Coexistence*. New York: Praeger, 1974, p. 304; Louis Fischer, *Russia's Road From Peace to War*. New York: Harper & Row, 1969, pp. 423–426.

7) Walter Millis, ed. *The Forrestal Diaries*. New York: Viking Press, 1951, quoted p. 387.

8) U.S. Army Air Force, "AAF Headquarters Intelligence Policy and Programs, (1946?), paragraph 1. Released by Air Force Historical Office, January 2, 1979.

9) National Security Council, NSCID No. 3, "Co-ordination of Intelligence Production," 13 January 1948 (declassified December 15, 1976).

10) Central Intelligence Agency, DCID 3/2, "Policy Governing Concurrences in National Intelligence Reports and Estimates," 13 September 1948. Cf. DCID 3/1 "Standard Operating Procedures for Departmental Participation in the Production and Co-ordination of National Intelligence," same date (both declassified December 15, 1976).

11) National Security Council, "The Central Intelligence Agency and National Organization for Intelligence" (Dulles-Jackson-Correa Report) 1 January 1949 (declassified June 13, 1976), p. 68.

12) Ibid., p. 69.

13) William L. Langer, *In and Out of the Ivory Tower.* New York: Neal Watson Academic Publications, 1977, p. 220.

14) Ray Cline, *Secrets, Spies and Scholars.*

Washington: Acropolis Press, 1976, p. 122.

15) Central Intelligence Agency, DCID 3/5, "Production of National Intelligence Estimates," Jan. 9, 1953 (declassified December, 1976), para. 5, p. 2.

CHAPTER TWO: INTERCONTINENTAL ATTACK

1) Georgi K. Zhukov, *The Memoirs of Marshal Zhukov.* New York: Delacorte Press, 1971, quoted pp. 474–475.

2) Arnold Kramish, *Atomic Energy in the Soviet Union.* Palo Alto: Stanford University Press, 1959, p. 41.

3) In view of the protracted and acrimonious debate in the United States about "atomic espionage" and the Rosenberg case, it is significant that all this development in the Soviet atomic program occurred *prior* to the date at which the Soviets are thought to have begun receiving information on American atomic achievements.

4) David Dallin, *Soviet Espionage.* New Haven: Yale University Press, 1955, pp. 458–459.

5) Daniel Yergin, *Shattered Peace.* Boston: Houghton Mifflin, 1978, quoted p. 135.

6) Robert Gilpin, *American Scientists and*

Nuclear Weapons Policy. Princeton: Princeton University Press, 1962, quoted p. 75.

7) Robert G. Joseph, *Commitments and Capabilities: United States Foreign and Defense Policy Coordination 1945 to the Korean War.* Ph.D. Dissertation: Columbia University, 1978, quoted fn. p. 234.

8) David E. Lilienthal, *Journals: II: The Atomic Energy Years 1945–1950.* New York: Harper & Row, 1964, p. 486.

9) Reprinted in Thomas Etzold & John L. Gaddis, ed. *Containment.* New York: Columbia University Press, 1978, p. 365.

10) Herbert York, *The Advisors: Oppenheimer, Teller and the Superbomb.* San Francisco: W. H. Freeman, 1976, p. 42.

11) FRUS 1950, v. I, pp. 415–416.

12) FRUS 1950, v. VIII, p. 310.

CHAPTER THREE: INTELLIGENCE RESOURCES

1) Data on agent operations is understandably anecdotal and fragmentary. Among the limited sources currently available are: Harry Rositzke, *The CIA's Secret Operations.* New York: Reader's Digest Press, 1977, pp. 18–38; Thomas Powers, *The Man Who Kept the Secrets.* New York: Knopf, 1979, pp. 37–47; E. H. Cookridge, *Gehlen: Spy of the Century.* New York: Random House, 1971, pp. 237–264; Peer de Silva, *Sub Rosa.* New York: Times Books, 1978, pp. 54–61; and Stewart Steven, *Operation Splinter Factor.* New York: Lippincott, 1974, passim.

2) Victor Marchetti and John D. Marks, *The CIA and the Cult of Intelligence.* New York: Dell Books, 1974, p. 34. A notable new source on the Berlin Tunnel is David Martin, *A Wilderness of Mirrors.* New York: Harper & Row, 1980, pp. 72–90. See also NYT April 24, 1956, April 25, 1956. An interesting periodical account is in Ian Fleming, "The Great Tunnel into the East Zone," WP, October 2, 1960. For other popular accounts see Andrew Tully, *CIA: The Inside Story.* Greenwich (Conn.): Fawcett Books, 1962, pp. 10–12; Cookridge, *Gehlen,* op. cit., pp. 397–406; Cook-

ridge, *The Many Sides of George Blake Esq.* Princeton: Vertex Books, 1970, pp. 157–158; Heinz Hohne and Hermann Zolling, *The General Was a Spy.* New York: Coward McCann, 1971, pp. 306–312. For comments from within CIA see Allen Dulles, *The Craft of Intelligence.* New York: New American Library, 1965, p. 193; Cline, *Secrets, Spies and Scholars,* op. cit., pp. 161–162; and Leonard Mosley, *Dulles.* New York: Dell Books, 1979, pp. 401–404.

3) An excellent account of photographic intelligence in World War II is Constance Babington-Smith, *Air Spy: The Story of Photo Intelligence in World War II.* New York: Ballantine Books, 1957. Cf. Andrew J. Brookes, *Photo Reconnaissance,* London: Ian Allen, 1975; R. V. Jones, *The Wizard War.* New York: Coward McCann, 1978.

4) Quoted from Eisenhower Oral History transcript in Herbert S. Parmet, *Eisenhower and the American Crusades.* New York: Macmillan, 1972, p. 538.

5) Versions differ on whether Eisenhower's approval covered a flight program of ten days' or two weeks' duration. See Mosley, *Dulles,* op. cit., p. 398; and also Powers, *The Man Who Kept the Secrets,* op. cit., p. 96.

6) "Memorandum of Conversation," no date. DDEL: ACWD, box 9, folder "October 1957."

7) Central Intelligence Agency, DCID 3/4 "Production of Scientific and Technical Intelligence," 14 August 1952 (declassified December 15, 1976), paragraph 1 and Annex B.

CHAPTER FOUR: THE BOMBER GAP

1) Yergin, *Shattered Peace,* op. cit., quoted in fn. 39, p. 454.

2) Valentin L. Sokolov, "Soviet Use of German Science and Technology 1945–1946." New York: Research Program on the USSR, Occasional Paper, 1955, pp. 1–2, 5–10, 26, 31; quoted from p. 2.

3) Leslie C. Stevens, *Russian Assignment.* Boston: Little, Brown, 1953, p. 387.

4) NYT, May 14, 1955.

5) Central Intelligence Agency, NIE 11-3-55, "Soviet Capabilities and Probable Causes of Action Through 1960," 17 May 1955 (declassified March 16, 1978), p. 31 & Table III; quoted from paragraph 116, p. 31.

6) Department of State *Bulletin,* March 24, 1960, p. 414. Soviet aircraft production facilities at the time were deemed to include some four hundred airframe, engine, machine tool, and assembly plants that employed between 500,000 and 750,000 workers.

7) USC(84/2) Senate Armed Services. *Hearings: Study of Airpower.* Washington: GPO, 1956, Wilson quoted from p. 1767; Radford from p. 1467. Cf. pp. 1510–1525; also, Charles A. Cannon, "Interest and Ideology: The Senate Airpower Hearings of 1956," *Armed Forces and Society,* v. 3, no. 4, August 1977, pp. 595–608.

8) Department of the Air Force, Report to the President of the United States by the Chief of Staff, USAF, "Visit of the U.S. Air Delegation to the USSR 23 June 1–July 1956" (declassified October 19, 1976), p. 1 (hereafter cited as Twining Report). DDEL: ACWF: AP, box 1, folder: "Air Force, Dept. of (1)."

9) Twining Report, p. 2.

10) Robert K. Gray, *Eighteen Acres Under Glass.* New York (Garden City): Doubleday, 1962, quoted p. 132. The senior Soviet official is not directly identified but from internal evidence may have been Marshal Zhukov.

11) General Thomas S. Power and Albert A. Arnhym, *Design for Survival*. New York: Coward McCann, 1964, p. 42.

12) USC(85/1) House Appropriations. *Hearings: Department of Defense Appropriation for 1958, Pt. 1*. Washington: GPO, 1957, p. 1063. Quarles was referring to Symington's Subcommittee on Airpower.

13) Andrew Goodpaster Interview, p. 128. Columbia University: Office of Oral History, Eisenhower Project.

14) Central Intelligence Agency, NIE 11-4-57, "Main Trends in Soviet Capabilities and Policies 1957–1962," 12 November 1957 (declassified April 24, 1978), paragraph 137, p. 32.

15) Ibid., footnote 2, p. 33.

16) "Memorandum of Conference With the President," 18 June 1958 (declassified February 21, 1979). DDEL: ACWF: DDE Diaries, box 20, folder "Staff Notes June 1958."

17) William T. Lee, "Understanding the Soviet Military Threat: How CIA Estimates Went Astray," National Strategy Information Center, Agenda Paper no. 6, 1977, pp. 27–28.

CHAPTER FIVE: INSTANTANEOUS ATTACK

1) Raymond L. Garthoff, "Russia . . . Leading the World in ICBM and Satellite Development?" *Missiles and Rockets*, October 1957, quoted p. 72. The best English language sources on early Soviet rocket development are: Nicolas Daniloff, *The Kremlin and the Cosmos*. New York: Knopf, 1972; Michael Stoiko, *Soviet Rocketry: Past, Present and Future*. New York: Holt, Rinehart & Winston, 1970; and Albert J. Parry, *Russia's Rockets and Missiles*. New York (Garden City): Doubleday, 1960. For a biography of Tsiolkovsky see Parry, *The Russian Scientist*. New York: Macmillan, 1973.

2) Stoiko, op. cit., quoted p. 73.

3) NYT, April 24, 1956.

4) Asher Lee, *The Soviet Air Force*. New York: Harper & Brothers, 1950.

5) William W. Prochenau and Richard W. Larsen, *A Certain Democrat*. Englewood Cliffs (N.J.): Prentice-Hall, 1972, pp. 161–164.

6) Dwight D. Eisenhower, *The White House Years: Waging Peace 1956–1961*. New York (Garden City): Doubleday, 1965, p. 390.

7) Central Intelligence Agency, NIE 11-3-55, "Soviet Capabilities and Probable Soviet Courses of Action Through 1960," 17 May 1955 (declassified March 16, 1978), p. 25 and fn. 13. DDEL: WHO: OSANS, box 47, folder "NIE 11-3-55."

8) *New York Herald-Tribune*, January 21, 1956.

9) NYT, April 26, 1956.

10) Cline, *Secrets, Spies and Scholars*, op. cit., pp. 154–155.

11) Stewart Alsop, "How Can We Catch Up?" *Saturday Evening Post*, v. 230, no. 24, December 14, 1957, p. 27.

12) Reedy-Department of Defense, letter, October 11, 1957. LBJL:GERP, unboxed, folder "Reedy—Subcommittee."

13) Reedy-Johnson, memo, undated. LBJL: SP, box 421, folder "Reedy Memos—November 1957 (1)."

14) Reedy-Johnson, memo, November 19, 1957. LBJL: op. cit.

15) Italics in the original. Reedy-Johnson, memo, November 23, 1957. LBJL: SP, box 355, folder "Preparedness Subcommittee on Satellites-Hearings."

16) Central Intelligence Agency, NIE 11-4-57, "Main Trends in Soviet Capabilities and Policies 1957–1962," 12 November 1957 (declassified April 24, 1978), pp. 6, 26–27.

17) Johnson-Herbert Hughes, letter, January 9, 1958. LBJL: SP, box 1012, folder "Armed Services—Missile Investigation." *Newsweek,* December 9, 1957, pp.

58–59. Investigation ordered: undated handwritten note. DDEL: WHO: OS-ANS, box 60, folder "Missile Publicity."

CHAPTER SIX: MASSIVE ATTACK

1) Eisenhower-H. Rowan Gaither, letter, May 8, 1957. DDEL: WHO: PCU, box 16, folder "Security Resources Panel (2)."

2) USC(86/2) Senate Government Operations. *Hearings: Organizing for National Security,* v. I. Washington: GPO, 1961, p. 298 (hereafter cited as Jackson Committee Hearings).

3) Peter Lyon, *Eisenhower: Portrait of a Hero.* Boston: Little, Brown, 1974, quoted p. 756. The same statement has also been attributed to Robert Lovett (by Joseph Alsop) and to Robert Sprague.

4) Jackson Committee Hearings, v. I, p. 294.

5) USC(94/2) Joint Committee on Defense Production. *Hearings: Civil Preparedness and Limited Nuclear War.* Washington: GPO, 1976, p. 6.

6) Jerome Wiesner, *Where Science and Politics Meet.* New York: McGraw-Hill, 1965, pp. 174–175.

7) National Security Council, "Deterrence and Survival in the Nuclear Age," Report of the Security Resources Panel (Gaither Report), 7 November 1957 (declassified January 10, 1973), pp. 4, 15–16, 28; quoted from p. 14.

8) Gaither Report, table p. 23.

9) Eisenhower, *Waging Peace,* op. cit., p. 221.

10) National Security Council, "Group Visiting the President," 16 July 1957. DDEL: AP, box 11, folder "General Robert Cutler (2)."

11) Lyndon Johnson, "Memorandum of Discussions and Meetings with the Executive Branch on the Gaither Report," January 6, 1958. LBJL:GERP, un-

boxed, folder "Reedy—Subcommittee Statements."

12) Neil McElroy interview; transcript p. 85. Columbia University Office of Oral History, Eisenhower Project.

13) Goodpaster, "Memorandum of Conference with the President," 5 December 1957. DDEL: ACWF: DDE Diaries, box 16, folder "Staff Notes December 1957."

14) Department of State *Bulletin,* March 14, 1960, p. 414.

15) Arnold Horelick and Myron R. Rush, *Strategic Power and Soviet Foreign Policy.* Chicago: University of Chicago Press, 1966, passim.

16) Whalen was arrested and tried on espionage charges in 1966. He was convicted but, in poor health, was paroled in 1970. See NYT July 13, 1966, July 14, 1966, December 17, 1966. Cf. Marchetti and Marks, *The CIA and the Cult of Intelligence,* pp. 212–214.

17) Goodpaster, "Memorandum of Conference with the President," 17 April 1958 (declassified June 24, 1975), p. 2. DDEL: ACWF: DDE Diaries, box 19, folder "Staff Notes April 1958."

18) Cabinet Minutes, 3 January 1958. DDEL: ACWF: DDE Diaries, box 18, folder "Staff Notes January 1958."

19) Goodpaster, "Memorandum of Conference with the President," 4 February 1958 (declassified June 28, 1975). DDEL: ACWF: DDE Diaries, box 18, folder "Staff Notes February 1958."

20) James R. Killian, *Sputnik, Scientists, and Eisenhower.* Cambridge: MIT Press, 1977, p. 222.

21) *The United States in World Affairs.* 1958. New York: Council on Foreign Relations, 1968, quoted p. 104.

22) Goodpaster, "Memorandum of Conference with the President," 18 June 1958 (declassified February 21, 1978). DDEL: ACWF: DDE Diaries, box 20, folder "Staff Notes June 1958."

23) *New York Herald-Tribune*, August 1, 1958.

24) NYT, September 28, 1958.

25) NYT, December 17, 1957.

26) David Wise and Thomas B. Ross, *The Invisible Government*. New York: Vintage Books, 1964, pp. 212–213.

27) USC(86/1) Senate Appropriations. *Hearings: Department of Defense Appropriation, 1960, Pt. 1.* Washington: GPO, 1959, p. 9.

28) USC(86/1) Senate Armed Services and Committee on Aeronautical and Space Sciences. *Hearings: Missile and Space Activities.* Washington: GPO, 1959, p. 15.

29) John B. Martin, *Adlai Stevenson and the World*. New York (Garden City): Doubleday, 1978, p. 439.

30) Goodpaster, "Memorandum of Conference with the President," 14 January 1959 (declassified August 12, 1975). DDEL: ACWF: DDE Diaries, box 25, folder "Staff Notes January 1959."

31) NYT, March 25, 1959.

32) Killian, *Sputnik, Scientists and Eisenhower*, p. 172.

33) Central Intelligence Agency, "Memorandum for the President," 18 August 1959 (declassified November 18, 1976), p. 3 paragraph 5 and p. 1 paragraph 3. DDEL: AP, box 14, folder "Allen W. Dulles (1)."

34) George B. Kistiakowsky, *A Scientist at the White House*. Cambridge: Harvard University Press, 1976, p. 55.

35) Kistiakowsky, op. cit., p. 219.

36) NYT, January 20, 1960.

37) Goodpaster, "Memorandum of Conference with the President," 26 January 1960 (declassified December 6, 1977), p. 3. DDEL: ACWF: DDE Diaries, box 30, folder "Staff Notes January 1960 (1)."

38) Transcript, NYT January 27, 1960.

39) NYT, January 28, 1960.

40) General Thomas Power, *Design for Survival*. New York: Pocket Books, 1965, pp.149–150. Power's speech was supported by analysis done by Rodney Smith, chief of operations research at SAC headquarters. There was some additional support for such a view in a report issued in December 1959 by the Washington Center for Foreign Policy Studies, which found that four to six Soviet rockets would be necessary to have assurance of destroying each SAC base. See USC(86/1) Senate Foreign Relations. *Report: Developments in Military Technology and Their Impact on United States Strategy and Foreign Policy.* GPO, 1959, p. 58. Similar fears of vulnerability can be discerned in Albert Wohlstetter's "Delicate Balance" studies. It is remarkable that these were some of the earliest analytical studies to predict total force performance required for a given ICBM force to achieve a given outcome. See also Joseph Alsop, *New York Herald-Tribune*, January 25, 1960.

41) USC(86/2) House Appropriations. *Hearings: Department of Defense Appropriation for 1961, Pt. 1.* GPO, 1960, p. 23.

42) Department of State *Bulletin,* March 14, 1960, pp. 411–417.

43) National Security Council, "Notes of Conversation with Mr. John Steele of Time-Life," 27 January 1960. DDEL: WHO: PCU, box 7, folder "Memos for Record (2)."

44) NYT, February 2, 1960.

45) USC(86/2) Senate Armed Services and Committee on Aeronautical and Space Sciences. *Joint Hearings: Missiles, Space and Other Defense Matters 1960.* GPO, 1960 (hereafter cited as 1960 Joint Hearings), p. 404.

46) 1960 Joint Hearings, p. 120.

47) 1960 Joint Hearings, pp. 409, 411.

48) Chalmers Roberts, *First Rough Draft.* New York: Praeger, 1975, quoted pp. 151–152.

49) Department of State, "Intelligence Estimates of Soviet ICBM Strength," draft statement, no date (declassified May 10, 1979), p. 3. DDEL: ACWF: DDE Diaries, box 31, folder "Staff Notes February 1960 (2)."

CHAPTER SEVEN: INTELLIGENCE RESOURCES IN THE LATE 1950s

1) Sherman Adams, *Firsthand Report.* New York: Popular Library, 1962, quoted p. 447.

2) Francis Gary Powers, *Operation Overflight.* New York: Holt, Rinehart & Winston, 1970. Powers, "The Poison Pin Decision," *Rolling Stone* magazine, December 1, 1977, p. 52. Thomas Wise and David Ross, *The U-2 Affair.* New York: Random House, 1962. Leonard Mosley, *Dulles: A Biography of Eleanor, Allen, and John Foster and Their Family Network.* New York: Dial Press, 1978, pp. 454–456. Vladimir Petrov, "The Formation of Soviet Foreign Policy," *Orbis,* v. 17, no. 3, Fall 1973, p. 828. On the program versus single flight question, Gary Powers says that even before April he had known he would be the backup pilot on the April nine mission and then lead pilot on the next. There is also some evidence that the May Day mission was separately approved by the President (Bohlen, *Witness to History,* op. cit., p. 466). As for the incident itself it is still disputed whether Powers's U-2 was the victim of a SAM attack, an engine "flameout" due to malfunction, sabotage, or some combination of these. The SAM-2 is currently credited with an operational ceiling of sixty thousand feet. Senator Barry Goldwater, for one, believes that pilot error may have allowed the plane to descend to a height at which the Soviets could catch it (*With No Apologies.* New York: Berkeley Books, 1980, pp. 73–74). Powers was tried by the Soviets for espionage, convicted, and sentenced to ten years in prison.

3) Kistiakowsky, *A Scientist at the White House,* op. cit., p. 319. The words are those of the PSAC, not the President.

4) Bohlen, op. cit.

5) Robert Murphy, *Diplomat among Warriors.* Garden City (New York): Doubleday, 1964, quoted p. 440.

6) General Vernon A. Walters, *Silent Missions.* Garden City (New York): Doubleday, 1978, pp. 340–341. Parenthetically it might be noted that De Gaulle was one of a few foreign personalities (aside from the British) to have seen the U-2 photographs. He had been shown pictures of Soviet bomber bases around Vinnitsa in the Ukraine in 1959 when NATO officials were attempting to persuade France to join in an air defense network named NADGE.

7) Walters, quoted, p. 344.

8) WP, April 10, 1969.

9) Oleg Penkovsky, *The Penkovsky Papers* (tns. Peter Deriabin). New York: Avon Books, 1966. Greville Wynne. *Contact on Gorky Street.* New York: Atheneum, 1968. See also Richard Helms's speech reported in *The New York Times,* April 14, 1971.

10) Mosley, *Dulles,* op. cit., p. 432.

11) Goodpaster, "Memorandum of Conference with the President," 15 July 1959 (declassified August 11, 1975). DDEL: ACWF: DDE Diaries, box 27, folder: Staff Notes July 1959 (2).

12) Kistiakowsky, p. 45.

13) Ibid., p. 192.

14) Central Intelligence Agency, DCID 1/3 "Priority National Intelligence Objec-

tives," January 14, 1960 (declassified December 15, 1976), p. 1.

CHAPTER EIGHT: THE END OF THE MISSILE GAP

1) Kistiakowsky, p. 240.

2) Henry A. Kissinger, *The Necessity for Choice*. New York: Harper & Brothers, 1961, p. 15.

3) Ibid., p. 26.

4) Daniel O. Graham, "The Intelligence Mythology of Washington," *Strategic Review*, v. 4, no. 3, Summer 1976, pp. 59–61.

5) Andrew Tully, *The Super Spies*. New York: William Morrow, 1969, pp. 33–35.

6) Roger Hilsman, *To Move a Nation*. New York: Delta Books, 1967, pp. 192–193.

7) Central Intelligence Agency, "Current Status of Soviet and Satellite Military Forces and Indications of Military Intentions," 6 September 1961 (declassi-

fication date not available), pp. 3–5 DDRS-(75)-56-a.

8) Power, *Design for Survival*, p. 109.

9) USC(89/1) Senate Armed Services. *Hearings: Military Procurement Authorization Fiscal Year 1966, Pt. 1.* GPO, 1965, p. 43.

10) Lyman D. Kirkpatrick, *The Real CIA*. New York: Macmillan, 1968, p. 220. Italics in the original.

11) Raymond Garthoff, "On Estimating and Imputing Intentions." *International Security*, v. 2, no. 3, Winter 1977, p. 23.

12) Edgar Bottome, *The Missile Gap: A Study of the Formulation of Military and Political Policy*. Rutherford (New Jersey): Fairleigh Dickinson Press, 1971, p. 190.

CHAPTER NINE: MISSILES OF OCTOBER

1) Pierre L. Thyraud de Vosjoli. *Lamia*. Boston: Little, Brown, 1970, p. 296. Cf. NYT, November 27, 1972, p. 41. There is a fictionalized account of de Vosjoli's efforts in Leon Uris's novel *Topaz*. (New York: McGraw-Hill, 1967). The latter also portrays the Soviet defector Yuri Nosenko (see p. 373).

2) Graham Allison, *Essence of Decision*. Boston: Little, Brown, 1971, p. 190.

3) Walt W. Rostow, *The Diffusion of Power*. New York: Macmillan, 1972, quoted p. 259.

4) Central Intelligence Agency, OCI No. 3047/62 "Recent Soviet Military Aid to Cuba" (declassified October 26, 1977). DDRS (77)-266-f.

5) Kenneth Keating, "My Advance View of the Cuban Crisis," *Look* magazine, November 3, 1964.

6) USC(87/2) Senate Foreign Relations. *Hearing: Situation in Cuba*. GPO, 1962,

pp. 12–13. It is worth noting that Keating also seemed to think the Soviet SAM missiles could be modified to be used *offensively* against Florida, which in fact was much further distant than the range of the SAM-2.

7) Central Intelligence Agency, SNIE 85-3-62 "The Military Buildup in Cuba" (declassification date not available [1973]), paragraph 31, p. 8.

8) Victor Marchetti, "The Missile Crisis at CIA," in Linda R. Obst, ed. *The Sixties*. New York: Random House, 1977, pp. 76–77.

9) Edward Weintal and Charles Bartlett, *Facing the Brink*. New York: Scribner's, 1967, quoted p. 59.

10) Robert F. Kennedy, *Thirteen Days*. New York: New American Library, 1969, p. 24.

11) USC(95/2) Senate Intelligence. *Hearings: National Intelligence Reorgani-*

zation and Reform Act of 1978. GPO, 1978, p. 76.

12) Central Intelligence Agency, SNIE 11-18-62 "Soviet Reactions to Certain U.S. Courses of Action on Cuba," 19 October 1962 (declassification date not available [1973]), paragraph 5, p. 3.

13) Central Intelligence Agency, SNIE 11-19-62 "Major Consequences of Certain U.S. Courses of Action on Cuba," 20 October 1962 (declassification date not available [1973]), p. 9.

14) Elie Abel, *The Missile Crisis.* New York: Bantam Books, 1966, quoted p. 134.

15) *The Bedford Incident* (New York: Pocket Books, 1964) by Mark Rascovitch may have been loosely based upon the *Cecil* affair. Cf. *Time* magazine, June 28, 1963, p. 18.

16) Hilsman, *To Move a Nation,* op. cit., p. 188.

17) USC(88/1) Senate Armed Services. *Interim Report: The Cuban Military Buildup.* GPO, 1963, pp. 2, 3.

18) Klaus Knorr, "Failures in National Intelligence Estimates: The Case of the Cuban Missiles," *World Politics,* v. 16, no. 3, April 1964, pp. 455–467.

CHAPTER TEN: THREAT FROM DEFENSE

1) Freeman Dyson, *Disturbing the Universe.* New York: Harper & Row, 1979, p. 137.

2) Robert S. McNamara, Fiscal Year 1965 Posture Statement, February 3, 1964, p. 38.

3) Robert S. McNamara, Fiscal Year 1966 Posture Statement, January–February 1965, p. 52.

4) General Nikolai Talensky, "Anti-Missile Systems and Disarmament," in William R. Kintner, ed. *Safeguard: Why the ABM Makes Sense.* New York: Hawthorn Books, 1969, pp. 366, 370, 371–372.

5) An exo-atmospheric interceptor is the technical term for an ABM missile which engages an incoming ICBM above (or outside) the atmosphere. An "endo-atmospheric" ABM, by contrast, is designed to engage its target during final reentry within the atmosphere. In the Soviet system, Galosh was exoatmospheric; Tallinn, were it actually an ABM, would have been endo-atmospheric. In the U.S. systems after 1965, Nike-X was exo- and Sprint was endoatmospheric.

6) Robert S. McNamara, Fiscal Year 1967 Posture Statement, no date (January 1966?), pp. 59–60.

7) Lloyd Norman, "Nike-X: Big Chip in the Deadly Gamble of Nuclear Exchange," *Army* magazine, March 1967, quoted p. 30.

8) Michael Getler, "Soviet ABM Deployment Expected in Year," *Technology Week,* November 21, 1966, quoted p. 10.

9) Robert S. McNamara, Fiscal Year 1968 Posture Statement, January 23, 1967, p. 50.

10) Fiscal 1968 Hearings, Pt. 1, p. 490.

11) Ibid., p. 251.

12) Fiscal 1968 Hearings, Pt. 1, p. 490.

13) Clark M. Clifford, Fiscal Year 1970 Posture Statement, January 13, 1969, p. 87.

14) Ibid.

15) Alan Platt, *The U.S. Senate and Strategic Arms Policy 1969–1977.* Boulder (Colorado): Westview Press, 1978, quoted p. 12.

16) Daniel O. Graham, *Shall America Be Defended?* New Rochelle (New York): Arlington House, 1979, p. 95.

17) AWST, September 22, 1980, p. 15.

CHAPTER ELEVEN: INTELLIGENCE ORGANIZATION AND RESOURCES IN THE 1960s

1) For a technical discussion of satellite sensor systems, with mathematical expressions for calculation of ground resolution and other factors, see Ted Greenwood, "Reconnaissance, Surveillance, and Arms Control." London: International Institute of Strategic Studies, Adelphi Paper no. 88, June 1972. An informative but more general discussion is in Greenwood's "Reconnaissance and Arms Control," *Scientific American*, February 1973. An excellent and detailed account is also in Phillip J. Klass, *Secret Sentries in Space*. New York: Random House, 1971.

2) NYT, May 5, 1975.

3) The Defense Intelligence School has played an active role in developing expertise on military intelligence subjects. Not until 1964–1965 was there a single introductory text in strategic intelligence. Then a programed instruction manual was introduced consisting of units in five of the eight courses being taught at the school. The text was titled *Components of Strategic Intelligence*. A 1966 text, *The Intelligence Process*, contained what is described as a unique case study. In 1969 the Defense Intelligence School published further texts on the identification of Soviet and other military equipment. The school now runs a variety of intelligence courses under the Intelligence Career Development Program, listed in Defense Intelligence Agency, "Compendium of Training for General Intelligence Career Development Program (ICDP) Personnel," March 1977.

4) USC(88/1) Senate Appropriations. *Hearings: Department of Defense Appropriations for 1964*. GPO, 1963, p. 1038.

5) Trevor Armbrister, *A Matter of Accountability*. New York: Coward McCann, 1970, quoted p. 180.

6) Joint Chiefs of Staff, memorandum, General Maxwell Taylor–McGeorge Bundy, 24 December 1963 (declassified July 12, 1976). LBJL: Agency File, box 5,8,9,10 (consolidated), folder "CIA v.1."

7) National Security Council, memorandum McGeorge Bundy–Maxwell Taylor, 3 March 1964 (declassified July 12, 1976) ibid.

8) Central Intelligence Agency, USIB D1.2/1 "Reorganization of USIB," 16 March 1964 (declassified July 12, 1976) ibid.

9) Central Intelligence Agency, DCID 1/3 "Priority National Intelligence Objectives," 23 December 1964 (declassified December 15, 1976).

10) Central Intelligence Agency, DCID 1/3 "Priority National Intelligence Objectives," 1 July 1966 (declassified December 15, 1976).

11) Central Intelligence Agency, DCID 1/3 "Priority National Intelligence Objectives," 16 May 1968 (declassified December 15, 1976).

CHAPTER TWELVE: THE SOVIET MISSILE BUILDUP

1) Central Intelligence Agency, "Trends in the World Situation," 9 June 1964 (declassified CIA letter March 22, 1976, no NARS action date given), paragraphs 5 (p. 3), 9 (pp. 6–7). LBJL: NSF: Agency File, boxes 5,8,9,10 (consolidated), folder "CIA v. 1."

2) Penkovsky, *Penkovsky Papers*, op. cit., pp. 328, 329.

3) Freeman Dyson, *Disturbing the Universe*, op. cit., pp. 145–46.

4) Robert S. McNamara, Fiscal Year 1964 Posture Statement, February 3, 1963,

p. 29. All references to posture statements prior to 1972 (fiscal 1973) are to the classified versions unless otherwise noted. These were declassified in 1974.

5) Ibid.

6) Robert S. McNamara, Fiscal Year 1965 Posture Statement, March 4, 1964, p. 37.

7) *U.S. News and World Report,* April 12, 1965, p. 59.

8) NYT, November 18, 1965, from Soviet trade-union magazine *Trud.*

9) NYT, November 14, 1965.

10) Central Intelligence Agency, DCID 3/4 "Production of Guided Missiles and Astronautics Intelligence," 23 April 1965 (declassified December 15, 1976).

11) Melvin R. Laird, Fiscal Year 1972 Posture Statement, January 3, 1971, pp. 62–63, table p. 239.

12) Albert Wohlstetter, "Legends of the Strategic Arms Race," United States Strategic Institute, USSI Report 75–1, 1975; Wohlstetter, "Is There a Strategic Arms Race?" *Foreign Policy* no. 15, Summer 1974, pp. 3–20; Wohlstetter, "Rivals But No Race," *Foreign Policy* no. 16, Fall 1974, pp. 48–81; Wohlstetter, "Optimal Ways to Confuse Ourselves," *Foreign Policy* no. 20, Fall 1975.

13) Wohlstetter, "Legends of the Strategic Arms Race," p. 6.

14) Lawrence Freedman, *U.S. Intelligence and the Soviet Strategic Threat.* London: Macmillan, 1978, pp. 107–108.

CHAPTER THIRTEEN: THE SOVIET MIRV

1) Bureau of the Budget, memo "Minuteman-Polaris-Poseidon," 8 November 1965 (declassified December 13, 1976); National Security Council, memo Spurgeon Keeny-McGeorge Bundy, same subject (declassified May 23, 1977). LBJL: NSF: Agency File, boxes 14–17 (consolidated).

2) NYT, May 31, 1979, quoted p. A5.

3) Richard J. Whalen, "The Shifting Equation of Nuclear Defense," *Fortune* magazine, June 1, 1967, p. 87.

4) Center for Strategic Studies (Georgetown), "The Soviet Military-Technological Challenge, op. cit., p. 42.

5) USC(90/2) Senate Appropriations. *Hearings: Fiscal Year 1969 Department of Defense, Pt. 5.* GPO, 1969, p. 2666.

6) USC(91/1) Senate Armed Services. *Hearings: Authorization for Military Procurement. Research and Development Fiscal Year 1970 and Reserve Strength. Pt. 1.* GPO, 1969, pp. 126–127.

7) Fiscal 1970 Hearings, Pt. 1, p. 206.

8) Laird's statement was made to a closed session of the House Appropriations Committee on March twenty-second. It was reported in the press and later quoted in the hearing on "Intelligence and the ABM." See below.

9) At the time of writing (1980) there are still no public claims that the Soviets have achieved a retargeting capacity. American developments in this area are discussed in Chapter XIV. Foster's scenario is in Fiscal 1970 Hearings, Pt. 2, pp. 1713–1714. Cf. AWST, July 7, 1969.

10) Murphy Commission, op. cit., v. 7: *Appendix U: Intelligence Functions Analysis,* p. 47.

11) *Public Papers of the Presidents: Richard M. Nixon, 1969.* GPO, 1971, p. 301.

12) USC(91/1) Senate Foreign Relations. *Hearings: Strategic and Foreign Policy Implications of ABM Systems.* GPO, 1969, Pt. 1, p. 159.

13) Fiscal 1970 Hearings, Pt. 2, p. 1775.

14) Henry A. Kissinger, *White House Years.* Boston: Little, Brown, 1979, p. 37. Cur-

iously, while Kissinger mentions this episode in describing Helms, his chronological account of 1969 defense decision-making (pp. 197–198) is completely silent on the matter of the triplet and instead refers to Wohlstetter's *Legends of the Strategic Arms Race.*

15) USC(91/1) Senate Foreign Relations. *Hearing: Intelligence and the ABM.* GPO, 1969, pp. 53–54.

16) Ibid., p. vi.

17) Thomas Powers, *The Man Who Kept the Secrets,* op. cit., pp. 211–212.

18) USC(91/1) House Foreign Affairs. *Hearings: Diplomatic and Strategic Impact of Multiple Warhead Missiles.* GPO, 1969, pp. 255, 263.

19) Church Committee, Final Report, Bk. I, quoted p. 78.

20) Ibid., p. 79.

21) USC(95/2) Senate Intelligence. *Hearings: National Intelligence Reorganization and Reform Act of 1978.* GPO, 1978, p. 21.

22) Department of Defense, Report to the President and the Secretary of Defense on the Department of Defense by the Blue Ribbon Defense Panel (Fitzhugh Panel), Supplemental Statement, September 30, 1970, pp. viii–ix.

23) By 1980, with the Soviets having deployed another generation of ICBMs and being on the verge of testing another in the interval, no Soviet ICBM is yet thought to have attained a CEP as accurate as .15 nautical mile. Even pessimists like Paul Nitze, in 1979, claimed current Soviet CEPs of about .17 nautical mile and did not expect achievement of .15 nautical mile accuracies before 1982.

24) *Washington Star,* May 1, 1971.

25) USC(92/2) Senate Appropriations. *Hearings: Department of Defense Appropriation Fiscal Year 1973, Pt. 1.* GPO, 1972, p. 86.

26) Ibid., p. 539.

27) Fiscal 1973 Hearings, Pt. 3, pp. 230–231.

28) Edgar Ulsamer, "Increasing Momentum of Soviet Strategic Systems," *Air Force* magazine, March 1973, pp. 62–63.

29) USC(92/2) Senate Armed Services. *Hearings: Military Implications of the Treaty on the Limitations of ABM Systems and the Interim Agreement on the Limitation of Strategic Offensive Arms.* (Hereafter cited as SALT I Hearings). GPO, 1972, p. 385.

30) Ralph Lapp, *Arms Without Doubt.* New York: Cowles, 1970, p. 136.

31) *New York Times* Editorial, April 26, 1970.

CHAPTER FOURTEEN: MONITORING SALT

1) Richard Nixon, *RN: The Memoirs of Richard Nixon,* op. cit., v. 1, p. 422.

2) Kissinger, *White House Years,* op. cit., p. 11.

3) Ibid., p. 36.

4) Ibid. Cf. Roger Morris, *Uncertain Greatness.* New York: Harper & Row, 1977, pp. 77–85, 88; and Powers, *The Man Who Kept the Secrets,* op. cit., pp. 202–203.

5) John Newhouse, *Cold Dawn: The Story of SALT.* New York: Holt, Rinehart & Winston, 1973, p. 159.

6) Kissinger, p. 148.

7) Gerard C. Smith, *Doubletalk: The Story of the First Strategic Arms Limitation Talks.* Garden City (New York): Doubleday, 1980, p. 109. Interestingly enough, Smith's account makes no mention of the NSSM-28 fracas or his own motivations in recommending formation of the Verification Panel. General Wheeler, who was so harsh in criticizing the efforts of the ACDA-led NSSM-28 group, is described as an old friend of Smith's.

8) Newhouse, p. 149.

9) SALT I Hearings, pp. 398–399.

10) Ibid., p. 412.

11) "The Pike Report," New York *Village Voice*, February 16, 1976, p. 92, fn. 590.

12) Department of State *Bulletin,* January 5, 1976, p. 10. Cf. Roger P. Labrie, ed. *SALT Handbook: Key Documents and Issues 1972–1979.* Washington, DC: American Enterprise Institute, 1979, pp. 221–240; Richard Burt, "Soviet Sea-based Forces and SALT," *Survival* v. 17 no. 1, January–February 1975, pp. 9–13; and Leslie H. Gelb, "Washington Dateline: The Story of a Flap," *Foreign Policy* no. 16, Fall 1974, pp. 165–181.

13) James R. Schlesinger, Fiscal Year 1975 Posture Statement (unclassified), March 4, 1974, p. 45. The first full-range shots of the SS-19 also took place around this time—two launchings from Tyuratam into the Central Pacific. The SS-19 has never been tested other than with MIRVs, there is no single-warhead version.

14) Labrie, ed. *SALT Handbook,* p. 314.

15) Department of State *Bulletin,* July 29, 1974, p. 215.

16) Department of State *Bulletin,* January 5, 1976, p. 2.

17) USC(94/1) House Select Committee on Intelligence. *Hearings: U.S. Intelligence Agencies and Activities: Risks and Control of Foreign Intelligence Pt. 5* (hereafter cited as Pike Committee Hearings). GPO, 1975, p. 1934.

18) Pike Committee Hearings, p. 1951.

19) Department of State *Bulletin,* January 5, 1976, p. 3.

20) USC(95/2) Senate Intelligence. *Hearings: National Intelligence Reorganization and Reform Act of 1978.* GPO, 1978, p. 702.

21) USC(94/1) House International Relations. *Hearings: U.S.-Soviet Union-China: The Great Power Triangle.* GPO, 1976, p. 102. The syntax of the last sentence is reproduced as recorded in the transcript.

22) WP, June 18, 1980, quoted p. C23.

23) Arms Control and Disarmament Agency, "Verification: The Critical Element of Arms Control," ACDA Publication no. 85, March 1976, p. 30.

24) USC(96/1) Senate Foreign Relations. *Hearings: The SALT II Treaty, Pt. 1.* GPO, 1979, p. 226.

25) Gerard Smith, "Wrestling with the Plowshare Problem," NYT OpEd, January 16, 1976.

26) Senate Select Committee on Intelligence, "Principal Findings of the Senate Select Committee on Intelligence on the Capabilities of the United States to Monitor the SALT II Treaty," press release, October 5, 1979, p. 7.

27) Ibid.

28) David S. Sullivan, "Soviet SALT Deception." Boston (Virginia): Coalition for Peace Through Strength, 1979, pp. 1–2.

CHAPTER FIFTEEN: INTELLIGENCE ALARUM

1) A good summary of the issues is in Paul Cockle, "Analyzing Soviet Defense Spending: The Debate in Perspective," *Survival,* v. 20, no. 5, September–October 1978, pp. 209–219. Major criticisms are in William T. Lee, *The Estimation of Soviet Defense Expenditures 1955–1975.* New York: Praeger, 1977. For a different view of the "residuals" approach see Franklyn Holzman, *Financial Checks on Soviet Defense Expenditures.* Lexington (Massachusetts): Lexington Books, 1975.

2) Daniel O. Graham, "The Soviet Military Budget Controversy," *Air Force* magazine, May 1976, pp. 33–37. Also Henry S. Bradsher in *The Washington Star,* February 15, 1976. Cf. Lev Navrozov, "What the CIA Knows About Russia,"

Commentary, v. 66, no. 3, September 1978, p. 53. The Soviet secret statistical handbook, produced in only about four hundred copies and known to the CIA since 1972, is said to show Soviet defense spending in 1972 at 58 billion rubles.

3) Central Intelligence Agency, SR 76-10053 "A Dollar Comparison of Soviet and U.S. Defense Activities 1965–1975," February 1976 (unclassified). USC(94/1) Joint Economic Committee. *Hearings: Allocation of Resources in the Soviet Union and China 1975.* GPO, 1975.

4) William Colby, *Honorable Men,* op. cit., pp. 351–352.

5) USC(94/2) Joint Economic Committee. *Hearings: Allocation of Resources in the Soviet Union and China 1976, Pt. 2.* GPO, 1976, quoted p. 61.

6) NYT, December 26, 1976, quoted p. A14.

7) WP, January 2, 1977, quoted p. A1.

8) USC(95/2) Senate Intelligence. *Report: The National Intelligence Estimates A-B Team Episode Concerning Soviet Strategic Capability and Objectives.* GPO, 1978, p. 3ff.

9) Committee on the Present Danger, "Common Sense and the Present Danger," no date (January 1977), p. 1.

10) Donald H. Rumsfeld, Fiscal Year 1978 Posture Statement, January 17, 1977 (unclassified), p. 32.

11) Richard E. Pipes, "Why the Soviet Union Thinks It Could Fight and Win a Nuclear War," *Commentary,* v. 65, no. 1, July 1977, pp. 21–34.

12) For the Paisley incident see Tad Szulc, "The Missing CIA Man," *New York Times Magazine,* January 7, 1979. In 1980 it became known that the FBI considers the Paisley death a suicide with no foul play involved (NYT, April 24, 1980).

13) Senate Intelligence Committee, Staff Report on B Team, op. cit., p. 7.

14) Central Intelligence Agency, SR 80-10005 "Soviet and U.S. Defense Activities: A Dollar Cost Comparison," January 1980 (unclassified), p. 3.

15) Franklyn Holzman, "Are the Soviets Really Outspending the U.S. on Defense?" *International Security,* v. 4, no. 4, Spring 1980, pp. 86–104. It should also be noted that CIA considers the Soviets to be spending fifteen to twenty-five percent of their annual budget, evidently a growing percentage, on forces purely oriented against the People's Republic of China. If this were considered a further deflating factor, then U.S. budgets would show even better in comparison to the Soviet.

16) "Perspectives on Intelligence 1976–1981," reprinted in *Covert Action Information Bulletin* no. 6, October 1979, p. 15.

17) USC(96/1) House Appropriations. *Hearings: Department of Defense Appropriations for 1980, Pt. 3.* GPO, 1979, pp. 12–13.

18) NYT, September 5, 1971.

19) James R. Schlesinger, Fiscal Year 1975 Posture Statement, March 4, 1974 (unclassified), p. 47.

20) Glagolev, "The Soviet Decision-making Process on Arms Control Negotiations," op. cit., pp. 772–773.

21) Gerald R. Ford, *A Time to Heal,* op. cit., quoted p. 294.

22) William Colby, *Honorable Men,* op. cit., quoted p. 375, italics in the original.

23) AWST, October 18, 1976, p. 15.

24) Bonner Day, "Soviet Bombers: A Growing Threat," *Air Force* magazine, November 1978, quoted p. 86.

25) Donald H. Rumsfeld, Fiscal Year 1978 Posture Statement, January 17, 1977 (unclassified), p. 63.

26) Harold R. Brown, Fiscal Year 1979 Posture Statement, February 2, 1978 (unclassified), p. 47.

27) Backfire seems to have broken the Soviets' stricture against both mentioning

weapons characteristics at SALT and against their diplomats having access to such. Both Brezhnev and Gromyko have now commented in detail on this weapon. Statements on performance of Backfire have also been made on several occasions to both U.S. diplomats and political figures by the chief of the Soviet general staff, Marshal Nikolai V. Ogarkov.

28) Department of State, "SALT II Agreement, Vienna June 18, 1979," Selected Documents No. 12B, p. 58.

29) Brezhnev quoted by Strobe Talbott, *Endgame: The Inside Story of SALT II.* New York: Harper & Row, 1979, p. 15. Kosygin in WP, August 31, 1979, quoted p. A1. *Newsweek,* June 25, 1979, quoted p. 27.

CHAPTER SIXTEEN: SALT II

1) Leonid Brezhnev, *Peace, Détente, and Soviet-American Relations: A Collection of Statements.* New York: Harcourt Brace Jovanovich, 1979, pp. 148–149.

2) Interim Agreement on the Limitation of Strategic Offensive Arms, May 26, 1972, Article V.

3) Talbott, *Endgame,* p. 201.

4) Department of State, "SALT II Agreement, Vienna, June 18, 1979," Article XV. Selected Documents No. 12B, p. 44.

5) NYT, March 3, 1979.

6) Readers may recall that President Johnson remarked on reconnaissance satellites in a discussion in Nashville during 1967, saying that he didn't care how much the United States had spent on space, because now we *knew* how many missiles the Russians had. But Johnson's remarks were supposed to have been off the record and only inadvertently became part of it.

7) NYT, March 2, 1979, quoted p. A8.

8) NYT, March 9, 1979, quoted p. A5.

9) There have also been rumors of an offer from China to build a ground ELINT station there. Thoughts of reestablishing a ground station in Pakistan were entertained but dismissed after informal contacts with the Pakistani government evidently revealed a lack of enthusiasm in that quarter.

10) Trevor Armbrister, *A Matter of Accountability,* op. cit., quoted p. 182.

11) *Newsweek,* February 6, 1978, p. 30.

12) Department of State, "SALT II Senate Testimony, July 9–11, 1979," Current Policy Series no 72A, p. 3.

13) Ibid., p. 36.

14) Coalition for Peace Through Strength, "An Analysis of SALT II," May 1979, p. 41. My italics.

15) SALT II Hearings, Pt. 1, p. 209.

16) Senate Select Committee on Intelligence, "Principal Findings of the Senate Select Committee on Intelligence on the Capabilities of the United States to Monitor the SALT II Treaty," press release, October 5, 1979, pp. 2, 9, 10.

17) Ibid.

18) Edward Luttwak, "Why Arms Control Has Failed," *Commentary,* v. 65, no. 8, January 1978, p. 21.

19) USC(95/1) Joint Economic Committee. *Hearings: Allocation of Resources in the Soviet Union and China 1977, Pt. 1.* GPO 1977, p. 31.

20) For informed technical analyses of the requirements for directed-energy weapons see Richard L. Garwin, "Charged-Particle Beam Weapons?" *Bulletin of the Atomic Scientists,* October 1978, pp. 24–27; John Parmentola and Kosta Tsipis, "Particle Beam Weapons," *Scientific American,* April 1979, pp. 54–65; and G. Bekefi, B. T. Feld, J. Parmentola, and K. Tsipis, "Particle Beam Weapons—A Technical

Assessment," *Nature,* March 20, 1980, pp. 219–225.

21) USC(96/1) Senate Foreign Relations.

Fiscal Year 1980 Arms Control Impact Statements, March 1979. GPO, 1979, p. 17.

CHAPTER SEVENTEEN: CENTRAL INTELLIGENCE AND THE ARMS RACE

1) Les Aspin, "Debate over U.S. Strategic Forecasts: A Mixed Record," *Strategic Review,* v. 8, no. 3, Summer 1980, pp. 29–43.

2) Irving Janis in *Victims of Groupthink*

(Boston: Houghton Mifflin, 1972) describes how officials as members of a team become infected with common biases and are subject to peer-group pressures to conformity.

AFTERWORD

1) George V. Lauder, Letter to the Editor, *Foreign Policy,* no. 58, Spring 1985, p. 172.

2) On developments in intelligence organization see Stephen J. Flanagan, "Managing the Intelligence Community," *International Security,* v. 10, no. 1, Summer 1985, pp. 58–95. A more general historical view of organizational developments is Jeffrey T. Richelson, *The U.S. Intelligence Community.* Cambridge: Ballinger, 1985.

3) Lauder, op. cit. Lauder, the public affairs director at the CIA, was writing in response to a more critical assessment by former analyst Allen E. Goodman, "Dateline Langley: Fixing the Intelligence Mess," *Foreign Policy,* no. 57, Winter 1984–85, pp. 160–179. Lauder predictably paints a rosier picture, which Goodman rejects in his response to the editorial letter (*Foreign Policy,* no. 58, pp. 173–177). For the views of the NIO who resigned see John Horton, "Why I Quit the CIA," *Washington Post,* January 2, 1985.

4) USC(98/2) Senate Select Committee on Intelligence. *Report: January 1, 1983 To December 31, 1984.* GPO, 1985.

5) Caspar Weinberger, *FY 1986 Report of* [the] *Secretary of Defense,* GPO, 1985, p. 48. *Armed Forces Journal,* v. 123, no. 1, August 1985, pp. 14–16. Harold

Brown, *FY 1982 DOD Report.* GPO, 1981, table 4–2, p. 53.

6) NYT, July 19, 1985. Results derived from standard calculations using the General Electric Missile Effectiveness Calculator (more recent methods of calculation developed by DIA generally show even less effectiveness). At this resulting SSKP some seven warheads would be necessary to attain a ninety-five percent probability of destroying a Minuteman silo. Aside from the feasibility of laying down such large numbers of warheads against single targets, the SS-19 carries only *six* warheads in its most capable Mod-3 configuration, meaning that an attack requiring so many RVs per target would in fact disarm the SS-19 force instead.

7) For example, see Department of Defense, *Soviet Military Power* (3rd edition), April 1984, map p. 28.

8) *Washington Post,* December 22, 1984. International Institute of Strategic Studies, *Military Balance 1980–1981.* London: 1984, pp. 10, 11. IISS, *Military Balance 1984–1985.* London: 1984, pp. 17, 20, NYT, October 1, 1985.

9) AWST, January 3, 1983, p. 13. More extensive discussion is available in Bill Sweetman, "Blackjack: The Biggest Bomber By Far," *International Defense Review,* May 1984, pp. 549–552.

10) See Joel S. Wit, "Soviet Cruise Mis-

siles," *Survival*, v. 25, no. 61, November–December 1983, pp. 249–260; also, IISS, *Strategic Survey 1984–1985*. London: 1985, pp. 19–23.

11) NYT, October 30, 1981; *Soviet Military Power* (3rd edition), op. cit., pp. 36–39.

12) Paul H. Nitze, "SDI: The Soviet Program." Department of State, Current Policy no. 717, n.d. (July 1985); also NYT, July 12, 1985.

13) Gerard C. Smith, *Doubletalk: The Story of the First Strategic Arms Limitation Talks*. Garden City (New York): Doubleday, 1980. Also, Raymond L. Garthoff, *Detente and Confrontation: American-Soviet Relations From Nixon to Reagan*. Washington: Brookings Institution, 1985.

14) The following discussion is based on the paper "Verification, Compliance and Politics: The Case of Superpower Arms Control" (ms, 1985) prepared by the author and presented at the conference of the International Studies Association, March 1985.

15) Quoted respectively from *Newsweek*, May 9, 1983, p. 23; NYT, April 23, 1983, p. 9; NYT, February 2, 1985, p. 3.

16) Kenneth A. Adelman, "Arms Control With and Without Agreements," *Foreign Affairs*, v. 63, no. 2, Winter 1984–1985, p. 244.

17) Robert Gates, "Allocation of Resources in the Soviet Union and China 1984," Testimony before the Joint Economic Committee, November 21, 1984 (mimeo), especially pp. 12–16.

18) AWST, March 18, 1985, p. 101.

19) NYT, September 14, 1981. Department of State, Special Report no. 98, "Chemical Warfare in Southeast Asia and Afghanistan," March 22, 1982. Also, Department of State, Special Report no. 104, "Chemical Warfare in Southeast Asia and Afghanistan: An Update," November 1982.

20) Grant Evans, *The Yellow Rainmakers*. London: Verso, 1983.

21) Thomas D. Seeley, Joan W. Nowicke, Matthew Meselson, Jeanne Guillemin, and Pongthep Akratanakul, "Yellow Rain," *Scientific American*, v. 253, no. 3, September 1985, pp. 128–137.

22) Saul Hormats, "A Chemical Expert Who Doubts the Soviets Used Yellow Rain," *Washington Post*, February 26, 1982.

23) Alexander Haig, *Caveat: Realism, Reagan and Foreign Policy*. New York: Macmillan, 1984, p. 139.

24) NYT, June 6, 1985. Jack Anderson in the *Washington Post*, June 2, 1985: June 6, 1985; NYT, June 9, 1985.

BIBLIOGRAPHY

I. DOCUMENTS:

(Specific documents and originators are fully identified in the chapter notes. The following are documentary collections and a list of the congressional and miscellaneous documents consulted.)

a) *Dwight D. Eisenhower Library, National Archives:*
Administration Papers
Ann Whitman Diary
Ann Whitman File: DDE Diary Series
Cabinet Series
Official File
White House Office: Office of the Assistant for National Security: Project Clean-Up
U.S. President's Science Advisory Committee
Clifford C. Furnass Papers
Robert K. Gray Papers
Neil C. McElroy Papers
Donald A. Quarles Papers
Walter Bedell Smith Papers

b) *Lyndon Baines Johnson Library, National Archives:*
National Security File: Agency File
National Security File: Country File
National Security File: NSC Staff File
Senate Papers
Vice Presidential Security File
White House Central Office
George E. Reedy Papers

c) *Declassified Documents Reference Service* (DDRS): This is a microfiche documents collection first issued in 1975. It is organized in a Retrospective (R) series and subsequent annual series. In citations the series is given, followed by a card number and then an alphabetic document identifier (example: (R)-298-c).

d) *Freedom of Information Act:* documents cited with only the originating agency and a declassification date were obtained by the author or by other researchers using the Freedom of Information Act.

e) *Congressional Documents:*
(All such documents are cited by the Congress and session numbers (e.g., 95/2), the originating committee, and the title.)

USC(84/1) Senate Appropriations. *Hearings: Department of Defense Appropriation for 1956.* GPO, 1955.

USC(84/2) Senate Appropriations. *Hearings: Department of Defense Appropriation for 1957.* GOP, 1956.

USC(85/1) Senate Appropriations. *Hearings: Department of Defense Appropriation for 1958.* GPO, 1957.

USC(86/1) Senate Appropriations. *Hearings: Department of Defense Appropriation for 1960.* GPO, 1959.

USC(86/2) Senate Appropriations. *Hearings: Department of Defense Appropriation for 1961.* GPO, 1960.

USC(88/1) Senate Appropriations. *Hearings: Department of Defense Appropriation for 1964.* GPO, 1963.

USC(90/1) Senate Appropriations. *Hearings: Military Authorization and*

Defense Appropriation 1968. GPO, 1967.

USC(90/2) Senate Appropriations. *Hearings: Department of Defense Appropriations Fiscal Year 1969.* GPO, 1968.

USC(91/1) Senate Appropriations. *Hearings: Department of Defense Appropriations Fiscal Year 1970.* GPO, 1969.

USC(91/2) Senate Appropriations. *Hearings: Department of Defense Appropriations Fiscal Year 1972.* GPO, 1970.

USC(92/2) Senate Appropriations. *Hearings: Department of Defense Appropriations Fiscal Year 1973.* GPO, 1972.

USC(94/1) Senate Appropriations. *Hearings: Department of Defense Appropriations Fiscal Year 1976.* GPO, 1975.

USC(95/2) Senate Appropriations. *Hearings: Department of Defense Appropriations Fiscal Year 1979.* GPO, 1978.

USC(84/2) Senate Armed Services. *Hearings: Study of Airpower.* GPO, 1956.

USC(85/1&2) Senate Armed Services. *Hearings: Inquiry into Satellite and Missile Programs.* GPO, 1958.

USC(86/1) Senate Armed Services and Committee on Aeronautical and Space Sciences. *Joint Hearings: Missile and Space Activities.* GPO, 1959.

USC(86/2) Senate Armed Services and Committee on Aeronautical and Space Sciences. *Joint Hearings: Missiles, Space, and Other Major Defense Matters.* GPO, 1960.

USC(88/1) Senate Armed Services. *Hearings: Military Procurement Authorization Fiscal Year 1964.* GPO, 1963.

USC(88/1) Senate Armed Services. *Interim Report: The Cuban Military Buildup.* May 9, 1963. GPO, 1963.

USC(91/1) Senate Armed Services. *Hearings: Authorization for Military Procurement, Research, and Development, Fiscal Year 1970 and Reserve Strength.* GPO, 1969.

USC(92/1) Senate Armed Services. *Hearings: Fiscal Year 1972 Authorization for Military Procurement, Research and Development, Construction and Real Estate Acquisition for the Safeguard ABM and Reserve Strengths.* GPO, 1971.

USC(92/2) Senate Armed Services. *Hearings: Military Implications of the Treaty on the Limitation of ABM Systems and the Interim Agreement on Limitation of Strategic Offensive Arms.* GPO, 1972.

USC(93/1) Senate Armed Services. *Hearings: Amending the Central Intelligence Agency Retirement Act.* GPO, 1973.

USC(94/1) Senate Armed Services. *Hearings: Nomination of George Bush to be Director of Central Intelligence.* GPO, 1975.

USC(94/2) Senate Armed Services. *Hearing: Nomination of Daniel Orrin Graham.* GPO, 1976.

USC(95/1) Senate Armed Services. *Hearings: Fiscal Year 1978 Authorization for Military Procurement, Research and Development, and Active Duty, Selected Reserve, and Civilian Personnel Strengths.* GPO, 1977.

USC(87/2) Senate Foreign Relations and Armed Services. *Hearing: Situation in Cuba.* GPO, 1962.

USC(88/1) Senate Foreign Relations. *Hearings: Nuclear Test Ban Treaty.* GPO, 1963.

USC(91/1) Senate Foreign Relations. *Hearings: Strategic and Foreign Policy Implications of ABM Systems.* GPO, 1969.

USC(91/1) Senate Foreign Relations. *Hearing: Intelligence and the ABM.* GPO, 1969.

USC(92/2) Senate Foreign Relations. *Hearings: Strategic Arms Limitation Agreements.* GPO, 1972.

USC(94/1) Senate Foreign Relations. *Analyses of Effects of Limited Nuclear Warfare.* GPO, 1975.

USC(95/1) Senate Foreign Relations. *Hearings: United States/Soviet Strategic Options.* GPO, 1977.

USC(95/1) Senate Foreign Relations. *Analyses of Arms Control Impact Statements Submitted in Connection with the Fiscal Year 1978 Budget Request.* GPO, 1977.

USC(96/1) Senate Foreign Relations. *Fiscal Year 1980 Arms Control Impact Statements.* March 1979. GPO, 1979.

USC(96/2) Senate Foreign Relations. *Hearings: The SALT II Treaty.* GPO, 1979.

USC(96/1) Senate Foreign Relations. *Report: The SALT II Treaty.* GPO, 1979.

USC(96/2) Senate Foreign Relations. *Fiscal Year 1981 Arms Control Impact Statements.* May 1980. GPO, 1980.

USC(87/1) Senate Government Operations. *Hearings and Report: Organizing for National Security.* GPO, 1961.

USC(93/2) Senate Government Operations. *Hearings: Government Secrecy.* GPO, 1974.

USC(93/2) Senate Government Operations. *Hearings: Legislative Proposals to Strengthen Congressional Oversight of the Nation's Intelligence Agencies.* GPO, 1974.

USC(94/2) Senate Government Operations. *Hearings: Oversight of U.S. Government Intelligence Functions.* GPO, 1976.

USC(94/2) Senate Select Committee to Study Governmental Operations with Respect to Intelligence Activities: *Interim Report: Alleged Assassination Plots Involving Foreign Leaders. Final Report: I: Foreign and Military Intelligence IV: Supplementary Reports on Intelligence Activities VI: Supplementary Detailed Staff Reports on Foreign and Military Intelligence.* GPO, 1976.

USC(94/2) Senate Intelligence. *Hearing: Nomination of E. Henry Knoche.* GPO, 1976.

USC(95/1) Senate Intelligence. *Annual Report, May 1977.* GPO, 1977.

USC(95/2) Senate Intelligence. *Report: The National Intelligence Estimates A-B Team Episode Concerning Soviet Strategic Capability and Objectives.* February 16, 1978. GPO, 1978.

USC(95/2) Senate Intelligence. *Hearings: National Intelligence Reorganization and Reform Act of 1978.* GPO, 1978.

USC(96/1) Senate Intelligence. *Report to the Senate Covering the Period May 16, 1977–December 31, 1978.* May 14, 1979. GPO, 1979.

USC(96/1) Senate Intelligence. "Principal Findings by the Senate Select Committee on Intelligence on the Capabilities of the United States to Monitor the SALT II Treaty," press release, October 5, 1979.

USC(94/2) Joint Committee on Defense Production. *Hearings: Civil Preparedness and Limited Nuclear War.* GPO, 1976.

USC(95/1) Joint Committee on Defense Production. *Report: Civil Preparedness Review, II: Industrial Defense and Nuclear Attack.* April 1977. GPO, 1977.

USC(96/1) Joint Committee on Defense Production. *Study: Economic and Social Consequences of Nuclear Attack on the United States.* March 1979. GPO, 1979.

USC(94/1) Joint Economic Committee. *Hearings: Allocation of Resources in the Soviet Union and China 1975.* GPO, 1975.

USC(94/2) Joint Economic Committee. *Hearings: Allocation of Resources in* the Soviet Union and China 1976. GPO, 1976.

USC(95/1) Joint Economic Committee. Hearings: Allocation of Resources in the Soviet Union and China 1977. GPO, 1977.

USC(95/1) Joint Economic Committee. Study: Soviet Economic Problems and Prospects. August 8, 1977. GPO, 1977.

USC(95/2) Joint Economic Committee. Staff Study: Western Perceptions of Soviet Economic Trends. March 6, 1978. GPO, 1978.

USC(84/1) House Appropriations. Hearings: Department of Defense Appropriations for 1956. GPO, 1955.

USC(85/1) House Appropriations. Hearings: Fiscal Year 1958 Department of Defense Appropriation. GPO, 1957.

USC(85/1) House Appropriations. Hearings: Department of Defense: The Ballistic Missile Program. GPO, 1957.

USC(86/1) House Appropriations. Hearings: Department of Defense Appropriations for 1960. GPO, 1959.

USC(86/2) House Appropriations. Hearings: Department of Defense Appropriations for 1961. GPO, 1960.

USC(88/1) House Appropriations. Hearings: Department of Defense Appropriation 1964. GPO, 1963.

USC(96/1) House Appropriations. Hearings: Department of Defense Appropriation Fiscal Year 1970. GPO, 1969.

USC(96/1) House Appropriations. Hearings: Department of Defense Appropriations for 1980. GPO, 1979.

USC(96/1) House Armed Services. Hearings: Fiscal Year 1980 Military Posture, Research and Development. GPO, 1979.

USC(91/1) House Foreign Affairs. Hearings: Diplomatic and Strategic Impact of Multiple Warhead Missiles. GPO, 1969.

USC(91/1) House Foreign Affairs. Hearings: ABM, MIRV, SALT and the Strategic Arms Race. GPO, 1969.

USC(96/1) House Foreign Affairs. Special Study: Soviet Diplomacy and Negotiating Behavior: Emerging New Context for U.S. Diplomacy. GPO, 1979.

USC(94/1) House Select Intelligence. Hearings: U.S. Intelligence Agencies and Activities: Risks and Control of Foreign Intelligence, Pt. 5. GPO, 1975.

USC(95/2) House Permanent Select Intelligence. Hearings: Disclosure of Funds for Intelligence Activities. GPO, 1977.

USC(80/2) House Un-American Activities. Hearings Regarding Communist Espionage in the United States. GPO, 1948.

f) Miscellaneous Documents:

Arms Control and Disarmament Agency:
    Arms Control and Disarmament Agreements (annual series)
    Annual Reports.

"Verification: The Critical Element of Arms Control," Dept. of State Publication no. 85, March 1976.

Central Intelligence Agency: CIA reports and estimates are identified in the chapter notes along with the sources from which they have been drawn.

Commission on CIA Activities Within the United States (Rockefeller Commission), Report to the President, June 1975. GPO, 1975.

Commission on the Organization of Government for the Conduct of Foreign Relations (Murphy Commission), June 1975:

Final Report (1v plus 7v of appendices)
v.4: Appendix K: Adequacy of Current Organization, Defense and Arms Control.
v. 7: Appendix U: Intelligence Functions Analyses.

Congress. Office of Technology Assessment. *The Effects of Nuclear War.* Montclair (New Jersey): Allanheld, Osmun and Company, 1980.

Congressional Record.

Department of the Air Force:

Air Force Systems Command, "Air Force Systems Command," brochure, no date.

Air University Quarterly Review.

Soviet Military Thought Series:

No. 1: Colonel A. A. Sidorenko, *The Offensive.* (Moscow, 1970). GPO, no date (1974?).

No. 2: Colonel B. Byely, et al. *Marxism-Leninism on War and the Army.* (Moscow, 1972). GPO, no. date.

No. 3: Colonel-General N. A. Lomov, ed. *The Revolution in Military Affairs.* (Moscow, 1973) GPO, no date.

No. 4: V. Ye. Savkin, *The Basic Principles of Operational Art and Tactics.* (Moscow, 1972). GPO, no date (1975?).

No. 6: Colonel-General V. V. Druzhnin and K. S. Kontorov, *Concept, Algorithm, Decision.* (Moscow, 1972) GPO, no date.

No. 9: Dictionary of Basic Military Terms. (Moscow, 1965). GPO, no date.

No. 11: *Selected Soviet Military Writings 1970–1975.* GPO, no date (1976).

No. 12: Marshal A. A. Grechko, *The Armed Forces of the Soviet State.* (Moscow, 1975) GPO, no date (1977).

Studies in Communist Affairs Series:

v. 1: Joseph D. Douglass, Jr. *The Soviet Theater Nuclear Offensive.* GPO, 1977.

v. 2: Paul J. Murphy, ed. *Naval Power in Soviet Policy.* GPO, 1978.

Department of the Army:

Command and General Staff College. *Abstracts of Master of Military Art and Science (MMAS) Theses and Special Studies 1964–1976.* USCGSC, 1976.

FM 30-40. *Handbook on Soviet Ground Forces.* 30 June 1975.

FM 30-102. *Opposing Forces Europe.* 18 November 1977.

Vietnam Studies: Major General Joseph A. McChristian. *The Role of Military Intelligence 1965–1967.* GPO, 1974.

Department of Defense:

Blue Ribbon Defense Panel (Fitzhugh Panel), *Report of the Blue Ribbon Defense Panel to the President and the Secretary of Defense on the Department of Defense.* 1 July 1970. GPO, 1970.

Joint Chiefs of Staff: *Dictionary of Military and Associated Terms* (JCS Pub 1), 3 September 1974.

U.S. Military Posture for FY1980: An Overview by General David C. Jones, CJCS. GPO, 1979.

U.S. Military Posture for FY1981: An Overview by General David C. Jones, CJCS. GPO, 1980.

Office of the Secretary of Defense:

Historical Office: Alice C. Cole, et al., ed. *The Department of Defense: Documents on Establishment and Organization 1944–1978.* GPO, 1979.

Annual Posture Statements.

Department of State:

Current Policy 72A: "SALT II Senate Testimony, July 9–11, 1979."

Current Policy 92: "Soviet Troops in Cuba," speech October 1, 1979.

Foreign Relations of the United States, 1950, I: National Security Policy. GPO, 1978.

Selected Documents no. 7: "SALT One Compliance; SALT Two Verification," no date (March 1978).

Selected Documents no. 12B: "SALT II Agreement, Vienna, June 18, 1979."

Selected Documents no. 13, "Vienna Summit, June 15–18, 1979."

Special Report no. 55: "Compliance With SALT I," July 1979.

Special Report no. 56: "Verification of SALT II," August 1979.

Department of State *Bulletin.*

Marine Corps:
FMFM 2-1 *Intelligence.* GPO, 1977.

National Aeronautics and Space Administration:

EP-88: *Exploring in Aerospace Rocketry: An Introduction to the Fundamentals of Rocketry.* NASA Lewis Research Center. GPO, 1971.

SP-427: *High Altitude Perspective.* NASA Ames Research Center. GPO, 1978.

SP-4202: *Vanguard: A History,* by Constance M. Green and Milton Lomask. GPO, 1970.

Office of the President:

Public Papers of the President: Richard M. Nixon, 1969. GPO, 1971.

Public Papers of the President: Richard M. Nixon, 1972. GPO, 1974.

Report to Congress: U.S. Foreign Policy for the 1970s, February 18, 1970. GPO, 1970.

Report to Congress: U.S. Foreign Policy for the 1970s, February 25, 1971. GPO, 1971.

Report to Congress: U.S. Foreign Policy for the 1970s, February 9, 1972. GPO, 1972.

Report to Congress: U.S. Foreign Policy for the 1970s, May 3, 1973. GPO, 1973.

Weekly Compilation of Presidential Documents.

BOOKS

a) Ph.D. Dissertations:

Ball, Desmond J. *The Strategic Missile Program of the Kennedy Administration.* Australian National University, no date (1973?).

Ghebhardt, Alexander O. *Implications of Bureaucratic Process Models for Soviet ABM Decision-Making.* Columbia University, 1975.

Jayne, Edward R. *The ABM Debate: Strategic Defense and National Security.* Massachusetts Institute of Technology, 1969.

Josephs, Robert G. *Commitments and Capabilities: United States Foreign*

and Defense Policy Coordination, 1945 to the Korean War. Columbia University, 1975.

Moulton, Harland B. *American Strategic Power: Two Decades of Weapon Systems.* University of Minnesota, 1969.

b) Bibliographies:

Blackstock, Paul W., and Frank L. Schaf, Jr. *Intelligence, Espionage, Counterespionage, and Covert Operations: A Guide to Information Sources.* Detroit: Gale Research Company, 1978.

Department of the Air Force. *Intelligence,* by Norman E. Dakan. Pacific Air Forces Bibliography Series, April 1, 1962.

Department of the Army: *National Security, Military Power, and the Role of Force in International Relations.* DA PAM 550-19, September 1976.

Department of the Army: *USSR: Analytical Survey of the Literature* (1976 edition). DA PAM 550-6-1.

Hunter, David H. "The Evolution of Literature on United States Intelligence," *Armed Forces and Society* v. 5, no. 1, November 1978.

c) Other Books:

Abel, Elie. *The Missile Crisis.* New York: Bantam, 1966.

Acheson, Dean. *Present at the Creation: My Years at the State Department.* New York: New American Library, 1970.

Adams, Benson D. *Ballistic Missile Defense.* New York: Elsevier, 1971.

Adams, Sherman. *Firsthand Report: The Story of the Eisenhower Administration.* New York: Popular Library, 1962.

Aiken, George D. *Senate Diary.* Brattleboro (Vermont): The Stephen Greene Press, 1976.

Aliano, Richard A. *American Defense Policy from Eisenhower to Kennedy: The Politics of Changing Military Re-*

quirements. Athens (Ohio): Ohio University Press, 1975.

Allison, Braham T. *Essence of Decision: Explaining the Cuban Missile Crisis.* Boston: Little, Brown, 1971.

Alsop, Stewart. *The Center: People and Power in Political Washington.* New York: Harper & Row, 1968.

Anderson, Clinton P. *Outsider in the Senate: Senator Clinton Anderson's Memoirs.* New York: World Publishing Company, 1970.

Anderson, Jack, with George Clifford. *The Anderson Papers.* New York: Ballantine Books, 1974.

Anderton, David A. *Strategic Air Command: Two-Thirds of the Triad.* New York: Scribner's, 1976.

Armacost, Michael A. *The Politics of Weapons Innovation: The Thor-Jupiter Controversy.* New York: Columbia University Press, 1969.

Armbrister, Trevor. *A Matter of Accountability: The True Story of the Pueblo Affair.* New York: Coward McCann, 1970.

Aron, Raymond. *The Great Debate: Theories of War and Peace.* Garden City (New York): Doubleday, 1965.

Art, Robert J. *The TFX Decision: McNamara and the Military.* Boston: Little, Brown, 1968.

————, and Kenneth N. Waltz, ed. *The Use of Force: International Politics and Foreign Policy.* Boston: Little, Brown, 1971.

Ashby, W. Ross. *Design for a Brain.* London: Chapman and Hall, 1960.

Austin, Anthony. *The President's War.* New York: Lippincott, 1971.

Ayers, Bradley E. *The War That Never Was.* New York: Bobbs-Merrill, 1976.

Baar, James, and William E. Howard. *Polaris!* New York: Harcourt, Brace and Company, 1960.

Babington-Smith, Constance. *Air Spy: The Story of Photo Intelligence in World War II.* New York: Ballantine Books, 1957.

Bacchus, William I. *Foreign Policy and the Bureaucratic Process: The State Department's Country Director System.* Princeton: Princeton University Press, 1974.

Baldwin, Hanson W. *The Great Arms Race.* New York: Praeger, 1958.

Barghoorn, Frederick C. *Détente and the Democratic Movement in the USSR.* New York: Free Press, 1976.

————. *The Soviet Image of the United States: A Study in Distortion.* New York: Harcourt, Brace and Company, 1950.

Barnaby, C. F., and A. Boserup, ed. *PUGWASH: Implications of Anti-Ballistic Missile Systems.* New York: The Humanities Press, 1969.

Barron, John. *KGB: The Secret Work of Soviet Secret Agents.* New York: Bantam Books, 1974.

Baruch, Bernard. *The Public Years.* New York: Pocket Books, 1962.

Beam, Jacob D. *Multiple Exposure: An American Ambassador's Unique Perspective on East-West Issues.* New York: W. W. Norton, 1978.

Beard, Edmund. *Developing the ICBM: A Study in Bureaucratic Politics.* New York: Columbia University Press, 1976.

Beitzell, Robert. *The Uneasy Alliance: America, Britain, and Russia 1941–1943.* New York: Knopf, 1972.

Bergaust, Erik. *Rocket City: From Huntsville, Alabama, to the Moon.* New York: Macmillan, 1963.

Betts, Richard K. *Soldiers, Statesmen, and Cold War Crises.* Cambridge: Harvard University Press, 1977.

Bloomfield, Lincoln P., Walter C. Clemens, Jr., and Franklyn Griffiths. *Khrushchev and the Arms Race: Soviet Interests in Arms Control and Disarmament.* Cambridge: MIT Press, 1966.

Blumberg, Stanley A., and Gwinn Owens. *Energy and Conflict: The Life and Times of Edward Teller*. New York: Putnam's, 1976.

Bohlen, Charles E. *Witness to History 1929–1969*. New York: W. W. Norton, 1973.

Borklund, C. W. *The Department of Defense*. New York: Praeger, 1968.

———. *Men of the Pentagon: From Forrestal to McNamara*. New York: Praeger, 1966.

Bottome, Edgar M. *The Balance of Terror: A Guide to the Arms Race*. Boston: Beacon Press, 1971.

———. *The Missile Gap: A Study of the Formulation of Military and Political Policy*. Rutherford (New Jersey): Fairleigh Dickinson Press, 1971.

Boyle, Andrew. *The Fourth Man*. New York: Dial Press, 1979.

Brandon, Henry. *The Retreat of American Power*. Garden City (New York): Doubleday, 1973.

Branyan, Robert L., and Lawrence H. Larsen, ed. *The Eisenhower Administration 1953–1961: A Documentary History*. New York: Random House, 1971.

Braun, Werner von. *Space Frontier*. Greenwich (Connecticut): Fawcett, 1969.

Brecher, Michael. *Decisions in Israel's Foreign Policy*. New Haven: Yale University Press, 1975.

Brezhnev: Pages from His Life. Written under auspices of the USSR Academy of Sciences. New York: Simon and Schuster, 1978.

Brezhnev, Leonid. *Peace, Détente, and Soviet-American Relations: Public Statements*. New York: Harcourt, Brace Jovanovich, 1979.

Brodie, Bernard, ed. *The Absolute Weapon: Atomic Power and World Order*. New York: Harcourt, Brace, 1946.

———, and Fawn Brodie. *From Crossbow to H-Bomb*. Bloomington: Indiana University Press, 1973.

———. *Escalation and the Nuclear Option*. Princeton: Princeton University Press, 1966.

———. *Strategy in the Missile Age*. Princeton: Princeton University Press, 1965.

———. *War and Politics*. New York: Macmillan, 1973.

Brookes, Andrew J. *Photo Reconnaissance*. London: Ian Allen, 1975.

Buchheim, Robert W., ed. *Space Handbook: Astronautics and Its Applications*. New York: Random House, 1958.

Burleson, Clyde W. *The Jennifer Project*. Englewood Cliffs (New Jersey): Prentice-Hall, 1977.

Burrns, Thomas S. *The Secret War for the Ocean Depths*. New York: Atheneum, 1978.

Byrnes, James F. *All in One Lifetime*. New York: Harper & Brothers, 1958.

Campbell, John F. *The Foreign Affairs Fudge Factory*. New York: Basic Books, 1971.

Canan, James W. *The Superwarriors: The Fantastic World of Pentagon Superweapons*. New York: Weybright and Talley, 1975.

Carpozi, George, Jr. *Red Spies in Washington*. New York: Trident Press, 1968.

Carroll, John M. *Secrets of Electronic Espionage*. New York: Dutton, 1966.

Casserly, John J. *The Ford White House: The Diary of a Speechwriter*. Boulder: Colorado Associated University Press, 1977.

Cave Brown, Anthony, ed. *Dropshot: The United States Plan for War with the USSR in 1957*. New York: Dial Press, 1978.

———, and Charles B. MacDonald, ed. *The Secret History of the Atomic Bomb*. New York: Delta Books, 1977.

Center for the Study of Democratic Institutions. *Anti-Ballistic Missile: Yes or No?* New York: Hill and Wang, 1969.

Chayes, Abram, and Jerome B. Wiesner, ed. *ABM: An Evaluation of the Decision to Deploy an Antiballistic Missile System.* New York: Harper & Row, 1969.

CIA: The Pike Report. Nottingham (England): Spokesman Books, 1977.

Clark, Keith C., and Laurence J. Legere. *The President and the Management of National Security.* New York: Praeger, 1969.

Clark, Ronald. *The Man Who Broke Purple: The Life of Colonel William F. Friedman Who Deciphered the Japanese Code in World War II.* Boston: Little, Brown, 1977.

Clarke, Duncan L. *Politics of Arms Control: The Role and Effectiveness of the U.S. Arms Control and Disarmament Agency.* New York: Free Press, 1979.

Clemens, Walter C., Jr. *The Superpowers and Arms Control.* New York: Praeger, 1973.

Cline, Ray S. *Secrets, Spies and Scholars: Blueprint of the Essential CIA.* Washington, D.C.: Acropolis Press, 1976.

Colby, William E., and Peter Forbath. *Honorable Men: My Life in the CIA.* New York: Simon and Schuster, 1978.

Collins, John M. *American and Soviet Military Trends Since the Cuban Missile Crisis.* Georgetown: Center for Strategic and International Studies, 1978.

————, and Anthony H. Cordesman. *Imbalance of Power: Shifting U.S.-Soviet Military Strengths.* San Rafael (California): Presidio Press, 1978.

Cookridge, E. H. *Gehlen: Spy of the Century.* New York: Pyramid Books, 1971.

————. *The Many Sides of George Blake, Esq.* Princeton: Vertex, 1970.

Cooper, Chester L. *The Lion's Last Roar: Suez 1956.* New York: Harper & Row, 1978.

Corson, William R. *The Armies of Ignorance: The Rise of the American Intelligence Empire.* New York: Dial Press, 1977.

Coulam, Robert F. *The Illusion of Choice: The F-111 and the Problem of Weapons Acquisition Reform.* Princeton: Princeton University Press, 1977.

Cox, Arthur Macy. *The Myths of National Security: The Perils of Secret Government.* Boston: Beacon Press, 1975.

Cox, Donald, and Michael Stoiko. *Spacepower: What It Means to You.* Philadelphia: John C. Winston Company, 1958.

Cutler, John H. *Ed Brooke: Biography of a Senator.* New York: Bobbs-Merrill, 1972.

Cutler, Robert C. *No Time for Rest.* Boston: Little, Brown, 1966.

Daedalus, *Arms, Defense Policy, and Arms Control* v. 104 #3, Summer 1975.

Daniloff, Nicolas. *The Kremlin and the Cosmos.* New York: Knopf, 1972.

Davis, Lynn E. *The Cold War Begins: Soviet-American Conflict over Eastern Europe.* Princeton: Princeton University Press, 1974.

Davis, Vincent. *The Admirals Lobby.* Chapel Hill: University of North Carolina Press, 1967.

————. *Postwar Defense and the U.S. Navy 1943–1946.* Chapel Hill: University of North Carolina Press, 1966.

Dean, Gordon. *Report on the Atom.* New York: Knopf, 1954.

Deane, General John R. *The Strange Alliance: The Story of Our Efforts at Wartime Cooperation With Russia.* New York: Viking, 1947.

Deane, Michael J. *Political Control of the Soviet Armed Forces.* New York: Crane, Russak, 1977.

DeRivera, Joseph. *The Psychological Dimension of Foreign Policy.* Columbus (Ohio): Charles E. Merrill, 1968.

de Silva, Peer. *Sub Rosa: The CIA and the Uses of Intelligence.* New York: Times Books, 1978.

Desmond, James. *Nelson Rockefeller: A Political Biography.* New York: Harper & Row, 1964.

Detzer, David. *The Brink: The Cuban Missile Crisis 1962.* New York: Thomas Crowell, 1979.

Deutsch, Karl. *The Nerves of Government.* New York: Free Press, 1963.

Deutscher, Isaac. *Russia, China, and the West.* London: Oxford University Press, 1970.

Di Certo, J. J. *Missile Base Beneath the Sea: The Story of Polaris.* New York: St. Martin's Press, 1967.

Dietz, David. *Atomic Science, Bombs and Power.* New York: Dodd, Mead & Coy, 1954.

Dinerstein, Herbert S. *The Making of a Missile Crisis: October 1962.* Baltimore: Johns Hopkins University Press, 1976.

———. *War and the Soviet Union: Nuclear Weapons and the Revolution in Soviet Military and Political Thinking.* New York: Praeger, 1962.

Divine, Robert A. *Blowing on the Wind: The Nuclear Test Ban Debate 1954–1960.* New York: Oxford University Press, 1978.

———, ed. *The Cuban Missile Crisis.* Chicago: Quadrangle, 1971.

Donovan, Robert J. *Conflict and Crisis: The Presidency of Harry S Truman.* New York: W. W. Norton, 1977.

———. *Eisenhower: The Inside Story.* New York: Harper & Brothers, 1956.

Dornberg, John. *Brezhnev: The Masks of Power.* New York: Basic Books, 1974.

Dornberger, Walter. *V-2.* New York: Viking, 1958.

Dorwart, Jeffrey M. *The Office of Naval Intelligence: The Birth of America's Oldest Intelligence Agency, 1865–1918.* Annapolis: Naval Institute Press, 1978.

Downs, Anthony. *Inside Bureaucracy.* Boston: Little, Brown, 1967.

Drew, Elizabeth. *American Journal: The Events of 1976.* New York: Random House, 1977.

Dulles, Allen. *The Craft of Intelligence.* New York: New American Library, 1965.

Dulles, Eleanor Lansing. *American Foreign Policy in the Making.* New York: Harper & Row, 1968.

———. *John Foster Dulles: The Last Year.* New York: Harcourt, Brace & World, 1963.

Dyson, Freeman. *Disturbing the Universe.* New York: Harper & Row, 1979.

Easton, David. *The Political System.* New York: Knopf, 1953.

Eisenhower, Dwight D. *Mandate for Change: The White House Years 1953–1956.* New York: New American Library, 1965.

———. *Waging Peace: The White House Years 1956–1961.* Garden City (New York): Doubleday, 1965.

Emme, Eugene, ed. *The History of Rocket Technology: Essays on Research Development and Utility.* Detroit: Wayne State University Press, 1964.

d'Encausse, Hélène Carrère. *Decline of an Empire: The Soviet Socialist Republics in Revolt.* New York: Newsweek Books, 1979.

Endicott, John, and Roy Stafford, Jr., ed. *American Defense Policy.* Baltimore: Johns Hopkins University Press, 1974 ed., 1977 ed.

Enthoven, Alain C., and K. Wayne Smith. *How Much Is Enough? Shaping the Defense Program 1961–1969.* New York: Harper & Row, 1971.

Epstein, Edward J. *Legend: The Secret World of Lee Harvey Oswald.* New York: Ballantine Books, 1978.

Erickson, John, ed. *The Military-Technical Revolution*. New York: Praeger, 1966.

Etzold, Thomas H., and John L. Gaddis, ed. *Containment: Documents on American Foreign Policy and Strategy 1945–1950*. New York: Columbia University Press, 1978.

Evans, Rowland and Robert Novak. *Lyndon B. Johnson: The Exercise of Power*. New York: New American Library, 1966.

Fain, Tyrus G., Katharine Plant, and Ross Molloy, ed. *The Intelligence Community: History, Organization, and Issues*. New York: R. R. Bowker Company, 1977.

Farago, Ladislas. *War of Wits: The Anatomy of Espionage*. New York: Paperback Library, 1954.

Feis, Herbert. *Churchill-Roosevelt-Stalin: The War They Waged and the Peace They Sought*. Princeton: Princeton University Press, 1957.

Feld, Bernard T., et al., ed. *Impact of New Technologies on the Arms Race*. Cambridge: MIT Press, 1971.

Fitzgerald, A. Ernest. *The High Priests of Waste*. New York: W. W. Norton, 1972.

Ford, Corey. *Donovan of OSS*. Boston: Little, Brown, 1970.

Ford, Gerald R. *A Time to Heal: The Autobiography of Gerald R. Ford*. New York: Harper & Row, 1979.

Fox, William T. R. *The Superpowers*. New York: Harcourt, Brace and World, 1944.

Franck, Thomas M., and Edward Weisband, ed. *Secrecy and Foreign Policy*. London: Oxford University Press, 1974.

Freedman, Lawrence. *U.S. Intelligence and the Soviet Strategic Threat*. London: Macmillan, 1977.

Frye, Alton. *A Responsible Congress: The Politics of National Security*. New York: McGraw-Hill, 1975.

Gaddis, John L. *Russia, The Soviet Union and the United States: An Interpretive History*. New York: John Wiley & Sons, 1978.

Gantz, Lieutenant Colonel Kenneth L., ed. *The United States Air Force Report on the Ballistic Missile*. Garden City (New York): Doubleday, 1958.

Garthoff, Raymond L. *Soviet Military Policy: An Historical Analysis*. New York: Praeger, 1966.

————. *Soviet Strategy in the Nuclear Age*. New York: Praeger, 1958.

Gavin, Lieutenant General James M. (ret.). *War and Peace in the Space Age*. New York: Harper & Brothers, 1958.

Geelhoed, E. Bruce. *Charles E. Wilson and Controversy at the Pentagon, 1953 to 1957*. Detroit: Wayne State University Press, 1979.

Gehlen, Reinhard. *The Service: The Memoirs of General Reinhard Gehlen*. New York: Popular Library, 1972.

George, Alexander, and Richard Smoke. *Deterrence in American Foreign Policy: Theory and Practice*. New York: Columbia University Press, 1974.

Gervasi, Frank. *The Real Rockefeller*. New York: Atheneum, 1964.

Gibert, Stephen P., et al. *Soviet Images of America*. New York: Crane, Russak, 1977.

Gilpin, Robert. *American Scientists and Nuclear Weapons Policy*. Princeton: Princeton University Press, 1962.

Ginsburgh, Colonel Robert N., USAF. *U.S. Military Strategy in the Sixties*. New York: W. W. Norton, 1965.

Glass, Robert R., and Phillip D. Davidson. *Intelligence is for Commanders*. Harrisburg (Pennsylvania): Military Service Publishing Company, 1948.

Glasstone, Samuel, and Philip J. Dolan, ed. *The Effects of Nuclear Weapons*, third edition. GPO, 1977.

Goldman, Eric F. *The Tragedy of Lyndon Johnson*. New York: Dell Books, 1969.

Goldman, Thomas A., ed. *Cost-Effectiveness: New Approaches in Decision-Making.* New York: Praeger, 1967.

Goldwater, Senator Barry M. *With No Apologies: The Personal and Political Memoirs of a United States Senator.* New York: Berkeley Books, 1980.

Goodpaster, General Andrew J., USAR (ret.). *For the Common Defense.* Lexington (Massachusetts): Lexington Books, 1977.

Goulden, Joseph C. *Truth is the First Casualty.* Chicago: Rand McNally, 1969.

Goulding, Phil G. *Confirm or Deny: Informing the People on National Security.* New York: Harper & Row, 1970.

Gouré, Leon. *Civil Defense in the Soviet Union.* Berkeley: University of California Press, 1962.

————. *War Survival in Soviet Strategy.* Coral Gables (Florida): University of Miami Press, 1976.

Graham, Lieutenant General Daniel O., USAR (ret.). *Shall America Be Defended? SALT II and Beyond.* New Rochelle (New York): Arlington House, 1979.

Gramont, Sanche de. *The Secret War.* New York: Dell, 1962.

Gray, Colin S. *The Soviet-American Arms Race.* Farnsborough (Hampshire, UK): Saxon Books, 1976.

Gray, Robert Keith. *Eighteen Acres under Glass.* Garden City (New York): Doubleday, 1962).

Greenwood, Ted. *Making the MIRV.* Cambridge: Ballinger, 1975.

Grodzins, Morton, and Eugene Rabinowitch, ed. *The Atomic Age: Scientists in National and World Affairs.* New York: Basic Books, 1962.

Gromyko, Anatoli Andreievich. *Through Russian Eyes: President Kennedy's 1036 Days.* Washington, D.C.: International Publishers, 1973.

Groves, Major General Leslie R., USAR (ret.). *Now It Can Be Told: The Story of the Manhattan Project.* New York: Harper & Brothers, 1962.

Hadley, Arthur T. *The Nation's Safety and Arms Control.* New York: Viking Press, 1961.

Halberstam, David. *The Best and the Brightest.* New York: Random House, 1972.

Haldeman, H. R., with Joseph DiMona. *The Ends of Power.* New York: Dell Books, 1978.

Halperin, Morton H., with Priscilla Clapp and Arnold Kanter. *Bureaucratic Politics and Foreign Policy.* Washington, D.C.: Brookings, 1974.

Halpern, Manfred. *The Morality and Politics of Intervention.* New York: Council on Religion and International Affairs, 1963.

Harvey, Mose L., Leon Gouré, and Vladimir Prokofieff. *Science and Technology as an Instrument of Soviet Policy.* University of Miami: Center for Advanced International Studies, 1972.

Herring, George C., Jr. *Aid to Russia 1941–1946: Strategy, Diplomacy, the Origins of the Cold War.* New York: Columbia University Press, 1973.

Heuer, Richard J., Jr., ed. *Quantitative Approaches to Political Intelligence: The CIA Experience.* Boulder (Colorado): Westview Press, 1978.

Hewes, James E., Jr. *From Root to McNamara: Army Organization and Administration 1900–1963.* United States Army: Center for Military History, Special Study, 1975.

Hewlett, Richard G., and Francis Duncan. *Nuclear Navy 1946–1962.* Chicago: University of Chicago Press, 1974.

Higham, Robin, and Jacob W. Kipp, ed. *Soviet Aviation and Air Power: A Historical View.* Boulder (Colorado): Westview Press, 1977.

Hilsman, Roger. *Strategic Intelligence and National Decisions.* Glencoe (Illinois): Free Press, 1956.

————. *To Move a Nation: The Politics of Foreign Policy in the Administration of John F. Kennedy*. New York: Delta Books, 1967.

Hirsch, Richard, and Joseph J. Trento. *The National Aeronautics and Space Administration*. New York: Praeger, 1973.

Hilton, Ralph, ed. *Tales of the Foreign Service*. Columbia: University of South Carolina Press, 1978.

Hingley, Ronald. *The Russian Mind*. New York: Scribner's, 1977.

Hitch, Charles J., and Roland N. Mc-Kean. *The Economics of Defense in the Nuclear Age*. Cambridge: Harvard University Press, 1960.

Holmes, W. J. *Double-Edged Secrets: U.S. Naval Intelligence Operations in the Pacific During World War II*. Annapolis: Naval Institute Press, 1979.

Holst, Johan J., and William Schneider, Jr., ed. *Why ABM? Policy Issues in the Missile Defense Controversy*. New York: Pergamon Press, 1969.

Holzman, Franklyn D. *Financial Checks on Soviet Defense Expenditures*. Lexington (Massachusetts): Lexington Books, 1975.

Hoopes, Townsend. *The Devil and John Foster Dulles*. Boston: Little, Brown, 1973.

Horelick, Arnold, and Myron Rush. *Strategic Power and Soviet Foreign Policy*. Chicago: University of Chicago Press, 1966.

Hoxie, R. Gordon. *Command Decision and the Presidency*. New York: Reader's Digest Press, 1977.

Hubler, Richard G. *SAC: The Strategic Air Command*. Westport (Connecticut): Greenwood Press, 1977.

Hughes, Emmet J. *The Ordeal of Power* New York: Dell Books, 1962.

Huntington, Samuel P. *The Common Defense: Strategic Programs in National Politics*. New York: Columbia University Press, 1961.

————. *The Soldier and the State: The Theory and Politics of Civil-Military Relations*. New York: Vintage Books, 1957.

Hymoff, Edward. *The OSS in World War II*. New York: Ballantine Books, 1972.

Infield, Glenn B. *Unarmed and Unafraid*. London: Macmillan, 1970.

Irving, David. *The German Atomic Bomb: The History of Nuclear Research In Nazi Germany*. New York: Simon and Schuster, 1967.

————. *The Mare's Nest: The German Secret Weapons Campaign and Allied Countermeasures*. Boston: Little, Brown, 1964.

Jackson, Robert. *The Red Falcons: The Soviet Air Force in Action 1919–1969*. Brighton (UK): Clifton Books, 1970.

Jacobs, David M. *The UFO Controversy in America*. New York: New American Library, 1976.

Jacobsen, Carl G. *Soviet Strategy-Soviet Foreign Policy: Military Considerations Affecting Soviet Policy-Making*. Glasgow (UK): The University Press, 1972.

Jacobson, Harold K. *Diplomats, Scientists, and Politicians*. Ann Arbor: University of Michigan Press, 1966.

James, Peter N. *The Air Force Mafia*. New Rochelle (New York): Arlington House, 1975.

Janis, Irving L., and Leon Mann. *Decision Making: A Psychological Analysis of Conflict, Choice, and Commitment*. New York: Free Press, 1977.

————. *Victims of Groupthink*. Boston: Houghton Mifflin, 1972.

Jervis, Robert. *The Logic of Images in International Relations*. Princeton: Princeton University Press, 1970.

————. *Perception and Misperception in International Politics*. Princeton: Princeton University Press, 1976.

Johnson, Lyndon Baines. *The Vantage Point: Perspectives of the Presidency*

1963–1969. New York: Holt, Rinehart and Winston, 1971.

Jones, R. V. *The Wizard War: British Scientific Intelligence 1939–1945*. New York: Coward McCann, 1978.

Joubert, Air Marshal Sir Philip, RAF. *Rocket*. New York: Philosophical Library, 1957.

Kahan, Jerome H. *Security in the Nuclear Age: Developing U.S. Strategic Arms Policy*. Washington, D.C.: Brookings, 1975.

Kahn, David. *The Codebreakers: The Story of Secret Writing*. New York: Macmillan, 1967.

Kahn, Herman. *On Thermonuclear War*. New York: Free Press, 1969.

Kalb, Marvin, and Bernard. *Kissinger*. New York: Dell Books, 1975.

Kanter, Arnold. *Defense Politics: A Budgetary Perspective*. Chicago: University of Chicago Press, 1979.

Katz, James E. *Presidential Politics and Science Policy*. New York: Praeger, 1978.

Kaufmann, William W. *The McNamara Strategy*. New York: Harper & Row, 1964.

Kearns, Doris. *Lyndon Johnson and the American Dream*. New York: New American Library, 1976.

Keesing's Research Report. *Disarmament Negotiations and Treaties 1946–1971*. New York: Scribner's, 1972.

Kennedy, John F. *The Strategy of Peace* (ed. Allan Nevins). New York: Harper & Brothers, 1960.

Kennedy, Robert F. *Thirteen Days: A Memoir of the Cuban Missile Crisis*. New York: New American Library, 1969.

Kennan, George F. *The Cloud of Danger: Current Realities of American Foreign Policy*. Boston: Little, Brown, 1977.

Kent, Sherman. *Strategic Intelligence for American World Policy*. Princeton: Princeton University Press, 1949.

Khrushchev, Nikita S. *Khrushchev Remembers* (tns. Strobe Talbott). New York: Bantam Books, 1971.

———. *Khrushchev Remembers: The Last Testament* (tns. Strobe Talbott). New York: Bantam Books, 1976.

Killian, James R., Jr. *Sputnik, Scientists, and Eisenhower*. Cambridge: MIT Press, 1977.

Kinnard, Douglas. *President Eisenhower and Strategy Management*. Lexington: University of Kentucky Press, 1977.

Kintner, William R., ed. *Safeguard: Why the ABM Makes Sense*. New York: Hawthorn Books, 1969.

Kirk, Grayson, and Nils H. Wessell, ed. *The Soviet Threat: Myths and Realities*. Proceedings of the Academy of Political Science, v. 33 no. 1, 1978.

Kirkpatrick, Lyman B. *The Real CIA*. New York: Macmillan, 1968.

———. *The U.S. Intelligence Community*. New York: Hill and Wang, 1973.

Kissinger, Henry A. *The Necessity for Choice: Prospects for American Foreign Policy*. New York: Harper & Brothers, 1961.

———. *Nuclear Weapons and Foreign Policy*. New York: W. W. Norton, 1969.

———. *White House Years 1969–1973*. Boston: Little, Brown, 1979.

Kistiakowsky, George B. *A Scientist at the White House: The Private Diary of President Eisenhower's Special Assistant for Science and Technology*. Cambridge: Harvard University Press, 1976.

Klass, Phillip J. *Secret Sentries in Space*. New York: Random House, 1971.

Knorr, Klaus, ed. *Historical Dimensions of National Security Problems*. Lawrence: University Press of Kansas, 1976.

———. *Limited Strategic War*. Princeton: Princeton University Press, 1961.

Kolkowicz, Roman, Matthew P. Gallagher, and Benjamin S. Lambeth. *The Soviet Union and Arms Control: A Superpower Dilemma.* Baltimore: Johns Hopkins Press, 1970.

Kolodziej, Edward A. *The Uncommon Defense and Congress 1945–1963.* Columbus (Ohio): Ohio State University Press, 1966.

Korb, Lawrence J. *The Joint Chiefs of Staff: The First Twenty-five Years.* Bloomington: Indiana University Press, 1976.

Korol, Alexander G. *Soviet Research and Development: Its Organization Personnel, and Funds.* Cambridge: MIT Press, 1965.

Kramish, Arnold. *Atomic Energy in the Soviet Union.* Stanford: Stanford University Press, 1959.

Krock, Arthur. *Memoirs: Sixty Years on the Firing Line.* New York: Funk and Wagnalls, 1968.

Labrie, Roger P. *SALT Handbook: Key Documents and Issues 1972–1979.* Washington, D.C.: American Enterprise Institute, 1979.

Laird, Melvin R. *A House Divided: America's Strategy Gap.* Chicago: Henry Regnery, 1962.

Lang, Daniel. *From Hiroshima to the Moon.* New York: Dell Books, 1959.

Langer, William L. *In and Out of the Ivory Tower.* New York: Neale Watson Academic Publications, 1978.

Lapp, Ralph E. *Arms beyond Doubt: The Tyranny of Weapons Technology.* New York: Cowles Book Company, 1970.

————. *The Weapons Culture.* Baltimore: Penguin Books, 1969.

Larson, David L. *The Cuban Crisis of 1962: Selected Documents and Chronology.* Boston: Houghton Mifflin, 1963.

Lasby, Clarence G. *Project Paperclip: German Scientists and the Cold War.* New York: Atheneum, 1971.

Lasky, Victor. *JFK: The Man and the Myth.* New York: Macmillan, 1963.

Laurence, William L. *Men and Atoms.* New York: Simon and Schuster, 1959.

Leacacos, John P. *Fires in the In-Basket: The ABC's of the State Department.* Cleveland: World Publishing Company, 1968.

Lee, Asher. *The Soviet Air Force.* New York: Harper & Brothers, 1950.

————. *The Soviet Air Force.* New York: John Day, 1962.

————, ed. *The Soviet Air and Rocket Forces.* London: Weidenfield and Nicolson, 1959.

Lee, William T. *The Estimation of Soviet Defense Expenditures 1955–1975: An Unconventional Approach.* New York: Praeger, 1977.

Leites, Nathan. *The Operational Code of the Politburo.* New York: McGraw-Hill, 1951.

LeMay, General Curtis, USAF, with MacKinlay Kantor. *Mission with LeMay.* Garden City (New York): Doubleday, 1965.

Levine, Robert A. *The Arms Debate.* Cambridge: Harvard University Press, 1963.

Ley, Willy. *Rockets, Missiles, and Men in Space.* New York: New American Library, 1968.

Lieberman, Joseph I. *The Scorpion and the Tarantula: The Struggle to Control Atomic Weapons 1945–1949.* Boston: Houghton Mifflin, 1970.

Lilienthal, David. *Journals: II: The Atomic Energy Years 1945–1950.* New York: Harper & Row, 1964.

Lindsey, Robert. *The Falcon and the Snowman.* New York: Simon and Schuster, 1979.

Lowe, George E. *The Age of Deterrence.* Boston: Little, Brown, 1964.

Lucas, Richard C. *Eagles East: The Army Air Force and the Soviet Union 1941–1945.* Tallahassee: Florida State University Press, 1970.

McBride, James H. *The Test Ban Treaty: Military, Technological, and Political Implications.* Chicago: Henry Regnery, 1967.

McClellan, David, S. *Dean Acheson: The State Department Years.* New York: Dodd, Mead, 1976.

McGarvey, Patrick J. *CIA: The Myth and the Madness.* New York: Saturday Review Press, 1972.

McGovern, James. *Crossbow and Overcast.* New York: Paperback Library, 1964.

McGuire, Martin C. *Secrecy and the Arms Race: A Theory of the Accumulation of Strategic Weapons and How Secrecy Affects It.* Cambridge: Harvard University Press, 1965.

Mader, Julius. *Who's Who in the CIA.* (East) Berlin: Julius Mader, 1968.

Mandelbaum, Michael. *The Nuclear Question: The United States and Nuclear Weapons 1946–1976.* Cambridge: Cambridge University Press, 1979.

Mansfield, Edwin, ed. *Defense, Science, and Public Policy.* New York: W. W. Norton, 1968.

Marchetti, Victor, and John D. Marks. *The CIA and the Cult of Intelligence.* New York: Dell Books, 1974.

Martel, Lieutenant General Sir Giffard, British Army. *East versus West.* London: Museum Press Ltd., 1952.

Martin, David C. *A Wilderness of Mirrors.* New York: Harper & Row, 1980.

Martin, John B. *Adlai Stevenson and the World.* Garden City (New York): Doubleday, 1978.

Martin, Laurence. *Arms and Strategy: The World Power Structure Today.* New York: David McKay, 1973.

Masterman, Sir John C. *The Double-cross System.* New York: Avon Books, 1972.

Mastny, Vojtech. *Russia's Road to the Cold War: Diplomacy, Warfare, and the Politics of Communism.* New York: Columbia University Press, 1979.

Medaris, Brigadier General John B., USAR (ret.). *Countdown for Decision.* New York: Paperback Library, 1961.

Medvedev, Roy A., and Zhores A. *Khrushchev: The Years in Power.* New York: Columbia University Press, 1976.

Medvedev, Zhores A. *Nuclear Disaster in the Urals.* New York: W. W. Norton, 1979.

———. *Soviet Science.* New York: W. W. Norton, 1978.

Melman, Seymour, ed. *Inspection for Disarmament.* New York: Columbia University Press, 1958.

Meyer, Cord. *Facing Reality: From World Federalism to the CIA.* New York: Harper & Row, 1980.

Millis, Walter, ed. *The Forrestal Diaries.* New York: Viking Press, 1951.

Moore, Dan Tyler, and Martha Waller. *Cloak and Cipher.* Indianapolis: Bobbs-Merrill, 1962.

Morris, Joseph A. *Nelson Rockefeller: A Biography.* New York: Harper & Brothers, 1960.

Morris, Roger. *Uncertain Greatness: Henry Kissinger and American Foreign Policy.* New York: Harper & Row, 1977.

Mosely, Phillip E. *The Kremlin and World Politics.* New York: Vintage, 1960.

Mosley, Leonard. *Dulles: A Biography of Eleanor, Allen, John Foster, and Their Family Network.* New York: Dial Press, 1978.

Moss, Norman. *Men Who Play God.* New York: Harper & Row, 1968.

Moulton, Harland B. *From Superiority to Parity: The United States and the Strategic Arms Race 1961–1971.* Westport (Connecticut): Greenwood Press, 1973.

Murphy, Robert B. *Diplomat among Warriors.* Garden City (New York): Doubleday, 1964.

Neal, Roy. *Ace in the Hole: The Story of Minuteman.* Garden City (New York): Doubleday, 1962.

Nessen, Ron. *It Sure Looks Different from the Inside*. New York: Playboy Press, 1978.

Newhouse, John. *Cold Dawn: The Story of SALT*. New York: Holt, Rinehart and Winston, 1973.

Nixon, Richard M. *RN: The Memoirs of Richard Nixon*. New York: Warner Books, 1979.

"An Observer." *Message From Moscow*. New York: Knopf, 1969.

Ordway, Frederick III, and Mitchell R. Sharpe. *The Rocket Team*. New York: Thomas Y. Crowell, 1979.

Osborne, John. *The Last Nixon Watch*. Washington, D.C.: The New Republic Book Company, 1975.

———. *The Nixon Watch*. Washington, D.C.: The New Republic Book Company, 1972.

———. *The White House Watch: The Ford Years*. Washington, D.C.: New Republic Press, 1978.

Pachter, Henry M. *Collision Course: The Cuban Missile Crisis and Coexistence*. New York: Praeger, 1963.

Paine, Lauran. *The CIA at Work*. London: Robert Hale, Ltd., 1977.

Parmet, Herbert S. *Eisenhower and the American Crusades*. New York: Macmillan, 1972.

Parry, Albert. *Russia's Rockets and Missiles*. Garden City (New York): Doubleday, 1960.

———. *The Russian Scientist*. New York: Macmillan, 1973.

Payne, James L. *The American Threat: The Fear of War as an Instrument of Foreign Policy*. Chicago: Markham Publishing Company, 1970.

Pearson, Drew, and Jack Anderson. *U.S.A.—Second Class Power?* New York: Simon and Schuster, 1958.

Peeters, Paul. *Massive Retaliation: The Policy and Its Critics*. Chicago: Henry Regnery, 1959.

Penkovsky, Colonel Oleg. *The Penkovsky Papers* (tns. Peter Deriabin). New York: Avon Books, 1965.

Persico, Joseph E. *Piercing the Reich: The Penetration of Nazi Germany by American Secret Agents During World War II*. New York: Viking Press, 1979.

Petee, George S. *The Future of American Secret Intelligence*. Washington, D.C.: Infantry Journal Press, 1946.

Pfaltzgraff, Robert L. ed. *Contrasting Approaches to Strategic Arms Control*. London: Lexington Books, 1974.

Phillips, David Atlee. *The Night Watch: 25 Years of Peculiar Service*. New York: Atheneum, 1977.

Pipes, Richard, ed. *Soviet Strategy in Europe*. New York: Crane, Russak, 1976.

Platt, Alan. *The U.S. Senate and Strategic Arms Policy 1969–1977*. Boulder (Colorado): Westview Press, 1978.

Platt, Washington. *Strategic Intelligence Production*. New York: Praeger, 1957.

Poling, James, ed. *A Political Self-Portrait: The Rockefeller Record*. New York: Thomas Y. Crowell, 1960.

Polmar, Norman, ed. *Strategic Air Command: People, Aircraft, and Missiles*. Annapolis: Nautical and Aviation Publishing Company of America, 1979.

Possony, Stefan T., and J. E. Pournelle. *The Strategy of Technology*. New York: Dunellen, 1970.

Potter, William C., ed. *Verification and SALT: The Challenge of Strategic Deception*. Boulder (Colorado): Westview Press, 1980.

Power, General Thomas S. USAF (ret.). *Design for Survival*. New York: Pocket Books, 1965.

Powers, Francis Gary, with Curt Gentry. *Operation Overflight*. New York: Holt, Rinehart and Winston, 1970.

Powers, Thomas. *The Man Who Kept the Secrets: Richard Helms and the CIA*. New York: Knopf, 1979.

Pranger, Robert J., and Roger P. Labrie, ed. *Nuclear Strategy and National Security: Points of View.*
Washington, D.C.: American Enterprise Institute, 1977.

Primack, Joel, and Frank von Hippel.
*Advice and Dissent: Scientists in the
Political Arena.* New York: New Amer-
ican Library, 1974.

Prochenau, William W., and Richard
W. Larsen. *A Certain Democrat: Senator Henry Jackson, A Political Biography.* Englewood Cliffs (New Jersey):
Prentice-Hall, 1972.

Prouty, Colonel L. Fletcher, USAF
(ret.). *The Secret Team.* Englewood
Cliffs (New Jersey): Prentice-Hall, 1973.

Quade, E. S., ed. *Analysis for Military
Decisions.* Chicago: Rand McNally,
1964.

Quester, George H. *Nuclear Diplomacy.* New York: Dunellen, 1970.

Ramberg, Bennett. *The Seabed Arms
Control Negotiations: A Study of Multilateral Arms Control Conference Diplomacy.* Monograph Series in World
Affairs, University of Denver, 1978.

Raymond, Jack. *Power at the Pentagon.* New York: Harper & Row, 1964.

Ransom, Harry Howe. *Central Intelligence and National Security.* Cambridge: Harvard University Press,
1958.

———. *The Intelligence Establishment.*
Cambridge: Harvard University Press,
1970.

Riabchikov, Evgeny. *Russians in
Space.* Garden City (New York): Doubleday, 1971.

Roberts, Chalmers. *First Rough Draft:
A Journalist's Journal of Our Times.*
New York: Praeger, 1973.

———. *The Nuclear Years: The Arms
Race and Arms Control.* New York:
Praeger, 1970.

Roherty, James M. *Decisions of Robert
S. McNamara: A Study in the Role of

the Secretary of Defense.* Coral Gables:
University of Miami Press, 1970.

Roosevelt, Kermit. *Countercoup: The
Struggle for Control of Iran.* New York:
McGraw-Hill, 1979.

Rositzke, Harry. *The CIA's Secret Operations.* New York: Reader's Digest
Press, 1977.

Rostow, W. W. *The Diffusion of Power:
An Essay in Recent History.* New York:
Macmillan, 1972.

Rothstein, Robert L. *Planning, Prediction, and Policy-Making in Foreign Affairs: Theory and Practice.* Boston:
Little, Brown, 1972.

Russett, Bruce M., and Bruce G. Blair,
ed. *Progress in Arms Control?* San
Francisco: W. H. Freeman, 1979.

Sakharov, Andrei D. *My Country and
the World* (tns. Guy V. Daniels). New
York: Vintage Books, 1975.

———. *Sakharov Speaks.* New York:
Vintage Books, 1974.

Sakharov, Vladimir, and Umberto Tosi.
High Treason. New York: Putnam's,
1980.

Sanders, Ralph. *The Politics of Defense
Analysis.* New York: Dunellen, 1973.

Sapolsky, Harvey M. *The Polaris System Development: Bureaucratic and
Programmatic Success in Government.*
Cambridge: Harvard University Press,
1972.

Sarkesian, Sam C., ed. *Defense Policy
and the Presidency: Carter's First
Years.* Boulder (Colorado): Westview
Press, 1979.

Schelling, Thomas C. *Arms and Influence.* New Haven: Yale University
Press, 1966.

———, and Morton H. Halperin. *Strategy and Arms Control.* New York:
Twentieth Century Fund, 1961.

Schlesinger, Arthur F., Jr. *Robert Kennedy and His Times.* Boston: Houghton Mifflin, 1978.

————. *A Thousand Days: John F. Kennedy in the White House.* Greenwich (Connecticut): Fawcett, 1965.

Schorr, Daniel. *Clearing the Air.* New York: Berkeley Books, 1978.

Schwiebert, Ernest G. *A History of USAF Ballistic Missiles.* New York: Praeger, 1964.

Schwien, E. E. *Combat Intelligence.* Washington, D.C.: Infantry Journal Press, 1936.

Shelton, William. *Soviet Space Exploration: The First Decade.* New York: Washington Square Press, 1968.

Shepley, James R., and Clay Blair, Jr. *The Hydrogen Bomb: The Men, the Menace, the Mechanism.* New York: David McKay, 1954.

Sherry, Michael S. *Preparing for the Next War: American Plans for Postwar Defense 1941–1945.* New Haven: Yale University Press, 1977.

Shternfeld, Ari. *Soviet Space Science.* New York: Basic Books, 1959.

Singer, J. David. *Deterrence, Arms Control, and Disarmament.* Columbus: Ohio State University Press, 1962.

Sivachev, Nicolai V., and Nikolai N. Yakovlev. *Russia and the United States: U.S.-Soviet Relations from the Soviet Point of View.* Chicago: University of Chicago Press, 1979.

Smith, Bruce L. R. *The Rand Corporation.* Cambridge: Harvard University Press, 1966.

Smith, Gerard C. *Doubletalk: The Story of the First Strategic Arms Limitation Talks.* Garden City (New York): Doubleday. 1980.

Smith, Joseph Burkholder. *Portrait of a Cold Warrior.* New York: Putnam's, 1976.

Smith, Perry McCoy. *The Air Force Plans for Peace 1943–1945.* Baltimore: Johns Hopkins Press, 1970.

Smolders, Peter. *Soviets in Space.* New York: Taplinger, 1974.

Snyder, Glenn H. *Deterrence and Defense: Toward a Theory of National Security.* Princeton: Princeton University Press, 1961.

Sokolovsky, Marshal V. D. *Soviet Military Strategy* (tns. and ed. by Harriet Fast Scott). New York: Crane, Russak, 1975.

Sorensen, Theodore. *Kennedy.* New York: Bantam Books, 1965.

————. *Soviet Writings on Earth Satellites and Space Travel.* New York: Citadel Press, 1958.

Spadaro, Robert N., et al., ed. *The Policy Vacuum: Toward a More Professional Political Science.* Lexington (Massachusetts): Lexington Books, 1975.

Spielmann, Karl F. *Analyzing Soviet Strategic Arms Decisions.* Boulder (Colorado): Westview Press, 1978.

Stein, Harold, ed. *American Civil-Military Decisions.* Birmingham: University of Alabama–Inter-University Case Program, 1963.

Steinbruner, John D. *The Cybernetic Theory of Decision: New Dimensions of Political Analysis.* Princeton: Princeton University Press, 1974.

Stevens, Vice Admiral Leslie C. (ret.). *Russian Assignment.* Boston: Little, Brown, 1953.

Stockholm International Peace Research Institute (SIPRI): World Armaments and Disarmament Yearbook (annual) Bhuprenda M. Jasemi, *Outer Space—Battlefield of the Future?* London: Taylor and Francis, 1978. Andrzej Karkoszka, *Strategic Disarmament Verification and National Security.* London: Taylor and Francis, 1977.

Stockwell, John. *In Search of Enemies: A CIA Story.* New York: W. W. Norton, 1978.

Stoessinger, John G. *Henry Kissinger: The Anguish of Power.* New York: W. W. Norton, 1976.

Stoiko, Michael. *Soviet Rocketry: Past, Present, and Future*. New York: Holt, Rinehart and Winston, 1970.

Strauss, Lewis L. *Men and Decisions*. Garden City (New York): Doubleday, 1962.

Strong, Major General Sir Kenneth, British Army. *Intelligence at the Top*. Garden City (New York): Doubleday, 1967.

———. *Men of Intelligence*. New York: St. Martin's Press, 1971.

Sulzberger, Cyrus L. *An Age of Mediocrity*. New York: Macmillan, 1973.

———. *The Last of the Giants*. New York: Macmillan, 1970.

Szulc, Tad. *The Illusion of Peace: Foreign Policy in the Nixon Years*. New York: Viking Press, 1978.

Talbott, Strobe. *Endgame: The Inside Story of SALT II*. New York: Random House, 1979.

Tatu, Michel. *Power in the Kremlin: From Khrushchev to Kosygin*. New York: Viking Press, 1969.

Taylor, John W. R., and David Mondey. *Spies in the Sky*. New York: Scribner's, 1972.

Taylor, General Maxwell D., USAR (ret). *Precarious Security*. New York: W. W. Norton, 1976.

———. *The Uncertain Trumpet*. New York: Harper & Brothers, 1959.

Teller, Edward and Allen Brown. *The Legacy of Hiroshima*. Garden City (New York): Doubleday, 1962.

terHorst, Jerald F. *Gerald Ford and the Future of the Presidency*. New York: The Third Press, 1974.

Thomas, John R., and Ursula M. Kruse-Vaucien, ed. *Soviet Science and Technology: Domestic and Foreign Perspectives*. Washington, D.C.: George Washington University (for the National Science Foundation), 1977.

Thomas, Lowell J., and Edward Jablonski. *Doolittle: A Biography*. Garden City (New York): Doubleday, 1976.

Trewhitt, Henry L. *McNamara*. New York: Harper & Row, 1971.

Truman, Harry S. *Memoirs: I: Year of Decisions; II: Years of Trial and Hope*. New York: New American Library, 1965.

Tsipis, Kosta, Anne H. Cahn, and Bernard T. Feld, ed. *The Future of the Sea-based Deterrent*. Cambridge: MIT Press, 1973.

Tucker, Samuel A., ed. *A Modern Design for Defense Decision: A McNamara-Hitch-Enthoven Anthology*. Washington, D.C.: Industrial College of the Armed Forces, 1966.

Tully, Andrew. *CIA: The Inside Story*. Greenwich (Connecticut): Fawcett, 1962.

———. *The Super Spies: More Secret, More Powerful Than the CIA*. New York: William Morrow, 1969.

———. *White Tie and Dagger*. New York: William Morrow, 1967.

Turner, Gordon B., and Richard D. Challener, ed. *National Security in the Nuclear Age*. New York: Praeger, 1960.

Twining, General Nathan F. USAF (ret.). *Neither Liberty nor Safety*. New York: Holt, Rinehart and Winston, 1966.

Ulam, Adam B. *Expansion and Coexistence: Soviet Foreign Policy 1917–1973*, second edition. New York: Praeger, 1974.

Varner, Roy, and Wayne Collier. *A Matter of Risk*. New York: Random House, 1978.

Valeriani, Richard. *Travels With Henry*. Boston: Houghton Mifflin, 1979.

Voss, Earl H. *Nuclear Ambush: The Test Ban Trap*. Chicago: Henry Regnery Company, 1963.

Wagner, Ray, ed. *The Soviet Air Force in World War II* (tns. Leland Fetzer). Garden City (New York): Doubleday, 1973.

Walters, Lieutenant General Vernon A. USAR (ret.). *Silent Missions.* Garden City (New York): Doubleday, 1978.

Warburg, James P. *Disarmament: The Challenge of the 1960s.* Garden City (New York): Doubleday, 1961.

Weintal, Edward, and Charles Bartlett. *Facing the Brink: An Intimate Study of Crisis Diplomacy.* New York: Scribner's, 1967.

Weisband, Edward, and Thomas M. Franck. *Resignation in Protest.* New York: Grossman Publishers, 1975.

Welch, William. *American Images of Soviet Foreign Policy: An Inquiry into Recent Appraisals from the Academic Community.* New Haven: Yale University Press, 1970.

Whetten, Lawrence L., ed. *The Future of Soviet Military Power.* New York: Crane, Russak, 1976.

————, ed. *The Political Implications of Soviet Military Power.* New York: Crane, Russak, 1977.

White, Theodore H. *The Making of the President 1960.* New York: Pocket Books, 1960.

Wicker, Tom. *JFK and LBJ: The Influence of Personality upon Politics.* New York: Penguin Books, 1978.

————. *On Press.* New York: Berkley Books, 1979.

Wiesner, Dr. Jerome B. *Where Science and Politics Meet.* New York: McGraw-Hill, 1965.

Wilensky, Harold L. *Organizational Intelligence.* New York: Basic Books, 1967.

Williams, Phil. *Crisis Management: Confrontation and Diplomacy in the Nuclear Age.* New York: John Wiley & Sons, 1976.

Willrich, Mason, and John B. Rhinelander, ed. *SALT: The Moscow Agreements and Beyond.* New York: Free Press, 1974.

Windchy, Eugene E. *Tonkin Gulf.* Garden City (New York): Doubleday, 1970.

Wise, David, and Thomas B. Ross. *The Espionage Establishment.* New York: Random House, 1967.

————. *The Invisible Government.* New York: Vintage Books, 1964.

————. *The U-2 Affair.* New York: Random House, 1962.

Witcover, Jules. *Marathon: The Pursuit of the Presidency 1972–1976.* New York: New American Library, 1978.

Wohlstetter, Roberta. *Pearl Harbor: Warning and Decision.* Stanford: Stanford University Press, 1962.

Wolanin, Thomas R. *Presidential Advisory Commissions: Truman to Nixon.* Madison: University of Wisconsin Press, 1975.

Wolfe, Thomas W. *Soviet Power and Europe 1945–1970.* Baltimore: Johns Hopkins Press, 1970.

Wukelic, George E. *Handbook of Soviet Space Research.* New York: Gordon and Breach, 1968.

Wyden, Peter. *Bay of Pigs: The Untold Story.* New York: Simon and Schuster, 1979.

Yanarella, Ernest J. *The Missile Defense Controversy: Strategy, Technology, and Politics 1955–1972.* Lexington: University of Kentucky Press, 1977.

Yergin, Daniel. *Shattered Peace: The Origins of the Cold War and the National Security State.* Boston: Houghton Mifflin, 1978.

York, Herbert F. *The Advisors: Oppenheimer, Teller, and the Superbomb.* San Francisco: W. H. Freemen, 1976.

————. *Race to Oblivion: A Participant's View of the Arms Race.* New York: Clarion Books, 1971.

Zacharias, Capt. Ellis M., USN (ret.). *Secret Missions.* New York: Putnam's, 1946.

Zhukov, Marshal Georgi K. *The Memoirs of Marshal Zhukov.* New York: Delacorte Press, 1971.

Zlotnick, Jack. *National Intelligence.* Washington, D.C.: Industrial College of the Armed Forces, 1964.

Zumwalt, Admiral Elmo R. USN (ret.). *On Watch: A Memoir.* New York: Quadrangle Books, 1976.

III. Articles and Papers:

Abel, Christopher A. "A Breach in the Ramparts," United States Naval Institute *Proceedings,* v. 106, no. 7, July 1980.

Academy for Interscience Methodology (Museum of Science and Industry, Chicago). "Development of Models for Analysis of the Influence of Mobile Nuclear Forces on Arms Control Agreements," ACDA AIM 70-T-6, December 1970.

Aldridge, Robert C. "The Counterforce Syndrome," Transnational Institute, Pamphlet no. 7, 1978.

Alexander, Arthur J. "Decision-Making in Soviet Weapons Development," International Institute of Strategic Studies (London): Adelphi Paper no. 147–148, Winter 1978–1979.

———. "R & D in Soviet Aviation." Rand R-589-PR, November 1970.

Allison, Graham. "Cold Dawn and the Mind of Henry Kissinger," *Washington Monthly,* v. 6, no. 1, March 1974.

Alsop, Joseph. "The New Balance of Power," *Encounter* magazine, v. 10, no. 5, May 1958.

Alsop, Stewart. "How Can We Catch Up?" *Saturday Evening Post,* v. 230, no. 24, December 14, 1957.

———. "Our Gamble With Destiny," *Saturday Evening Post,* v. 231, no. 46, May 16, 1959.

American Security Council, "The Changing Strategic Military Balance USA/USSR," Washington, D.C.: American Security Council, 1967.

Art, Robert J. "Bureaucratic Politics and American Foreign Policy: A Critique," *Policy Sciences,* v. 4, 1973.

Aspin, Les. "Debate Over U.S. Strategic Forecasts: A Mixed Record," *Strategic Review,* v. 8, no. 3, Summer 1980.

———. "The Verification of the SALT II Agreement," *Scientific American,* v. 240, no. 2, February 1979.

Astor, Gerald. "Henry Kissinger: Strategist in the White House Basement," *Look* magazine, v. 33, no. 6, August 12, 1969.

Baldwin, Hanson. "The Future of Intelligence," *Strategic Review,* v. 4, no. 3, Summer 1976.

Ball, Desmond. "Déjà-Vu: The Return to Counterforce in the Nixon Administration," Southern California Seminar on Arms Control and Foreign Policy, December 1974.

———. "United States Strategic Doctrine and Policy—With Some Implications for Australia," in Robert O'Neill, ed. *The Strategic Nuclear Balance—An Australian Perspective.* Australian National University, 1975.

———. "Research Note: Soviet ICBM Deployment," *Survival,* v. 22, no. 4, July–August, 1980.

Barnds, William J. "The Foreign Affairs Kaleidoscope." New York: Council on Religion and International Affairs, 1974.

———. "Intelligence and Foreign Policy: Dilemmas of a Democracy," *Foreign Affairs,* January 1969, v. 47, no. 2.

———. "The Right to Know, to Withhold and to Lie," New York: Council on Religion and International Affairs, 1969.

Barnett, Roger W. "Trans-SALT Soviet Strategic Doctrine," *Orbis,* v. 19, no. 2, Summer 1975.

Belden, Thomas G. "Indication, Warning and Crisis Operations," *International Studies Quarterly,* v. 21, no. 1, March 1977.

Bennett, Bruce. "Fatality Uncertainties in Limited Nuclear War," Rand R-2218-AF, November 1977.

Ben-Zvi, Abraham. "Hindsight and Foresight: A Conceptual Framework for the Analysis of Surprise Attacks," *World Politics,* v. 28, no. 3, April 1976.

Berman, Robert P. "Soviet Air Power in Transition." Washington, D.C.: Brookings, 1978.

Bernstein, Barton J. "The Week We Almost Went to War," *Bulletin of the Atomic Scientists,* v. 32, no. 8, February 1976.

Betts, Richard K. "Analysis, War, and Decision: Why Intelligence Failures Are Inevitable," *World Politics,* v. 31, no. 1, October 1978.

Blackstock, Paul W. "The Intelligence Community Under the Nixon Administration," *Armed Forces and Society,* v. 1, no. 2, February 1975.

Blechman, Barry M., et al. "The Soviet Military Buildup and U.S. Defense Spending," Washington, D.C.: Brookings, 1977.

Block, Colonel Emil N., USAF. "President Nixon's National Security Council System," National War College: *National Security Affairs Forum* no. 14, 1971.

Bloomfield, Lincoln P., Walter C. Clemens, and Franklyn Griffiths. "Soviet Interests in Arms Control and Disarmament: The Decade Under Khrushchev 1954–1964." Massachusetts Institute of Technology: CENIS Reports C/65-1 and C/65-2, February 1, 1965.

Bowie, Robert R. "Analysis of Our Policy Machine," *New York Times Magazine,* March 1, 1958.

Bresler, Robert J., and Robert C. Gray. "The Bargaining Chip and SALT," *Political Science Quarterly,* v. 92, no. 1, Spring 1977.

Brower, Brock. "Why People Like You Joined the CIA," *Washington Monthly,* v. 8, no. 9, November 1976.

Brown, Dr. Harold. "Planning Our Military Forces," *Foreign Affairs,* v. 45, no. 1, January 1967.

Brown, Thomas A. "Number Mysticism, Rationality and the Strategic Balance," *Orbis,* v. 21, no. 3, Fall 1979.

Burt, Richard. "Soviet Sea-based Forces and SALT," *Survival,* v. 17, no. 1, January–February 1975.

Caldwell, Dan, ed. "Department of Defense Operations During the Cuban Crisis: A Report by Adam Yarmolinsky," *Naval War College Review,* v. 32, no. 4, June–July 1979.

———. "A Research Note on the Quarantine of Cuba, October 1962," *International Studies Quarterly,* v. 22, no. 4, December 1978.

Cannon, Charles A. "The Politics of Interest and Ideology: The Senate Airpower Hearings of 1956," *Armed Forces and Society,* v. 3, no. 4, August 1977.

Center for Strategic Studies. "The Soviet Military-Technological Challenge," Georgetown University, Special Report no. 6, September 1967.

Chan, Steve. "The Intelligence of Stupidity: Understanding Failures in Strategic Warning," *American Political Science Review,* v. 73, no. 1, March 1979.

Cline, Ray. "Policy Without Intelligence," *Foreign Policy* no. 17, Winter 1975–1976.

Coalition for Peace Through Strength. "An Analysis of SALT II," 2nd edition, Boston (Virginia): American Security Council, May 1979.

Cockburn, Andrew, and Alexander. "The Myth of Missile Accuracy," *New York Review of Books,* v. 27, no. 18, November 20, 1980.

Cockle, Paul. "Analyzing Soviet Defense Spending: The Debate in Perspective," *Survival,* v. 20, no. 5, September–October 1978.

Cooper, Chester L. "The CIA and Decision-Making," *Foreign Affairs,* v. 50, no. 2, January 1972.

Costick, Miles. "The Strategic Dimensions of East-West Trade," American

Council for World Freedom: Task Force on Strategic Trade, 1978.

Cox, Arthur Macy. "The CIA's Tragic Error," *New York Review of Books,* v. 27, no. 17, November 6, 1980.

Crane, Robert D. "Soviet Nuclear Strategy: A Critical Appraisal," Georgetown University: Center for Strategic Studies, 1963.

Davis, Lynn E., and Warner R. Schilling. "All You Ever Wanted to Know About MIRV and ICBM Calculations but Were Not Cleared to Ask," *Journal of Conflict Resolution,* v. 17, no. 2, June 1973.

————. "Limited Nuclear Options: Deterrence and the New American Doctrine," International Institute of Strategic Studies: Adelphi Paper no. 121, Winter 1975–1976.

Day, Bonner. "Soviet Bombers: A Growing Threat," *Air Force* magazine, v. 61, no. 11, November 1978.

Destler, I. M. "Can One Man Do?" *Foreign Policy,* no. 5, Winter 1971–1972.

Dick, James C. "The Strategic Arms Race 1957–1961: Who Opened the Missile Gap?" *Journal of Politics,* v. 34, no. 4, November 1972.

Dinerstein, Herbert S. "The Revolution in Soviet Strategic Thinking," *Foreign Affairs,* January 1958, v. 36, no. 2.

Dornberger, Walter R. "Can Russian Missiles Strike the United States?" *Collier's* magazine, v. 135, no. 1, January 7, 1955.

Drew, Elizabeth. "A Reporter At Large: Brzezinski," *The New Yorker,* v. 54, no. 1, May 1, 1978.

Ellsworth, Robert F., and Kenneth Adelman, "Foolish Intelligence," *Foreign Policy* no. 36, Fall 1979.

Epstein, Edward J. "The Spy War," *New York Times Magazine,* September 26, 1980.

————. "The War Within the CIA," *Commentary* magazine, v. 66, no. 2, August 1978.

Erickson, John. "Soviet-Warsaw Pact Force Levels," United States Strategic Institute, USSI Report 76-2, 1976.

Eustace, Harry F. "Changing Intelligence Priorities," *Electronic Warfare/Defense Electronics,* v. 10, no. 11, November 1978.

Fallows, James. "Crazies by the Tail: Bay of Pigs, Diem and Liddy," *Washington Monthly,* v. 6, no. 7, September 1974.

Fellwock, Perry. "U.S. Electronic Intelligence: A Memoir," *Ramparts,* v. 11, no. 2, August 1972.

Fenlon, Captain Leslie K. USN (ret.). "The Umpteenth Cuban Confrontation," United States Naval Institute *Proceedings,* v. 106, no. 7, July 1980.

Frank, Lewis Allen. "Soviet Nuclear Planning: A Point of View on SALT," Washington, D.C.: American Enterprise Institute, 1977.

Garn, Senator Jake. "Soviet Superiority: A Question for National Debate," *International Security Review,* v. 4, no. 1, Spring 1979.

Garrett, Stephen A. "Détente and the Military Balance," *Bulletin of the Atomic Scientists,* v. 33, no. 4, April 1977.

Garthoff, Raymond. "How the Russians Run Their Missile Program," *Air Force* magazine, v. 40, no. 12, December 1957.

————. "On Estimating and Imputing Intentions," *International Security,* v. 2, no. 3, Winter 1977.

————. "Russia—Leading the World in ICBM and Satellite Development?" *Missiles and Rockets,* v. 2, no. 12, October 1957.

————. "SALT and the Soviet Military," *Problems of Communism,* v. 24, no. 1, January-February 1975.

————. "SALT I: An Evaluation," *World Politics,* v. 31, no. 1, October 1978.

————. "Mutual Deterrence and Strategic Arms Limitation in Soviet Policy."

International Security, v. 3, no. 1, Summer 1978.

Garwin, Richard L., and Hans A. Bethe. "Antiballistic Missile Systems," *Scientific American,* March 1968.

———. "Antisubmarine Warfare and National Security," *Scientific American,* July 1972.

———. "Effective Military Technology for the 1980s," *International Security,* v. 1, no. 2, Fall 1976.

Gazit, Shlomo. "Estimate and Fortune Telling in Intelligence Work," *International Security,* v. 4, no. 4, Spring 1980.

Gelb, Leslie H. "Muskie and Brzezinski: The Struggle over Foreign Policy," *New York Times Magazine,* July 20, 1980.

———. "Schlesinger for Defense, Defense for Détente," *New York Times Magazine,* August 4, 1974.

———. "Washington Dateline: The Story of a Flap," *Foreign Policy* no. 16, Fall 1974.

George, Alexander. "The Case for Multiple Advocacy in Making Foreign Policy," *American Political Science Review,* v. 66, no. 1, September 1972.

———. "The Operational Code: A Neglected Approach to the Study of Political Leaders and Decision-making," *International Studies Quarterly,* v. 13, no. 2, June 1969.

Getler, Michael. "Arms Control and the SS-9," *Space/Astronautics,* v. 52, no. 6, November 1969.

Glagolev, Igor S. "The Soviet Decision-Making Process in Arms Control Negotiations," *Orbis,* v. 21, no. 4, Winter 1978.

Gouré, Leon. William G. Hyland, and Colin S. Gray. "The Emerging Strategic Environment: Implications for Ballistic Missile Defense," Tufts University: Fletcher School and Institute for Foreign Policy Analysis, December 1979.

Graham, Lieutenant General Daniel O., USAR (ret.). "Estimating the Threat: A

Soldier's Job," *Army* magazine, v. 23, no. 4, April 1973.

———. "The Intelligence Mythology of Washington," *Strategic Review,* v. 4, no. 3, Summer 1976.

———. "U.S. Intelligence at the Crossroads," United States Strategic Institute, USSI Report 76-1, 1976.

———. "The Soviet Military Budget Controversy," *Air Force* magazine, v. 59, no. 5, May 1976.

Gray, Colin S. "Détente, Arms Control, and Strategy: Perspectives on SALT," *American Political Science Review,* v. 70. no. 4, December 1976.

———. "The Future of Land-Based Missile Forces," International Institute for Strategic Studies: Adelphi Paper no. 140, Winter 1977.

———. "Gap Prediction and America's Defense: Arms Race Behavior in the Eisenhower Years," *Orbis,* v. 16, no. 1, Spring 1972.

———. "Soviet Rocket Forces: Military Capability, Political Utility," *Air Force* magazine, v. 61, no. 3, March 1978.

———. "War and Peace: The Soviet View," *Air Force* magazine, v. 59, no. 10, October 1976.

Greenwood, Ted. "Reconnaissance and Arms Control," *Scientific American,* February 1973.

———. "Reconnaissance, Surveillance, and Arms Control," International Institute for Strategic Studies, Adelphi Paper no. 88, June 1972.

Gwertzman, Bernard. "Cyrus Vance Plays It Cool," *New York Times Magazine,* March 18, 1979.

Halperin, Morton H. "Clever Briefers, Crazy Leaders, and Myopic Analysts," *Washington Monthly,* v. 6, no. 7, September 1974.

———. "The Decision to Deploy the ABM: Bureaucratic and Domestic Politics in the Johnson Administration," *World Politics,* v. 25, no. 1, October 1972.

―――. "The Gaither Committee and the Policy Process," *World Politics,* v. 13, no. 3, April 1961.

Handel, Michael. "Surprise and Change in International Politics," *International Security,* v. 4, no. 4, Spring 1980.

Hellman, Martin E. "The Mathematics of Public Key Cryptography," *Scientific American,* August 1979.

Hersh, Seymour M. "The Angleton Story," *New York Times Magazine,* June 25, 1978.

Hoag, David D. "Strategic Ballistic Missile Guidance: A Story of Ever Greater Accuracy," *Astronautics and Aeronautics,* v. 16, no. 5, May 1978.

Hoeber, Francis P. "Slow to Take Offense: Bombers, Cruise Missiles and Prudent Deterrence." Georgetown University: Center for Strategic and International Studies, February 1977.

Holsti, Ole R. "The 'Operational Code' Approach to the Study of Political Leaders: John Foster Dulles' Philosophical and Instrumental Beliefs," *Canadian Journal of Political Science,* v. 3, no. 1, March 1970.

Holzman, Franklyn D. "Are the Soviets Really Outspending the U.S. on Defense?" *International Security,* v. 4, no. 4, Spring 1980.

Hughes, Thomas L. "The Fate of Facts in a World of Men: Foreign Policy and Intelligence-Making," New York: Foreign Policy Association, Headline Series no. 233, December 1976.

Ikle, Fred C. "Can Nuclear Deterrence Last Out the Century?" *Foreign Affairs,* v. 51, no. 2, January 1973.

Jacobs, Walter Darnell. "Soviet Strategic Effectiveness," *Journal of International Affairs,* v. 26, no. 1, Summer 1972.

Johnson, Loch. "Congress and the CIA: Monitoring the Dark Side of Government," Paper presented to the American Political Science Association, Washington, D.C.: September 1979.

Kahn, David. "Big Ear or Big Brother?" *New York Times Magazine,* May 16, 1976.

―――. "Cryptology Goes Public," *Foreign Affairs,* v. 58, no. 1, Fall 1979.

Kalish, Robert B. "Air Force Technical Intelligence," *Air University Review,* v. 22, no. 5, July-August 1971.

Kaplan, Fred M. "Dubious Specter: A Second Look at the Soviet Threat," Washington, D.C.: Transnational Institute, pamphlet no. 6, December 1977.

―――. "Our Cold War Policy—Circa 1950," *New York Times Magazine,* May 18, 1980.

―――. "The Soviet Civil Defense Myth," *Bulletin of the Atomic Scientists,* v. 34, nos. 3 & 4, March and April 1978.

Katz, Amrom. "The Soviets and the U-2 Photos—An Heuristic Argument," Rand RM-3584-PR, March 1963.

Keating, Senator Kenneth. "My Advance View of the Cuban Crisis," *Look* magazine, v. 28, no. 22, November 3, 1964.

Kemp, Geoffrey. "Nuclear Forces for Medium Powers," International Institute for Strategic Studies, Adelphi Paper no. 107, Autumn 1974.

Kemp, Representative Jack F. "Congressional Expectations of SALT II," *Strategic Review,* v. 8, no. 1, Winter 1979.

Kent, Sherman. "Estimates and Influence," *Foreign Service Journal,* v. 46, no. 4, April 1969.

Kistiakowsky, George B. "The Arms Race: Is Paranoia Necessary for Security?" *New York Times Magazine,* November 21, 1977.

―――. "False Alarm: The Story of SALT II," *New York Review of Books,* v. 26, no. 4, March 22, 1979.

Knebel, Fletcher. "Washington in Crisis," *Look* magazine, v. 26, no. 29, December 18, 1962.

Knorr, Klaus. "Failures in National Intelligence Estimates: The Case of the

Cuban Missiles," *World Politics*, v. 16, no. 3, April 1964.

———. "Foreign Intelligence and the Social Sciences," Princeton University: Center for International Studies Monograph no. 17, 1964.

———. "Is the American Defense Effort Enough?" Princeton University: Center for International Studies Memorandum no. 14, December 23, 1957.

———. "National Power and its Sources," National War College: *National Security Affairs Forum*, no. 23, Fall–Winter 1975.

———. "Political Conjecture in Military Planning," Princeton University: Center for International Studies, Policy Memorandum no. 35, November 1968.

Krasner, Stephen D. "Are Bureaucracies Important? (Or Allison Wonderland)." *Foreign Policy* no. 7, Summer 1972.

Laird, Melvin R. "Arms Control: The Russians Are Cheating," *Reader's Digest*, December 1975.

———. "Is *This* Détente?" *Reader's Digest*, July 1975.

Lamb, John. "Verification and Strategic Security," unpublished paper, Columbia University, Fall 1977.

Lambeth, Benjamin S. "Deterrence in the MIRV Era," *World Politics*, v. 24, no. 2, January 1972.

———. "The Political Potential of Soviet Equivalence," *International Security*, v. 4, no. 2, Fall 1979.

Leacacos, John P. "Kissinger's Apparat," *Foreign Policy* no. 5, Winter 1971–1972.

Lee, William T. "Debate Over U.S. Strategic Forecasts: A Poor Record," *Strategic Review*, v. 8, no. 3, Summer 1980.

———. "Intelligence: Some Issues of Performance," in Francis P. Hoeber and William Schneider, ed. *Arms, Men, and Military Budgets*. New York: Crane, Russak, 1978.

———. "The Politico-Military-Industrial Complex of the USSR," *Journal of International Affairs*, v. 26, no. 1, Spring 1972.

———. "Soviet Defense Spending: Planned Growth 1976–1980," *Strategic Review*, v. 5, no. 1, Winter 1977.

———. "Soviet Targeting Strategy and SALT," *Air Force* magazine, v. 61, no. 9, September 1978.

———. "Understanding the Soviet Military Threat: How CIA Estimates Went Astray," New York: National Strategy Information Center, Agenda Paper no. 6, 1977.

Leighton, Richard M. "The Cuban Missile Crisis of 1962: A Case in National Security Crisis Management," National Defense University, GPO, 1978.

Libby, Willard F., William J. Thaler, and General Nathan F. Twining. "USSR vs. USA: The ABM and the Changed Strategic Military Balance," Washington, D.C.: Acropolis Press, 1969.

Licklider, Roy. "The Missile Gap Controversy," *Political Science Quarterly*, v. 35, no. 4, December 1970.

London, Michael P. "Safeguard: Is There a Choice?" *Space/Astronautics*, v. 52, no. 6, November 1969.

Lord, Carnes. "Verification and the Future of Arms Control," *Strategic Review*, v. 6, no. 1, Winter 1978.

Lowenhar, Herman. "ABM Radars: Myth vs. Reality," *Space/Astronautics*, v. 52, no. 6, November 1969.

McCone, John A. "Why We Need the CIA," *TV Guide*, January 10, 1976.

Margerison, Tom. "Spy in the Sky," *Survival*, v. 2, no. 5, September–October 1960.

Masters, Colonel Barry, USAR. "The Ethics of Intelligence Activities," National War College, *National Security Affairs Forum*, Spring–Summer 1976.

Morris, Roger. "Kissinger and the Brothers Kalb," *Washington Monthly*, v. 6, nos. 5–6, July–August 1974.

Moynihan, Senator Daniel Patrick. "Reflections: The SALT Process," *The New Yorker,* v. 55, no. 40, November 19, 1979.

Muckerman, Colonel Joseph E., USAR. "Hedging on a Strategic Gamble," *Army* magazine, v. 21, no. 9, September 1967.

Murphy, Charles J. V. "The Embattled Mr. McElroy," *Fortune* magazine, v. 59, no. 4, April 1959.

———. "Khrushchev's Paper Bear," *Fortune* magazine, v. 70, no. 6, December 1964.

———. "The New Air Situation," *Fortune* magazine, v. 52, no. 3, September 1955.

———. "The U.S. as a Bombing Target," *Fortune* magazine, v. 48, no. 5, November 1953.

———. "The White House since Sputnik," *Fortune* magazine, v. 57, no. 1, January 1958.

Nacht, Michael, "The Delicate Balance of Error," *Foreign Policy* no. 19, Summer 1975.

Nathan, James. "Did Kissinger Leak the Big One?" *Washington Monthly,* v. 6, no. 7, September 1974.

Navrozov, Lev. "What the CIA Knows About Russia," *Commentary* magazine, v. 66, no. 3, September 1978.

Newhouse, John. "Reflections: The "SALT Debate," *The New Yorker,* v. 55, no. 44, December 17, 1979.

Nitze, Paul. "Assuring Strategic Stability in an Age of Equivalence," *Foreign Affairs,* v. 55, no. 2, January 1976.

———. "Deterring Our Deterrent," *Foreign Policy* no. 25, Winter 1976–1977.

———. "The Strategic Balance Between Hope and Skepticism," *Foreign Policy* no. 17, Winter 1975.

Nocera, Joseph. "The Art of the Leak," *Washington Monthly,* v. 11, nos. 5–6, July–August, 1979.

Norman, Lloyd. "Mr. Laird and the No War Strategy for the 1970s," *Army* magazine, v. 21, no. 2, February 1971.

———. "Nike-X: Big Chip in the Deadly Game of Nuclear Exchange," *Army* magazine, v. 17, no. 3, March 1967.

Nove, Alec. "Soviet Defense Spending," *Survival,* v. 13, no. 10, October 1971.

Panofsky, Wolfgang H. "Arms Control and SALT II," Seattle: University of Washington Press, 1979.

———. "The Mutual Hostage Relationship Between America and Russia," *Foreign Affairs,* v. 52, no. 1, October 1973.

Panyalev, Georg. "Backfire and SALT II," *International Defense Review,* v. 10, no. 2, April 1977.

Parry, Albert. "What the Russians Tell . . . And What They Don't Tell," *Missiles and Rockets,* v. 2, no. 2, February 1957.

———. "Why Should We Have Been Surprised?" *The Reporter,* v. 17, no. 8, October 31, 1957.

———. "Will the Russians Beat Us to the Moon?" *The Reporter,* v. 14, no. 10, November 18, 1954.

Paxon, E. W. "Computers and Strategic Advantage: III: Games, Computer Technology and a Strategic Power Ratio," Rand R-1644-I-PR, May 1975.

Pederson, Lieutenant Commander Gary, USN. "Soviet Reporting of the Cuban Crisis," United States Naval Institute *Proceedings,* v. 91, no. 10, October 1965.

Peterson, Lieutenant Harries-Clichy, USMC. "Bringing the 'Spooks' Into the Light," *Marine Corps Gazette,* v. 60, no. 7, July 1977.

Peterson, Phillip A. "American Perceptions of Soviet Military Power," *Parameters: Journal of the Army War College,* v. 7, no. 4, Winter 1977.

Petrov, Vladimir. "Formation of Soviet Foreign Policy," *Orbis,* v. 17, no. 3, Fall 1973.

Phillips, John. "The Days of the Dulleses," *New York Review of Books,* May 4, 1978.

Phillips, Brigadier General Thomas W., USAR. "The Growing Missile Gap," *The Reporter*, v. 18, no. 17, January 8, 1959.

Potter, William C. "Coping With MIRV in a MAD World," *Journal of Conflict Resolution*, v. 22, no. 4, December 1978.

Ransom, Harry Howe, "Strategic Intelligence and Foreign Policy," *World Politics*, v. 27, no. 1, October 1974.

Reed, Leonard. "The Budget Game and How to Win It," *Washington Monthly*, v. 10, no. 10, January 1979.

Reed, Thomas C. "The Soviet Backfire and SALT II: An Appraisal," *International Security Review*, v. 4, no. 1, Spring 1979.

Roberts, Adam. "The CIA: Reform Is Not Enough," *Millennium: Journal of International Studies*, v. 6, no. 1, Spring 1977.

Rositzke, Harry, "America's Secret Operations: A Perspective," *Foreign Affairs*, v. 53, no. 2, January 1975.

Ross, Denis, "Rethinking Soviet Strategic Policy: Inputs and Implications," *The Journal of Strategic Studies*, v. 1, no. 1, May 1978.

Rowen, Henry S. "The Need for a New Analytical Framework," *International Security Review*, v. 1, no. 2, Fall 1976.

Rudins, George. "Soviet Research on Semiconductor Thin Films: A Survey," Rand R-1181-ARPA, February 1973.

———. "Russia's Guided Missile Program," *Missiles and Rockets*, v. 2, no. 2, February 1957.

Ryan, Lieutenant Kathleen, USMC. "Intelligence and the Great Technology Race," *Marine Corps Gazette*, v. 62, no. 3, March 1978.

Scoville, Herbert, Jr. "Is Espionage Necessary for Our Security?" *Foreign Affairs*, v. 54, no. 3, April 1976.

———. "The Limitation of Offensive Weapons," *Scientific American*, January 1971.

———. "The SALT Negotiations," *Scientific American*, August 1977.

———. "A Soviet First Strike?" *New Republic*, October 2, 1971.

———. "Upgrading Soviet SAM," *New Republic*, October 9, 1971.

Scowcroft, Colonel Brent, USAF. "Deterrence and Strategic Superiority," *Orbis*, v. 13, no. 2, Summer 1969.

Serfaty, Simon. "Play It Again Zbig," *Foreign Policy* no. 32, Fall 1978.

Shlaim, Avi. "Failures in National Intelligence Estimates: The Case of the Yom Kippur War," *World Politics*, v. 28, no. 3, April 1976.

Silberman, Charles E., and Sanford S. Parker. "The Economic Impact of Defense," *Fortune* magazine, v. 57, no. 6, June 1958.

Smith, Gerard C. "Negotiating With the Russians," *New York Times Magazine*, February 27, 1977.

———. "SALT After Vladivostok," *Journal of International Affairs*, v. 29, no. 1, Spring 1975.

Smith, Richard K. "The Violation of the *Liberty*," United States Naval Institute *Proceedings*, v. 104, no. 6, June 1978.

Snyder, Richard E. "The Soviet Sojourn of Citizen Oswald," *Washington Post Magazine*, April 1, 1979.

Sokolov, Valentin A. "Soviet Use of German Science and Technology 1945–1946," New York: Research Program on the USSR, 1955.

Spex, Milton, "How To Steal Government Secrets," *Washington Monthly*, v. 10, no. 11, February 1979.

Spielmann, Karl F. "Defense Industrialists in the USSR," *Problems of Communism*, v. 25, no. 5, September–October 1976.

Steinbruner, John D., and Thomas M. Garwin. "Strategic Stability: The Balance Between Prudence and Paranoia," *International Security*, v. 1, no. 1, Summer 1976.

Steiner, Barry H. "On Controlling the Soviet-American Nuclear Arms Competition," *Armed Forces and Society*, v. 5, no. 1, November 1978.

———. "On Evaluating Estimates of Soviet Strategic Procurement—Without a Clearance," Paper presented at American Political Science Association, Chicago: September 2, 1976.

Stone, Jeremy J. "The Case Against Missile Defenses," International Institute of Strategic Studies: Adelphi Paper no. 47, April 1968.

Stovall, Colonel Don O., USAR. "U.S.-Soviet Détente: The Nature of the Relationship and Soviet Aims," National War College, *National Security Affairs Forum* no. 24, Spring-Summer 1976.

Sullivan, Cornelius D., et al. "The Soviet Military-Technological Challenge." Georgetown University: Center for Strategic Studies, Special Report no. 6, September 1967.

Sullivan, David S. "The Legacy of SALT I: Soviet Deception and U.S. Retreat," *Strategic Review*, v. 8, no. 1, Winter 1979.

———. "Soviet Deception and SALT," Boston (Virginia): Coalition for Peace Through Strength, 1979.

Szulc, Tad. "The Missing CIA Man," *New York Times Magazine*, January 7, 1979.

———. "Shaking Up the CIA," *New York Times Magazine*, July 29, 1979.

Thayer, Harry E. T. "The China Factor in the ABM Debate: Chronicle of a Rationale," National War College, *National War College Forum* no. 14, Winter 1971.

Treverton, Gregory F. "Reforming the CIA," *Millennium: Journal of International Studies*, v. 5, no. 3, Winter 1976–1977.

Trofimenko, Henry. "The Theology of Strategy," *Orbis*, v. 20, no. 3, Fall 1977.

Tsipis, Kosta, "The Accuracy of Ballistic Missiles," *Scientific American*, July 1975.

Turn, R., and Nancy Nimitz. "Computers and Strategic Advantage: I: Computer Technology in the United States and the Soviet Union," Rand R-1642-PR, May 1975.

Ulsamer, Edgar. "Increasing Momentum in Soviet Strategic Systems," *Air Force* magazine, v. 56, no. 3, March 1973.

Veater, Major Jimmie, USMC. "Photo Mission 1980," *Marine Corps Gazette*, v. 59, no. 3, March 1975.

Welles, Benjamin. "H-L-S of the CIA," *New York Times Magazine*, April 18, 1971.

Wells, Samuel F., Jr. "Sounding the Tocsin: NSC-68 and the Soviet Threat," *International Security*, v. 4, no. 1, Fall 1979.

Weymouth, Lally. "Foundation Woes: The Saga of Henry Ford: Part II," *New York Times Magazine*, March 12, 1978.

Whalen, Richard J. "The Shifting Equation of Nuclear Defense," *Fortune* magazine, v. 75, no. 6, June 1, 1967.

Wilbur, Commander Ted, USN. "Space and the United States Navy," Chief of Naval Operations: *Naval Aviation News*, October 1970.

Wilson, Major William T., USAF. "A New Vitality in Soviet 'Defense' Posture," *Air University Review*, v. 20, no. 5, July–August 1969.

Wohlstetter, Albert. "The Delicate Balance of Terror," *Foreign Affairs*, v. 37, no. 2, January 1959.

———. "Is There a Strategic Arms Race?" *Foreign Policy* no. 15, Summer 1974.

———. "Legends of the Strategic Arms Race," United States Strategic Institute, USSI Report 75-1, 1975.

———. "Optimal Ways to Confuse Ourselves," *Foreign Policy* no. 20, Fall 1975.

———. "Rivals But No Race," *Foreign Policy* no. 16, Fall 1974.

————, F. S. Hoffman, R. J. Lutz, and H. S. Rowen. "Selection and Use of Strategic Air Bases," Rand R-266, April 1954.

Wohlstetter, Roberta. "Cuba and Pearl Harbor: Hindsight and Foresight," *Foreign Affairs*, v. 43, no. 4, July 1965.

Wolfe, Thomas W. "The SALT Experience: Its Impact on U.S. and Soviet Strategic Policy and Decisionmaking," Rand R-1686-PR, September 1975.

————. "Signs of Stress in Soviet Political-Military Relations," Rand P-2877, March 1964.

————. "Soviet Military Power and European Security," Rand P-3429, March 1964.

————. "Soviet Strategy at the Crossroads," Rand Memorandum RM-4085-PR, April 1964.

Yergin, Daniel J. "The Arms Zealots," *Harper's* magazine, v. 254, no. 1525, June 1977.

York, Herbert F. "The Debate over the Hydrogen Bomb," *Scientific American*, October 1975.

————. "Reconnaissance Satellites and the Arms Race," in David Carlton and Carlo Schaerf, ed. *Arms Control and Technological Innovation.* New York: John Wiley & Sons, 1976.

————, and G. Allen Greb. "Strategic Reconnaissance," *Bulletin of the Atomic Scientists*, v. 33, no. 4, April 1977.

INDEX

Aaron, David, 272, 277
Acheson, Dean, 15, 20, 149
Adams, Sherman, 97
Advanced Research Projects Agency (ARPA), 106–7, 109
aerial reconnaissance, 26, 27, 29–35, 175–6, 275; of China, 136; of Cuba, 143–4, 145–6; of Soviet, 58, 62, 63, 85, 96–102; Soviet, 273–4. *See also* reconnaissance satellites; U-2 flights
aerospace industry, 105, 264
Afghanistan, 282
Africa, 176, 242, 278
Air Force and Air Force intelligence, 8, 18–19, 25, 26, 57, 68, 69, 83, 110, 116, 124, 201; aerial reconnaissance, 29, 33, 34, 97, 138, 141, 143, 176; Air Technical Intelligence Center (ATIC), 201; Ballistic Missile Division (BMD), 108; ballistic missile early-warning radar network, 68; and the "bomber gap," 38, 41, 43–50; conflict with CIA, 176, 178, 202, 259; and Cuban crisis, 130, 138, 139, 142, 143; Foreign Technologies Division (FTD), 201, 208, 270; Iran stations, 273; on military space programs, 201, 202, 203; Minuteman, 80, 81; on the "missile gap," 93, 113, 115–16, 117, 118–19, 125, 126; nuclear defenses, 70, 71; reconnaissance satellites, 105, 106, 108; Science Advisory Board, 105, 287; on Soviet ABMs, 157, 161; on Soviet ballistic missiles, 57, 58–59, 60, 61, 62, 81–82, 84, 292; on Soviet beam weapons, 286–7; on Soviet first-strike capability, 220; on Soviet heavy bomber, 258, 259–60, 264, 267; on Soviet MIRV, 206, 208, 236; on Soviet missile buildups, 186, 189, 196; spacecraft, 173. *See also* American bombers; bomber gap; Strategic Air Command
Air Policy Commission, 39

Alaska, 36, 80, 144
Aleutian Islands, 270
Allen, Richard V., 253
Allison, Royal B., 229
Alsop, Joseph, 61, 78, 84
American air defense network, 266
American antiballistic missiles, *see* antiballistic missiles (ABMs)
American bombers, 69, 70–71, 169; B-29s, 38, 39; B-52s, 43, 219, 259, 264; B-70s, 175; Carter policy, 266–7; FB-111, 260, 261, 267. *See also* Air Force; bomber gap
American intelligence network, *see* intelligence; intelligence community; intelligence disputes; intelligence estimates; names of agencies
American missiles and missile development: ABMs, *see* antiballistic missiles; Atlas, 69, 72, 80, 81, 92, 105, 238; Eisenhower policies, 88, 152, 205, 292; ICBMs, 57, 59, 69, 71, 78, 80, 114, 120–2, 153, 159, 189, 194, 200, 205, 238, 254; IRBMs, 72, 73; Johnson programs, 92–95, 161, 162, 163, 205; Jupiter, 105; Minuteman, *see* Minuteman missile; Polaris, 72, 80, 156, 160, 208; Poseidon, 161, 205; MIRV, 158, 159, 161, 168, 171, 195, 205, 207; MX, 279, 284, 289, 290, 297; SLBMs, *see* submarine-launched ballistic missiles; Titan, 80, 114, 119, 174
American satellites, 64, 104–9; Anna, 172; Corona/Discoverer, 106, 107–8, 113; Early-Warning, 106, 109, 275; Eisenhower policies, 106, 111; Sentry, 106, 108
American Security Council, 279
Amory, Robert, 48, 72, 100, 130
Anderson, George W., 249
Anderson, Rudolf, 143, 149
antiballistic missiles (ABMs): Laird policies, 209–16; Nike, 68, 158, 159, 160, 161–2,

Library of Congress Cataloging-in-Publication Data

Prados, John.
  The Soviet estimate.

  Reprint. Originally published: New York: Dial Press, 1982.
  Bibliography: p.
  Includes index.
  1. United States. Central Intelligence Agency. 2. Intelli-
gence service—United States. 3. Strategic forces—Soviet
Union. I. Title.
JK468.I6P72 1986   327.1′2′0973   85-43379
ISBN 0-691-07685-5 (alk. paper)
ISBN 0-691-02235-6 (pbk.)